Chicago
and the
American
Century

THE 100 MOST
SIGNIFICANT
CHICAGOANS
OF THE
TWENTIETH
CENTURY

F. RICHARD CICCONE

CB
CONTEMPORARY BOOKS

Library of Congress Cataloging-in-Publication Data

Ciccone, F. Richard.
   Chicago and the American century : the 100 most significant
Chicagoans of the twentieth century / F. Richard Ciccone.
     p. cm.
  Includes bibliographical references.
  ISBN 0-8092-2675-8
   1. Chicago (Ill.)—Biography. 2. Chicago (Ill.)—History—20th
century. I. Title.
F548.25.C56 1999
920.0773911—dc21
[B]
                                                  98-26990
                                                  CIP

For my mother

Jacket design by Kim Bartko
Cover photographs courtesy *Chicago Tribune*
Interior design by Impressions Book and Journal Services, Inc.

Published by Contemporary Books
A division of NTC/Contemporary Publishing Group, Inc.
4255 West Touhy Avenue, Lincolnwood (Chicago), Illinois 60646-1975 U.S.A.
Copyright © 1999 by The Chicago Tribune Company
Printed in the United States of America
International Standard Book Number: 0-8092-2675-8
98 99 00 01 02 03 LB 17 16 15 14 13 12 11 10 9 8 7 6 5 4 3 2 1

■ ■ ■ CONTENTS

There is never enough history. History can be verbatim, interpretive, revisionist, and repetitive. Chicago's fascinating history has been told many times in many ways, but rarely do all of the remarkable people who made it the "city of the century" get a satisfactory treatment. The thought behind this book was that Chicago's story could be told through the stories of the one hundred Chicagoans who had the greatest impact on America during the twentieth century.

On further thought it seemed worthwhile to consider ranking those accomplishments. That immediately led to conflicts. How can one measure the impact of Michael Jordan against the influence of Richard J. Daley? The solution was to select individuals by category and limit the number to no more than ten in the most obvious categories: politics, sports, crime, business, media, law, performing arts, literature, and architecture, with a final category reserved for those singularly successful individuals who did not fit neatly into the other categories.

Some of the people selected have had entire libraries devoted to them. Others have only a few yellowed scraps of newsprint to mark their presence and, more likely, their passing.

Although readers are encouraged, even implored, to debate the rankings, remember the author's intent was to consider the individuals' value to all of America—not only who was the richest, smartest, most popular, or most powerful in Chicago, but which of them most affected the way people lived and thought in places as disparate as Barton, Vermont, or Billings, Montana.

The rankings in these chapters were, of course, subjective. They were also necessary logistically to determine which of these people deserved the most of the writer's words and the reader's time. Many sources and many people were consulted, and in some cases there probably is little debate as to the group at the top or the bottom, although there is no clear justification for minor differentiations between those ranked first or second or third, or perhaps ninth and tenth. It could be just as easily the other way around.

The one dilemma in compiling these lists was the determination of who should be counted as a Chicago figure. It was not a question of birthplace. Walt Disney and William Paley were born in Chicago and went to high school here. So did Supreme Court Justice John Harlan. But Disney's fame is linked to Hollywood. Paley built the Columbia Broadcasting System in New York, and Harlan went east to college and never returned, ascending to the high court through the federal courts in New York. What about Louis Armstrong, a citizen of the world? Enrico Fermi won a Nobel Prize in 1938, four years before he arrived in Chicago. Theodore Dreiser wrote all his books about Chicago after he moved. The best approach seemed to apply to everyone the formula for writers that H. L. Mencken described seventy years ago:

> Find a writer who is indubitably American . . . who has something new and peculiarly American to say and who says it in an unmistakable American way and nine times out of ten you will find that he has some sort of connection with the gargantuan and inordinate abattoir by Lake Michigan—that he was bred there, or got his start there or passed through there in the days when he was young and tender.

There is also a gender and racial gap in the listings. Generally, the people who did the most and meant the most were white men. The contemporary current of political correctness cannot change the reality that for most of the twentieth century minorities and women were given no opportunities in business or government or almost any other endeavor.

Some of the people who were especially thoughtful and helpful in the creation of this book include David Axelrod, John Blades, Gene Callahan, Richard Christiansen, Dorothy Collin, Jack Fuller, Paul Green, William Griffin, Kenan Heise, Dan Houlihan, Blair Kamen, Rick Kogan, George Langford, Paul Lis, Abner Mikva, Newton Minow, Howard Reich, Thomas Reynolds, Dan Rostenkowski, Robert Schmuhl, James Strong, and Thomas Tully.

The bulk of the research material used was found in the *Chicago Tribune* library, where Alan Peters was again indispensable.

Several hours of videotaped interviews that went into the selecting and writing of *Chicago and the American Century* are available on the *Chicago Tribune*'s Internet site at chicago.tribune.com.

The most helpful people, as always, were Joan and Cristin and Richard.

POLITICS' TOP TEN

Of all the hyperbole that can be splashed over just about anything in Chicago there is little to boast of in the city's ill-chosen, inappropriate, toneless, and wistful motto: City in a Garden.

While the city's turn-of-the-century rogues were fixing everything in sight, including the direction of the river, they might have taken the time to do away with the Latin *Urbs in Horto* and adopt the more fitting phrase of Finley Peter Dunne's fictitious saloon keeper, Mr. Dooley: "Politics ain't bean bag."

Advocates of architecture and business, and science and education, can hotly debate which discipline produced Chicago's most tangibly significant contributions to the American Century. It can be argued that the machine gun and the jump shot were the dominant images that made Chicago unique in such diverse periods as the twenties and the nineties.

But the art and romance of Chicago has always been its politics and the amazing array of people who practiced the craft. Chicago-style politics was the standard for the rest of American cities. If there was corruption in Albany, it was never as bad as in Chicago. If there was a machine in Memphis, it was never as efficient as the one in Chicago. If there were statesmen of great vision in New York, they were never as eloquent as those from Chicago. If there were kingmakers in Cleveland, they were never as powerful as the ones in Chicago. In no other American city did the nation's destiny turn on the decisions of handfuls of men who gathered in the Chicago hotels a dozen times to pick the presidents who presided over the American Century.

Best of all, in Chicago, politics was fun.

It is true that no Chicagoan has ever reached the Oval Office. That seems absurd when seven callow fellows born in Ohio have gone to the White House. California sent an actor and a future felon. Even Georgia and New Hampshire and Missouri can boast of native sons who became president.

Chicago undoubtedly sent better politicians to prison than other states sent to Pennsylvania Avenue.

Not that Chicago didn't have men who wanted to be president. Adlai Stevenson wanted to be and might have been. Governors like Frank Lowden and Dwight Green and Dan Walker and James Thompson thought they could be. If Richard Daley the Elder didn't think he could be, most Chicagoans thought he should be. Mayor William "Big Bill" Thompson wanted to be president, but unlike Daley, most Chicagoans didn't even think he should be mayor. There were newspaper publishers like Colonel Robert R. McCormick and Colonel Frank Knox who thought about being president. And William Randolph Hearst started a newspaper here to help him get to be president, and it didn't matter to him whether he would have run from California, New York, or Chicago. It mattered so little to everyone else that he was never considered. There were senators who wanted to be president: Everett Dirksen and Paul Simon. And there was Jesse Jackson.

Chicago politics in this century began with the corrupt images of "Hinky Dink" Kenna and "Bathhouse John" Coughin, a pair of rascals who ran the city's First Ward, which for most of the twentieth century enveloped the bars, brothels, and businesses whose kickbacks fueled the Democratic Party. It continued through the reign of Daley père and Daley fils, interrupted by the brief, heralded appearance of Jane Bryne and the brief, lamentably short era of Harold Washington.

In between there were bosses like Roger Sullivan, Anton Cermak, Ed Kelly, and Jake Arvey. There were governors such as Len Small, Henry Horner, William Stratton, and Otto Kerner. There were Senators J. Hamilton Lewis, Scott Lucas, C. Wayland Brooks, Charles Percy, Adlai Stevenson III, Alan Dixon, and Carol Moseley-Braun.

There was Adolph Sabath and Sid Yates, who between them represented Chicago in Congress for all but a few years of the entire twentieth century.

And the mayors. No city has had a greater collection of local politicians who became national figures for many different reasons. "Big Bill" Thompson gave the keys of the city to Al Capone and earned national notoriety for threatening to punch the king of England in the nose. Tony Cermak became a footnote to the New Deal by taking a bullet for president-elect Roosevelt and was briefly memorialized when a Chicago newspaperman made up a quote, "I'm glad it was me." Chicago pols who had watched the immigrant Bohemian coal miner muscle his way to the top of the Democratic machine laughed. There was Ed Kelly, the confidante of Roosevelt who created the "voice from the sewer" chant that steamrolled FDR to an unprecedented third nomination in 1940.

And there was Richard J. Daley, who more than anyone in the latter half of the twentieth century personified Chicago. Revered as the man who made Chicago work, feared as the boss of the last machine, and scorned as the defiant opponent of the 1968 peace pilgrims, Daley was as much a part of Chicago's image as the lake, the skyscrapers, and the smell of the stockyards.

John F. Kennedy boosted Daley's national stature by crediting him for electing JFK in 1960, but that was more myth than reality. The Chicago Democratic machine undoubtedly stole some votes and unquestionably delivered the massive Democratic turnout that helped Kennedy carry Illinois by less than eight thousand votes. As it turned out, he could have lost Illinois and still won. But both Kennedy's fable and Daley's reputation were bulwarked by the legend of Chicago politics and its ghost voters, disappearing ballot boxes, and robber precinct captains.

Chicago had corruption. Running for office in Chicago automatically included a visit from the U.S. attorney. There have been more aldermen convicted of more things in Chicago than anywhere else. They were nailed for vote fraud and kickbacks and ghost payrollers and extortion and bribery and mail fraud and perjury. If there was a criminal statute, some alderman was certain to violate it. The federal government has just about run out of names for the sting operations in Chicago. The last was Silver Shovel. The biggest was Greylord, which had every judge, every person who had been a judge, and everyone who wanted to be a judge awaiting a grand jury summons. In other cities, officials retire to Florida. In Chicago, city clerks and city treasurers routinely go to Lexington, Kentucky, Terre Haute, Indiana, or Oxford, Wisconsin, where the federal government runs minimum-security institutions. Chicago politicians aren't necessarily violent, just crooked.

Senator William J. Lorimer was one of the worst. Lorimer certainly deserves mention in any listing of those who had impact on America. He is the reason senators are directly elected. Until 1916, state legislatures chose U.S. senators. But in 1910, the *Chicago Tribune* discovered that Lorimer had paid off enough state representatives to get the job. Lorimer was eventually thrown out of the Senate and took whatever money he didn't hand to his bagman for an extended trip to South America. He returned in 1928 to support a protégé, Len Small, for governor. Small had been governor for two terms, winning reelection in 1924 despite being indicted for using state money to collect personal interest.

Illinois also had a governor who had been a U.S. attorney. He was convicted by a U.S. attorney who then became governor. The names: Otto Kerner and James Thompson. Kerner's predecessor, William Stratton, was indicted for misuse of campaign funds after he left the governor's office. He beat the rap. Dan Walker was indicted for bilking a savings and loan after he left office. He didn't beat the rap. Harold Washington, of course, was elected mayor despite having served time for failure to file income-tax returns. Oh, his taxes were paid from withholding, but the government got impatient with his habit of forgetting to mail in a return. He forgot for nineteen straight years.

Almost everyone who serves on the zoning board or the sanitary district gets indicted sooner or later. Mayor Ed Kelly, who was chief engineer of the sanitary district before ascending to city hall, somehow escaped indictment during one of the great pilferages of public funds in the 1920s. He died a millionaire. Congressman Dan Rostenkowski went to jail for giving away rocking chairs.

Chicago politics has been a century of carnival, with hucksters and shillmen and promises of exotic wonders for whoever pays the price.

Still, in terms of charting the course of a nation, raising its aspirations, creating the vision to deal with the real and imagined threats of foreign aggression and domestic upheaval, providing the voice of opposition and the songs of patriotism, there were Chicago pols who contributed significantly to the American Century.

I

THE EGGHEAD:
ADLAI STEVENSON

They didn't invent the word *egghead* because Adlai Stevenson was bald. In fact, Stevenson was one of the most romantic men in American politics. He did not run up scores of one-night stands like some Democratic presidents are reputed to have done, but his life was filled with women who passionately cared about him and who he loved in return. His name was linked with glamorous women like Ava Gardner, Lauren Bacall, and Marlene Dietrich, and political women like Dorothy Fosdick and Marietta Tree, and powerful women like *Newsday* publisher Alicia Patterson, whom he loved for many years.

Once it was rumored he would marry Eleanor Roosevelt. "I'm too old for her," he joked graciously.

Stevenson did so many things graciously that he was the most admired loser in American presidential history.

Certainly a great deal of his appeal was that Stevenson seemed to appear as many things, but never a politician. He was labeled an "egghead," the phrase his Republican opponents coined for the 1952 presidential campaign to disparage his intellectual image. He was an internationalist, a social liberal, and an economic moderate. He was a writer and one of the last men in American public life to cherish the language he used to attack Republicans, alert Americans to nuclear folly, and create a vision for a new society. In an era of "hawks" and "doves" he was neither. He was a critic of American affluence and public apathy, and an advocate of developing the third-world nations not out of altruism but out of common sense. He was a witty man who most enjoyed the last laugh on himself.

He hardly seems to fit as a Chicago politician. But he was. Adlai Stevenson also had pedigree. One of his ancestors was Bloomington lawyer Jesse Fell, who excepting *Tribune* founder Joseph Medill worked harder than anyone to make Abraham Lincoln president. His grandfather, the first Adlai E. Stevenson, was Grover Cleveland's vice president and an unsuccessful candidate for governor of Illinois in 1908. His father, Lewis Stevenson, was a defeated candidate for Illinois secretary of state in 1916.

Stevenson was a Princeton man who meandered in and out of several Washington appointments during the New Deal and World War II, always returning to Chicago, where he had his law office and a political base at the top of the Council of Foreign Relations, writing papers and delivering speeches on the need for America to adopt a global view. He was not considered a player in the Cook County Democratic Party because he was snobbish, educated, worldly, and he never asked for anything, which made him suspect. It was this last trait that made friends from Harry Truman to Richard Daley want to wring his neck.

The problem with Stevenson was that he *did* want something, but he never could make up his mind what it was. In 1948, Jake Arvey, chairman of the Democratic Party, looking for a blue-ribbon ticket to allay the eternal charges of corruption in the Democratic regime, put Stevenson and former maverick alderman Paul Douglas on the Democratic ticket for governor and senator. Douglas had wanted to be governor, but his rash displays of integrity during his council days made him unacceptable to party leaders, whose lips drooled at the thought of the patronage in the governor's office. Stevenson, a former special assistant to two U.S. secretaries of state, wanted the Senate slating. After some weeks of soul-searching and Arvey's blandishments he accepted the governor's nomination and was elected.

Four years later, Arvey was back with a demand that Stevenson seek the Democratic presidential nomination. Harry Truman summoned him to the White House and begged him to take the nomination. Democrats all over America told him he was the only one who could save the party. On the eve of the nomination battle at the 1952 party convention in Chicago, Stevenson went to the Illinois caucus and proclaimed: "I just don't want to be nominated for president. I just couldn't . . . wouldn't . . . didn't want to be a candidate. I have no ambitions, no fitness either mentally, temperamentally or physically for the job as president. . . . What I personally wanted is to run for governor. I ask you to abide by my wishes and not to nominate or vote for me should I be nominated."

The next day, Adlai Stevenson was nominated. Whatever his misgivings, he began one of the most thoughtful and inspiring campaigns in American history. The bad news was he had to make it against Dwight "Ike" Eisenhower, the most popular hero of the most popular war in American history.

Adlai Stevenson did not have a long and distinguished term as an officeholder. He was never directly responsible for the landmark legislation that presidents and congressmen can claim. His one term as governor was impressive but not remarkable. Yet, in two presidential campaigns when Americans still longed to hear ideas rather than sound bites, Adlai Stevenson set the tone for the future of the Democratic Party, issued a history lesson on the glories of democracy, and treated the country to its last luxurious eloquence.

Stevenson began his campaign with the uncharacteristic rhetoric that would distinguish him from all other politicians: "Even more important than winning the election is governing the nation. . . . Let's talk sense to the American people. Let's tell them the truth, that there are no gains without pains, that we are now on the eve of great decisions, not easy decisions . . . but a long costly struggle which alone can assure triumph over the great enemies of man—war, poverty and tyranny—and the assaults upon human dignity which are the grievous consequences of each."

It was all on television. The 1952 election was the first campaign the American public watched nightly in their homes. Television was in some ways costly to Stevenson. The technology was new and his speeches often ran too long. But in most ways it was a boon. The campaigns paid relatively cheap amounts to purchase blocks of time so that the candidates could speak for fifteen minutes or even an hour.

They weren't restricted to the twenty-second sound bites of the 1980s and 1990s. Stevenson began the campaign as a virtually unknown midwestern governor and ended it wearing the mantle of a national patriot. There was no question that Stevenson's eloquence and sensibility overrode Ike's stoic, choppy, partisan appeal for votes. There also was no question that the Republicans had, after twenty years of Democratic rule, the right slogan: It's time for a change.

When attacked by red-baiting Senator Joseph McCarthy and Richard Nixon, who served as Ike's hatchet man, Stevenson chose to respond to charges that he was soft on communism in the hostile arena of an American Legion convention: "Patriotism is not the fear of something, it is the love of something."

On the eve of the election, he spoke to the nation: "Win or lose, I have told you the truth as I see it. I have said what I meant and meant what I said. I have not done as well as I should like to have done, but I have done my best; no man can do more, and you are entitled to no less."

Stevenson lost in every way possible. He told reporters, "It hurts too much to laugh. I am too old to cry."

Unlike other overwhelmed candidates, he did not disappear. He remained the leader of the Democratic Party and was again chosen to run another ill-fated campaign against Eisenhower in 1956. And again, he did not disappear. Most influential Democrats wanted to give him a third crack at the Oval Office. Mayor Richard Daley sought to learn early in the spring of 1960 whether his friend wanted yet another chance. Stevenson flatly rejected the offer. But when the Democrats gathered in Los Angeles, Stevenson had another change of heart, and Daley had to cruelly tell him he had no chance to derail the John Kennedy express.

Stevenson's final dallying created great animosity in the Kennedy camp and probably cost him the job he wanted most after the presidency—the secretary of state. But Kennedy found a consolation prize. He raised the position of ambassador to the United Nations to cabinet level and gave it to Stevenson.

From 1952 until his death in London in 1965, Stevenson traveled the world and spoke to America about its place in it. A generation of

Stevenson Democrats grew up to meld into the New Frontier and Great Society. Another generation has learned to respect his vision of free nations competing in a global economy no longer dominated by the nightmare of nuclear holocaust.

Even those who held him at arm's length from the power he envied understood that his noble view of the political system had inspired them.

Lyndon Johnson, who also ignored Stevenson's wish to be secretary of state, said at his death, "For an entire generation of Americans, he imparted a nobility to public life and a grandeur to American purpose which has already reshaped the life of the nation and will endure for many generations."

He educated and reminded America of its unique heritage with speeches embodying the beliefs of Jefferson, Madison, and Wilson— that the great experiment of a democracy is a commitment that the people ultimately shall decide and a trust that the good common sense of the American voter will do what is right. Even if they did it to him twice.

2

THE COLONEL:
ROBERT R. MCCORMICK

It would surprise both of them, a generation after their passing, if someone observed that Adlai Stevenson and Colonel Robert R. McCormick had much in common.

Underlying the bombastic, irrational, eccentric, and cruel diatribes that McCormick unleashed in print and on the airwaves for nearly a half century was the same relentless belief that Stevenson shared in the American sense of right and wrong and an unremitting resolve to defend individual liberties from government intrusion.

The main difference between the two men was that the individual liberties McCormick was most concerned with were his own and those that threatened the *Chicago Tribune,* which he shaped into one of the great newspaper franchises in America as he simultaneously warped its credibility.

McCormick was not a one-dimensional isolationist, conservative scold. His lash crossed party lines, ideologies, and on occasion contradicted his strong personal conviction that government should never interfere with the efforts of the wealthy to become wealthier.

For that matter, he didn't think government should interfere with the efforts of the poor to become wealthy, either.

For the millions who despised his railings against the New Deal, his pathological tirades against the British, and his furious detestations of internationalism, it would have helped them to understand had they realized Robert R. McCormick began his professional life as an alderman.

It is easy to conclude that no other alderman in Chicago history ever matched McCormick's achievements as one of America's mightiest publishers, or one of Chicago's most successful entrepreneurs. But those accomplishments do not merit McCormick's place on a list of political figures of significance in the twentieth century, although they certainly deserve notice in other categories.

The fact is that no Chicago alderman, congressman, mayor, or senator ever achieved the national influence that McCormick enjoyed as the most outspoken critic of Democratic White Houses for twenty years, and as the lonely, resolute voice that held the Republican Party together in the wake of Roosevelt landslides and what McCormick and his followers viewed as the disastrous encroachment of government on American values.

The critics who reveled in the description of McCormick as "one of the greatest minds of the nineteenth century" were not misdirected. McCormick was a publishing dinosaur. He was the last of the journalistic autocrats who believed a newspaper's role was advocacy, not objectivity, and that the publisher's role was to guide American destiny, including the selection of its political leaders. This was commonplace in the nineteenth century, when men such as McCormick's grandfather, Joseph Medill, brokered Lincoln into the nomination of the newly minted Republican Party. Editors and publishers continued to dominate both political parties into the 1900s. The 1920 election pitted two Ohio editors, James Cox and Warren Harding. But that year was the swan song of most journalistic political incest. Except for McCormick. He used the *Tribune* as the oracle of the Republican Party, which he believed, with some justification, he had inherited along with the *Tribune*.

Moreover, his publishing acumen had made the *Tribune* the voice not only of Chicago but of a great portion of the Heartland, where its echoes of manifest destiny and rugged individualism were welcomed. The *Tribune* became a political bible in Illinois, Indiana, Wisconsin, and out on the Great Plains, where the heyday of the railroads coincided with the colonel's desire to blanket Middle America with his editorial views.

His anti-internationalist stance had become well known in the early 1920s, when he was a fiery opponent of Woodrow Wilson's

League of Nations. After Franklin Roosevelt captured the White House in 1932, the Republican Party was bereft of leadership. Its last three presidents were of no help. Harding was disgraced and dead, Coolidge a recluse, and Hoover an embarrassment. The Democrats ruled the urban East and rural South. The West was no factor. McCormick became the voice of the GOP and the often disloyal opposition to the New Deal.

He became the rallying point for Republicans. He personally selected and shaped Alf Landon as the GOP's 1936 presidential candidate. His editorials and nationally broadcast speeches helped keep a scattering of Republicans in office. He adored isolationist Senator Arthur Vandenberg of Michigan and found just the man he wanted when Robert A. Taft was elected to the Senate in 1938 from Ohio.

He was courted by every Republican in America when it came time to select presidential nominees. He disliked almost all of them. He wanted the popular crime buster Tom Dewey of New York in 1940 but gave in to Wall Street's preference for Wendell Wilke. He decided Dewey had succumbed to the internationalist factor and fought against him in 1944 and 1948, stalking out of the GOP convention in the latter year, declaring, "Dewey can't win." His support for Taft in 1952 was thwarted by the GOP's desire to return from the political wilderness after twenty years of exile. The Republicans wanted a winner, and they picked Eisenhower without really knowing if he was a Republican. McCormick thought it the end of the world as he knew it, or at least as he wanted it to be.

Every president from Harding to Eisenhower tried to conciliate McCormick. He went to the White House to see the Republicans whom he found lacking. He ignored the Democrats for two reasons. He didn't think they would listen to him, and he thought it would be unseemly to be their guest and then return home to label them as traitors, socialist conspirators, communist sympathizers, and despots, all of which he did regularly and without regret.

In the world of instant news delivery, satellite, cable, and computer, it now seems implausible that someone armed only with a midwestern newspaper and the early technology of radio could have been an imposing national figure whose notoriety would rival today's political, sports, and media stars. But McCormick was exactly that. He was known not only throughout America but in Europe, particularly in England, where prime ministers and ambassadors feared his constant disdain for Great Britain would have a persuasive negative effect on its relationship with the United States. And it often did. When McCormick traveled abroad he was treated with more pomp than the secretary of state. When he spewed his military history along with his anti–New Deal venom on his WGN radio show, Americans from Maine to the Rockies listened.

His celebrity would be equal to a modern Rush Limbaugh, Larry King, and Dan Rather combined. No political figure in America today, save the president, is as renowned in these times as McCormick was in his.

It could be argued that since McCormick never succeeded in electing the president he wanted, he was not as influential as other Chicagoans who were vital to the elections of Wilson, Roosevelt, Truman, and Kennedy. But McCormick in defeat was louder than any of them in victory.

3

THE LAST BOSS:
RICHARD J. DALEY

He may not have influenced Americans from the Atlantic to the Pacific the way some others did, but no one, not Al Capone or Michael Jordan or Robert McCormick or Cyrus McCormick or Marshall Field, dominated Chicago with his presence as much as Richard J. Daley.

No one had more to do with changing Chicago's image from the town that invented the one-way ride to the city that works. No one equaled his reign of two decades as the most powerful and effective mayor of twentieth-century America. No local or regional political leader of the 1960s was held in higher esteem by two Democratic presidents. No Chicago political leader ever accomplished so much for his city.

Richard Daley, the "kid from the stockyards," hosted kings and queens and presidents and prime ministers and was more impressed by a good precinct captain. He was John Kennedy's first White House guest and Lyndon Johnson's constant telephone pal.

He took over a city that hadn't seen any new construction in a quarter-century and transformed it into one of America's greatest shopping venues. He protected the lakefront and filled it with civic extravaganzas. He understood bread and circuses.

There are two national images of Richard J. Daley. The first is the stocky, perfectly tailored middle-aged mayor to whom John Kennedy said he owed his presidency. The second is the aging, heavy-jowled autocrat screaming perceived profanities from the floor of the beleaguered 1968 Democratic convention. Neither image is quite accurate.

From 1953, when he became chairman of the Democratic Party—two years before his first mayoral victory—until his death in 1976, Daley was the most powerful boss of the last most powerful machine. But even by 1960, the Cook County Democratic Party was not the organization that through patronage and piracy could produce the 90 percent pluralities it delivered for Franklin Roosevelt in the 1930s. In 1960, Daley produced an enormous Chicago turnout that ultimately preserved Kennedy's eight-thousand-vote margin in Illinois. But it was his timing rather than his totals that mattered.

Daley produced his vote early enough so that television commentators put Illinois in the Kennedy victory column and apparently gave him enough electoral votes to capture the White House. By the next dawn, Richard Nixon had pulled ahead, and it wasn't until noon that Kennedy's Illinois victory was official. By that time, Texas had gone to the Democratic column and California was declared for Kennedy. When the results of the closest presidential election in history were finally tallied days later, Kennedy had lost California, but it didn't matter. What was often overlooked is that he could have lost Illinois as well and still won. But JFK had proclaimed Daley his savior, and the nation's political press repeated it for years along with constant reminders of the unbeatable machine that Richard Daley ruled in Chicago. In later years, when Lyndon Johnson was debating a second term, he told his friends he wasn't worried about the antiwar challengers. "With Dick Daley on your side you don't worry about people like Bobby Kennedy and Gene McCarthy."

The ruthless image of 1968 was just as misleading and just as indelible. Richard Daley had been against the Vietnam War for a long time, and he tried many times to get Lyndon Johnson to end American involvement. But he never told anyone. In public, Daley steadfastly remained loyal to his friend and president. He vowed that peace demonstrators would not take over his city and mar the Democratic convention. He called in the army and the FBI and the National Guard and had his police force ready for battle as though the Vietcong were encamped on the lake. He overreacted. He was frightened. In April of 1968 he was stunned almost to incapacity by the looting and burning of the West Side following the murder of Martin Luther King Jr. He had reports of attempted assassinations on himself and the president.

At an earlier time in his career, he might have scoffed, but after seeing so much of his beloved city in embers, he was almost in shock. He feared not the bearded, backpacking, foulmouthed, antiwar crowd. He feared a black uprising that would replicate in Chicago the burning of Watts, Newark, and Detroit in previous summers.

He also was a forlorn political leader. Lyndon Johnson had called Daley to tell him he would not seek another term. Daley wanted to draft Johnson. He begged the president to reconsider. Robert Kennedy was assassinated in Los Angeles. Edward M. Kennedy would not run. The Democrats were in disarray. Chicago was under siege. The clash between police and antiwar crowds in front of the Hilton Hotel was broadcast nationally, and antiwar followers of Senators Eugene McCarthy and George McGovern jeered Daley inside the convention arena. His response was to shout back, threaten, intimidate, demand— all the tools he used to rule Chicago politics for a generation. And the surly, angry visage of "the boss" flickered in every American living room.

In the aftermath of 1968, the political parties changed their rules to rid themselves of the power brokers that had run things for one hundred years and whose legacy was now solely personified by Richard Daley. In one sense, Daley's performance in 1968 perhaps influenced the future of American politics more than any other Chicagoan could have. The reforms ended for all time the convention battles over nominees, ushered in the primary system—which has produced far more mediocrities than the smoke-filled rooms—and reduced voter interest to embarrassing proportions.

But the cultural revolution that Daley and others of his generation could not restrain would have achieved those same results. His role in 1968 was only the first wave in the ocean of social change. His role as master politician and administrator is far more memorable.

Daley, who could stammer, shout, mutter, scream, and giggle in the space of a five-minute news conference, was the finest civic leader of his time. Even after his death, when the Rust Belt cities of the North fell into such fiscal disrepute that the federal government refused to back a New York City bond issue, Chicago survived, then thrived.

Daley, whose apprenticeship in government included courses in the offices of the city council, county clerk, county treasurer, state

revenue director, and state legislature, was arguably the most knowl-
edgeable person in America about municipal affairs. He knew budgets
and tax-anticipation warrants as well as he understood vote totals and
voter registration figures. He isolated agencies such as the school
board and the county hospital and the transit system. Unlike other
cities, where the failure of one unit could doom government, Daley
insulated Chicago against municipal wildfires. He also was canny
about the balance of power. He never minded Republicans holding
key state offices, which enabled him to make the kind of deals that
benefited both sides publicly and reinforced his power privately.

In the tradition of Chicago political giants, he often was silly. He
once talked of putting gondolas in the Chicago River. He was often
folksy. He told Queen Elizabeth II to "bring the kids" the next time she
visited Chicago. He was politically ruthless. In 1975, he not only won
an overwhelming primary victory, he plugged so many precinct workers into his Republican opponent's ward that the doleful John Hoellen
lost his aldermanic seat six weeks before he was scheduled to be
Daley's sixth and final mayoral election victim.

In Democratic circles, he was called the "Man on Five," because of
his fifth-floor office in city hall. Mike Royko called him "the Great
Dumpling." Other writers called him "the Great Buddha." He hated
being called "the Last Boss." Twenty years after his death, histories of
the period merely say, "Daley of Chicago." He would have liked that.

4

THE GRAND OLD CHAMELEON:
EVERETT DIRKSEN

Everett McKinley Dirksen thought of himself as a man of the future. His critics believed he belonged in the nineteenth century. It was a fitting compromise that he occupied the American political stage for the middle third of the American Century.

Dirksen represented both the old and the new, and he built his political strength by discarding old principles and amending new positions. He was the last of the Heartland voices whose eloquence dominated Congress for a century with stentorian lectures on the preservation of the union that they were convinced was rooted in the prairie states, whose virtues were conservative politics, a free-market economy, and a stubborn spirit of self-reliance that they encouraged the rest of the nation and world to embrace.

Everett Dirksen was the last of the county fair stem-winders and the first politician to star in the midcentury miracle of television. He was as comfortable and appealing in front of the camera as he was at the Farm Bureau and Rotary Club meetings where he spent a great deal of his half century in politics.

He believed fervently in God and Abraham Lincoln. He was an isolationist who became an internationalist. He defended Joe McCarthy's unpardonable "witch hunts" but played a most critical role in passing the historic civil rights legislation of the 1960s. He opposed all of Franklin Roosevelt's efforts to involve America in World War II and supported Lyndon Johnson's immersion in Vietnam. He despised deficit budgets and government bureaucracy but won his first congressional election promising federal relief for farmers.

He unquestionably had more to do with the fate of his nation than any other Illinoisan who served in Congress during this century.

And he had more to say than anyone else who ever served there.

Had history not branded Henry Clay as the Great Compromiser the title could have been affixed to Dirksen's tombstone. He would have shuddered and undoubtedly had ten or twenty thousand well-chosen words to say about the recent political gridlocks that have sporadically paralyzed the federal government.

Dirksen went to Congress in 1932 and was elected to the first of four Senate terms in 1950. He served as Republican Senate minority leader for ten years, longer than any GOP senator led that party until Bob Dole ended his Senate career in 1996 after twelve years as the party's spokesman. In all Dirksen's years in the minority, beginning with his first term in Congress in 1932, he never believed his role was obstructionist. He was a magician of minority politics.

He was a godsend to political reporters.

During the 1960 presidential campaign, Dirksen observed that the Democratic candidate, his senatorial colleague, John F. Kennedy, was seldom in attendance. Pointing to Kennedy's seat he intoned, "We call this the emptiest saddle in the New Frontier," Dirksen observed.

A typical Dirksen greeting to the assembled media: "I am happy to be back in the broad fertile bosom of Illinois in the resurrection of spring."

He startled his wife-to-be, Louella, on Christmas Eve of 1926 by announcing his intention to marry her with the question, "Would you like a ring or a radio?"

But in almost fifty years of political life, none of the thousands of memorable words Dirksen spoke ever matched the impact of his appearance at the first nationally televised political convention in 1952.

Dirksen, already a budding GOP star after two years in the Senate, was fervently supporting Ohio's Senator Robert Taft for the Republican nomination, although the favorite was Dwight Eisenhower, who had the backing of the eastern wing of the GOP, which was led by New York Governor Thomas A. Dewey, who had lost the presidential elections in 1944 and 1948.

Rising to argue for Taft on a parliamentary issue intended to block Ike's first-ballot nomination, Dirksen appeared for the first time in millions of American homes and to many millions more in saloons and restaurants. It was their first look at the gray curls that grew in different directions to form the leonine mane crowning his lined face and jutting ears. They watched as he pointed a long, bony finger from the podium to the very front row where Dewey was sitting with his New York delegation and exhorted, "We followed you before and you took us down the path to defeat."

There had never been a moment like it in American politics. The convention erupted into pandemonium, with Eisenhower supporters booing Dirksen, and Taft backers jeering at Dewey and the Ike forces. The shouts and taunts continued until Dirksen pleaded, "Will the delegates take their seats. This is no place for Republicans to be booing other Republicans." He was booed louder. There had been raucous moments at American political gatherings, but never with 20 million people watching. Dirksen became a national celebrity.

That appearance was merely a prelude to future starring roles. After Kennedy began using the televised press conference as his personal forum, Dirksen and House minority leader Charles Halleck of Indiana were given rebuttal time for the GOP. The act was dubbed the "Ev and Charlie Show," and when Gerald Ford succeeded Halleck as minority leader in 1966 he joined the show. But Dirksen was as born to stagecraft as to statecraft.

Dirksen's biggest stage was the U.S. Senate. For nearly twenty years Dirksen was the man presidents sought to work out a compromise. Even before he became the GOP leader in 1959, Dirksen was critical to the passage of every important bit of legislation in the Senate. Eisenhower, leery of the GOP old guard of Taft, William Knowland of California, and Styles Bridges of New Hampshire, often bypassed them to consult with the junior senator from Illinois. Dirksen, who had been against Eisenhower receiving the GOP nomination, had loyally rallied to his party's leader and used every weapon in his massive vocabulary arsenal to praise Ike.

Under Democrats it was the same thing. Both Kennedy and Dirksen's close friend Lyndon Johnson valued his role as leader of the loyal opposition. Dirksen often stated, "The minority has the same stake in the well being of the whole country as the majority." In times of crisis, Dirksen believed it mandatory to abandon personal convictions to support the president no matter what the issue. "We cannot as a minority show a disunited spirit to the world."

He was accused of being too cozy with Kennedy and even closer to Johnson, but Dirksen never wavered in his belief that his job was to pass legislation, not to thwart it.

One of his biggest challenges involved Kennedy's attempt to pass a nuclear test–ban treaty in 1963. Dirksen and the rest of the GOP "Cold War Warriors" argued that for America to unilaterally stop nuclear testing would be madness. Kennedy disagreed and asked Dirksen to help pass the treaty.

When Dirksen rose to cast his vote, everyone listened. "One of my age thinks about his destiny a little," he said. "I should not like to have written on my tombstone, 'He knew what happened at Hiroshima, but he did not take a first step.'" The treaty passed.

In 1964, southern Democrats planned to filibuster to death the Civil Rights Bill. The Democrats controlled the Senate by a 67–33 margin but President Johnson, knowing he could not count on the support of southern Democrats, needed at least twenty-five GOP votes to provide the necessary two-thirds to shut off the debate. He needed Everett Dirksen. Dirksen didn't have to be persuaded. His Lincolnian political heritage had always pushed him toward civil rights. But many of his GOP colleagues from the Great Plains and the West saw the issue as a fratricidal one among Democrats and were reluctant to help the Democratic president. First, Dirksen worked with the White House on the language of the bill, reducing as many objections as possible. Then he began his personal lobbying. Dirksen never traded votes. He never promised quid pro quos. His reasoning was always persuasive and logical, and he never threatened. When it was time to declare, he rose again in the Senate and after his usual eloquent oratory he concluded, "Nothing is eternal except change."

The bill passed. Dirksen had brought twenty-seven of his GOP colleagues to the table.

Lyndon Johnson publicly applauded him. The press applauded him. The *Chicago Defender*, never a friend, wrote, "We doff our hats to him for the grand manner of his generalship behind the passage of the best civil rights measure that has ever been enacted into law since Reconstruction."

He was first called a "chameleon" by his opponent in the 1950 Senate race, and critics never ceased attacking him for his seamless ability to switch positions. Dirksen simply called it politics.

In the closing years of his Senate career, Dirksen worked tirelessly to overturn the Supreme Court decision banning school prayer. Dirksen was a devout man. He credited God with saving his sight after he suffered from eye cancer in 1948, and he prayed daily in the garden of his Maryland home, which was filled with the flowers he loved and the vegetables he had learned to grow as a small boy in Pekin. He never succeeded in overturning the Court's ruling.

Despite his advancing age and declining body—he suffered from emphysema and the effects of various broken bones—he never lost his sense of humor or beauty. While defending LBJ's Vietnam War and finding himself a pariah among the antiwar counterculture youth, Dirksen found time to wage a campaign to name the marigold the national flower. He would often amuse the Senate with floral poetry.

After his death at Walter Reed Hospital on September 7, 1969, his body lay in state in the Capitol rotunda, only the fifth member of the Senate so honored. Gerald Ford said, "He left an indelible imprint on many major laws that will live in the statute books for many, many years." Barry Goldwater called him "one of the greatest men ever produced in this country."

Dirksen's record is secure. His statesmanship was historic. But in an era of twenty-second sound bites and computer-packaged position papers, the absence of that remarkable sound, the human voice used as an instrument of persuasion, argument, and entertainment, is perhaps a greater loss. *Time* magazine described it once: "He speaks, and the words emerge in soft, sepulchral baritone. They undulate in measured phrases, expire in breathless wisps. He fills his lungs and blows word-rings like smoke. The sentences curl upward. They chase each other around the room in dreamy images of Steamboat Gothic."

5 ▪

THE CONSCIENCE:
PAUL DOUGLAS

Of all the political bodies in the world, the one least likely to produce anyone of influence in the twentieth century was the Chicago City Council. Oh, there were dozens of aldermen convicted of influence peddling, and dozens more jailed for fraud, bribery, kickback schemes, and almost any sort of official malfeasance that was against the law. Not every alderman went to jail. Most of them just got rich. But not even every alderman got rich. Some were simply too stupid to be successfully corrupt.

Few of the great names in Illinois political history were tainted by service in the city council. Neither Richard Daley the Greater nor Richard the Lesser deigned to serve there. Several aldermen were handed their keys to the treasury in the form of aldermanic seats after they served time in Congress. Few ever rose higher. No governor of Illinois ever served in the council chambers, although a few served time in jail.

And of all the significant figures in Chicago's twentieth century, the one least likely to have gotten his political start as an alderman was the one man whose national reputation for honesty, integrity, and moral courage soared above any of his contemporaries—Paul H. Douglas.

It is to his credit that he didn't stay one long.

Paul Douglas was a scholar, a humanist, a conservationist, an economist, a marine, a Quaker, a reformer, a rebel, a liberal, and for eighteen years was widely recognized as the "conscience of the U.S. Senate."

Hubert Humphrey, a liberal soulmate who shared in many of the honorable and often hopeless battles Douglas waged, said in 1966, "Back in the days when they almost had no chance of enactment, Paul Douglas was a sponsor of Medicare, federal aid to elementary education, aid to higher education, the immigration bill, the water pollution bill—there is no member of the Senate today who has his name stamped on more major issues, major bills and major legislation than Paul Douglas . . . he is a giant of a man, a giant of a senator."

Paul Douglas stood a few inches past six feet and weighed more than two hundred pounds when he arrived in Chicago in 1919 to teach economics at the University of Chicago. He resembled in appearance and spirit the rocky countryside of the remote Maine farmland where he was born and raised. For twenty years he earned a reputation as a scholar in theories involving wages and benefits and salaries and profits. He was a rebel among economists who argued that the free market and corporate profits were the only keys to national greatness. He believed a country could prosper by offering fair wages and employee inducements. He believed a nation of riches should be able to afford to help those unable to participate in the rewards of business. He gloried in the principles of the New Deal. He was asked by Franklin Roosevelt to help draft the first Social Security legislation, and he wandered the neighborhoods of his beloved Hyde Park with petitions aimed at curing all the social ills he saw in Chicago's corrupt Roaring Twenties.

In 1939, do-gooder Douglas and his allies were stumped for a candidate for alderman from Hyde Park, so he, at age forty-seven, reluctantly filed for the office. In one of those odd fits of brilliance that only rarely have struck Chicago political bosses, Mayor Edward Kelly decided to embrace the maverick's candidacy. With the support of the Democratic organization, Douglas was elected. The "boys" immediately knew what a mistake Kelly had made. Douglas objected to almost everything the business-as-usual council attempted. He even spoke out against their time-honored tradition of demanding a few thousand in cash before granting anyone a permit to build a driveway.

After three years of being the "one" in an endless number of 49–1 votes, Douglas rebelled and challenged the organization candidate for the 1942 U.S. Senate nomination. As expected, he lost. Unexpectedly, the fifty-year-old Douglas joined the Marine Corps the day after the election. He startled his eighteen-year-old boot camp companions by winning prizes for pistol shooting and bayonet techniques. He wrangled his way out of a rear-echelon desk job in the Pacific and wound up in some of World War II's bloodiest battles on Peleliu and Okinawa. He received the Bronze Star and, while sitting on the edge of a bunker discussing Keynesian economics in Okinawa, also received a piece of Japanese shrapnel that left his left arm paralyzed and, he often joked, "good only for a paperweight."

Douglas returned to his teaching after the war, but if he was through with the Democratic Party of Cook County, it wasn't through with him. An old adversary in the council, Jake Arvey, had returned from the war with the rank of colonel, which he now used for his first name. He had taken over the party's chairmanship from Kelly and scored a big win by replacing the faltering Mayor Kelly with reformer Martin Kennelly, who won the important patronage office in 1947. Now, Arvey was looking for a blue-ribbon ticket in 1948 on the theory that, one, the Republicans led by incumbents Governor Dwight Green and Senate Majority Leader Wayland "Curly" Brooks were going to win, and, two, he could appease the party regulars by offering up as sacrificial lambs a couple of intellectual pains in the ass—Adlai Stevenson and Paul Douglas.

Stevenson, a marvelous phrasemaker, had become a favorite of the Council of Foreign Relations crowd and was very interested in the Senate. Douglas said he would go for the governor's post. But as the Democrats neared the decision, Arvey remembered how Douglas had winced at every council motive he deemed unpure. It was unlikely that he would be compliant in the patronage-rich governor's office. Arvey switched the ticket.

Despite little financial backing from the party, Douglas toured the state in a jeep equipped with a loudspeaker. He was part of Harry Truman's miracle comeback of 1948. Truman carried Illinois by 31,000 votes. Douglas won by 407,000.

Even before winning, he had gone to the 1948 party convention in Philadelphia and stood in awe as his friend, Humphrey, led a Democratic stampede to a civil rights platform with his memorable demand, "We must move out from the shadow of states rights into the bright sunshine of human rights."

It was to be Douglas's credo for the next eighteen years. He began fighting for a civil rights bill from the moment he entered the Senate in 1949. Within two years, he was named the nation's best senator by the Washington press corps. Within four years he was the unchallenged leader of the liberal wing of the party, fighting the lonely battle against the intransigent southern bloc and their ability to filibuster to death any civil rights bill.

But each term, for fifteen years, Douglas took up his cudgel, often going head to head with Illinois's junior senator, Everett Dirksen. There was a great deal of respect but not much affection between the two men, although Douglas did acknowledge the critical role Dirksen played when, finally, in 1964, the Civil Rights Bill won passage.

But Douglas had many other irons in the fire. Almost immediately upon joining the Senate, he battled to save the Marine Corps, which President Truman, an old army man, wanted to collapse. Next, he started a long crusade for a truth-in-lending bill. All that small print at the bottom of automobile ads and the even smaller words on credit card solicitations are Paul Douglas's fault.

He fought just about every Republican effort to dismantle New Deal programs during the Eisenhower years and was no friend of Lyndon Johnson. Unlike his colleague Dirksen, who was skilled at befriending presidents, Douglas seemed enthralled with the thought of challenging them. Except when it came to communism.

Douglas supported Truman in Korea, Eisenhower anywhere the red scare arose, and Johnson in Vietnam. He had visited Russia in 1926 and had voted to allow the Soviet Union in the United Nations. The first act caused him to be labeled a "pink" and fellow traveler throughout his career. He eternally regretted the second and became a firm disciple of the "domino theory," fearing any communist encroachment would ultimately lead to regional domination.

He was a confidante of Martin Luther King during the early 1960s civil rights protests. His second wife, Emily Taft Douglas, walked with King in Alabama protest marches. Douglas stood next to King at the podium in front of the Lincoln Memorial when the civil rights leader made his historic "I have a dream" speech.

Five years before Rachel Carson awakened the dormant environmental spirit of Americans with *Silent Spring*, Douglas began his most cherished crusade, to save the Indiana Dunes.

He first tried to convince a pair of Republican senators from Indiana to fight for their state's natural resources but quickly learned that the state party hierarchy was part of the cabal that intended to let steel companies create a massive harbor and replace the sandy Lake Michigan beach with a huge industrial complex. Despite the opposition of Indiana's congressional delegation, Douglas lobbied for nearly a decade, enlisting the help of western environmentalists such as his friend from Alaska, Ernest Gruening, and Interior Secretary Stewart Udall. He was stunned when President Kennedy—who while in the Senate sponsored similar legislation to make Cape Cod a national parkland—seemed lukewarm to saving the Indiana Dunes. Douglas finally bypassed all the White House bureaucracy and confronted Kennedy in the Oval Office.

Still, it was not Kennedy, but another Massachusetts Democrat, Speaker John McCormack, who ultimately pushed through the bill in 1966 when it was clear Douglas was going to lose his bid for a fourth Senate term.

By 1966, Paul Douglas, despite his enthusiasm and zest, had begun to look and act his seventy-four years. He was opposed by Charles Percy, a Chicago business wunderkind. In the midst of the campaign, Percy's twenty-one-year-old twin daughter was murdered in Percy's Kenilworth mansion. The combination of sympathy and the tumult of the antiwar movement, which turned on the Senate's greatest contemporary liberal, led to a humiliating defeat.

Paul Douglas was revered throughout the nation, but the institutions of his hometown never appreciated his greatness until his time had passed. The Democratic Party usually ignored him, and Richard Daley often succeeded in bypassing him to get federal appointments for friends. The *Chicago Tribune* opposed him in every election for every office for thirty years. "At least they are consistent," Douglas mused.

He would have been shocked at the *Tribune*'s editorial following his death in 1976:

> Paul Douglas was in many ways ahead of his time. And to be ahead of one's time calls for the sort of courage which Mr. Douglas displayed in abundance. . . . He was justly called the "fighting liberal" but when he felt the liberals were wrong, he fought against them. . . . Mr. Douglas was always his own man. He put his foot down for what he thought was right, no matter whose toes got in the way. And these, after all, are the qualities most essential to a "giant of a man."

6 ▦

THE CHAIRMAN:
DANIEL ROSTENKOWSKI

Danny Rostenkowski scared people. He knew it and he enjoyed doing it. For more than a decade from the Reagan revolution to the Clinton new age, the most powerful congressman in the United States was Danny Rostenkowski of Chicago, and no one from Chicago's political world ever had so much impact on so many Americans.

"No one from Chicago was ever more effective nationally than Danny," said Gene Callahan, a onetime political reporter who watched Rostenkowski during the 1980s from his perch as the top aide to Senator Alan Dixon.

As chairman of the Ways and Means Committee from 1980 to 1994, Rostenkowski was the gatekeeper to America's public money. No tax was passed, no dollar spent, that didn't get massaged by his huge hands. He was courted by presidents in the same way they pleaded with Everett Dirksen. Reagan depended on him. Bush was an old friend. Bill and Hillary were the "kids" he showed the ropes. No appropriation could make its way to the floor of the House until the hulking, scowling, threatening, deal maker from Chicago had his say, and most often, his way.

He was the man most responsible for the 1986 tax act that some say made the rich richer. Others would say it built the framework for the great economic boom of the 1990s. Rostenkowski traded billions for the special interests to get the concessions he needed to get the bill passed.

"If I had a secret, it was that I never let anybody know what I really wanted," Rostenkowski once said.

During the 1980s and 1990s, George Mitchell headed the Senate and Tom Foley was Speaker, but everyone in Washington knew who was the supreme deal maker. Congress has fifty committees, but no one ever had to ask who was being discussed when someone mentioned "the chairman."

He put the heads of Fortune 500 companies on hold as though he were dealing with a precinct captain back in Chicago. He scolded Clinton like he was talking to his alderman. He brought billions in federal money to Chicago, and he raised a campaign war chest that stunned reformers.

But he passed bills. Despite his image as a raw power player, Rostenkowski was far more complex than he was given credit for by the media, who treated him as a dinosaur in the age of processed politicians and media manipulation.

For thirty-six years, Dan Rostenkowski thought politics was about results. His political baptism was in the Illinois General Assembly, where the legendary rogue Paul Powell once explained, "We take care of the people's business first and then we take care of ourselves."

Rostenkowski succeeded his father, Joe, as committeeman of the 32nd Ward on the northwest side and went to Congress in 1958, a beefy thirty-year-old who learned fast and played hard. His rough edges, Chicago syntax, and intimidating bulk made him a stereotype of the Chicago machine Democrats who the Washington media enjoyed portraying as mere stooges of Mayor Richard J. Daley.

Rostenkowski was much more than that. He went to school under House Speaker John McCormack and became a close colleague of Tip O'Neill, who would later become Speaker. He admired the way Lyndon Johnson ran the Senate and would be a personal favorite of LBJ when Johnson took over the White House. That ultimately created a near-fatal detour in his Washington career. During the raucous Democratic National Convention of 1968, Johnson was infuriated that House Speaker Carl Albert of Oklahoma, the convention chairman, allowed the antiwar delegates to dominate the nationally televised proceedings, embarrassing the president. He ordered Rostenkowski to take over the gavel to quiet the proceedings. Nothing ever got really quiet in 1968, and a year later Albert got even by dumping Rostenkowski from the leadership group, sending him into temporary oblivion. But Rostenkowski climbed back up the ladder and rose to the number-two spot on Ways and Means. When Al Ullman lost a reelection bid in the 1980 Reagan landslide, Rostenkowski became "chairman."

He helped Reagan get his first tax cut and emerged as one of the Capitol's elite after he pushed through the 1986 tax act. In 1993, Clinton won a bitter battle to pass NAFTA and praised the vital role Rostenkowski played. But to get the votes he needed, Rostenkowski had promised tobacco-state Democrats he would take care of them in the upcoming battle on health care. When Clinton began the health care debate by suggesting taxes on a package of cigarettes should be hiked to two dollars, Rostenkowski was livid. He was viewed by the Clinton White House as the critical player in the attempt to pass national health care legislation in 1994, and when a federal indictment forced his resignation as "chairman" the bill's chances evaporated.

Danny Rostenkowski didn't begin life as an aspiring politician, despite growing up in a political house. He wanted to be a baseball player. His father persuaded him that life in politics was good. What Rostenkowski saw of politics was that it helped people. His father got people jobs. Danny got people jobs. Despite his lofty status in Washington, Rostenkowski was a committeeman at heart. During the 1973 oil crisis, he conducted a regular meeting in the 32nd Ward headquarters. Half the office space was filled with service-station operators begging Rostenkowski to get the government to do something before they were put out of business. On the other side of the room, his aides were passing out garbage cans. Rostenkowski never strayed too far from the politics of the streets. In the end, it was his undoing.

In 1991 he became a target of the Justice Department, which was investigating his use of congressional funds to hire people, pay office rent, lease cars, and send gifts. They were particularly interested in the House Post Office, where congressmen often traded stamp vouchers for cash. They said that over the years Rostenkowski used about fifty thousand dollars in stamp money for personal expenses.

Like his anachronistic zest for wheeling and dealing, Rostenkowski's lifestyle resembled that of old-time politicians. He was never seen jogging or eating bean sprouts. He ate steaks and drank martinis.

He was often someone's guest. Just as often, he reached for the tab. The government said he reached for too many of them.

Rostenkowski could have resigned in 1992 and kept $1 million in campaign money, a provision in the law that expired the following year. Friends thought the Justice Department might lose interest in pursuing its investigation if he no longer held one of the most powerful jobs in Washington. Chicago pols were certain he would quit.

He didn't. He insisted he had done nothing wrong. People had been doing these things ever since he went to Washington during the Eisenhower presidency.

And he loved his job. He loved the tradition and the history. He spent a great deal of time and taxpayer money on a film commemorating the two-hundredth anniversary of the House Ways and Means Committee.

Once he spent a half hour explaining to a visitor how he found Davy Crockett's old desk in a government warehouse and had it restored for his use. He walked around the desk a dozen times, touching the edges. "Imagine, me sitting in Davy Crockett's desk!"

He was defeated for election in 1994, pleaded guilty to government charges in 1996, and was sentenced to seventeen months. Not even the Washington press corps chortled over another Chicago pol ending his career in prison. Rostenkowski was not a plunderer in the Chicago tradition. He did not collect graft or arrange phony contracts. He lamented to a friend, "I'm going to jail for sending a guy a rocking chair."

7

THE REVEREND:
JESSE JACKSON

When the Reverend Jesse Louis Jackson decided to run for president in 1988 it was baffling to those who had spent twenty years more or less observing the flamboyant, peripatetic, handsome, boisterous, demanding, articulate, obnoxious, and charming civil rights leader. Frankly, being Jesse Jackson seemed a much better job than being president.

Some would argue that Jesse Jackson was not a politician, never having been elected to anything. Others would say that Jesse Jackson, although having a residence in Chicago for more than thirty years, was really a citizen of whatever destination was written on the airline ticket in his pocket.

In most white enclaves of Chicago, Jesse Jackson rated only vile epithets. There were some black enclaves where the epithets were more vile.

It was in one of those white enclaves in the summer of 1966 that Jesse Jackson became a media figure on his way to being a media star on his way to being Jesse Jackson.

Martin Luther King Jr. had declared his nonviolent war on Chicago, leading open housing protests in the city's white neighborhoods where ethnic residents feared black neighbors would devalue their cherished bungalows and two-flats. Leading the marchers was a tall, handsome native of South Carolina who was not at all reticent to talk to the white media desperately trying to find a spokesman for the new civil unrest.

Jesse was always good copy. "All these people marching behind me got plenty of money to buy homes. Real estate dealers won't take it. GMAC will. Why do you think there are so many Cadillacs in the ghetto?"

Jesse on crime and the absence of black fathers: "You take a young boy in Cabrini Green when he sees a screwdriver for the first time. He thinks it's a weapon. He's never seen anybody use a screwdriver to turn screws."

After King's murder in 1968, Jackson, with his rhythmic limerick speech, became the most visible figure in the civil rights movement, and many said, the most ambitious. He formed Operation PUSH (People United to Save Humanity) in 1971 and began his globe-trotting with Chicago as a base. He traveled to South Africa to speak out against apartheid and toured Israel to promote a Palestinian state. Jesse Jackson had his own foreign policy. He led protests against companies that didn't hire enough blacks or promote the ones they had. Some businessmen privately called him an extortionist. Liberal audiences in Los Angeles, San Francisco, and New York adoringly paid him ten thousand dollars a speech.

For years, an unusual geographical rule applied in Jackson's case: the more distance he put between himself and Chicago, the stronger his support and his recognition. His Chicago opponents viewed him as a meddler and perennial problem, a character who thrived on creating confrontations that only he could resolve, who developed strategies just this side of scams, advancing his own interests in their resolution.

Through the chaotic political period following Mayor Daley's death, Jackson was expected to run for mayor or seek some prominent Illinois office. He never did, and opponents said he was wise enough to know he couldn't win.

His entrance in the 1984 presidential race was viewed as little more than a token, a historical footnote, ill-funded and unorganized as well as ill-timed in the face of Republican President Ronald Reagan's overwhelming popularity.

But 1988 was different. The Democrats thought they could beat George Bush. They didn't think they could do it with Jesse Jackson.

But Jackson ran and ran better than any white candidate except Michael Dukakis, and after the results of the November election were counted it wasn't certain that Jackson might not have been the better Democratic candidate.

Jesse Jackson made history in 1988 by building on a strong black base in the presidential primaries to come in second, collecting 7 million votes in the process. Wherever he spoke, so long as it wasn't in Chicago, the crowds cheered him as though he were the nominee. In his last stop before election day, more than five thousand people packed an arena in Dayton. The old geographical rule was at work again. His personal popularity was as strong as ever.

After Dukakis had clinched the nomination, the major political question of 1988 was not whether he could beat George Bush; it was, as *Time* and *Newsweek* covers inquired, "What does Jesse want?"

No other African American in history had produced such an impact on America's national politics. Even if, as they always said, he couldn't get elected dogcatcher in Chicago.

8

THE FIRST BOSS:
ROGER SULLIVAN

Lost in the creation of Cermak, the success of Kelly-Nash, and the legend of Daley, is Roger Sullivan, the first boss of the Democratic Party in Chicago. True to the tradition of those who would follow him, Sullivan built the foundations of the Democratic machine on one of the great political scams of all time. If he had lived longer he would have been as famous as his successors. Had he lived in their times he would have gone to jail.

Roger Sullivan was a first-generation Irishman born in Belvidere. He was orphaned in his early teens and made his way to Chicago, where he began working in the trolley yards and quickly became a member of the fledgling unions, earning a spot in the Democratic party rank and file. He worked for Grover Cleveland in the 1884 election and was rewarded with a federal patronage post, then was elected clerk of the probate court in 1890, a post that made him part of the Democratic inner circle. A fellow Cleveland supporter was John P. Hopkins, who happened to be handy during the 1893 world exposition when Mayor Carter Harrison was assassinated. Sullivan helped engineer the selection of Hopkins to serve out the unexpired term of mayor.

Sullivan, a disciple of the "I seen my chances and I took 'em" school of politics, decided what Chicago needed was a competitor to the Peoples Gas, Light and Coke Company. He formed the Ogden Gas Company in 1896 and with the help of Mayor Hopkins obtained a franchise from the city council. To anyone's knowledge the Ogden Gas

Company did not own any gas, did not lease any gas, did not build any pipelines, and had no customers. But it had a franchise, which meant it could someday do all of those things, which wasn't in the best interests of Peoples Gas. So Peoples Gas did the prudent thing and paid Roger Sullivan $1 million for his franchise. Mayor Hopkins got a cut.

By now, Sullivan controlled the state Democratic apparatus but would battle for twenty years with factions led by Carter Harrison II and Edward Dunne for control of Chicago Democratic politics. He was chairman of the Democratic convention delegations from 1900 to 1916 and would have chaired the 1920 delegation had he not died a few months before the convention. The zenith of his national influence came in 1912 when the Democrats were deadlocked for more than one hundred ballots in Baltimore. His nemesis, Harrison, was a staunch supporter of Missouri's Champ Clark. William Jennings Bryan, another Sullivan enemy, was backing Woodrow Wilson. Sullivan liked neither man, but set a pattern that would be followed by Cermak, Kelly, and Daley, remaining silent until the crucial moment when the opportunity arose to become a kingmaker. He threw the Illinois delegation to Wilson, who often credited Sullivan for making him president. Sullivan's most ambitious personal effort failed in 1914 when he was defeated for the U.S. Senate. But with Wilson's sponsorship and a free hand with all Illinois's federal patronage, he finally overcame the Harrison-Dunne factions and united the Chicago Democrats under his undisputed rule. The politics of the American Century would not be the same, or as colorful, without the myth and reality of the Chicago Democratic machine. Without Roger Sullivan, there would have been no machine.

Sullivan High School is named for him. They should have renamed the gas company, too.

9

THE BUILDER:
WILLIAM HALE THOMPSON

A turn-of-the-century Republican asked to sponsor the profligate son of a prominent party contributor told his colleagues, "The worst you can say about him is that he's stupid."

He was wrong. Before William Hale Thompson, that young profligate, completed his three disconnected terms as mayor of Chicago there were plenty of worse things that were said about him. He was corrupt, an oaf, arrogant, and a fool. But he was not stupid.

Thompson was an early practitioner of coalition politics and consensus politics. He won his first mayoral term in 1915, attacking his Democratic opponent's German heritage at a time when stories of Hun rape in Belgium filled the newspapers. He sensed the midwestern mood of isolationism growing in apprehension of American troops being sent to the trenches in France and began damning the English in time for his 1919 reelection. His anglophobic diatribe caused a national stir when he promised to punch King George in the nose if the British monarch ever set foot in Chicago. But he was not all bombast. Thompson also won in 1919 by wooing the newly arrived black migrants who settled on the South Side and, to his credit, installed a number of black politicians in city hall.

Another 1919 strategy was boostering Chicago by shaking down businessmen for a $1 million fund to proclaim the city's glories. He called himself "Big Bill the Builder." He started the Michigan Avenue bridge construction, which paved, literally, the growth of America's most magnificent shopping strip, and he built Navy Pier as a recreation area that ultimately became a military installation, a college campus, and, in the Chicago spirit of "what goes around, comes around," a recreation center once again.

He was vilified by the *Chicago Tribune*'s Colonel McCormick and sanctified by William Randolph Hearst. He failed to win a U.S. Senate seat in 1924 and impossibly toyed with running for president in 1928. Undoubtedly, he was Chicago's most colorful mayor, but more than that, he was Al Capone's best friend.

"Big Bill" did not have many moral scruples. He was a politician. In his first term he undid all the reforms of the progressives who had shuttered the brothels and gambling dens that cluttered the Loop. When a civic backlash occurred, he flipped and closed down saloons on Sunday. When no one was looking, he allowed them to reopen. He was the perfect mayor for the mob.

Without Thompson, Chicago would never have emerged as the icon of the Roaring Twenties. The machine-gun warfare, the hundreds of unsolved murders, the elaborate gangland funerals, the thousands of speakeasies and brothels that literature and cinema have used to provide the texture of the Prohibition era never flourished elsewhere in America the way they did in Bill Thompson's Chicago. Certainly, the crime bosses were in Chicago before Thompson and Prohibition triggered a national wave of acceptable law-breaking, but nowhere did criminals operate so openly and with the tacit approval of city hall.

Capone was so distraught when Thompson wisely decided not to seek a third term in 1923 that he moved his crime empire to Cicero. He was so enthralled at Thompson's political reentry in 1927 that he provided a half-million dollars to Big Bill's campaign.

Thompson's final election inspired Capone to new heights in gangland warfare, culminating in the St. Valentine's Day Massacre and the murders of prominent political figures standing in the way of mob rule.

Not even Chicagoans used to the most unimaginable crimes wanted more of this, and Thompson was sent to permanent retirement when he tried unsuccessfully to win a fourth term in 1931. He spent his last years avoiding indictment and counting his money. His name is on the dedication plaque at the Michigan Avenue bridge. He did not invent the symbol of the 1920s that also was named Thompson, but without Big Bill the machine gun and Chicago would never have been synonymous.

THE IRON HORSE:
ADOLPH SABATH

In the winter of 1953 a new congressional appointee arrived in Washington from Chicago. Jimmy Bowler, seventy-seven, committeeman from the 7th Ward, was asked why he was coming to Washington at such an advanced age. "It was my turn," snorted the septuagenarian, adding another layer to the myth of Chicago Democratic politics.

Bowler hardly left a shadow in his brief passage through the Capitol rotunda, but for some time it appeared that the man he was appointed to replace wasn't going to ever leave.

Bowler was appointed to fill the vacancy caused by the death of Adolph J. Sabath, not one of the names bandied about in Chicago Democratic lore, but it should be. In the arts, in literature, in sports, and in politics, longevity counts for something. At the time of his death in November 1952, Adolph Sabath had served continuously longer than any other person Americans ever sent to Congress.

He was first elected in 1906 and won his twenty-fourth consecutive term a few hours before his death. His record stood until House Speaker Sam Rayburn won his twenty-fifth term in 1960. Sabath's mark never brought him any kind of notoriety. It was the same as the lack of attention paid to Ty Cobb's three-thousandth hit. At the time, no one knew it was a milestone.

Adolph Sabath was born in Zabori, Bohemia, in 1866. At age fifteen he emigrated to America and saved money to bring his parents, five sisters, and five brothers to Chicago. He clerked and became a salesman for a sash and door company and graduated from Chicago

Law School in 1890. He turned his business interests to real estate and became wealthy until the 1893 financial panic. A Bohemian and a Jew, Sabath was supported in 1906 for a judgeship by the southwest side Democratic organization, but he turned it down to run for Congress. He won and won and won and won.

He became a social progressive, supporting the earliest forms of welfare legislation in the Woodrow Wilson administration. He became a champion of immigration rights. While 15 million Europeans— many of them Jewish—migrated to America in the first two decades of the century, there were constant attempts to halt the flow of new Americans. Sabath fought them all. After World War I, new restrictions were passed limiting severely the numbers of immigrants. But Sabath remembered his own experiences and fought until after World War II, when the laws were eased and many displaced victims of the war—and many survivors of the Holocaust—were welcomed to America.

As chairman of the powerful House Rules Committee during the New Deal and until his death, Sabath became one of Washington's most powerful politicians, pushing the "go" button for every Democratic bill and bottling up Republican legislation.

Although he was anathema to the GOP, his district was so staunchly Democratic that only nominal and frivolous opponents lined up to challenge him every two years. While Sabath is not a name that echoes in local Democratic lore like Hinky Dink Kenna, Paddy Bauler, or other great rogues, the man who last had a chance to beat him had a theory that rivals any ghost-voter story.

Manny Stein, then a forty-two-year-old store owner, was the Republican challenger in 1952. "I got into the race figuring the son-of-a-bitch would die. . . . Sabath died about seven days before the election. . . . They kept him on ice in the hospital under the orders of Mayor Kennelly. . . . It was a (Republican) landslide. I automatically would have been declared the winner. . . . No write-in candidate could have beaten me as a printed candidate on the ballot."

No one ever paid attention to Stein's claims. That doesn't mean it didn't happen.

II

SPORTS'
TOP TEN

In the beginning there were the Black Sox. In the end there was Michael Jordan. In between were some of the most historic and memorable players and performances, individuals and events that did as much to create the American myth and mystique of sport as any other place in the country.

It is ironic, however, that Chicago, which triumphed like no other city of the twentieth century, earned its niche in the American sports myth because of its penchant for defeat. It has been the scene of great individual triumphs, but its teams, with rare exception, only led the league in profits.

Chicago hosted bicycle races when that sport was a national craze, track meets when the sprinters and hurdlers were amateurs, wrestling matches when it was a sport not an act, classic thoroughbred matches when the sport of kings was also the sport of saloon keepers, and some of the most artistic and brutal boxing dramas. Of course, it had to have the most famous mistake.

Of all the fights in all the world, from Shelby, Montana, to Kinshasha, Zaire, none is more famous than the 1927 "long count" at Soldier Field. The greatest fighter of them all, Jack Dempsey, failed to regain his heavyweight championship when the referee ignored a flattened Gene Tunney for somewhere between four and twelve seconds while chasing Dempsey to a neutral corner.

Chicago has not, sadly, seen many World Series, but it has made the most of them. The last time the fall classic visited Chicago was not unusual in that the Los Angeles Dodgers made short work of the White Sox. It was the prelude that is memorable. When the Sox clinched the American League pennant in 1959 the ebullient fire commissioner set off sirens all over the city, sending many residents to their basements with visions of Soviet missiles approaching the lakefront.

The Cubs last played in a World Series when baseball was diluted by World War II service. The best thing about that matchup with the equally ordinary Detroit Tigers was sportswriter Warren Brown's famous prediction: "Neither team can win."

Neither 1959 nor 1945 compare historically with the previous arrival of the World Series. That was in 1919, when seven White Sox players on what was considered the finest baseball team ever decided to throw the World Series. In keeping with Chicago's inept sporting tradition, three of the players never got paid off by the gamblers and three of them took the money but played to win. Either way, they all were banned from the game for life, and although Commissioner Kenesaw Landis didn't mention it, the World Series apparently was banned from Chicago as well.

The Cubs, of course, are most famous for their futility, summed up by broadcaster Jack Brickhouse: "Anyone can have a bad century." But the Cubs are not alone. Most Chicago teams have been losers. And there have been lots of them. Until the 1990s, the Bulls certainly belonged to this group, and the 1990s notwithstanding, the Black Hawks. There also were the Cardinals and the Rockets and the Hornets, and there was the Sting and before them the Gears, the Stags and Packers, and the Zephyrs and the Wind and the Blitz and the Fire. There were Whales and Mustangs and Owls. Lately there is the Wolves, who may or may not be related to the Cougars. They both played hockey. The Zephyrs and the Wind were not, to anyone's knowledge, related since they played different sports but compiled equally dismal records.

Whoever they were or whatever they played, they lost.

But Chicago has had its share of superstars, men who played their games as well or better than anyone else, at any other time or in any other place. And Chicago has had men whose contributions to sports transformed both the games and American society far more than can be measured by counting home runs, touchdowns, slap shots, or slam dunks.

PAPA BEAR:
GEORGE HALAS

"The weather was perfect. So were the Bears."

The day was December 8, 1940, and that is how Arthur Daley of the *New York Times* began his description of the most devastating offensive display in the history of National Football League championship play.

The Chicago Bears, owned, coached, and nurtured by George Stanley Halas, had defeated the Washington Redskins 73–0. The National Football League wasn't the multibillion-dollar industry it became by the 1990s. It was argued by many fans that the professional teams of the 1940s were not in the same league with the college teams. The professionals were regarded as little more than an upgrade of the semipro town teams that had been popular since the turn of the century, playing in places like Taylorville or Hinckley, Rock Island, Duluth, Pottsville, Portsmouth, and Providence. These were teams made up of players who might one weekend be earning fifty dollars at Canton and turn up the next Sunday playing for Massillon. Although the league had solidified and mostly moved into major cities during the 1930s, the majority of American ticket buyers were skeptical.

But what the Bears did to the Redskins on that balmy late-autumn afternoon changed a lot of minds. It also changed forever the way the game would be played.

George Halas was not the greatest athlete in Chicago's twentieth century, but he was one of them. He played three sports at Crane High School and at the University of Illinois. He was most valuable player of the 1919 Rose Bowl, and that same summer he started in right field for the New York Yankees. He lost his job the following year when New York traded for an outfielder named Babe Ruth. He played both ways at end for his Chicago Bears from 1919 to 1929. He played semipro basketball in his thirties. But George Halas does not top the list of Chicago sports figures of the twentieth century for his athletic skills.

George Halas did not invent professional football any more than Henry Ford invented the automobile. But just as Ford created the process that would produce a billion cars, it was George Halas who built professional football from a shady and curious blue-collar pastime to the national phenomenon that has turned American Sundays into a television obsession.

Halas started out with a team called the Decatur Staleys. He coached and starred for the Staleys and in 1920 joined a dozen other pro football enthusiasts in a Hupmobile showroom in Canton, Ohio, where they formed what would become the National Football League. "There weren't enough chairs so I sat on the running board," said Halas. One of the founders was Jim Thorpe, who would be the league's first president and who was perhaps the greatest American athlete of all. Of the rest, only Halas would find sports immortality. In 1921 he bought the Staleys and moved the team to Chicago. He arranged to play games in Wrigley Field, where he stayed for nearly sixty years and almost decided to name his team after his baseball landlords, the Cubs. But he concluded football players were bigger and more rugged than Cubs so he dubbed them the Bears.

The first year the team made seven dollars.

On Thanksgiving Day, 1925, Halas started professional football on its spiraling climb to the top of the sports world. He brought college football's most celebrated player, Harold "Red" Grange of Illinois, into Wrigley Field and thirty-six thousand people came out to watch him. A week later at the Polo Grounds, seventy thousand turned out to watch the Galloping Ghost. Halas barnstormed across the country, taking Grange and the sport on a whirlwind tour that established both of them. Crowds showed up at train stations to see Grange and went away talking about professional football.

For a few years the team made modest profits, but during the Depression, Halas kept the fledgling league alive by helping other owners with loans and players, and went in debt to everyone he knew and every bank that wasn't closed. And he won several championships with such sports legends as Bronko Nagurski.

Halas personally anointed the NFL's next president, Joe Carr, and then chose an old friend, Bert Bell, to become Carr's successor. While other teams floundered and other owners gave up, Halas was indomitable in his ambition to build professional football. He was innovative in his coaching and a visionary for the league. When the collegiate establishment complained in the 1920s about the professionals luring young men from the campus before their graduation, Halas pushed the NFL to stop the practice, and the pros had a hands-off policy toward undergraduates until the federal courts changed that in the 1990s. It was Halas who, although his Bears were dominant, agreed in 1935 to create the NFL draft so that the unsuccessful teams would have first crack at the top collegiates and create a parity that would ensure more competition. In the 1940s, when a new league surfaced, Halas quickly forged an expansion policy to co-opt the most successful franchises. Again in the 1960s, when the American Football League was created with the unending supply of Texas oil money, Halas was among the first to call for a merger. He put the Bears on radio in the 1930s and in the 1950s had a television network extending from the Dakotas to the Okefenokee to advertise his Bears. Of course, he didn't televise the games in Chicago. With the advent of the lush network-television contracts in the 1960s and the 1970s, it was Halas who agreed to revenue sharing for all teams even though he and the Mara family, which owned the New York Giants, could have insisted on hogging the pie as the baseball moguls in New York and Chicago do to this day.

There is no doubt that for all his altruistic innovations George Halas was trying to get rich. And he did. But all those years of struggling left indelible traits that in his final decades rewarded him with a reputation as a greedy, self-indulgent owner who cared more about his gate receipts than his team's success.

Halas had many idiosyncrasies. He was a man of contradictions. He was cheap but he was generous. He was a bully but he was a soft touch. He demanded excellence but accepted incompetence. He was a zealot but he was practical.

It was the Chicago Bears who first began training camps. It was the Bears who forced the rule change to allow passing from anywhere behind the line of scrimmage. It was the Bears who argued for years against making a fumbled lateral a live ball. His critics would note that at the time only the Bears threw the ball from far behind the line of scrimmage and only the Bears had a wide array of lateral plays. It was the Bears who first created the man-in-motion. It was the Bears who perfected the spacing of linemen and numbered the spaces to identify the play calls. It was Halas who authorized the first NFL rules book and created a league office to measure the consistency of field officials.

But it was also Halas who remembered the only profits that carried his early Bears were the ten-cent program sales. It was Halas who in the 1940s was still withholding a percentage of every player's salary until the end of the season. He argued that he didn't want his boys to spend all their pay and not have money to last until the next season. His players knew he was earning interest on their money.

It was Halas who installed temporary bleachers in Wrigley Field to boost capacity by another ten thousand seats, with some of the benches placed right on the field. One of his players once left a game and returned to his spot on the bench only to find a stranger sitting there. "And he had a ticket, too."

He kept his faithful friends on the payroll for forty years and turned against his greatest stars. He went to court to avoid paying Dick Butkus a promised salary after Butkus's knees had given out during a career that made him one of the most celebrated and ferocious players in the game and, coincidentally, made the Bears one of the nation's most attractive teams.

He underpaid one of his brightest assistant coaches, George Allen, and then sued to prevent Allen from accepting a job to head the Los Angeles Rams. When the judge ruled in Halas's favor, he promptly gave Allen permission to go to Los Angeles.

He won the first NFL playoff in 1932, when the Bears defeated the Portsmouth, Ohio, Spartans 9–0 in the only indoor title game ever played before the advent of modern domed stadiums. A snowstorm prompted Halas to move the game from Wrigley Field to Chicago Stadium, where they played on an eighty-yard field. His championship teams of 1940 and 1941 were so awesome they were called the Monsters of the Midway, the only nickname of prowess ever given any Chicago team.

The years were good to the sport Halas created, but not so good to the team he owned. After forty years of running the Bears from the sidelines, Halas stepped down from coaching. He subsequently proved that while he knew how to coach, he didn't know much about hiring those who claimed they did. Somehow, even in their odd successful season for the remainder of the century, the Bears were never quite the same without the scowling man in the fedora and tinted glasses roaming the sidelines, slapping the helmets of players, shoving referees, and counting the gate.

He won ten championships and shortly before his death hired a coach who would lead the Bears to their only Super Bowl, although Halas did not live to see it. He left Chicago with a rich tradition of football success and a legacy of penury that haunts his family, who still runs the team. More than that, George Halas left America with a game that is a multibillion-dollar industry and an integral part of American society.

2 ▪

BE LIKE MIKE:
MICHAEL JORDAN

Perhaps the most compelling aspect of America's fascination with sports is the enduring debates that the performers and the teams perpetuate. Not even in the most serious undertaking of men is there the controversy that can be stirred with a simple statement such as "Jack Dempsey was the greatest fighter ever." Has anyone ever heard a bar fight or a university forum compare armies? "Robert E. Lee would have stomped Napoleon." "Caesar's legions would have kicked the hell out of Rommel's Panzers." In these endeavors, we are content to let history record the victors. Not so in sports.

When baseball celebrated its one-hundredth season Joe DiMaggio was named the greatest baseball player of all, but the fans of Ty Cobb, Babe Ruth, and Willie Mays issued a formal protest. No native of Brooklyn will ever concede the Yankees of 1927 were better than the Dodgers of 1955.

Everyone was certain Bobby Jones was the greatest golfer, until Jack Nicklaus. And now Nicklaus may be surpassed by Tiger Woods. But Arnold Palmer would collect more locker room votes even if he won less tournaments.

Chicago hasn't had many contenders for "greatest." It has had Walter Payton and Gale Sayers, but they usually come in behind Jimmy Brown when the discussion is about running backs. There was Bobby Hull, but where does he stack up against the Great Gretzky, Mario LeMieux, or the older Gordie Howe and Rocket Richard? Ernie Banks was magnificent, but he didn't rate a call on the centennial baseball squad.

Another century may go by before anyone takes too seriously an argument that Michael Jordan is not the greatest basketball player who ever lived. There are some provincials who want to argue for the freakish Wilt Chamberlain, who played against men a foot shorter, or the gifted all-around skills of Magic Johnson, or the deadly clutch shooting and passing of Larry Bird. But Chamberlain's scoring was mundane albeit historic, and Magic's popularity was abetted by the glitz of Los Angeles and the second-best smile in the NBA. It helped Larry's legend that he was white.

Michael Jordan was not a transforming figure in basketball. Chamberlain forced rules changes about dunking the ball and caused the foul lane to be stretched to twelve feet. Bill Russell's shot-blocking and rebounding elevated defensive play, and his passing evolved the half-court offense. Julius Erving created the "above the basket" game. But the summation of all modern basketball is Michael Jordan. He scored more effectively than anyone. Chamberlain still holds the one hundred-point-game mark and tallied far more games above fifty points than Jordan, but he did it in an era when NBA contests routinely totaled 250 to 275 points, and with the exception of Russell there were few big men to stop him. Still, Jordan has led the league in scoring more times than Chamberlain and has a career thirty-point average in an era when a dozen less will make a player worth $100 million. In playoff and championship games, no one, not Chamberlain, or Magic, or Bird, approaches Jordan's scoring. Of the seven all-time highest playoff point totals, Jordan has four of them. If Russell invented the defensive game, Jordan perfected it. He has been the premier defensive player of his time. He has more steals than any other player who averaged thirty points for his career, and he has more points than any other player who averaged two steals a game throughout his career. And of all those players with record steals he has more rebounds. Of those players who have more rebounds, he has more assists.

Unlike Chamberlain, he has won many championships. As many as anyone excepting the flock of Celtics who were part of their great runs of the 1960s. And he did it playing in Chicago, where championships of any sort are as rare as spring.

And he had the smile and the leaking tongue and the tomahawk dunk. Like Babe Ruth and Muhammad Ali he became the most recognized figure in the world. A Chicagoan traveling in northern Burma in 1995 was jogging early in the morning in a remote village when he spotted an elderly man sitting by a well. This village did not receive cable TV and there were no telephone lines to surf the Internet. The man was wearing a Michael Jordan T-shirt.

All this with almost two years wasted on missing curveballs.

No one has more charming commercials. No athlete has made more money. It's just as well George Halas was gone. He would have died of envy.

But Michael Jordan was not Halas. He was not a creator, an inventor. The NBA had become well established with the Magic-Bird rivalry. It did not need Jordan to save it, but it welcomed the revenues he escalated by the perpetual appearance of the Bulls on television as often as possible during the regular season and during a decade of playoffs.

More than any other basketball player and like his peers in other sports, Jordan had an intangible, almost mystical flair for the dramatic moment.

Henry Aaron may have surpassed Babe Ruth in number of home runs, but he never called his shot. Perhaps Marciano or Dempsey or Joe Louis could have beaten Ali, but they wouldn't have predicted the round.

Michael Jordan in the fourth quarter was a mix of Arnold Palmer hitching up his pants on the back nine and Red Grange taking the snap in the last two minutes. There was the skinny freshman with a patch of fuzz on his head popping the jump shot to give North Carolina its NCAA title in 1982. There was the brash young Bull soaring and driving past Bird and all the other Celtics for sixty-three points in his first playoff season. There was the shot at Cleveland in 1989 that made the Bulls serious. There was the spree of three-point shots and the "Only God knows how good I am" shrug that buried Portland for the 1993 championship. And there was the tomahawk dunk against Los Angeles that ignited the four-game sweep after the Lakers had won game one in 1991. "I don't think about how I do it, I just do it."

No one else has ever done it as well.

3

THE GALLOPING GHOST:
RED GRANGE

They don't make nicknames like that anymore.

Harold "Red" Grange may not have been the greatest football player who ever lived, but in one amazing quarter against Michigan in 1924 he became the greatest player anyone ever heard about. The numbers he left in the record books are monumental, but the number 77 on his jersey was indelible. Grange became a household name in America when most households didn't know there was a game called football. His gifts were his ability to run, cut, slash, and dash, but his mystique was timing. Red Grange was part of the golden age of American sport.

"Red Grange made Jack Dempsey move over," Paul Sann wrote in *The Lawless Decade*. "He put college football ahead of boxing as the Golden Age picked up momentum. He also made some of the ball yards obsolete; they couldn't handle his crowds. He made people buy more radios: how could you wait until Sunday morning to find out what deeds Red Grange had performed on Saturday?"

If Grange didn't exactly push Jack Dempsey out of history, he certainly made room for himself in the sports pantheon of the twenties. He was right there with Babe Ruth, Man O' War, Bobby Jones, and Bill Tilden.

America of the 1920s was a payoff for the great wave of immigrants of the 1890s. They didn't work seven days a week anymore. There were a few dollars left for fun. And there were new heroes performing new games. It was, for perhaps the first time in civilized history, an opportunity for the lowest class of citizens to enjoy being spectators at something other than wars or public hangings. Boxing, a sport as old as Cain and Abel, was something everyone understood, and the various ethnic fighters served as figures of national pride to the Irish, German, Italian, and Jewish Americans. Baseball, with its daily shows from April until October, its bucolic holiday appeal, and its relative low cost, was quickly seized on by everyday Americans as a cheap form of leisure. So the Jack Dempseys and the Babe Ruths became instant heroes.

But college football was elitist. It was glamorous. It arrived in fancy roadsters and wore raccoon coats, and its players were surrounded by pretty rich girls waving yellow pom-poms. It all somehow belonged to Harvard and Yale and those institutions that in the 1920s clearly separated the American establishment from the hordes who arrived in steerage.

Red Grange changed all that.

It began in Wheaton, Illinois, where Grange, the son of the police chief, won sixteen letters in four sports and used his dazzling speed to score seventy-three touchdowns in three high school seasons. In the 1990s, his modest house would have been swamped by coaches, recruiters, sports agents, and lawyers. One of the many avaricious NFL owners would be in court trying to reverse the NFL law against signing high school players. But the 1920s were not the 1990s. Grange, whose summer job delivering ice had earned him one nifty sobriquet—the Wheaton Iceman—wandered off to the University of Illinois, where his older brother was on the varsity. Grange wasn't sure he would try out for football. He thought at five-foot-ten and 165 pounds he wasn't big enough. But in 1923 against a powerful Nebraska team that would later defeat Notre Dame and its Four Horsemen, Grange, a sophomore, scored three touchdowns in an Illinois victory. The *Chicago Tribune* noted: "Grange Sprints to Fame."

The following autumn, Illinois prepared to open its new seventy thousand–seat Memorial Stadium against mighty Michigan, the only midwestern football team that had gained equity with the Ivy League teams, which as the progenitors of the sport were considered the finest in the land. Michigan, with its legendary coach Fielding Yost, had already inaugurated a quaint New Year's Day tradition in the sleepy California town of Pasadena by playing in the 1903 Rose Bowl.

Michigan was expected to defeat Illinois, although there was considerable interest among the eastern press in the speedy Illinois back who had stunned Nebraska the previous year.

Some legends take a lifetime to gather. This one took just twelve minutes.

Michigan kicked off and Grange took the ball at his ten yard line, zigged, zagged, and raced ninety yards for a touchdown. On the Illini's next possession Grange found a hole outside his right end and raced seventy yards for a score. The next time Illinois got the ball he went around the left end for fifty-seven yards. Grange had to rest against the goalpost after his third touchdown, but moments later Illinois had driven to the Michigan forty-seven yard line and the Galloping Ghost broke it the rest of the way. Four touchdowns in twelve minutes.

The game was delayed for five minutes at the end of the first quarter when Coach Bob Zuppke took Grange out to a standing ovation that wouldn't stop.

But Zuppke must have decided the game had gotten boring, so he put Grange back in in the third quarter and number 77 promptly ran sixty-four yards for a fifth score. He then passed for a sixth. His day's work included 402 yards rushing and 64 more passing.

Grange would always remember one aspect of the famous game. "When I got to the bench, Zuppke said, 'You should have had another touchdown. You didn't cut right on one play.' "

More than eight hundred thousand people saw Red Grange play twenty football games at Illinois. He scored thirty-one touchdowns and ran for more than thirty-six hundred yards. He transformed the game into a Saturday spectacle that demanded huge arenas and commanded lifetime loyalties.

Then he did it again.

In 1925, professional football was an oddity. George Halas was struggling to show a profit with his Bears, probably the only successful team in the ever changing league. But the day after Grange played his last collegiate game, at Ohio State before a record crowd of eighty-five thousand, Halas signed him for one hundred thousand dollars—a figure that then rivaled the millions tossed at professional athletes of the 1990s.

Grange played his first professional game on Thanksgiving Day, 1925, and drew thirty-six thousand to Wrigley Field. Three days later, another twenty-eight thousand came to watch Grange and the Bears defeat the Columbus Tigers. Two days later Halas unveiled Grange in St. Louis, and by Saturday they were in Philadelphia to play before thirty-five thousand. On Sunday, Grange and professional football both arrived in New York. More than seventy thousand showed up at the Polo Grounds to see Red Grange. In all, Halas barnstormed with Grange for nineteen days, during which the Bears played ten games and box office receipts totaled more than $1 million. Grange earned his one hundred thousand dollars. Professional football now had its star.

Grange also was an original in the "show me the money" league. Before 1925 was over he had signed a contract for three hundred thousand dollars to appear in a movie, took another fifty thousand dollars for endorsing various small appliances, and was paid by a tobacco company that used his name but did not say in the advertisements that he smoked.

Grange played eight years in the NFL, starring as often with his defense or passing as his running. An injury in that very first week of the barnstorming tour had ruined his ability to cut. He was the main attraction wherever the Bears played, but he never repeated the dazzling runs he had made at Illinois.

He was named the greatest running back of the first half-century in a 1950 poll of sportswriters, and he might be named the greatest runner of the century when they poll again. He wore the most famous number in sports, and he was the first college star to turn his talents into a million-dollar enterprise. If Halas gave birth to the NFL, Red Grange gave it adolescence. His impact on both college and professional football was unparalleled. But for those who never saw him run there is Paul Gallico's epistle:

> Above all, we remember that wizard, red-haired young man sweeping us to our feet with his elegant eluding, avoiding and side-stepping, whipping the huge stadium to a screaming pitch of hysterical excitement as, spinning like a tee-totum from one hairbreadth escape to another, he climaxed his poetically rhythmic run with a touchdown.

They don't make sportswriters like that anymore, either.

4

THE OLD ROMAN:
CHARLES COMISKEY

They called it the national pastime. It was the game of farm boys and city kids and coal miners and cowboys. It was the game that gave every major city a picnic with entertainment and every small town a local nine whose players were community idols. It gave America its first sports heroes. Its intricate scoring and mountains of statistics gave every fan fodder for ceaseless discussion and appraisal and argument. They wrote poems about Tinker to Evers to Chance. They wrote volumes about Cobb and Ruth. They wrote songs about Mantle and Mays. Baseball was as American as the flag. It was the consuming topic of men and boys through the long winters before the fortuitous mixture of professional football, basketball, and television. It was the sport that provided hours of entertainment on radio for millions of Americans who had never been to New York or Philadelphia or Chicago but were able, from the cotton fields of Alabama and the corn fields of Nebraska, to visualize Yankee Stadium and Wrigley Field, the edifices that became the symbols of the great cities and the playgrounds of great warriors.

Baseball was *The Sporting News* and the local kid the Cardinals had signed to an obscure Class D minor league team in Opelousas, Louisiana, or Merced, California. Baseball was the local semipro coach who once batted against Walter Johnson in spring training. Baseball was the priceless autograph of Joe DiMaggio that the kid next door got from his uncle in Newark, who went to see the Yankees every Sunday. Baseball was men known as Giants and Tigers and Pirates. And yes, players known as Cubs.

From the beginning, it all went wrong in Chicago.

Baseball in Chicago has been a century of ineptitude. There were a few World Series triumphs back before anyone alive today can remember. There were a handful of great stars, though not very many. The last Chicago player to get three thousand hits was Cap Anson in 1897. The last Chicago team to win a World Series was the Sox in 1917. Oakland has won as many World Series as both Chicago teams in this century, and it didn't have a major league team until 1968. Teams from Canada have won more pennants than both Chicago teams in the last fifty years. Since World War II, Chicago has produced five Hall of Fame players. In the same period, six were produced in Brooklyn, which disappeared from baseball in 1958. In the entire century only four Chicago pitchers have made it to the Hall of Fame. The Cleveland Indians had three in 1954 alone. For most of America, baseball tradition has meant winning. It means that in Minnesota and Atlanta, in Los Angeles and St. Louis. Even Pittsburgh and Cincinnati and, of course, New York. The national image of Chicago baseball has become the ivy-covered walls of Wrigley Field and the only American sports cult that depends on losing.

And, the biggest scandal in American sports history.

Charles A. Comiskey, the Old Roman, gets the most blame—or credit—for this national embarrassment. But P. K. Wrigley will not go unnoticed.

Comiskey is noted in baseball history for being the first man to play off the first-base bag in the 1880s, when his love for the budding game of baseball was so intense he couldn't believe someone would pay him fifty dollars a week to play. Comiskey carried that attitude for the rest of his life, and his inability to understand that other players didn't feel quite the same about it led to baseball's darkest moments. Comiskey, the son of a rich contractor-politician, was also the key figure in the founding of the American League. He was an owner of a team in the American Association that refused to remain subservient to the established National League and began raiding players at the turn of the century. By 1903, the American League had gained equal footing and the first World Series was held. Comiskey had no qualms about spending money on acquiring players. His niggardliness only applied to paying them. The same was true about his ballpark, at least the private dining room known as the Bards Room, where he lavished food and drink on political cronies, business associates, and the loyal sportswriters who in turn praised his ball club in general and the Old Roman in particular.

When his "Hitless Wonders" defeated the Cubs in the 1906 World Series—some thought this was a harbinger of all the "city" series that would follow—Comiskey stunned his players by handing out fifteen thousand dollars to be split among the team. Coupled with their share of the World Series gate, each jubilant player wound up $1,874 richer. Their jubilance lasted only until the following spring, when Comiskey announced that he considered the World Series booty as part of their 1907 salary.

Comiskey shelled out seventy-five thousand dollars to bring Hall of Famer Eddie Collins from the Philadelphia Athletics in 1915, and he paid thirty thousand dollars to get Shoeless Joe Jackson from Cleveland. Collins and Jackson were the nucleus of the 1917 World Series champs, the last baseball title Chicago has won. In 1919, the Sox were the best team in baseball. Eddie Cicotte had won twenty-nine games but lost his chance at a bonus for winning thirty when Comiskey ordered the manager not to start him for two weeks in September. Collins was still getting paid fifteen thousand dollars, but the rest of the players would have been richer working the coal mines. When the 1919 Sox clinched the pennant, Comiskey sent a case of champagne from the Bards Room to the dressing room. It was warm. It tasted worse when the manager announced the bubbly represented the bonus Comiskey had promised the team for winning the pennant.

For the only time in the history of Chicago baseball, one of its teams was about to become part of the American myth. Seven Sox players threw the World Series to the underdog Cincinnati Reds. "Say it ain't so, Joe," the apocryphal lament of the small child to Joe Jackson, became the most famous five words in baseball. The myth grew larger when the seven were banned from baseball by newly anointed commissioner Kenesaw Landis. The lords of baseball were frantic that their sport and their personal wealth would disappear if baseball failed as a gate attraction. They needed something to get the fans excited about the game and not the crooked World Series. They hyped up the baseball just in time for Babe Ruth to hit it out of every ballpark in

America. The White Sox, depleted of their stars and their spirit, stumbled to oblivion in the 1920s while Ruth and the Yankees established a dynasty that would endure for four decades. Comiskey died in 1931, bitter, reclusive, and rich.

His heirs could never reverse the evil fortunes that befell the White Sox after the 1919 scandal. But they were faithful to Comiskey's belief that players should be paid as little as possible. After various owners tried to put the pieces back together, Bill Veeck surfaced as a possible savior in the 1950s, winning a pennant in 1959 that represents Chicago's last league championship title. There were the raucous days of Frank "Trader" Lane, whose bold moves got the White Sox to respectability, and the hopeful days of the 1980s, when the team got into the playoffs. But even with the Jerry Reinsdorf spend-a-million philosophy of the 1990s, the Sox legacy of failure has endured. Even worse, the Sox are a cipher nationally. They have been so mediocre so long, with so few interesting players, that most of America's baseball fans rarely think of them. And when a true talent such as Frank Thomas comes along, he arrives with such a morose personality that even his hitting skills cause little excitement. It is certain that when the century reaches its end, the White Sox will be best known for being the Black Sox.

5

P.K.:
PHILIP WRIGLEY

Unlike the White Sox, the Cubs are national darlings. For all the wrong reasons. The Tribune Company, which has owned the team since 1980, has done a good job of keeping the Cub image strong. It provides through its WGN superstation a steady supply of nationally televised scenes of beautiful Wrigley Field. At the end of each season, the Cubs have failed again to win. But the ballpark always sells out. The bottom line is black. The Tribune Company did somehow win divisional titles in 1984 and 1989. Although those achievements were two steps from glory, it seemed the Cubs were about to break their shackles of disappointment. But, happily for a century's worth of tradition, it hasn't happened.

And the ghost of P. K. Wrigley couldn't care less.

Philip Knight Wrigley loved baseball. He loved baseball fans. He loved the Cubs. But he never got worked up about winning. Unlike Charley Comiskey, P.K. was never bitter. He was reclusive and rich.

He once built a massive house on an Arizona mountain with only one bedroom. "There's no reason for anyone to stay overnight," he explained. P. K. Wrigley didn't like people. P. K. Wrigley liked to sell chewing gum from the factory he inherited from his daddy. He liked machines. He loved cars. He would have liked to have been an inventor. He invented Ladies Day. He once tried to wire warm-up jackets with a heating system so his pitchers wouldn't get cold. He cut the size of Wrigley Field boxes from ten seats to eight to make things more comfortable for his fans. He always kept seventeen thousand reserved seats available for sale on game day to ensure anyone could get into the park. He was a successful businessman, but when it came to baseball he cared more about customer service than the bottom line. He once went into the bar of Chicago's most famous building, his Wrigley Building, and ordered all the double-martini glasses smashed after he measured them and discovered they actually didn't hold two single drinks. He liked to make fudge.

P.K. inherited the Cubs from his father, and in his first year as president, 1935, the Cubs won a pennant. They did it again in 1938 and 1945. P.K. was proud that during the last World Series the Cubs have played in he was never seen at the ballpark. For most of his last thirty years he only watched the team on television. But it was his imprint that created the lovable losers.

Wrigley made the chewing gum company he inherited from his father one of America's most successful businesses. He was an avid believer in advertising, and often wrote some of the ad copy for Doublemint and Juicyfruit. But his love of Wrigley Field was greater. In the 1930s, baseball fences were covered with advertising. Wrigley ordered all the signs removed and covered his walls with ivy. At the time, it seemed like a silly decision that would cost revenues. But over the decades it enhanced the value and the legend of Wrigley Field far more than the signs advertising men's suits with two pairs of pants.

Like his contemporary George Halas, Wrigley often made decisions for the best interest of his sport rather than his team. He encouraged the Boston Braves to move to Milwaukee—encroaching on the Cubs' fan base—because he said baseball could not afford to allow a team to go bankrupt. He gave away his minor league franchise in Los Angeles so Walter O'Malley could move the Dodgers there in 1958 because he believed baseball needed to expand. He was the first to allow radio broadcasts of his team's games and then advocated television as a way to advertise his product. And, most famously, he refused to install lights at Wrigley because he didn't want the nearby residents disturbed by crowds at night games. For most of the two decades after 1945, they wouldn't have been disturbed much. Cubs crowds in the 1950s and 1960s often numbered less than five thousand. The teams were terrible.

Wrigley, who knew about four-barrel carburetors and fan comfort, knew nothing about the game. But he always held veto power on important trades and contracts. He was not afraid to be wrong, and he usually was.

He also was the prototype of the modern sports franchise owner whose fortunes have come from other enterprises, who often apply the same business practices they used in their previous ventures to their athletic teams. Wrigley refused to invest one penny of the William Wrigley Company money into the Cubs. He, like the Tribune Company today, insisted the team pay its own way.

But he was also eccentric. In the 1930s he paid five thousand dollars to a man who swore he could put a hex on the Cubs' opponents. Wrigley paid for the man to travel with the team and promised him another twenty-five thousand dollars if the Cubs won the pennant. They didn't.

He never paid his players much, but he was, like Halas, paternalistic toward them. He fretted so much every time he had to fire a manager that he came up with a scheme to avoid the problem. He instituted a rotating college of coaches who would take turns running the ball club and then revert to pitching batting practice. Eight different men ran the team over a five-year period in the early 1960s, and the Cubs lost more games than any team in baseball.

In 1963 he hired an air force colonel to lead the team in fitness exercises. Colonel Robert Whitfield also concocted special vitamin drinks he forced the players to drink. The Cubs finished last again.

Between them, Wrigley and White Sox owner Charles Comiskey dominated Chicago baseball for the first seventy years of the century. Chicago baseball dominated nothing.

6 ■

SWEET GEORGIA BROWN:
ABE SAPERSTEIN

It was not common in the America of the 1920s to see a plump, curly haired Jewish man driving a Model T with five black men stuffed in beside him. But that's how one of the most enduring successes of American sports began.

The year was 1927, and the white man driving the Ford was Abe Saperstein. The five blacks with him were the touring basketball team he called the Harlem Globetrotters.

Their first game was in Hinckley, Illinois, and the take from the gate was five dollars. It paid for the next day's meals. Over the next three-quarters of a century the Harlem Globetrotters would play more than twenty thousand games in more than one hundred countries. There were times when the Trotters were the best team in professional basketball. They always were the funniest.

Abe Saperstein was born in London in 1903 and moved with his family to the West Side of Chicago three years later. Saperstein was a sports nut, playing baseball, football, and basketball, but at five-foot-five he wasn't built for excellence. He became a gym rat, hanging around playgrounds and gymnasiums looking for a game. He was hired to coach a Negro Legion basketball team in 1926. The team played in places like the Savoy Ballroom but rarely got paid. Saperstein decided to take over the club and take it on the road, literally.

That road would showcase the talent of black athletes in front of white audiences all over America, and ultimately lead to blacks playing in the National Basketball Association, a league they have dominated for the past two decades.

Saperstein was serious about basketball, but he was more serious about earning a living for himself and his players. Although from the start the Globetrotters could play excellent basketball, it was clear that beating up on local teams wasn't going to fill their pockets or stomachs. They needed to make it entertaining.

They began to practice fancy passing routines, and Saperstein would play a recording of "Beer Barrel Polka" while his players went through their pregame routines. When the professionals of the 1930s and 1940s were perfecting the bounce pass and two-hand set shot, the Globetrotters were dunking, inventing the high and low post, the three-man weave, the three-point shot, the fast break, the full-court press, the behind-the-back pass, and the through-the-legs dribble.

They did it all before Dr. J, Magic, and Michael.

Their stars were Inman Jackson, Goose Tatum, Leon Hilliard, Marques Haynes, and Meadowlark Lemon. They worked on football routines, lining up in a T-formation and tossing the ball around the make-believe backfield. They had a baseball routine in which the players would pretend they were manning first, second, and third base at three corners of the basketball court and Tatum, whose arms hung almost to his ankles, was the spoof pitcher. They hid the basketball in their shorts and bounced it off opponents' heads into the basket. They had vaudeville routines with the officials. "You're walking," a referee would shout. "You want me to fly," Tatum would retort.

They used phony basketballs with rubber bands attached. They sometimes deflated the ball in the middle of the game. And they kept improving the speed of their pregame routine. Later, Saperstein would replace "Beer Barrel Polka," with a rhythmic whistling tune of the early 1940s.

The Globetrotters survived the Depression with their mix of slapstick and basketball, but Saperstein yearned to show the world that his team was not simply about show business.

He got his chance in 1940 when an open tournament was held in Chicago to determine a world professional basketball champion. The Globetrotters were one of fourteen teams invited. Another all-black team, the New York Rens, was the favorite. The Globetrotters won, defeating the host Chicago Bruins for the title.

In 1948, the Minneapolis Lakers, led by former DePaul star George Mikan, won the first of three NBA titles. They played the Globetrotters at the end of the season. The Trotters won. The next year the Lakers repeated as NBA champs and the Trotters repeated as champs of the Lakers.

The Reverend Jesse Jackson said, "That was the classic game. It was to basketball what the Joe Louis–Max Schmeling fight was to boxing, what Jesse Owens and the Berlin Olympics was to track. It was one of those giants in history that went on to disprove the inferiority of blacks."

The stunning success of professional basketball in the 1990s belies its early years. In the late 1940s, the Globetrotters were often the featured attraction at basketball doubleheaders. An NBA game would follow their premeditated drubbing of their perennial victims, the Washington Generals, but it was the Trotters, not the NBA, that drew the crowds. In 1950, the Globetrotters began a twelve-year series with a college all-star team that included every great name of the era. For twelve years the Globetrotters annually won the series. In 1962, the Globetrotters won fifteen of the sixteen games.

By then, the days were waning when the Trotters could be truly competitive with the established NBA. By the 1960s, the NBA was on the road to success with the Boston Celtic dynasty and such stars as Wilt Chamberlain (a former Globetrotter), Bill Russell, Oscar Robertson, and many other black athletes. Never again would the Globetrotters be able to attract the best black basketball players, and their future would be strictly in entertainment.

In 1950 the Trotters played to seventy-five thousand in Berlin, still the largest crowd ever to see a basketball game. They played in a special audience before Pope Pius XII. By the 1970s, the Trotters were regulars on television, appearing on *Sesame Street* and starring in their own *Harlem Globetrotter Popcorn Machine* show, a mix of comedy and educational motivation.

Saperstein continued to experiment with the game he loved. He started the American Basketball League in 1962 as a rival to the NBA. His league began the three-point rule for shots made from beyond twenty-one feet. The gimmick was later adopted by another NBA rival, the American Basketball Association, and later in the 1980s by the NBA when they absorbed many teams from the ABA.

Saperstein also played with a red-white-and-blue basketball that has not been adopted by anyone. He owned a piece of the NBA's Philadelphia Warriors at the time of his death in 1963.

His legacy is secure if somewhat clouded by historical revision.

The Globetrotters did change basketball and did much for black self-image when they were beating white teams regularly at a time when blacks weren't allowed to eat in most restaurants. The team also did even more for the way people thought about blacks in sports. The first black signed to an NBA contract was Nat "Sweetwater" Clifton, one of the Globetrotter stars of the 1940s.

But there were critics who thought Saperstein had turned the black ball players into "sambos." Author James Michener thought the clowning and slapstick invoked all the negative stereotypes of blacks as irresponsible and fickle.

By the civil rights era of the 1960s, the Trotters may indeed have carried comedy too far, but that cannot overshadow the role Saperstein played in opening the way for blacks in professional basketball.

"Saperstein, in his way, was as much a force in bringing the black athlete into the game as Branch Rickey [in baseball]," said Jesse Jackson.

And, for the Magic Johnsons and Michael Jordans whose shoes and T-shirts are sold throughout the world, it is doubtful anyone in Asia, Africa, or Europe would know exactly what game they played if the Harlem Globetrotters hadn't shown them fifty years ago.

Fittingly, more than twenty years after Saperstein's death in 1963, the Globetrotters finally had an appropriate player to showcase when the loudspeakers began to whistle their theme song.

Lynette Woodward, an all-American at Kansas, became the first woman professional player when she joined the Globetrotters in 1986. They had their very own "Sweet Georgia Brown."

7 ■

THE GOLDEN JET:
BOBBY HULL

They don't make nicknames like that anymore, either.

Championships have been so rare in Chicago during the twentieth century that just about anyone who delivered one could rightly be included on a list of the city's significant sports figures.

But Bobby Hull was more than the star of the 1961 Chicago Black Hawks who brought the city its only Stanley Cup in the last sixty years.

If Michael Jordan was not the greatest basketball player ever, he is undoubtedly the greatest basketball player of the 1990s. Chicago's only other professional athlete who unarguably was the best of his time was Bobby Hull.

And for the pure excitement he generated on the ice, he was incomparable. Chicago fans have filled the stadiums and ballparks, and with an anticipation that somehow the unexpected might happen: that a Chicago team or Chicago player might actually perform beyond their wildest beliefs. It occasionally happened. An Ernie Banks home run here, a Looie Aparicio stolen base there, an occasional Bears victory over Green Bay. For the first six decades of the century, it always was a surprise.

With Bobby Hull it was different. The crowds that returned to Chicago Stadium in the 1960s knew something was going to happen before they found their seats. When the puck bounced behind the Black Hawks goal and the blond number 9 swooped along the boards to gather it onto the curved blade of his stick, then moved his powerful thighs once or twice, sending his body hurling up the ice, quickly passing two or three defenders, swerving toward the blue line, cutting back and winding up for his almost invisible slap shot it was a rush, a thrill that few Chicagoans had ever experienced. They came every night expecting him to score. And he did.

Bobby Hull was the Babe Ruth of hockey in the 1960s. The game was still dominated by the Canadian teams, Montreal and Toronto, and they played with finesse and speed. They scored in patterns of passing and checking and moving the puck closer and closer to the goal until the play was climaxed by a rush of players jamming into the crease of the net and a quick flip off an anonymous stick slid past a beleaguered goalie. It was a game that had little popular interest in the United States except in those areas adjacent to the Canadian border and in New York, Boston, Detroit, and Chicago, where they had National Hockey League teams. No one in Atlanta or Anaheim cared about hockey.

Bobby Hull made the difference. Bobby Hull didn't need to be close to the goal. If Hull had the puck on his stick and he was inside the rink, the goal could come at any time from any distance. Television networks never had any interest in hockey until Bobby Hull arrived. If the 1920s were sport's golden age, the 1960s might have been the silver era. There was the golfing rivalry of Arnold Palmer and Jack Nicklaus. There was Vince Lombardi and the Green Bay football legend. Baseball had Mantle, Maris, Mays, and Aaron. Muhammad Ali, née Cassius Clay, restored boxing's worldwide popularity with a combination of speed and power never seen before on the canvas. And joining them regularly on the cover of sports magazines was the Golden Jet. He was named the NHL player of the 1960s. He was the league's MVP twice, and he broke the fifty-goal barrier three times, setting the all-time mark for the then six-team league with fifty-eight goals in the 1968–69 season.

In his prime, no one skated faster and fired harder than Bobby Hull. He was timed at 30 miles per hour on the ice, and his slap shot was measured at nearly 120 miles per hour—nearly 30 miles per hour faster than the average NHL shooter.

Hull played sixteen years and scored 610 goals, surpassed only by Gordie Howe, who played ten more years and in nearly six hundred more games, and the modern stars Wayne Gretzky and Phil Esposito, who benefited from the expansion of the NHL from six superior teams to twenty-four suspect squads. Had Hull played in the 1980s he might have scored one hundred goals in a season.

And had it not been for Bobby Hull, there would have been no Stanley Cups in Edmonton, Philadelphia, Long Island, Calgary, Pittsburgh, and Colorado.

Like all established leagues, the NHL had been constantly challenged by new leagues throughout its history. But it successfully rebuffed them until the World Hockey Association was formed in 1972.

The owner of the new Winnipeg franchise, Ben Hatskin, believed the new league would suffer the same fate of its predecessor challengers unless it included the biggest star in hockey. He went after Bobby Hull.

On June 27, 1972, Hull signed a $2.5 million contract to play for the new Winnipeg team, which immediately named itself the Jets. Consistent with Chicago's sports tradition, Arthur Wirtz, the owner of the Black Hawks, refused to match the offer to keep hockey's greatest star. Hull became the highest-paid performer in sports, matching Wilt Chamberlain's $250,000 a year and topping the $200,000 paid to baseball's premier hitter, Hank Aaron.

Hull's presence gave the WHA credibility and enabled it to survive until 1979, when the NHL finally surrendered and took in four WHA clubs in the same fashion that the NFL ultimately merged with teams from the All American Conference and later with the American Football League.

For better or worse, had there been no Bobby Hull there would be no Anaheim Mighty Ducks.

8

TARZAN:
JOHNNY WEISSMULLER

Somewhere from the Renaissance to the Roaring Twenties man decided that water was only good to drink. Beginning in the Middle Ages and lasting until the mid–twentieth century, bathing was at best a weekly affair and in some civilizations it was only by accident. One theory poses that during the European plagues of the Middle Ages the belief arose that such diseases were caused by stagnant pools and polluted rivers. By the beginning of this century, indoor plumbing had made bathing a more comfortable if not altogether daily occurrence. Swimming in the water was something only the savages of remote Pacific Islands enjoyed. Swimming pools were symbols of the very rich or the very famous Hollywood stars of the silent film era.

But in the last several Olympiads, swimming has become the glamour sport. Television spends more hours chronicling backstrokes, butterflies, medleys, relays, and sprints than any other competition. First one to the wall gets to be a millionaire. Mark Spitz, Janet Evans, Don Schollander, Donna de Varona, Summer Saunders.

The emergence of swimming as a sport and a recreation started on the Oak Street beach with a skinny kid named Peter John Weissmuller.

Stricken with polio at age nine, Weissmuller began swimming as therapy. When he retired from the sport he was the reigning world champion in every event he ever tried, and he tried all of them.

The former altar boy at St. Michael Church on West Eugenie Avenue was the star of the 1924 and 1928 Olympics. But like his contemporaries of the 1920s he had a charm and a dramatic flair that brought new devotees to his sport.

Weissmuller began swimming competitively in 1919 with the Illinois Athletic Club. When he retired ten years later he held every world freestyle record from 100 yards to a half-mile. He won the national outdoor 100- and 440-yard titles in 1922, 1923, 1925, 1926, 1927, and 1928. He would have won in 1924, but the events were not held.

In the 1924 Olympic Games in Paris he set records for the 100 and 400 meters. Four years later at Amsterdam he set a new 100-meter record that would not be broken for seventeen years.

Before Weissmuller, swimming ranked in popularity with skeet shooting. After Weissmuller, it was the rage.

Of course, there are millions of Americans who think the only time Johnny Weissmuller ever went swimming was to rescue Jane from a hungry crocodile.

In 1930 Weissmuller was given a screen test to play the chest-thumping, tree-swinging king of the jungle, Tarzan.

"I went to the back lot at MGM, they gave me a G-string and said, 'Can you climb a tree? Can you pick up that girl?' I could do all that."

There were other Tarzans before and after, but Weissmuller and his famous ape call was the most popular. He made eighteen Tarzan films between 1930 and 1947, then starred as Jungle Jim, a white hunter in the movies and in a television serial.

He did all his own stunts. Once he jumped from a tree to the back of a rhinoceros and rode the horned beast a considerable distance before he jumped off.

"It was easier riding it than spelling it," he confessed.

Weissmuller was stricken with heart and lung disease in his last years, and in a sad but amusing note was evicted from a nursing home in 1979 when other patients complained they were being awoken late at night by a Tarzan yell.

He died in 1984. One of his records makes him truly unique in the annals of Chicago sports: he never lost a race.

9

THE BIGGEST DRAW EVER:
BILL DECORREVONT

Sometime in January of 2001 one television network will announce that 200 million people watched the Super Bowl, the most widely viewed sports event in the world. But some other network will say the Academy Awards were watched by people in three hundred countries. Satellites and the microchip have made such distinctions meaningless for the twenty-first century. Because a television is turned on or a satellite is flashing a signal across the stars doesn't really mean everyone *watched* the event.

There was a time when *watching* meant attending, actually getting on the train or piling into the station wagon and traveling to one of the huge concrete stadiums where boys and men ran, passed, kicked, blocked, and tackled in the sun or the rain or the snow, on the grass and in the mud.

The most people who ever watched a football game in America were not drawn to the stadium by the Super Bowl. The biggest crowd to ever march through the turnstiles did not go to see Red Grange or Jimmy Brown or O. J. Simpson or Walter Payton. The classic Army-Navy battles of the post–World War II years, when 10 million veterans argued over bragging rights, routinely drew one hundred thousand soldiers, sailors, and others to Franklin Field in Philadelphia, but they were not the biggest crowds. Notre Dame and Southern California have staged classic brawls for sixty years in the mammoth Los Angeles Coliseum, but only occasionally has the crowd topped one hundred thousand.

The biggest crowd to ever watch a football game in America came to watch Bill DeCorrevont.

Bill DeCorrevont never won a Heisman Trophy, never signed a million-dollar contract, never even made all-American. But in the fall of 1937, Bill DeCorrevont was the most exciting football player in America and the most highly publicized schoolboy who ever played the game.

On November 27, 1937, more than 125,000 paid one dollar each to jam Soldier Field for the Prep Bowl between DeCorrevont's Austin team and the Catholic League champion, Leo.

The game, dubbed the Kelly Bowl because of the fanatical interest and sponsorship of Mayor Edward Kelly, was always a big draw. More than ninety thousand had watched Austin and Fenwick play to a tie the previous year. Tickets were sold in every city firehouse, and the firemen did their best to help the mayor make the game a success.

But the 1937 game was special.

Almost every football fan in America knew about Bill DeCorrevont. He was written about in the New York and Philadelphia and Boston newspapers. *Time* magazine wrote about him. Movie theater newsreels featured him.

DeCorrevont was the most exciting schoolboy runner since Red Grange. He scored thirty-five touchdowns in ten games in 1937. Against McKinley, he touched the ball ten times and scored nine touchdowns in Austin's 93–0 rout.

On a perfect autumn Saturday at Soldier Field, DeCorrevont did not disappoint. Jazz king Paul Whiteman led one thousand high school band members in playing "The Star-Spangled Banner," and then DeCorrevont led Austin with touchdown runs of forty-seven, one, and three yards. He passed for the fourth score in Austin's 26–0 victory.

DeCorrevont was offered many inducements, including cash, to take his football talents to various universities, but he chose to remain close to home, attending Northwestern, where he was the starting tailback until his senior year, when he shared the position with Otto Graham, the future NFL Hall of Famer from the Cleveland Browns.

After serving in the navy in World War II, DeCorrevont played professional football with Washington, Detroit, the Chicago Cardinals, and the Chicago Bears. He later established a successful rug- and furniture-cleaning company and spent the last years of his life living in Florida before his death in 1995.

For one day, in one place, he was the biggest draw in the history of football.

10 ▤

"LET'S PLAY TWO":
ERNIE BANKS

For all its collective futility, Chicago has had some remarkable performers. Their skills and their desire kept Chicago fans content, if not rewarded, for one hundred years. There was the acrobatic durability of Walter Payton and the magic of Gale Sayers in the open field, and before them, Charley Trippi and George McAfee. There was the brute force of Bronko Nagurski and the innovative precision of Sid Luckman. If there were no Michael Jordan, Scottie Pippen would be by far the finest basketball player who ever worked the Chicago Stadium. The ferocity of Dick Butkus is indelible, but so was the defensive genius of Bill George and George Connor. No one in Chicago sports, and few people elsewhere, ever had a year like Hack Wilson in 1930, whose 190 runs batted in may be the most unreachable record in all of sport. And there was Sammy Sosa.

But none of these wonderful athletes had the impact on American sport that those profiled in this section had. Sports nuts will demand that Payton be included, citing his longevity and the certainty that he will be the all-time leading rusher in the twentieth-century history of the NFL. But even among the most loyal Bears fans there would be as many votes for Sayers. Unless someone has such undeniably superior skills, such as Jordan and Hull, it is difficult to assess the significance of team performers and avert succumbing to provincialism. Butkus could have been the greatest linebacker ever, but no one in New York who watched Sam Huff invent the position would agree. Butkus might have been the most vicious linebacker, but no Green Bay devotee of

Ray Nitschke would concede that dubious honor. Had Sayers been able to run longer he might have been mentioned in the same breath with Jimmy Brown, but even the father of the premier runner of the 1990s, Barry Sanders, regularly tells his kid that Brown was better.

In baseball, even the loudest Chicago fan has little to say. It took a ten-year campaign to get the best White Sox player of the last half century, Nellie Fox, into the Hall of Fame, while other cities line up regularly to enshrine their heroes.

But like the St. Valentine's Day Massacre and the Great Fire of 1871, there are some events and people that come to signify a place and a time. In Chicago sports that was Ernie Banks.

Ernie Banks symbolized for the nation the cheerful spirit with which Chicago has served as a playground for its eclectic, eccentric teams and the men who run them. Ernie Banks was the best baseball player Chicago had in the twentieth century. He hit more home runs and drove in more runs than anyone. He was twice named most valuable player on teams where three of them wouldn't have helped. He played better for longer than any other athlete in Chicago's history.

Ernie Banks was often criticized for refusing to take any stand in the civil rights unrest of the 1960s. He was not a clubhouse leader like Jack Robinson or Curt Flood or other black superstars of the 1960s. His temperament was perfect for the first black baseball star in a city that had racial attitudes as convincing as any southern hamlet. But he had the quickest wrists in the game and he was an ambassador of beautiful Wrigley Field. Ernie Banks was like the ivy. He was a throwback for the millions of Americans who grew up long before television and basketball and soccer and hockey. He was an echo of the time when every boy in America raced out to the nearest sandlot to play baseball.

In the dwindling days of the century, no athlete in any sport will ever say something outrageous like "Let's play two," unless it's in the contract. Ernie Banks played as though he had no contract. He made Chicago feel good. He made America feel good about Chicago.

CRIME'S
TOP TEN

An argument can and has been made that of all the cities in all the world the one that truly was the city of the twentieth century was Chicago. Growth, energy, excitement, prosperity, lakefront, art, literature, politics, architecture, railroads, airports, athletes, scientists, musicians, and museums—Chicago had it all.

But it also can be said that beyond Carl Sandburg and Richard Daley, above Mies Van de Rohe and Enrico Fermi, equal to the symphony and the stockyards, twentieth-century Chicago filled the world's imagination with the most shocking, chilling crimes of the century. They were fiendish in their contemplation. They were brutal in their execution. There were lonely slayings and mass murders and serial butchery. There were gangs of killers and solitary madmen. In almost every decade of the century from the deadly 1920s to the anxious 1990s Chicago interrupted the world's sanity with a new tale of morbidity.

Chicago's destiny of death started long before Al Capone, although he was a big help.

From the very beginning, when Chicago was a tiny village with a few dozen men, one of them, John Kinzie, killed another, Jack Lalime. A few weeks later in that year of 1812 a band of Pottawattomies massacred eighty-six soldiers and civilians just south of where the Hilton Hotel now overlooks the lake.

Kinzie was Chicago's first killer and the Pottawattomies ran up the biggest score, but one was ruled self-defense and the other was war. Neither even approaches the infamous list of Chicago's greatest crimes.

THE PERFECT CRIME:
LEOPOLD AND LOEB

In 1924 the Drake Hotel, Soldier Field, and the Michigan Avenue bridge opened. Louis Armstrong was playing trumpet at the Lincoln Gardens on East Thirty-First Street, and Earl Hines was playing jazz at the nearby Elite Club. Radio stations WLS (World's Largest Store), owned by Sears, Roebuck, and WGN (World's Greatest Newspaper), owned by the *Chicago Tribune*, provided music for those who didn't travel to the South Side. Chicago's Edna Ferber won the Pulitzer Prize. Harold "Red" Grange of Wheaton and the University of Illinois scored four touchdowns in twelve minutes against Michigan. Oscar Mayer began to sell sliced bacon in a package. Calvin Coolidge was nominated by the Republicans to continue the presidency he inherited from Warren Harding. Most of all, 1924 was a great year for the coroner.

On April 1, Frank Capone was killed in Cicero's famous "bullets and ballots" election. Brother Al intoned that he was glad Frank had given his life for the Republican ticket, which won. Capone rival Dion O'Banion was so elated over the Cicero election shoot-out that he ordered twenty thousand dollars' worth of flowers in anticipation of the gangland funerals. In November, O'Banion was shredded in his flower shop across from Holy Name Cathedral. He would have loved the florist bill for his own wake. There were other crimes. A cabaret singer named Belva Gaertner was tried in April for the murder of a car salesman found dead in her Nash sedan. "I was drunk," the accused sighed. The *Chicago Tribune* had a dilemma with the abduction and mutilation of taxi driver Charles Ream. "Glandular Theft" said the newspaper, too delicate to use the word *castration*.

But the crime neither the coroner nor the world would ever forget in 1924 took place in May. It began as a perfect crime.

The dread that soon would terrify a city, a nation, and a generation of parents began with Jacob Franks. Franks was sixty-seven years old the night that his youngest son, Bobby, fourteen, never came home. It was Wednesday, May 21. Franks lived at 5052 Ellis Avenue in Kenwood, an enclave of large homes and mansions where many of Chicago's wealthiest Jewish families lived. Franks built his fortune in real estate and utilities investments, but his bankroll had come from his days as a pawnbroker, a friendly "Uncle Jake" who staked many of the city's gambling figures. That, and his decision to become a Christian Scientist, excluded him from the Jewish social set. There was also another skeleton in Franks's closet. Before he married Flora, who was his second wife, a French dressmaker, Mme. Sobra, sued him for seventy-five thousand dollars on a breach of promise. The jury decided it was nothing but a "shake down" scheme. Franks was a widower at the time. Franks and Flora had two other children, Josephine, seventeen, and Jack, fifteen, but Bobby was their sweet, gentle baby, rather elfin and innocent looking, although a neighbor youth referred to him as a "cocky son of a bitch."

Bobby Franks attended the prestigious, private Harvard School at 47th and Ellis, only a few blocks from his home. But on May 21, he was not home by dinnertime. Flora Franks called all his friends' homes, but no one knew anything about the youngster's whereabouts. Franks telephoned his close friend Samuel Ettelson, a former city corporation counsel who lost his job when the reform ticket swept Mayor William "Big Bill" Thompson out of office the previous year.

Franks and Ettelson walked to the Harvard School to see if Bobby had somehow been locked in the building. He had not. While they were walking back to the Franks home, Flora received a telephone call. "Your son has been kidnapped."

The caller said the Franks would receive further instructions in the morning.

Bobby Franks was already dead, his skull crushed by a chisel only moments after his abduction by two men whose names would be linked irreversibly in the annals of crime: Leopold and Loeb.

At 9:30 A.M. on Thursday, May 22, a special-delivery letter arrived at the Franks home. It was a typed letter demanding ten thousand dollars for the safe return of the boy. It said additional information would be delivered by telephone at 1 P.M.

As Franks and Ettelson began preparations to pay the ransom, a Pennsylvania Railroad repair crew riding a handcar near 115th Street and Wolf Lake saw a man standing on the single track waving frantically. The crew, headed by German immigrant Paul Korff, stopped by the man, who was speaking rapidly in Polish and pointing under the culvert. Korff and his men looked down and saw two bare feet sticking up from the shallow drainage. They waded into the murky water and lifted out the nude body of a young boy. One of the men took a piece of canvas from the handcar and wrapped the body. They loaded it on the handcar and began moving back up the track to Hegewisch. They thought the boy had gone swimming and drowned. Korff noticed a pair of eyeglasses on the ground. He assumed they belonged to the boy. He put them in his pocket. A few hours later at a funeral parlor in Hegewisch, the body found in the marsh was identified as Bobby Franks.

On Friday, May 23, 1924, the *Chicago Tribune* blared:

KIDNAP RICH BOY; KILL HIM

An Associated Press dispatch read, "Police call the crime the strangest and most baffling in Chicago's history."

The *Tribune* speculated, "If the theory that one or more of the kidnapper-murderers was a moron is the correct one, the police have several suspects in mind."

The telephone call and subsequent ransom note were ruses. There had never been a kidnapping. What made the killing of little Bobby Franks the most terrifying crime in American history was that it was not done for money; it was not an act of passion or revenge or jealousy or hate. Those were the common motives for murder in an America that only recently had left its frontier violence behind, and while accounts of the Lucy Borden ax murders and other grisly crimes titillated readers, few people were terrified they might become victims of such horrors. Crime was not unusual in America, but it was not personal. The heritage of the bloody Civil War left few

American families strangers to the loss of life or limb. Even kidnapping and premeditated slayings were not rare. The advent during Prohibition of mob-style slayings inured most people to violence. But the slaying of Bobby Franks was different. And it scared the hell out of American parents for years to come. A small child was taken, not for money, but chosen as a random victim. He was not murdered as part of a bungled crime. He was not the victim of insanity. He was not murdered because of who or what he was. He was murdered simply because he was there.

Nothing like that had ever happened anywhere.

But there was much more that made the murder of Bobby Franks the "first" crime of the century. It occurred during one of the sporadic media explosions of the century. Chicago had six newspapers with new editions flying off presses every hour of the day, updating, even fabricating, events as quickly as readers could absorb them. There was also the new technology of radio, poised to present live voices of authority revealing details of the crime in a far more dramatic fashion than the printed word.

The detective work in the ten days following the murder unfolded with a fascination that would provide material for mystery writers and screenplays for years.

The trial, which in reality was a sentencing hearing, was the first of several sensational murder trials that have enthralled America, from the Lindbergh case of the 1930s to the Sam Sheppard "fugitive" defense of the 1950s and the high-tech circus of O. J. Simpson's trial in the 1990s.

None of those trials had a star equal to Clarence Darrow, the most famous defense lawyer of the century. The trial was the first to unveil a gaggle of psychiatrists, known then as alienists, who opened the doors to every mental competency defense for the next seventy-five years. The controversy over the use of these experts quickly faded as their testimony delved into the backgrounds of the confessed killers, linking childhood episodes with hints of future violence, private writings with undertones of perversity, and candidly discussing their homosexual relations, which had been taboo in American conversation.

The myth of investigative reporting began with Leopold and Loeb. Two *Chicago Daily News* reporters won a Pulitzer Prize for linking the ransom note to a typewriter Leopold had borrowed. Reporters sat in with police as they interrogated the two suspects. Reporters rode in police cars with Leopold when he retraced the crime. Only the satellite feed of O.J.'s wild Bronco ride into 90 million households could match the media coverage of the Bobby Franks story.

The murders that captivated America in the twentieth century seemed mostly to involve money, fame, and sex.

Nathan Leopold and Richard Loeb were rich, brilliant, and homosexual.

Leopold was already a distinguished ornithologist and linguist. Loeb had graduated at age sixteen from the University of Michigan. Both were attending the University of Chicago when they plotted their perfect crime.

It was a warm spring day when Leopold and Loeb cruised in their rental car through the Kenwood neighborhood searching for their victim. A few days earlier they had fixed on Bobby Asher, a neighbor of Loeb's, but the fourteen-year-old had gone to baseball practice. At 3 P.M. on Wednesday, May 21, they parked at the Harvard School. Loeb strolled the parking lot and encountered Johnny Levinson, nine, the son of a prominent lawyer. Levinson often played with Loeb's younger brother, and Loeb had struck him a few weeks earlier. He quickly shied away from Loeb's invitation to take a ride. Loeb returned to the car and the two men drove north on Ellis Avenue. They spotted Irving Hartman Jr., the son of a furniture manufacturer. He was two blocks away. Then they saw Bobby Franks. It could have been any of the children. It was that senseless.

Ten days after Franks's body was discovered the police got their first break. The manufacturer of the eyeglasses found near the body sorted through fifty-four thousand records and determined that only three eyeglasses with the specific horn rims found at the culvert had been sold in Chicago. One pair was sold to Nathan Leopold.

Almost at the same time, a *Daily News* reporter had obtained from some of Leopold's friends copies of class notes Leopold had typed for them. The newspaper hired a printing expert who confirmed that the class notes had been typed on the same Underwood used to write the ransom note. The *Daily News* turned the information over to the state's attorney.

On May 31, Leopold and Loeb were taken into custody for questioning. They were interrogated separately at the LaSalle Hotel, where they stuck to their alibi that they had been joyriding in Leopold's car, done some drinking, and were looking for girls. The prosecutors took them to dinner at the Drake Hotel.

Shortly after midnight, June 1, prosecutors told Loeb their alibi was a lie. Leopold's chauffeur had sworn the family car had never been used the day of the Franks slaying. Loeb confessed.

A few hours later, Leopold confessed. Both men said the other had wielded the chisel that killed Bobby Franks. They never recanted their accusations.

Chicago was stunned by the news that two wealthy Jewish scions had committed such a crime, but the world was shocked by the motive Leopold admitted: "We did it for a thrill."

After their confessions, the only question was whether they would hang or be sent to prison for life. Public sentiment favored the gallows. State's Attorney Robert Crowe, with an eye on his November reelection bid, was determined they should hang. The Leopold and Loeb families conferred and begged Clarence Darrow to save their boys' lives.

Darrow was aging and tired, in his own words, "sixty-eight years old and very weary . . . tired of standing in the lean, lonely front line and facing the greatest enemy that ever confronted man—public opinion." But the man who had championed the causes of the poor was persuaded to take the case, not by the promise of a huge fee, but by his sense of fairness. He believed that if the two young men had not been wealthy, their confessions would have been accepted in return for a life sentence. "In a terrible crisis, there is only one element more helpless than the poor. And that is the rich."

Leopold and Loeb were arraigned July 21, 1924, at the Criminal Courts Building at the corner of Dearborn and Hubbard Streets. The hearing was held on the sixth floor, and the courtroom, the building, and the sidewalks outside were jammed by hundreds peering to see the ruthless killers and their famous attorney.

The chief justice of the criminal court, John R. Caverly, was assigned to the case. Shortly after 10 A.M., Darrow rose and stunned the court by entering a plea of guilty. Darrow believed that to try to plead not guilty by reason of insanity would require a jury trial, and he had no hopes of convincing twelve people to spare the lives of the young men. He elected to take his chances for mercy to Judge Caverly. He would argue that the youth and mental condition of the confessed killers demanded a sentence of life imprisonment. It was an unprecedented strategy. While insanity had been used as a defense, it had never been offered to mitigate a sentence.

For more than a month, the hearing dragged on. State's Attorney Crowe, infuriated that Darrow had made a guilty plea, nevertheless called every witness involved in the crime as though he were still trying to prove guilt. Then the parade of alienists for both sides took the witness stand. Finally, it was time for Darrow.

On Friday, August 22, the largest crowd of reporters in American history to that time filled every nook of the courthouse. The crowd of six hundred newspeople that had recently covered the Democratic convention in New York were believed to have arrived in Chicago en masse. Darrow began his plea, which would take two days. He concluded, "Your honor stands between the future and the past. You may hang these boys. You may hang them by the neck until they are dead. But in doing it, you will turn your face toward the past."

Judge Caverly said he would deliver his sentence on a Saturday, but in a weird and wonderful vignette of how Chicago worked in 1924, Genevieve Forbes, one of many *Tribune* reporters who had been covering the trial, raced into the judge's chambers and told him he had to change the sentencing date.

"I'm getting married and both you and Mr. Darrow have been invited to the wedding," Forbes reminded the judge.

Caverly returned to the bench and announced the sentence would be delayed until the following week. On September 10, 1924, Judge Caverly sentenced both men to life in prison.

Leopold served nearly thirty-four years until he was paroled in 1958 to spend the rest of his life working in a hospital in Puerto Rico, where he died in 1971 at the age of sixty-seven.

Loeb was slashed to death in a prison shower room in 1936 by an inmate who complained that Loeb had been making homosexual advances toward him. Whether that was true or not, it provided an opportunity for one of the *Chicago Daily News*'s finest correspondents, Edwin A. Lahey, to pen one of the most memorable leads in the rich history of Chicago journalism:

"Richard Loeb, a brilliant college student and master of the English language, today ended a sentence with a proposition."

2

MY FUNNY VALENTINE:
AL CAPONE

For years, the grimy garage on North Clark Street was an object of the peculiar ambivalence that is Chicago's history. It was an emblem of civic shame and an icon of the corrupt and violent past in which many Chicagoans took a warped sense of pride. But until they knocked it down in 1967 the dirty brick building was a far more popular sightseeing landmark than any of the remarkable and historic buildings that made the city's skyline a national architectural treasure.

In American cinema the garage on North Clark has been re-created more than any other structure except, perhaps, the flimsy wooded rails that formed the O.K. Corral. The story of the O.K. Corral originally pitted good guys against bad guys. Later historians have argued that the bad guys were really the good guys and vice versa. The garage on North Clark was simply filled with bad guys.

But what one bunch of bad guys did to the other bunch of bad guys symbolized Chicago to the entire world for a half century.

In Chicago's 1920s the baddest bad guy was Al Capone. He was the biggest crime lord of the American Century. Capone did not invent organized crime, but he did put it on the front page.

The underworld in Chicago had gotten a foothold long before Capone showed up in 1920 as a thug with a scarred cheek he earned in his brawling Brooklyn youth. The first crime boss in Chicago was Mike McDonald, an Irish saloon and brothel keeper of the 1890s who became the city's biggest gambler and bag man. Everyone who was anyone was on McDonald's payoff list, including Mayor Harvey

Doolittle Colvin. The next big crime lord was Diamond Jim Colosimo, who ran a famous restaurant, the Four Deuces, as a hobby and earned his living running the city's biggest string of brothels. The city's intermittent fits of reform rarely interfered with Colosimo's profits.

Neither the saga of Chicago or Al Capone could have occurred without the infamous experiment of Prohibition. It turned out to be an American nightmare, but it was the underworld's most cherished dream. Criminals usually prospered by taking things that other people wanted. Now they would become wealthy by giving other people what they wanted. Despite congressional approval and the ratification of thirty-six states, the Eighteenth Amendment was a joke to the American big cities with their huge ethnic populations. The idea that Germans would stop drinking beer or that Italians would stop making wine was preposterous. The opportunity to sell outlaw booze was irresistible to men like Jim Colosimo.

The script was ready for Chicago to become the epitome of 1920s violence. Hollywood never matched the cast of real characters. Never had the public been treated to such an array of scoundrels marching across the front pages in their mayhem: Dion O'Banion, the florist whose fight to control the North Side booze rackets made him second only to Capone in deadliness; the five ferocious Genna brothers, who ran the illegal stills in the Italian community and all wound up dead; George "Bugs" Moran, heir to O'Banion; John Scalisi and Albert Anselmi, deadly assassins; "Machine Gun Jack" McGurn, a psychopathic killer; and Mike Merlo, "Smoots" Amatuna, Patsy Lalordo, and Tony Lombardo, the lords of the local chapter of the Mafia.

Besides Al, there were brothers Ralph and Frank Capone and the mob's first accountant, Jake "Greasy Thumb" Guzik. Chicago newspapers ranted on their editorial pages about lawlessness, but their city rooms were filled with reporters who reveled in the chance to chronicle the daily outrages ignited by the mob warfare. And Chicagoans bought their illegal whiskey and beer regardless of what rivaling faction sold it.

The more than three hundred gangland murders that took place in the 1920s—all of them unsolved—began appropriately with the assassination of Colosimo. As with so much of the slaughter, no one knows for sure why someone was murdered or by whom. The myriad of movies and books about the Roaring Twenties offer many theories for many things. Colosimo might have been murdered by his underlings, Johnny Torrio and Capone, who were impatient to take over. O'Banion might have feared Colosimo was reaching for too much of the newly discovered bootleg business. It doesn't matter.

As the profits grew to more than $100 million annually in illegal booze, the fights became bloodier. O'Banion declared war on the Gennas: "To hell with them Sicilians." Anselmi and Scalisi dispatched O'Banion in his flower shop. Hymie Weiss shot up the Sicilians. Capone dispatched McGurn to blow Weiss in half in front of Holy Name Cathedral. Weiss's men cut down Torrio with a shotgun. He survived and retired to Italy. Almost everyone who won the prized post of head of the Unione Siciliana—the Mafia—was killed by one of the differing factions.

Two of Moran's gunmen, Frank and Pete Gusenberg, trapped McGurn inside a phone booth on Rush Street. He was hit several times but lived.

Capone was shot at so often some people believed him when he lamented, "I'd like to quit the rackets."

Capone had moved his headquarters to Cicero following the decision by his political patron, Mayor William Hale Thompson, not to seek reelection in 1923. But in 1927 Thompson was back with two hundred fifty thousand dollars of Capone's money to fund another winning campaign. Thompson spent most of the next two years vacationing in Michigan or touring the Mississippi River flood area while Capone ruled Chicago. Never before, or since, had a criminal boss held so much power in a major American city.

Capone wanted more.

He had agreed to a division of territories with the other gangs, but he never planned to keep his part of the bargain. By 1928, the only opposition was the North Side cartel headed by Bugs Moran. Capone believed Moran had ordered the killing of Capone ally Tony Lombardo earlier that year. It was the excuse he needed to order the elimination of Moran and his key henchmen.

While Capone retired for the winter to his Palm Island retreat off Miami, his henchmen, principally McGurn, made plans for Moran's funeral. They rented an apartment on North Clark Street across from the SMC Cartage Company, which was located in a one-story garage at 2122 North Clark. The garage was a clubhouse for the Moran gang.

At about 10:30 A.M. the morning of February 14, 1929, four men, two of them wearing police uniforms, wheeled up in front of the Clark Street building housing the SMC Cartage Company. They arrived in a Cadillac touring car with a large Klaxon gong on the running board similar to those used by police detectives. Barging into the long, narrow garage the four men surprised seven members or followers of the Moran gang and got the drop on them with tommy guns and shotguns. The seven were lined up against the north wall with their hands raised above their heads.

The occupants of the garage turned and faced the bricks with a minimum of protest, no doubt thinking it was just another innocuous police raid. Then the counterfeit cops opened fire with military precision, sending as many as one hundred rounds of ammunition into the unsuspecting victims as they collapsed in bloody heaps.

Police Captain Thomas Condon, Sargeant Thomas J. Loftus, and Detectives Joseph Connelley and John Devane of the old Thirty-Sixth District, who were assigned to investigate the savage homicides, turned in the following report:

Dead:

Peter Gusenberg, 434 Roscoe St., 40 years, American, no occupation.

Frank Gusenberg, 2130 Lincoln Park West, 36 years, American, no occupation, married.

John May, 1249 W. Madison St., 35 years, American, mechanic, married.

Adam Heyer, 2024 Farragut St. (Ave.), 40 years, American, accountant, married.

Albert Weinshank, 6320 Kenmore Ave., 26 years, American, cleaner and dyer, married.

Albert Kachellek, alias James Clark, 40 years, German, no occupation, married, 6036 Gunnison St.

Reinhardt Schwimmer, 2100 Lincoln Park West, 29 years, American, optometrist, single.

Time of Death:
Frank Gusenberg, 1:30 P.M. Feb. 14, 1929.
All others at 10:40 A.M. Feb. 14, 1929.
Place of Death:
Frank Gusenberg at Alexian Brothers Hospital.
All others at 2122 N. Clark St.
Cause of Death:
Numerous Bullet Wounds.

Frank Gusenberg, alias "Hock," who lived nearly three hours with fourteen bullets in him but refused to tell his friend Sergeant Loftus who shot him, was a top Moran lieutenant. His brother, Pete, known as "Goosey," had been a member of the North Side mob for three years.

May was identified as a North Side gangster with a lengthy police record who worked as a fifty-dollar-a-week mechanic on Moran's beer trucks. Heyer, alias Frank Schneider, the gang's business manager, leased the garage, where Moran maintained his fleet. Weinshank did cleaning work for the gang. Kachellek (Clark) was Moran's brother-in-law and an associate since early gangster days.

Dr. Schwimmer, who had offices at Wabash Avenue and Congress Street, was a gangland aficionado who had apparently just stopped by to chat with the guys he might have considered folk heroes.

Police investigating the massacre determined that the Moran group was set up by the Capone mob. Six of Moran's henchmen had assembled in the garage to await what they had been led to believe would be a clandestine shipment of high-grade hooch.

Moran should have been the seventh victim, but he was late. He spotted the "police car" in front of his place as he came down the street, and took off in the opposite direction. The unfortunate optometrist took his place in death.

After the shooting, the killers in police uniforms marched their two accomplices out at gunpoint, as though they were making an arrest. When they got to their bogus squad car, one of the "prisoners" in civilian clothes got behind the wheel as the other three climbed in, and they drove off.

The mass murder all but wiped out Moran's North Side gang, leaving the territory wide open for the ambitious Capone.

Loftus, who was the first legitimate lawman at the scene, found the bleeding Frank Gusenberg crawling across the floor.

"For heaven's sake, Tom, get me to a hospital," he said Gusenberg pleaded.

"Who did this?" Loftus asked the dying man.

"I won't talk," Gusenberg said.

As the result of the police investigation, "Machine Gun Jack" McGurn and John Scalisi were charged with the seven murders. Both were indicted, but neither ever went to trial.

Police and FBI reports later indicated that an imported gunman, Fred Burke, was one of the shooters. And in 1995, a pair of law-enforcement experts concluded that another was Anthony Accardo, the slight, private, éminence grise of the Chicago mob from the 1940s until his death of natural causes in 1992.

Arthur Bilek, a former law-enforcement official and associate director of the Northwestern Traffic Institute, said Accardo's participation in the St. Valentine's Day Massacre "was the start of his rise from Capone bodyguard sitting in the Lexington Hotel with a machine gun in his lap to boss of the Chicago mob."

Former FBI agent William Roemer, author of a book about Accardo, supported Bilek's identification of the shooters. "I am convinced Accardo was there," said Roemer, explaining that an FBI microphone he helped hide in a Chicago tailor shop in 1959 had recorded mobster Murray "The Camel" Humphreys talking about the St. Valentine's Day Massacre.

"On more than one occasion, Humphreys was heard saying Accardo had been there," Roemer said. "Mob guys themselves just accepted it (Accardo's presence) as fact."

Unlike Accardo, others suspected of being the garage triggermen didn't fare so well in mob hierarchy.

On May 8, 1929, only three months after the massacre, the bodies of Scalisi and Anselmi were found near Wolf Lake, just over the Indiana line. Capone had invited them over for dinner, and had personally beaten the men senseless with a baseball bat, after which they were stabbed and shot to death.

On February 15, 1936, the dapper McGurn was gunned down in a bowling alley at 805 North Milwaukee Avenue. As the three gunmen left the bowling alley, with twenty slack-jawed witnesses looking on, they left behind a comic valentine.

The garage killings inspired another famous newspaper lead: "The mob has graduated from murder to massacre."

The slaughter made every front page in America. But the day McGurn picked made it history: the St. Valentine's Day Massacre.

It was Capone's pièce de résistance. It was his undoing. The national outrage over such lawlessness prompted the federal government to go after Capone, since it was obvious that Chicago law authorities lacked either the ability or inclination to do so. Two years after the St. Valentine's Day executions, Capone was convicted of tax evasion and sent to prison for eight years, most of them at Alcatraz. He was released in 1941, his mind destroyed by the ravages of syphilis. He died in 1947.

3

BORN TO RAISE HELL:
RICHARD SPECK

Leopold and Loeb had shocked the world by the callow, senseless, and random selection of their victim. The St. Valentine's Day Massacre shocked a nation with its magnitude. In July 1966, the South Side of Chicago was the scene of a crime that combined the most horrifying aspects of both.

The 1960s were the years of the "long, hot summers" in urban America. Beginning with Watts in 1965 and continuing with the burning and looting of Newark and Detroit and then Chicago in 1967, black militants mingled with black activists to protest years of discrimination. Sometimes they marched. Sometimes they burned.

Martin Luther King Jr. had made Chicago his target in 1966, and from May until September his disciples marched to protest the racist real-estate patterns of the city. In August, King was stoned by a mob in Marquette Park. In September, a march to suburban Cicero required thousands of National Guardsmen to prevent wholesale bloodshed.

In July, the firebombing, stoning, and sniping that took place so often in urban America that year struck the West Side after several black children defied a police order to turn off a fire hydrant they were using to cool off from the hot summer at the corner of Roosevelt and Throop.

The militia and the police ringed the West Side, arresting looters and firing back at rooftop snipers. A dozen people were killed in four nights of violence.

It was while the city's attention was focused on the anger of its black population that an outsider wandered in to create unimaginable terror for nine student nurses living in a townhouse on the far southeast side near the Calumet harbor.

He came at midnight with a knife and a gun and pried open a screen, entered through the back door, and moved slowly upstairs, where he found the first of the six girls who were home. He spoke softly and said he only wanted money so he could leave Chicago for New Orleans. He tore bedsheets to bind and gag the first girl, then moved to each of the four bedrooms until he had tied up six girls. Three others came home, one by one, just before their 12:30 A.M. curfew. They also were tied.

During the next four hours, he picked one girl at a time and raped, stabbed, and strangled until they all were dead. The victims were:

Gloria Jean Davy, 23, president of the Illinois State Student Nurses Association, an aspirant for the Peace Corps

Suzanne Bridget Farris, 22, once a recreation leader in the Chicago Parks system, engaged to be married to Phillip Jordan, the brother of another victim

Mary Ann Jordan, 22, who chose nursing as a career because "In this way I can best serve others"

Patricia Ann Matusek, 21, who loved children and planned to work at Children's Memorial Hospital in Chicago

Nina Jo Schmale, 23, queen of the student nurses' dance the previous spring, engaged to a high school sweetheart

Pamela Lee Wilkening, 22, a sports enthusiast and humanitarian, who went into nursing because she hated to see people suffer

Merlita Gargullo, 21, from Manila, one of a group of exchange students from the Philippines

Valentina Pasion, 23, another exchange student, from Luzon, who worked at a Manila hospital before emigrating to America

The ninth victim, another exchange student, twenty-three-year-old Corazon Amurao, had slithered under a bed, and the killer had lost count of his victims. She lay there hardly breathing. She heard the sounds of the killer raping Miss Davy on the bed above her, and she listened in terror to the brief struggles for breath from her strangling roommates. She heard what sounded like punches but were the sounds of stabbing.

At 5 A.M. an alarm clock rang, shattering the terrible silence. It rang and rang. Then it ran down, slowly. Again, silence. Miss Amurao lay utterly still for another twenty minutes, heard no sound. Then she wriggled free of her bonds, crawled out from under the bed, and opened the bedroom door.

The spectacle was unbelievable. Farris lay in a pool of blood in the hallway. Pasion, Schmale, and Gargullo lay dead in one front bedroom; Wilkening, Matusek, and Jordan in the other. Blood was everywhere. All had been stabbed repeatedly, or slashed, or strangled, or all three. Downstairs, Davy lay naked on the living room couch, strangled.

Crazed with fear, Miss Amurao ran past the bodies of her friends, burst through the screen of one of the front bedroom windows to a ledge outside, and screamed: "My friends are all dead! Help! Help! I'm the only one left alive!" A few doors away, Mrs. Alfred Windmiller heard her. So did another neighbor, Robert Hall, who was out walking his dog. Mrs. Windmiller hailed a passing squad car. Patrolman Daniel R. Kelly, twenty-five, radioed for assistance and rushed to the townhouse. He helped Miss Amurao down off the ledge and to a neighbor's house. Then he went to the townhouse. He saw Davy's body on the couch. By tragic coincidence, he knew her personally, had dated her sister. Kelly went upstairs, saw the scene of horror, ran to his squad car, and radioed the news. Then he questioned the hysterical survivor briefly and radioed this information, which was flashed to the Chicago police teletype wire:

Wanted: male, white, 25, 6 feet, 170 pounds, short hair, black coat waist-length, dark trousers, no hat. Stated he wanted money to go to New Orleans. May be armed with revolver or knife.

Detectives began their methodical neighborhood survey. One found a service station attendant who said a stranger had left two suitcases there two days ago while he went to look for a room. He had returned yesterday morning to pick them up.

Next stop was the Maritime Union Hall across the street from the nurses' quarters. Yes, such a man had been there three days ago, looking for a job on a ship bound for New Orleans. The union agent remembered he had written the name on a piece of paper, which he tossed into a garbage can by his desk. The garbage can had not been emptied. Detectives sorted through the wastepaper. They found the scrap. The name on the paper was Richard Speck. A small, coin-machine photograph was attached. The man had left the phone number of a sister, where he could be reached in case a job turned up. It was 2 P.M., only eight hours after the murders had been discovered. A detective dialed the number Speck had left. A woman answered. The detective told her, tell your brother to call the union hall. At 3:10 P.M., Richard Speck returned the call. Posing as a union official, the detective told him to come to the hall immediately, a job was waiting for him. Richard Speck said he would be there right away. Speck did not return to the union hall. Instead he gathered his belongings, caught a cab, and headed for another part of town.

At the crime lab, technicians examined fingerprints lifted at the townhouse. They isolated three that didn't match those of the girls who lived there. The FBI supplied Richard Speck's file from the Maritime Commission. Technicians compared his fingerprints with those found at the townhouse. They matched all three. The morning after the killings, detectives went to Miss Amurao's hospital room. A police artist sketched a picture from the girl's description. It looked remarkably like Richard Speck. They showed Miss Amurao about two hundred photos from police files. Then, casually, a detective handed her three more, including one of Speck. She fingered the picture. "That's the man."

Police released the artist's sketch, but not the photograph. They didn't want to alert Speck, who they believed was still in the area, that they had identified him. But Speck had left the South Side. Less than twenty-four hours after he entered the townhouse he was in a saloon near the Loop, where he picked up a prostitute and took her to a cheap hotel. Later, in the early hours of July 15, he wandered to a North Side slum area and found another prostitute, who he took to the Raleigh Hotel on North Dearborn. When she left the hotel at 8 A.M., she told the desk clerk that the man she had been with had a gun. The clerk called the police. A patrolman went to Speck's room and confiscated the pistol without realizing he was confronting the man who had put an entire city in a state of door-locking terror.

Speck checked out of the Raleigh and headed for the Madison Avenue dives west of the Loop. He paid ninety cents for a room in the Star Hotel and began drinking. At nearly the same time, Police Superintendent O. W. Wilson held a news conference to announce that fingerprints lifted from a door in the townhouse had identified a merchant seaman, Richard Speck, as the intruder who butchered eight girls.

Speck was one of eight children. His father died when he was six. He lived in Monmouth, Illinois, then Dallas, Texas, where he got into trouble as a juvenile and went to jail for stealing a friend's paycheck in 1963. He was released and arrested again in 1965 after he threatened a woman with a butcher knife. He found work as a seaman on Great Lakes ships but visited Monmouth in June 1966, where he was sought for questioning in connection with a burglary.

He was now the most wanted man in the world.

The National Guardsmen were still patrolling the West Side. The weather was hot. In every home, Chicagoans watched the late newscasts dedicated almost entirely to the nurses' murders and the search for Speck, who had a tattoo on his arm reading, "Born to Raise Hell." His pockmocked face glared from television sets in living rooms, saloons, restaurants, bus stations, airports, and waiting rooms of every kind in the city.

At 11 P.M. on Saturday, July 17, Speck called out to the wino in the adjoining cubicle. "You've got to come see me. I done something bad." Speck was covered with blood. He had cut the veins in his wrist and arm with a broken bottle. The night clerk called police. A patrolman arrived, fashioned a tourniquet, and placed the apparent derelict in a police van for the short ride west to Cook County Hospital.

The police driver dropped the drifter in the emergency room and left, not knowing the identity of his passenger. The resident surgeon, Dr. LeRoy Smith, looked at the latest arrival. He wiped his face and asked a nurse to get the newspaper with Speck's picture dominating the front page.

"Call the police," Smith said. He washed the caked blood from the arm wound. The letters of a tattoo appeared. *B-O-R-* . . .

"What is your name?" Smith asked.

"Richard. Richard Speck."

At his trial, held in Peoria in April the following year, Richard Speck was sentenced to eight separate death penalties. In 1971 the Supreme Court threw out the death-penalty verdict on a technicality and ordered Speck to serve life in prison. He died there of a heart attack in 1991.

America had seen mass murders. In 1949 a deranged World War II veteran killed thirteen people on the street in Trenton, New Jersey. Before the turn of the century, Chicago's Dr. H. H. Holmes (Herman Mudgett) confessed to killing twenty-seven women and children over a period of years. And, of course, there was the slaughter in the Clark Street garage.

But the sudden act of a madman, tragic as it was, caused no nightmares. It was as much an accident of nature as an earthquake or flood. The mobsters, for the most part, preyed on each other. Even the Holmes murders, few of which he ever described in detail, seemed remote.

The night of terror for the eight student nurses was different. America shuddered in trying to imagine what it must have been like for the nurses in that townhouse. Gagged and bound and waiting for death, its certainty more obvious with the disappearance of each colleague. Nearly five hours of mental agony for the last victims.

Chicagoans did not sleep well that summer.

4

BEFORE I KILL MORE:
WILLIAM HEIRENS

On June 30, 1942, while America was celebrating its great naval victory at Midway and thousands of Chicago youths were heading off to fight the war, the *Chicago Tribune* ran a small story about a thirteen-year-old boy confessing to eleven burglaries. He told the judge he was inspired by listening to crime stories on the radio. The boy was sentenced to attend a private school in Indiana. Almost exactly four years later, the boy was arrested again.

After Leopold and Loeb, and before Richard Speck, there was William George Heirens, who committed what still ranks as the most grisly murder in Chicago history, and a few more that were almost as chilling.

On January 6, 1946, a government official named John Degnan, who had recently moved his family from Baltimore to Chicago, tucked in his plump, curly haired six-year-old daughter, Suzanne, with a reminder that the next day was the first day of school after the holiday break.

The next day was the most horrifying any American parent could imagine.

Little Suzanne was not in her bed when her father went to wake her in the morning. Her window, normally closed, was wide open. The parents called the police. Two detectives arrived and almost immediately found an oil-stained piece of foolscap on the floor. On the paper was scrawled:

> *Get $20,000 Ready & Waite for Word.*
> *Do Not Notify FBI or Police.*
> *Bills in 5's and 10's.*

Police arranged for Degnan to make a radio broadcast saying he would raise the ransom. "Please don't hurt her. She's only a little girl." The broadcast was recorded and run throughout the day. Early editions had headlined the kidnapping, and all Chicago began to pray with the transcribed voice begging for his daughter's safe return.

Fifty teams of detectives were assigned specific areas to search near the Degnan home at 5943 North Kenmore Avenue. Chief of Detectives Walter Storms wanted every alley, basement, porch, garbage can, sewer, and rubbish pile checked.

It was almost dark by 5 P.M. on January 7 when detectives Lee O'Rouke and Harry Benoit noticed the soil had been pried loose around a sewer cover in an alleyway between 5860 and 5900 North Kenmore. They lifted the lid and turned a flashlight into the sewer. They saw a little blond head floating on the water.

"Maybe it's a doll," O'Rouke said.

"It's no doll," Benoit softly replied.

In the next several hours parts of Suzanne Degnan's body were recovered in various sewers in the neighborhood. A left leg was found in another sewer. Her torso and the other leg was found in a shopping bag. It would be six weeks before a utility company crew found her arms floating in an open sewer three blocks south of the Degnan home.

Chicago was seized with terror. Mayor Edward Kelly made constant radio appeals to request calm, assuring the public that the killer would be caught. He promised to hire one thousand additional policemen.

From the moment Chief Storms saw the ransom note and learned from neighbors' reports of noises and dogs barking that the killer may have spent as long as two hours in the Degnan home, he felt a dreaded certainty that the child was already dead.

Among the unsolved murders Storms had on his desk was the December 10, 1946, slaying of Frances Brown, thirty, a secretary who had just returned from three years of service as a Wave. Her nude body was found in the bathroom of her apartment at 3941 Pine Grove

Avenue. A bread knife had been shoved all the way through her neck. She had been shot in the head and arm. On a mirror in the living room, written in lipstick, was this bizarre plea:

Catch Me Before I Kill More

When Storms had arrived at the scene he noted that the body had been washed clean despite the blood strewn about the apartment. He immediately recalled the murder in June 1946 of Josephine Ross, a forty-three-year-old widow who had been repeatedly stabbed in the face and neck. But her killer had wiped all the blood from her body and covered some of the cuts he had inflicted with adhesive tape.

Storms was certain the same person had killed both women. Neither woman had been sexually assaulted. The killer had spent time with both women. Both bodies were cleaned. He also was certain the same person who wrote "Catch Me Before I Kill More" had written the Degnan ransom note. The letter *e* appeared on both the living room mirror and the ransom note as it appears when typed, rather than the way a handwritten lowercase *e* is usually printed. Fingerprint experts had found one print on the ransom note, but the FBI could not match it in its files of known criminals. No prints were found at the scene of the Brown or Ross killings.

Almost six months after the Degnan slaying Storms still had a task force of thirty detectives assigned to the case. But they were baffled. They needed a break.

On June 26 a burglar was spotted in a Rogers Park apartment building. A resident and the building's janitor tried to apprehend him, but he threatened them with a revolver and fled. The police had been called, and the scuffle delayed the burglar long enough for Detective Tiffin Constant to spot him running from the building. Constant cornered the man on a second-floor porch at 1320 Farwell Avenue. The burglar tried to shoot down the steps at Constant, but the gun misfired. Constant grabbed him. The two men grappled until Abner Cunningham, an off-duty policeman returning from the beach in swim trunks, saw the scuffle and raced to the scene. He spotted a clay flowerpot and struck the burglar on the head three times. The burglar fell unconscious. He was taken to a hospital and transferred to the Bridewell prison hospital at 26th and California. Papers in his wallet said he was William Heirens, but all the arresting officers knew was that he was a seventeen-year-old University of Chicago student from suburban Lincolnwood who had been caught breaking into an apartment.

Captain Michael Ahearn of the Rogers Park police station thought differently. He had arrested Heirens four years earlier when the thirteen-year-old was a one-man burglary gang. He alerted Storms.

The Heirens case predated all the Supreme Court rulings regarding the rights of suspects. Storms sent police technicians to the Bridewell Hospital at Cook County Jail the next morning to take Heirens's fingerprints. Heirens apparently had not regained consciousness, although prison officials thought he was faking. When the technicians grabbed his hands he had to be restrained, then lapsed back into his "coma" when they departed.

At 6 P.M. on June 27, 1947, the telephone rang in Storms's office.

"The little finger on Heirens's left hand matches the print on the kidnap note."

The police were certain they had caught the killer of Suzanne Degnan. But the Heirens case got even stranger.

Heirens refused to answer any questions about the killings for three days. Finally, in desperation and in violation of every criminal procedure in effect today, police ordered that Heirens be given sodium pentothal, the so-called truth serum discovered during World War II.

The injection was administered, and with police and prosecutors present, Heirens was asked if he killed the Degnan girl.

"No, George did it," he said. Then he proceeded to exactly describe the kidnapping, dismemberment, and dispersal of body parts, alleging that his friend George Murman was the killer. It turned out that "George" was the alter ego Heirens subconsciously created, a situation that is now common in crime fiction and reality but was a startling revelation fifty years ago.

When the Heirens family obtained defense counsel, it was suggested that Heirens plead guilty to avoid the death penalty. Prosecutors, especially those who had heard the "George" alibi, were afraid that Heirens would be declared insane if he went to trial. They agreed to a guilty plea.

Heirens pleaded guilty September 7, 1947, and was sentenced to three consecutive life terms. He has spent more than fifty years in Illinois prisons and is the state's longest-serving prisoner.

He has recanted his confession many times and claims he was framed. Every Illinois governor from Otto Kerner to James Edgar has heard his plea for freedom. No one has granted it.

5

KILLER CLOWN:
JOHN WAYNE GACY

After deranged World War II veteran Howard Unruh murdered thirteen people in Trenton, New Jersey, in 1949, America was relatively
unscathed by mass murders until Richard Speck's rampage seventeen
years later. There was the usual array of interesting crimes: the Sam
Sheppard Case; the weird slaying of millionaire William Woodward,
shotgunned at the foot of his stairs by a wife who thought she heard a
burglar; and reclusive Ed Gein, the Wisconsin woodsman who dug up
a few bodies for dinner now and again.

But after Speck, a new era of crime began. People began to kill
each other in bunches. There was Charles Whitman, the Texas Tower
sniper who killed sixteen, then Juan Corona, the labor contractor who
chopped up twenty-five migrant workers with a machete and buried
them in orchards around Yuba City, California. Post offices and
McDonald's became massacre scenes. And America was invaded by a
new depraved species, the serial killer. These were people who did not
kill in large batches, they murdered slowly and over a long period of
time and were almost invisible. There was the Boston Strangler and
Hillside Strangler and the Son of Sam in New York and the Zodiac
Killer in San Francisco. There was handsome, friendly, and deadly Ted
Bundy. There was the shocking Elmer Henley, who killed twenty-
seven teenage boys in a sex and murder spree in Houston. Later, there
would be the gruesome Jeffrey Dahmer.

Of course, the record was set in Chicago.

One of the aftershocks of postwar affluency and the social revolution of the 1960s was the breakdown of the traditional American family. By the 1970s, divorce and remarriage were common. Illegitimacy was rising to record numbers. Children grew up in extended families with stepparents and step siblings and caretaker boyfriends. In the 1970s, children began to run away from home in astonishing numbers. The disappearance of a child, especially a teenager, was no longer treated by police in America as a possible kidnapping. There were too many reports to run down, and the reality was that most of these kids were not victims of anything other than a social upheaval. But some of them became victims of pimps and perverts who used them in ways society pretended to ignore. More than a few of them, unfortunately, met John Wayne Gacy.

John Butkovich, seventeen, was not a runaway. He was a teenager looking for work in the summer of 1975 when he was hired at five dollars an hour by P.D.M. Contractors, a building company that Gacy operated from his modest home at 8213 West Summerdale Avenue in an unincorporated area of Norwood Park bordering Chicago's northwest side.

Butkovich seemed to be enjoying his job. His mother, Theresa, recalled, "He was doing interior decorating and he slept over there several nights. We met Gacy and he seemed like a nice guy."

That's what everybody thought about John Gacy, who threw theme parties in his yard, barbecuing special dishes for an Italian party, a Polish picnic, and a bicentennial celebration where he dressed as Uncle Sam with the same self-evident joy he displayed when he dressed as a clown and entertained at children's parties and senior citizens' homes. He had learned several magic tricks and was especially fond of escaping from a specially made set of handcuffs. He often challenged friends to try and get loose. They couldn't. He did a lot of "gofer" work for the Democratic Party and had stationery printed awarding himself the title of precinct captain even though he wasn't. His neighbors, even his two ex-wives, thought he was a nice guy, although his second wife, the former Carole Hoff, later revealed their marriage had ended after John began bringing home magazines with pictures of naked men. About the only other bad thing anyone could say about Gacy was that there was a strange odor in his house. His mother-in-law had complained, "It smells like dead rats." Gacy claimed there was stagnant water in the crawl space.

That was a hint of the other side of John Wayne Gacy, one that had surfaced years earlier in Waterloo, Iowa. Gacy had moved to Waterloo with his first wife, whom he married in Springfield, Illinois, where he worked as a shoe salesman. They relocated in 1966 so Gacy could work for her father, who ran a string of Kentucky Fried Chicken franchises. Gacy quickly became a popular guy in Waterloo. But in 1968 he was convicted of sodomy with a sixteen-year-old boy and served eighteen months in prison. His wife divorced him while he was in jail, and after his parole Gacy returned to Chicago, where he had been born in 1942. Gacy grew up on the North Side and after a series of odd jobs after high school had moved to Springfield in 1962.

Gacy quickly got into trouble back in Chicago. On February 12, 1971, he was arrested after a teenage runaway complained that Gacy had picked him up at a Greyhound bus station, took him to his apartment, and tried to force him to have oral sex.

The charge was dropped when the teenager disappeared.

In 1975, Gacy formed P.D.M. Contractors and began hiring young men cheaply. He also began hitting on them. Although most of his friends were not aware of his sexual proclivities, Gacy pulled no punches with his employees. He bragged to the young boys about the sexual experiences he had.

On July 31, 1975, Butkovich told his mother he was going to pick up two weeks' pay from Gacy. He was never seen again. Marko and Theresa Butkovich reported their son was missing. Chicago police said they would file a report. The parents reported his disappearance a second time and told police he was last seen with a contractor named John Wayne Gacy. They reported it a third time. They never heard from the police department. Kids were always running away in the 1970s.

Greg Godzik had also disappeared. So had James Mazzara and Frank Landingin.

On December 11, 1978, Mrs. Harold Priest drove to the Des Plaines drugstore where her son, Robert, fifteen, worked. She had come to drive him home for her forty-sixth birthday party. The boy asked her to wait a few minutes because he was going to talk to a man about getting a construction job for five dollars an hour—twice what he earned at the drugstore. Mrs. Priest waited for nearly two hours and then drove home and reported Robert's disappearance to the police.

The following day, Lieutenant Joseph Kozenczak of the Des Plaines police saw the report. He had a fifteen-year-old son. He did not think every teenager was a potential runaway. He ordered a full-scale investigation. On December 13, Des Plaines police questioned John Wayne Gacy. He denied knowing anything about the Priest boy's disappearance. The police were not satisfied. They went to Gacy's home and found a receipt for a roll of film that had been left for developing at the drugstore where Priest worked. They learned that the film belonged to a friend of Robert's. Kozenczak ordered that Gacy be placed under twenty-four-hour surveillance. For the next four days, police questioned every friend and associate of Gacy they could turn up. They followed him in teams around the clock. Gacy seemed to his friends on the verge of a breakdown. He told his closest friend, "I been a bad boy." On December 19, Gacy filed a $750,000 civil suit against the Des Plaines police, charging harassment and illegal searches and seizures. On December 20, the Des Plaines police found out what the Chicago police could have learned at any time over the previous four years when Gacy's name was linked to a missing person's report: he had served time for sodomy in Iowa.

On December 21, the Des Plaines police, armed with a search warrant and accompanied by several Cook County sheriff's investigators, confronted Gacy again in his home. They accused him of holding the Priest boy captive and threatened to tear apart the house to find him.

Gacy blurted out that he once killed a man in self-defense and led the officers to his garage, where he took a can of spray paint and marked the concrete under which he said the body was buried. In the house, other investigators entered the crawl space. They found three bodies. The body in the garage was John Butkovich, missing nearly four years.

On December 22, Gacy told police that during the past six years he had killed thirty-two young men and boys after having sexual relations with them. He killed them so they couldn't report him to the police. He often persuaded them to try on his trick handcuffs, and then with a board or rope he beat or strangled them to death.

Over the next week investigators from the Cook County Medical Department went through the sickening task of uncovering body parts from the crawl space. Gacy had buried twenty-seven bodies in his home. He finally ran out of space. He tossed five other bodies into the Des Plaines River. The body of Robert Priest, the thirty-third and final victim, was recovered from the river a week after Gacy's arrest.

Gacy was convicted of Robert Priest's murder in March 1980 and sentenced to death. He spent fourteen years appealing the sentence. On March 10, 1994, he was executed by lethal injection.

"I wish he could have suffered more," said Eugenia Godzik, the sister of a Gacy victim. "The punishment didn't fit the crime."

Nothing could have.

6

UNSOLVED:
THE TYLENOL MURDERS

The 1980s were America's go-go decade: high-tech, merger mania, downsizing, and greed. Given that backdrop, it should not have been surprising that Chicago's habit of being the world's trendiest crime scene was the setting for an eerie string of deaths, bloodless and without any of the usual, banal accoutrements of machine gun, pistol, knife, or bludgeon.

The first victim was Mary Kellerman.

Mary Kellerman would have been thirty years old at the turn of the century, probably married, perhaps a mother, maybe a career woman or a graduate student. But in the autumn of 1982 she got a cold, and like millions of Americans the twelve-year-old Elk Grove Village child went to the medicine cabinet. She took a few capsules and then she died.

Every time someone curses while trying to unseal a bottle of non-prescription medication they should remember young Mary Kellerman and six other Chicago-area residents who died violently in a forty-eight-hour national nightmare that began September 29, 1982.

They were the victims of a madman who laced several bottles of Extra Strength Tylenol with cyanide in what remains the single most deadly unsolved crime in Chicago history.

"He wanted a lot of people to die in a short period of time," said one investigator.

Mary Kellerman was pronounced dead at 9:56 A.M. on September 29 at Alexian Brothers Hospital. Doctors thought little Mary Kellerman had a stroke, although that would be rare in a twelve-year-old. Shortly before noon, ten miles away in Arlington Heights, Adam Janus, a twenty-seven-year-old Polish-born postal worker, complained of chest pains. He took Extra Strength Tylenol. By 3 P.M., he was dead. His doctor, Thomas Kim, noted his symptoms were those of cyanide poisoning: dizziness, headaches, nausea, convulsions, and unconsciousness.

In DuPage County, two women became the next victims. Mary Reiner, twenty-seven, of Winfield, had just come home from the hospital, where she had given birth to her third child. She was feeling dizzy. She took Extra Strength Tylenol. She was dead by morning. In Elmhurst, Mary McFarland, thirty-one, a divorced mother of two sons, was at work in the Yorktown Shopping Center when she told a colleague she had a "tremendous headache." After she was pronounced dead at Good Samaritan Hospital in Downers Grove, police found a bottle of Extra Strength Tylenol in her purse and two other bottles in her home.

Two other DuPage residents, Stanley Janus and his wife, Theresa, had left their home in Lisle to rush to Arlington Heights, where Stanley's brother, Adam, had been stricken. Adam Janus was dead by the time they arrived. They joined family members in shock and disbelief in the Janus home. A bottle of Extra Strength Tylenol was on the kitchen table. Stanley and Theresa each took two.

That evening, Paula Jean Prince, a thirty-five-year-old flight attendant from Chicago, stopped at a Walgreens drugstore at North Avenue and Wells Street, where she bought a bottle of Extra Strength Tylenol. "We knew Paula was supposed to fly out again on Thursday, so we didn't miss her," her sister, Carol, said later. "But on Friday, when we couldn't locate her, we got concerned." She and a friend went to Paula's apartment at 5:15 P.M. and found her dead on the bathroom floor.

Police were now conducting five separate investigations into mysterious deaths in the northwest suburbs of Elk Grove Village and Arlington Heights, in the western suburbs of Winfield and Lombard, and in Chicago itself.

The common thread that tied the macabre cases together was discovered by accident as suspicions arose between two off-duty firemen who were stumped by the cases. Phillip Cappitelli of Arlington

Heights had heard about the deaths in the Janus family while monitoring fire-department radios in his home. His mother-in-law had told him of hearing about the death of the Kellerman girl.

Cappitelli called firefighter Richard Keyworth in Elk Grove Village, who knew about the circumstances of the little girl's death. The two men talked. Keyworth said Mary Kellerman had taken Tylenol before going into convulsions.

"This is a wild stab," Keyworth said. "Maybe it's Tylenol." They relayed the information to Dr. Thomas Kim, who passed it along to Arlington Heights Police Sergeant Michael Ossler, who was at the hospital. Ossler telephoned Elk Grove investigator Richard Cribben, who was holding the bottle of Tylenol Mary Kellerman had used. On the other end, Ossler had the bottle from the Janus kitchen. They read the labels. Both bottles were lot number MC 2880.

The race was now on to determine where the victims, or their families, had purchased the Tylenol. Adam Janus had obtained his medication at a Jewel store in Arlington Heights. Other bottles of Tylenol laced with cyanide were found still on the shelves in stores in Schaumburg, Wheaton, and Chicago. All of the tainted containers were from lot number MC 2880. Johnson & Johnson's McNeil Laboratories, manufacturer of the product, quickly pulled the product from the market and offered refunds to customers who had purchased containers from that lot. Walgreens, Jewel, Osco, F. W. Woolworth, and other stores removed Tylenol from their shelves.

At McNeil's plant in Ft. Washington, Pennsylvania, samples from lot MC 2880 were tested and found to be pure. Clearly, the Tylenol had been tampered with after it left the factory. The terror quickly spread across the country in the form of copycat poisonings and false alarms. The FBI entered the case as the Tylenol manufacturer posted a one hundred thousand dollar reward for information leading to the arrest and conviction of whoever tampered with the medication.

Investigators surmised that the killer put the contaminated capsules on all the shelves on the same day, September 28. All of the poisoned packages were up front on the shelves, where a customer would reach for them first.

"Whoever laced the capsules with cyanide did an amateurish job. Some capsules were not even rejoined properly," said Illinois Attorney

General Tyrone Fahner, who was in charge of the investigation. "There is no meaningful way you can deal with a madman hell-bent on doing something like this."

It was not long before it appeared that the murders might not be the work of a madman but of an old-fashioned extortionist in a high-tech world.

The week after the deaths, Johnson & Johnson received a letter demanding $1 million to "stop the killing." The letter, which bore a New York postmark, touched off a manhunt by hundreds of New York detectives and FBI agents. It was eventually traced through handwriting analysis to James Lewis, thirty-five, who was wanted by postal inspectors for credit card fraud in Kansas City, Missouri, where he had also been indicted in 1978 for the murder of an elderly resident. He was freed in the homicide case on legal technicalities.

Lewis and his wife, LeAnn, fled Kansas City in December of 1981 as U.S. Postal Service inspectors converged on their bungalow with a search warrant to obtain evidence in the credit card scheme. The couple came to Chicago, where they changed their names to Robert and Nancy Richardson. Lewis got a job preparing tax returns but was fired after a violent outburst in the office where he worked. The couple left Chicago and moved to New York in September of 1982, the same month the Tylenol deaths occurred.

Under questioning by federal authorities, Lewis admitted sending the million-dollar extortion letter to Johnson & Johnson but denied going around to Chicago and suburban stores and slipping cyanide into random Tylenol containers.

Lewis was returned to Kansas City, where he was convicted of credit card fraud and sentenced to ten years in prison. He was then convicted in federal court in Chicago for extortion in the Tylenol case and sentenced to another ten years.

In a 1992 prison interview, Lewis acknowledged that he had told police how the killer might have infused drug capsules with cyanide, spreading the poison onto a cutting board and then carefully brushing it through holes into capsules beneath the board.

"They asked me to show how it might have been done and I tried, as a good citizen, to help," he said. "It was a speculative scenario. I could tell you how Julius Caesar was killed, but that does not mean I was the killer."

The file remains open. The one hundred thousand dollar reward still stands.

Johnson & Johnson recalled 100 million dollars' worth of the capsules, and federal and state governments everywhere passed laws requiring tamper-proof packaging of over-the-counter medications. In terms of its effect on the entire population, perhaps no crime in Chicago's sordid history had a greater impact than the Tylenol murders. None remains more mysterious.

7

A KILLING IN KENILWORTH:
VALERIE PERCY

In the North Shore suburbs of Chicago, a number of small, wealthy communities look across narrow, private beaches to the gray-blue waves of Lake Michigan. One of the communities is Kenilworth, named for Sir Walter Scott's novel, and one of the beaches belonged in the fall of 1966 to Windemere, the estate of Charles H. Percy. At eighteen, Percy had been a stock clerk; at thirty, he had been president of Bell and Howell and on his way to amassing a fortune to be counted in the millions. At forty-seven, he was Republican candidate for United States senator from Illinois and regarded as one of the bright young hopes of his party nationally. There were those already forecasting a Percy run at the presidency.

On September 18, Mrs. Percy and the family's three girls—Valerie and Sharon, twenty-one-year-old twins, and Gail, thirteen—dined at home with two men who were working on the Percy campaign. One son, Mark, eleven, was on a camping trip and the other, Roger, nineteen, was at college in California. Roger and the twins were Percy's children by his first wife, who had died in 1947.

Sharon went out after dinner, returned at 11:30, and visited her twin's room to return a borrowed raincoat. Valerie was watching television. Charles Percy came home after midnight from a campaign rally in Chicago. He checked the bedrooms on the second floor of the seventeen-room Norman mansion. Everything was quiet.

Then, as dawn came with murky haze, a man knelt on the flagstone patio facing the lake and silently chopped through the screen of a French door. With a glass cutter, he chipped a square from the door pane and admitted himself to the music room. He walked around the piano and climbed the eighteen steps of a circular staircase. He passed Sharon's room and opened the door to Valerie's room.

Lorraine Percy, Valerie's mother, would recall: "I heard a noise, someone on the steps, I think. The next thing I heard was low moaning; it sounded as if one of the children was sick. I got out of bed and walked down the hall toward the girls' rooms. I saw a light coming from under the door. I called out, 'Val.' And then I opened the door.

"Over her bed was a man. All I could see was his dark outline. I could tell he had on a light shirt, but I could not see anything to distinguish him by. I was frozen for a moment; he was shining his flashlight in my face. Then I screamed."

The scream awakened Charles Percy. He telephoned police, ran to Valerie's room, and then down the stairs. The front door was still chained, the back door still latched, and there was no sign of an intruder. Percy phoned Dr. Robert Hohf, a neighbor. Mrs. Percy was with Valerie; she used a pillowcase to wipe blood from the girl's head and face.

Hohf arrived and the family assembled downstairs. Chief Robert Daley of the Kenilworth police arrived. Dr. Hohf came downstairs and said somberly, "Valerie is gone." It was 5:15 A.M.

Next came Captain Daniel Dragel and four men from the Chicago Crime Laboratory. They lifted fingerprints, combed the grounds, vacuumed the floors, took photographs. They filled seventeen bags with possible evidence.

The coroner said Valerie had been killed by four blows on the left side of her head, struck with an arrow-shaped weapon. She had been struck on the head, arms, and chest more than sixty times. She had been stabbed ten times in the head, throat, and chest. A burglary theory was discounted: sixty dollars in a wallet on Valerie's dresser was untouched.

The savagery of the attack made many detectives believe this was a deliberate, hateful killing, not a bungled home invasion. There were theories that a campaign worker spurned by Valerie had extracted a vicious revenge. There were, as there always is, suggestions that the murder was committed by a family member, perhaps the stepmother.

That rumor was fueled by the unfortunate wording of a Michigan Avenue neon news ticker, which during the coroner's inquest tapped out: "Lorraine Percy tells of daughter's murder."

Nothing ever came of any theory.

A dozen volunteers took lie-detector tests. More than one thousand leads were investigated; three hundred persons were fingerprinted. The state police assigned Sergeant Robert Lamb to continue the open investigation, and he kept at it for more than twenty years until his retirement.

On September 21, 1966, a private funeral service was held for Valerie Percy. Seven weeks later, Percy was elected to the first of three U.S. Senate terms. He was a prominent national figure who emerged as the leader of the GOP moderate wing. He was considered a likely candidate for the 1976 Republican presidential nomination until Richard Nixon's resignation made Gerald Ford an accidental incumbent president.

The murder of Valerie Percy was never solved.

8

THE LADY IN RED:
JOHN DILLINGER

In Chicago, the good guys often were killers. And the lady in red really wore orange.

In the Depression of the 1930s, Chicago schoolteachers went unpaid, the transit lines went broke, and unemployed men sold apples at every corner of the Loop. America was angry at the politicians, at the dust storms, at Wall Street, and at the banks.

John Dillinger robbed banks. He became a folk hero to a public hungry for any form of free entertainment, which Dillinger and others of the era like Bonnie and Clyde, Ma Barker, and Alvin Karpis provided with daring robberies and bloody gun battles with police and federal agents.

Dillinger was not really a Robin Hood to most Americans. They knew he was a common crook, but there was a perverse side of public opinion that admired someone who was defying the establishment and getting away with it. Most Americans would not have wanted to emulate John Dillinger, but that didn't stop them from rooting for him.

There wasn't much else to cheer for in the dismal 1930s.

One man who despised the public acclaim for Dillinger was J. Edgar Hoover, not yet the legendary power broker who blackmailed presidents and senators and spied on Americans from Ernest Hemingway to Martin Luther King. In the 1930s Hoover was the ambitious head of the fledgling Federal Bureau of Investigation, whose agents looked as inept as the cops in Charlie Chaplin comedies whenever they were matched with Dillinger.

A major FBI fiasco came at a northern Wisconsin resort, Little Bohemia, where Dillinger and his gang escaped in a blazing shoot-out on April 22, 1934. The Dillinger gang killed one federal agent. The FBI killed a civilian and wounded two others.

Dillinger was laying low in Chicago in the summer of 1934, posing as Jimmie Lawrence, a Board of Trade clerk, dating Polly Hamilton, who could be described either as an attractive waitress who turned tricks at night, or a full-time prostitute who worked tables during the day. They both lived in a building at 2420 Fullerton Avenue owned by Anna Sage, a Rumanian immigrant who had been a successful madam in Gary, Indiana, until a reform administration asked the government to deport her back to eastern Europe. Sage knew "Jimmie Lawrence" really was public enemy number one, the most wanted man in the history of America.

Everyone was after Dillinger. Hoover had two FBI agents in Chicago charged with the Dillinger hunt. One was Sam Cowley, head of the Chicago FBI, and the other was Melvin Purvis, self-appointed head of the Dillinger chase who had botched the Little Bohemia trap.

Captain John Stege headed one of two Chicago police task forces searching for Dillinger. And just across the state line, there were task forces in Gary and East Chicago, Indiana, where Dillinger had killed a policeman during a bank robbery.

The cops, Anna Sage, and John Dillinger all came together on Sunday night, July 22, 1934, at the Biograph Theatre on Lincoln Avenue, not far from Sage's apartment building at 2420 Fullerton Avenue.

At 10:30 P.M. Dillinger, Sage, and Polly Hamilton walked out of the theater, where they had watched Clark Gable in *Manhattan Melodrama*. Purvis and a dozen FBI agents had surrounded the theater. Some East Chicago policemen were there. Gunshots were fired. Dillinger was struck in the back and side and fell dead in an alleyway next to the movie house.

The details of the capture-ambush-execution are as hazy sixty-five years after the hot July night as they were then. Purvis was acclaimed the hero, but he may not have fired the fatal shots. Police produced a gun they said Dillinger had pulled from his pocket. It had not been fired. Police said there was only seven dollars in Dillinger's pockets, but his associates said the nation's number-one bank robber always had several thousand on him. As usual when police and Dillinger tangled, two innocent people were wounded by gunfire.

Within minutes a crowd materialized. Women dipped handkerchiefs in the blood stain under Dillinger's body. Radio stations broke into their programming to announce the death of public enemy number one.

The morbidness continued the next day at the Cook County morgue, where the body was taken. The crowds trying to view the corpse were so large that police feared they would break into the building and finally agreed to allow the gawkers inside.

John Dillinger was dead in the streets of Chicago, but Chicago police had nothing to do with it. The bizarre killing of Dillinger was set up by Anna Sage. She went to her old friends in the East Chicago police department and offered to give up Dillinger if they would halt the deportation proceedings. One of the East Chicago cops was a former Sage lover, Martin Zarkovich. The East Chicago cops brought the deal to Captain Stege with a stipulation: they wanted Dillinger shot dead in revenge for their slain colleague. Stege refused. The East Chicago cops next approached the FBI.

Hoover maintained for years that the FBI refused such a deal and said he had ordered that Dillinger be taken alive if possible. But the fact that the Indiana police and the FBI went ahead and planned a trap for Dillinger without informing the Chicago police department raised serious doubts as to whether Hoover cared how Dillinger was taken. It was also odd that Purvis agreed to wait for Dillinger to appear in a public place rather than simply raid Sage's apartment building earlier in the day.

There was probably no truth to the myth that Sage recognized Dillinger from newspaper pictures. Their illicit roots were in northwest Indiana, and it's certain they had known each other earlier. There also is no truth to the "Lady in Red" fable.

When Sage agreed to lure Dillinger to his doom, she told Purvis she would wear a white blouse and brightly colored skirt so he could easily identify her at the theater. Sage, who remained a public figure of sorts throughout the proceedings that ultimately led to her deportation in 1936, spent a lot of time insisting that the skirt she wore while leading Dillinger to his doom was really orange. It was only under the flickering neon lights of the Biograph marquee that it looked blood red.

The death of John Dillinger in Chicago virtually ended the wild, lawless era of the 1930s and cemented the legend of the FBI as the ultimate "good guys," a myth that Hoover nurtured and perpetuated in movies and literature for the next thirty years. It was a myth that protected the bureau and its director from any public criticism for its misdirected communist "witch hunts" of the 1950s and its invasion into the lives of any American who Hoover disapproved of and, in many instances, tried to destroy.

9

YUMMY:
ROBERT SANDIFER

Police found the hit man's body under a viaduct at 108th and Dauphin in the South Side neighborhood of Roseland and immediately surmised that the gang had taken him out because of the heat over a botched killing. Instead of killing his targets, the hit man had killed a fourteen-year-old girl. Now, he was lying dead with two bullets in the back of his head. A gangland execution, pure and simple.

Chicago has had more than one thousand unsolved gangland killings in its violent history, so why did this particular killing on August 31, 1994, attract worldwide attention?

Probably because the "hit man" found executed was a sixty-eight-pound, eleven-year-old boy.

Even Chicago's reputation for the most sordid and often inexplicable rages of death had never gotten down to kids.

About an hour before his execution, Robert Sandifer cowered in the shadows of a street corner, just blocks away from home. An unassuming youngster with a slight build, the eleven-year-old fugitive, who with the help of his Black Disciple brothers had eluded an intense police hunt for three days, was spotted suddenly by a friend and her mother out for a walk about 10:30 P.M. on Wednesday, August 31.

They approached Robert and spoke with him briefly. They then offered to get help for the boy, wanted for questioning in the murder of fourteen-year-old Shavon Dean, who had been killed three days earlier only fifty feet from her home by a gunman who fired six shots at several boys playing football on the corner of 108th Street and Wentworth Avenue. Another youth had been wounded on the same corner a few hours earlier.

The woman called the boy by his nickname, Yummy. Visibly shaken, he came to her and asked the woman to call his grandmother so she could turn him in to police. Yummy also asked for prayer. At about 11 P.M., the woman took Robert into her home, where they prayed briefly. She then left her house to use a telephone to call his grandmother.

Not long after, Robert spotted a van belonging to his family. He pointed down the street and said it was his "grandma," the woman recalled. She walked down the street to inspect the vehicle and recognized from broadcast news reports a woman in the van as Robert's grandmother. But when they returned to the house, Robert was gone.

What the woman did not see was Derrick Hardaway, sixteen, who had emerged from a nearby walkway. He told Robert to come with him, that the gang was going to take care of him, that "he had to go out of town."

The boys walked down the alley to a waiting car, a late-model Oldsmobile. Derrick's brother, Cragg, was behind the wheel. Robert was told to get in the back seat of the car, face down. The Hardaway brothers, who later were convicted of murdering Sandifer, had been hiding him for three days in an abandoned building until they were ordered by Black Disciple leaders to kill the child before he was arrested and fingered gang bosses.

The three boys drove several blocks to a viaduct at 108th Street and Dauphin Avenue. Derrick told police that his brother and Robert got out of the car. Derrick said he was told to keep the car running and that when he heard shots to be ready to drive. After hearing three shots a short time later, Derrick told authorities he saw Cragg running from the tunnel with his right hand covering his pocket, although he reportedly did not see a weapon. Cragg had a different story. He said he walked Robert into the tunnel, where another gang member named Kenny waited. Cragg told police he left the tunnel and then heard shots. Turning around, he said he saw Robert on the ground, bleeding. Cragg said he ran to the car.

Robert "Yummy" Sandifer's record was extensive, averaging a felony a month over the last eighteen months of his abbreviated life. The boy's criminal history as a juvenile included twenty-three felonies and five misdemeanors from January 1992 to July 1994. Robert was the second of seven children Lorina Sandifer had, the first four by the same man. He was abused as a two-year-old. His scrawny body bore evidence of cigarette burns and beatings with electrical cords.

"This is horrible, horrible," said Public Guardian Patrick Murphy. "He never had a chance."

Neither did Shavon Dean or Kianta Britten, sixteen, who wears leg braces and walks with a cane because of two bullets that ripped through his stomach while he was playing basketball a few hours before Shavon's killing.

"I knew it was Yummy," he said. "I saw his face before he shot me."

10

THE BABY:
ERIC MORSE

Nine-year-old Derrick Lemons wore a powder blue suit and a white turtleneck sweater when he took the witness stand on October 18, 1995.

He was asked about the day a year ago when his five-year-old brother, Eric, died.

Derrick remembered everything.

On October 13, 1994, he and his brother were going to visit their aunt when they were stopped by four youths near the Ida B. Wells complex at 3833 South Langley Avenue.

"Want to go see our clubhouse?" one of the youths asked the boys. "Yeah," said Eric. The boys went to the fourteenth-floor apartment, which had metal bars partially covering one window and a wood board over a second window. An eleven-year-old boy tore the wood board off the window while a twelve-year-old grabbed Eric and dangled him outside the window. Derrick grabbed his little brother's arms and pulled him back to safety. Another boy told Eric to go to another window to look at a fight occurring on the ground below.

"If you don't look, I'll hit you in the head with a brick," one of the youths threatened Eric. The two boys again pushed Eric toward the open window. Derrick again tried to save his little brother. One of the boys bit him on the hand.

Eric was thrown over the side.

The packed juvenile courtroom was silent as Derrick said, "I ran downstairs. I tried to catch him."

The two assailants, ages eleven and twelve, were convicted of first-degree murder and sentenced to an out-of-state, locked residential facility for juvenile offenders until they are twenty-one years old.

Prosecutors who questioned the young murderers said they had asked the five-year-old to steal candy for them and he refused.

Eric Morse was tossed to his death only several weeks after the execution of Robert "Yummy" Sandifer. Sandifer's killers were sixteen and fourteen. Eric's assassins were eleven and twelve.

Sandifer's death was not as shocking as his own role as a child hit man. He was a gang member. He was killed by gang members.

Eric Morse was a baby killed by babies.

In a city that gave the world new forms of depravity in almost every decade of the century, Eric Morse became the most merciless victim in the shameful tradition of Chicago crime.

■ ■ ■ ■ IV

BUSINESS'S TOP TEN

Ernest Hemingway was always looking for the one true sentence. Calvin Coolidge, of all people, said it: The business of America is business. Businesspeople are salesmen, innovators, marketers, hucksters, charlatans, distributors, managers, promoters, or advertisers. They are rarely statesmen or inventors. Only a few inventors ever had their names planted on great American businesses—Alexander Graham Bell, the first American to invent the telephone, and Thomas Edison, who invented everything else.

With rare exception the brand names that Americans purchase belonged to peddlers with great ideas and great determination. There has been nothing new in business since the first toolmaker traded a sharpened flint to the first hunter for a slab of mastodon ribs. Supply and demand. But some of the merchant princes who became household names in America were simply better at it than anybody else for a variety of reasons. Some of them had great ideas about how to sell something. Some of them had sound principles and integrity. Most of them were always a few steps ahead of the competition. Some of them were only a few steps ahead of a grand jury.

It would seem, at first glance, much easier to deal with the great businessmen of Chicago's nineteenth century, men who established great companies that are still thriving on the eve of the twenty-first century. But none of them brought to the world anything particularly new other than the way they did it. Before Marshall Field opened his first store on Lake Street, R. H. Macy had opened a similar one in

New York. The Willard Hotel in Washington was serving great bourbon to presidents before Potter Palmer rented his first room. P. D. Armour and Gus Swift didn't invent slaughtering hogs, they were just the first who never threw anything away. It is even doubtful that Cyrus McCormick invented the reaper, although his claim was always vindicated in courts. If any McCormick invented the reaper, it probably was Cyrus's father. None of the great robber barons of the last century were much different than their Chicago peers. Cornelius Vanderbilt didn't invent railroads. He bought them. John D. Rockefeller didn't make oil. God did, although Rockefeller apparently never was convinced of that.

While Armour and Swift certainly changed the eating habits of America, the two Chicago companies that had the greatest impact on the country at the end of the last century were Montgomery Ward and Sears, Roebuck. It would be easy to say that Aaron Montgomery Ward, who began the catalog that brought needles and thread and pots and pans and stoves and irons to rural America, had the most significant impact on the nation of any Chicagoan of his era. A dozen years later, a natural huckster named Richard Sears set out to beat Ward at his own game, and by the turn of the century he did. Ward was a man of principle who believed he was doing people a needed service. When he retired from actively running his company, he spent the last dozen years of his life spending millions in legal suits to stop anyone from building anything on Chicago's lakefront. It was Ward who saved the lakefront, not Dan Burnham's pithy admonition "Make no small plans" in his Chicago plan that created the lakefront parks system.

Richard Sears, on the other hand, would have been jailed if truth-in-advertising laws existed.

But Sears's store prevailed to become the single largest retail giant in America for most of the century, and the men who followed Sears were obviously of great significance in the twentieth century. And for a brief while, so was one of Ward's successors.

As in the areas of law, sports, and media, Chicagoans who were merely successful at making money or keeping it did not necessarily impact America. There are a slew of them. The Crowns, the Pritzkers, John D. MacArthur and W. Clement Stone in insurance, Nathan Cummings and the Levy brothers in food, Dan Rice and Richard Dennis in commodities, and a whole new breed of venture capitalists and real estate moguls such as William Farley and Sam Zell. And then there are the successors to the great fortunes: the Morton salt folks, the McCormick harvester folks, the Armours, and the Swifts. The inflated salaries of corporate chieftains in the 1990s do not equate to national or world influence. Rising to the helm of a Fortune 500 company in the 1990s was not quite the same as building one from scratch. If annual income were the criteria of greatness, the entire Chicago Bulls bench and the middle of the White Sox batting order would rank ahead of the CEOs of Abbott, G. D. Searle, Motorola, and all the rest.

But the most influential businessmen of Chicago's twentieth century shared something very much in common with their predecessors of the previous century; they were always aware of how Americans were changing the way they lived, the way they worked, the way they played. One man changed what people ate all over the world.

THE FRANCHISER:
RAY KROC

In 1997, Thomas Friedman of the *New York Times* observed that not one of 106 countries around the globe had gone to war since they opened a McDonald's restaurant. Friedman was not necessarily crediting Big Macs and Egg McMuffins for world peace. His premise was that the presence of the Golden Arches underscored the fact that these nations were developing successful internal economies, which they worried would be reversed by armed conflict.

Ray Kroc would have worried if the restrooms were clean.

Ray Kroc did not concern himself with world peace. He did not concern himself with almost anything except selling hamburgers to more people in more places than anyone had ever conceived. He wanted to sell hamburgers faster than anyone else and do it in places that were cleaner than anywhere else, and, most importantly, he wanted every one of the billions of hamburgers sold to be exactly the same size and shape and sold at exactly the same price.

Ray Kroc was a salesman, a dreamer. When the fifty-two-year-old former piano player and food-industry peddler offered to franchise a San Bernardino, California, hamburger stand for a couple of brothers named McDonald, he did not know that his dream of a national fast-food franchise would be the perfect fit for a society that would undergo dramatic changes over the next half century. But he had a hunch.

In 1954, Ray Kroc could not know President Eisenhower was going to create an interstate highway system that made Americans the most mobile society in history, but he did know that Americans were in love with all the chrome and horsepower Detroit was sending them. He did not know that the Levitttowns popping up all over America to alleviate the crowding of inner cities would surpass the inner cities in population, but he did know that the corner store was a thing of the past. When Ray Kroc was looking for places to build the early McDonald's stores he advised his agents, "Look for a church steeple." Kroc wanted to sell to families, the 1950s families composed of a working father, a housewife, and 2.4 children. It is ironic that McDonald's became the kitchen of American families, which after the 1970s consisted of remote family units in which both parents worked and picked up dinner on the way home, or family units that did not have two parents, or family units that consisted of stepbrothers and half-brothers and weekends with dad. He did not know that shopping centers and malls and electronic entertainment would create a workforce of teenagers with their own disposable income. He could not have known that by the end of the century one of every sixteen teenage Americans would get their first job at McDonald's.

Ray Kroc's dream was to have one thousand McDonald's in America. By 1988, there were ten thousand. By 1998 there would be ten thousand McDonald's overseas and thirteen thousand McDonald's in the United States.

No one knows for sure, but it is doubtful if there is anyone in America who has never had something to eat or drink from McDonald's. It is certain there is no one who has never seen a McDonald's store or heard a television cajoling, "You Deserve a Break Today."

McDonald's was not the first hamburger joint in America. It was not the first fast-food stand in America. It was not the first franchise operation in America. It is not, at century's end, the only place where hurried mothers feed their children or senior citizens idle away the mornings with coffee refills. There is its chief rival, Burger King, and there is Taco Bell, Pizza Hut, Arby's, Wendy's, Hardee's, Dairy Queen, and thousands of local and regional fast-food places. But McDonald's is to fast food as Kleenex is to tissue.

Ray Kroc didn't know all that much about hamburgers in 1954. He knew about milk shakes. Kroc was sales manager of a small company that sold a machine that made five milk shakes at once. For fifteen years he had been selling those machines, one at a time, to all the soda fountains that proliferated on the corners of cities like Chicago and villages like Oak Park, where Kroc was born in 1902. But the post–World War II boom was creating subdivisions in places like Arlington Heights, where Kroc lived. These were isolated areas intentionally designed to be two, three, or four miles away from shopping areas. The age of the pedestrian who might take a break at a local snack shop was ending. Mass retailing was destroying small drugstores with big chains like Rexall and Walgreen. They began selling garden tools where the soda fountains used to be, and Kroc knew his business was in trouble. That's why he was curious about the McDonald brothers, whose California drive-in used eight of these milk shake machines. Initially, Kroc wasn't thinking big. His first instinct in wanting to franchise the McDonald brothers' unique system of speedy delivery and single-item menu was to create more markets to sell his multi-shake mixer.

But when he saw people standing in long lines from mid-morning until after midnight to buy a fifteen-cent hamburger, a ten-cent bag of fries, and a Coke, he knew he was seeing the future. "It has future," Kroc would tell his managers years later when he heard an idea that appealed to him.

Kroc made a deal with the McDonald brothers to franchise their restaurants, but Kroc had a whole new idea about franchising. "From his years in supplying the restaurant industry he had seen a thousand restaurants that failed and a thousand that succeeded. He knew the difference," said Richard Starmann, a senior vice president of McDonald's who worked closely with Kroc during the 1970s.

"He knew if people invested their own capital and worked the stores and followed his formula of quality, service and cleanliness, they would succeed."

Or disappear. The first McDonald's franchises were awarded for twenty years. Many operators who did not keep their premises as spotless as Kroc demanded or showed more interest in the golf course than their stores were not renewed. That included several of his old buddies from Rolling Green Country Club who he had signed up in his first desperate days of seeking franchisees.

Kroc risked everything to build McDonald's, which was why it was readily apparent over the years that he cared more about building his empire than profits, more about the opening of a new store than his company's selection as the first food retailer on the Dow Jones 30 list. Starmann recalled that as a young manager he brought a group to Kroc's office in San Diego, where the boss was chatting with President Gerald Ford. "He actually told the President—wait a minute, Jerry—and called me to say hello, introduced us to the President and told his bartender to take good care of the boys from Oak Brook. That was Kroc, he cared more about the boys from Oak Brook than the President."

Kroc used his home equity, borrowed on his life insurance, and put himself totally in debt at age fifty-five to build his first McDonald's in Des Plaines. A few years later, he put his cash-poor company totally in debt to buy out the McDonald brothers for $2.7 million. A few years after that, McDonald's stock went public and Ray Kroc was worth $32 million. At his death in 1984, he was worth $500 million.

Before McDonald's there had been cheap hamburgers; White Castle began in 1921. Before McDonald's there had been national chain restaurants like Howard Johnson's. There were drive-ins like A&W root beer stands and Dairy Queen stands before Ray Kroc, but no one made it work like Kroc.

"He could see the future and he could pick the right people," Starmann said. The first person Ray Kroc picked was Harry Sonneborn, the man who made McDonald's profitable. Kroc's arrangement with the McDonald brothers was a financial disaster. No matter how many stores were opened and how many hamburgers were sold, the brothers would reap the majority of the rewards. Sonneborn put McDonald's into the real estate business. He leased land for restaurants and then re-leased it at a 40 percent profit to the franchisees. In time, McDonald's began buying land and leasing it to the operators. In 1985, McDonald's surpassed Sears, Roebuck as the largest retail real-estate owner in the country.

Kroc knew better than anyone else that people would flock to quality, service, and cleanliness. He didn't know what they would eat. While independent operators never were permitted to add anything to the standard menu, Kroc trifled with it. He tried out Hulaburgers, a disaster. He suggested desserts such as triple ripple and strawberry shortcake, double disasters. The only successful McDonald's additions over the years—fish sandwiches, Big Macs, Egg McMuffins—were developed and tested by individual operators. Kroc even tried to diversify with a North Michigan Avenue gourmet hamburger palace called Ramon's, a Latino version of his name. Latino disaster. He and Sonneborn invested in a German restaurant. Kaput.

But he knew everything there was to know about how to keep McDonald's successful. In the last months of his life he would sit in the company's San Diego office, which overlooked a McDonald's store. He could see only out of one eye, and he used a telescope to time how long each car waited in the new drive-thru window. When a car sat too long he would telephone the manager screaming.

"We had to change managers at that store about every three months," Starmann laughed.

Ray Kroc bought himself a baseball team, the San Diego Padres, and once got so frustrated at its ineptness he got on the stadium loud-speaker to tell the fans he thought the team was terrible.

"He was a dictator," Starmann said. "He would scream in that high-pitched voice and then a few minutes later he would say you were okay. I've walked with him when he would pick cigarette butts up in the parking lot and hand them to the store manager. He had great convictions about cleanliness. He lived that way. He cared more about the stores than money. He didn't think about getting rich, he thought about getting stores."

Kroc lived well, but he always believed in thrift, and he urged his employees to do the same. He sent out memos advising them to buy toilet paper by the case to save money. "I saw him refuse to buy a sportcoat that he liked because it was too expensive," Starmann recalled. "He was worth about $300 million at the time."

When Kroc was opening his first store in Des Plaines he was visited by a Coca-Cola salesman who Kroc had called for service. He told the salesman he wanted to buy orange and root beer as well as Coke. In the 1950s, Coke only made Coke, and the salesman said, "I'm sorry, we don't make anything but Coke." Kroc looked at him and said, "Well, you better start making it because someday I'm going to have a thousand of these stores."

By the year 2000 there will be twenty-five thousand McDonald's stores, and there will be millions of Americans whose first restaurant meal was a bagful of McDonald's fries, millions of Americans whose first ritual of passage from infancy to childhood was clutching a handful of coins at a McDonald's counter, millions of Americans whose first paycheck was stamped with golden arches, millions of Americans who never had to leave the car for lunch—millions of Americans who fervently believed that they deserved a break today.

Not even Ray Kroc had that kind of vision.

2

THE MANAGER AND THE GENERAL:
JULIUS ROSENWALD AND ROBERT WOOD

On January 25, 1993, Sears, Roebuck and Company killed the American Dream.

They canceled the big book, the Sears catalog that since 1896 had been America's wish list and the magic wand that brought technological affluence to farmers and blue-collar workers. The Sears catalog was an annual preview of the future and a measure of rural and immigrant America's climb to the middle class. If it was in the Sears catalog, it was for everyone. And everything was in the Sears catalog: the first electric irons and four-horsepower automobiles, prefabricated houses, and when electricity became available, refrigerators and washing machines and electric stoves. And dresses and shoes and watches. Over the century it grew from the 556 pages of the 1896 edition to the two-volume 1,600-page finale, which went to 13 million families. Even after Sears blanketed America with its retail stores, catalog sales amounted to one-fifth of its business.

The end of the catalog was the footnote to Sears's fall as America's leading retailer for ninety years. It was passed in total sales in 1990 by both Wal-Mart and K-Mart. But K-Mart almost immediately stumbled into financial problems, and no matter how successful Wal-Mart or any other successor might become, there will never be another store that so influenced and changed the American way of life for an entire century.

Two men in this century made it happen.

One of them was Julius Rosenwald, who between 1900 and 1930 made more money and gave away more money than any man in America.

The 1896 catalog was Rosenwald's first major contribution to the company, which had been founded a decade earlier by Richard Sears, a brilliant salesman and advertiser who got started in the mail-order business selling watches, then expanded to jewelry and whatever other items he could buy at a distress sale. Sears was a hustler whose colorful ads and innovative sales ideas—"Send No Money"—overcame his organizational impediments and a penchant for shading the truth.

Sears was an entrepreneur ready to sell anything to anybody, especially farmers, who made up the majority of the U.S. population in 1890. Julius Rosenwald had a different concept. He convinced Sears to be the "buyer for the American farmer." While Sears's earlier catalogs contained a variety of items, the catalog did not become a total buying service until Rosenwald became Sears's partner in 1895 with an investment of $37,500 that ultimately made him $150 million.

Rosenwald came with none of the trappings of most great entrepreneurs of this or any other century. He was not poor; his Jewish father and uncles were well established in the ready-made clothing business that prospered after the Civil War. Rosenwald, who grew up in Springfield, Illinois, owned his own clothing store in Chicago. He was not a man desirous of great power or filled with great vision, or the need to become famous. His gift was corporate management, creating without realizing it futuristic benchmarks for customer service and employee relations that Fortune 500 companies practice in the 1990s.

Over the next thirty years Rosenwald made Sears the nation's buyer and seller of everything. The 1896 catalog included work and dress clothing, buggies, harnesses, farm tools and equipment, plumbing supplies, toilets, stoves, dishes, cutlery, glasses, kerosene lamps, hunting supplies, patent medicines, dry goods, concrete blocks, guns, bicycles, musical instruments, soap, needles, thread, and thimbles.

It was as big as Montgomery Ward's catalog, which had been around since 1872. In five years Sears's revenues jumped from less than $1 million annually to $10 million in 1900. Sears passed Montgomery Ward and never looked back.

By then Rosenwald was fully in charge of the company. Richard Sears didn't like or understand all of Rosenwald's ideas, and an invalid wife kept him occupied until, in 1909, he sold his stock in the company and died in 1914. Rosenwald had already put into place the strategies that would make Sears a company with over $200 million in sales in 1920.

His first key strategy, which had major implications in trimming the distance between America's rich and poor, was to sell more for less, an idea Richard Sears never could quite comprehend but one that his store continued for more than a half century. Rosenwald convinced manufacturers to cut prices in exchange for greater volume. When 1 million bicycles were sold in 1904, one hundred thousand of them were sold by Sears at a lower price than anyone else could offer. A generation later, when electric refrigerators first appeared, costing about $350—the same as an automobile—Rosenwald's belief in volume cut the cost to $139, and more people bought their first refrigerator from Sears than anywhere else. The same could be said of almost anything.

Rosenwald invented "Satisfaction or Your Money Back," and besides obtaining better prices from manufacturers he believed the way to further lower prices was to cut the cost of selling. He streamlined the distribution and delivery systems, and invested in the world's largest business building on the West Side, with miles of railroad tracks running through and around it to hasten delivery. He sent salesmen out to bus stops to inquire casually if Sears was doing a good job, a preview of modern "focus groups." Sears didn't have to preselect respondents, since someone in half of America's families purchased something from Sears.

In 1916, he stunned the second-generation robber barons by introducing profit sharing for employees, and for a half century Sears enjoyed the public-relations coup of stories about spinster clerks and elderly elevator operators retiring with hundreds of thousands of dollars from Sears. It took many major companies seventy years to emulate Rosenwald.

It was about this time that he realized he was making so much money that he started to give it away in sums that made him known to future generations as a great philanthropist rather than a great businessman. He became a friend of Booker T. Washington in 1910 and gave huge amounts to Tuskegee Institute. He contributed to building almost five thousand elementary schools for black children in fourteen southern states. He insisted that his name not be placed on any of them, but they were known for decades as "Rosenwald schools." He gave $5 million to start the Chicago Museum of Science and Industry (his brother-in-law and fellow Sears millionaire Max Adler built the nation's first planetarium, which bears his name). The Julius Rosenwald Fund was established in 1917 and eventually gave away $35 million, and no one knows how much Rosenwald gave to Jewish appeal and refugee funds. When he died in 1932, at age sixty-one, he still had $33 million to leave his family.

Five years before his death he turned over Sears to General Robert E. Wood, the man who created suburbia.

Wood, one of the most colorful and eventually controversial chief executives in American business, was born in 1879 in Kansas City, Missouri. As a teenager he persuaded his congressman to send him to West Point, where he met a future friend and idol, Douglas MacArthur. Newly commissioned Lieutenant Wood fought the guerrillas in the Philippines and wound up as the chief procurement officer for the Panama Canal project, a mission that lasted until 1915 and supplied Wood with the administrative, logistic, and management skills that he would use in the future. He left the army and worked briefly for a DuPont company and a manufacturer of asphalt, but reentered the service during World War I and became quartermaster of the U.S. Army. At the end of the war he was recruited to join Montgomery Ward, where he was in line to head the company. Wood was never a good subordinate, and when his plans to move Ward out of the mail-order business into the retail-store business were ridiculed he went looking for another job, and he found it in 1924 at Sears.

Wood saw in 1924 a precursor of the growth that Ray Kroc saw thirty years later. He knew that mechanization would change farm life and move vast numbers of rural residents toward cities, and that the automobile would change society. He knew that the static shopping districts in New York and Chicago were built for consumers who walked or used mass transit. They could not accommodate cars. He convinced his superiors at Sears to invest in retail stores, not in cities, but on the edges of cities. He opened the first Sears retail store on February 2, 1925, on the first floor of the huge Chicago mail-order plant at Homan Avenue. He quickly opened seven more stores that year.

By 1929 there were 324 Sears stores. Ward's, under the leadership of Sewell Avery, had also changed its mind about the retail-store business and was opening locations faster than Sears. But Ward's made an ultimately fatal error by concentrating on small towns. Wood was surrounding the big cities. Even Sears insiders laughed at the huge parking lots he built, wondering when there would be enough cars to fill them.

But Wood continued his belief that the automobile would be the single most powerful driving force of America's society and economy, and in 1931 he founded the Allstate Auto Insurance Company, a cash cow for Sears over the next sixty years until California earthquakes and Florida hurricanes convinced Sears to sell it.

In the 1930s, Sears easily survived the Depression as Wood cut the prices of everything to allow his consumers to still ogle at the catalog and browse through his stores. Another thing happened in the 1930s. Homes were needed on the outskirts of cities. Tiny towns began to grow as middle-class Americans opted to leave crowded cities and apartment dwelling for the privacy and pleasure of a backyard. When they arrived, Sears was already there. The presence of a Sears store eliminated the need to shop in the central city. There was nothing except bread and milk that Americans couldn't buy at Sears.

In 1939, when Wood reached the retirement age of sixty-nine, he merely moved up to chairman and for fifteen years appointed a series of "tall, lean Sears men" to serve as president, which was merely a window-dressing job while Wood remained in charge. At the end of World War II he expanded stores everywhere, including Latin America, where he opened a store in Mexico City in 1947 and made quick advances to Venezuela, Brazil, Colombia, Peru, Cuba, and most Central American countries.

Sears stores in the United States were everywhere. In his classic study of Sears, *The Big Store*, Donald Katz noted that Sears's sales volume was bigger than that of the entire tobacco or furniture industry. "As huge shopping centers began to cover the landscape, entire developments were predicated on the presence of a Sears store, and fundamental alterations in surrounding markets occurred because of the corporate advertising that made the sound of Sears part of the background noise of everyday life."

When Wood finally left Sears in 1954 the company had nearly nine hundred stores, seventeen hundred catalog and sales offices, thirteen regional distribution centers, 124 warehouses, and nearly a half-million employees. A decade later, *Fortune* magazine declared, "It is number one in the U.S. and also number 2, 3, 4, and 5."

Wood's personal popularity had been in decline since 1939, when he joined with a pair of colonels, McCormick and Lindbergh, in forming the antiwar—and, many thought, anti-Semitic—America First committee.

But his legacy of creating the most successful and influential chain retail store in America was enormous. A variety of his successors sat smugly through the 1960s and 1970s unaware that the aberrations in American life that were making Ray Kroc's dream come true were destroying Sears: the extended and separated family, teenagers with disposable income, a growing disparity between the upper and lower classes, and a penchant for clothing that had names, not the Sears brand.

An effort to turn Sears into America's financial shopping center with the addition in the 1980s of the Dean Witter brokerage and the Coldwell Banker real estate firm didn't work. And in 1993 the catalog died. At least ten thousand people were quoted as saying, "It was always like Christmas when the Sears catalog arrived." Others remembered parties on isolated Rocky Mountain ranches where cowboys and farm wives would take turns looking at the catalog and the ranch foremen would collect the orders.

Rural schoolteachers short of textbooks used the catalog to teach arithmetic, letting children make imaginary shopping lists and then adding up the cost. Immigrants found it easier to learn how to read when every phrase was topped by a picture of the item.

For nearly a century it was hard to tell whether the seat of democracy was in Washington or at the nearest Sears store.

3

THE KING OF POWER:
SAMUEL INSULL

Thomas Edison invented the incandescent light and created the modern electrical system. Samuel Insull owned it.

Or most of it.

In 1930, Samuel Insull was the most powerful businessman in America. His utility empire was worth $3 billion. He controlled six thousand power generators in thirty-two states and produced one-eighth of all the electricity in America. He sat on the boards of eighty-five companies, chaired sixty-five of those boards, and was president of eleven companies. He owned textile mills, paper mills, a hotel, and a grand estate in Libertyville. The cornerstone of his empire was Commonwealth Edison, a company he put together in 1907. But he also owned Peoples Gas Company, and Public Service of Northern Illinois. He could plunge Chicago or any one of five thousand other communities into darkness on a whim. He ran the elevated railways and three interurban electric train systems that connected Chicago with its suburbs and with Wisconsin and Indiana. He was worth $150 million. He became the patron of opera in Chicago when he built the $10 million Civic Opera House inside a thronelike building at Madison Avenue and the Chicago River. He opened the building ten days after the October 1929 stock market crash.

By the end of 1932 he was broke and facing indictment on charges of fraud, embezzlement, and violation of federal bankruptcy laws. The real charge was that he deceived shareholders and bondholders who had jumped aboard his colossal utility juggernaut.

The man who built America's utility system was born in England in 1859 and was hired in 1881 to go to America as a private secretary for Edison, America's innovative genius who couldn't balance his checkbook. While Edison created the first lighting system at his home in Menlo Park, New Jersey, Insull was responsible for dealing with the men who would pay for it, primarily the banking house of J. P. Morgan and Company. A few years after Edison had proved electricity would provide power much cheaper than gas, Morgan and others financed him to build a generator manufacturing plant in Schenectady, New York. Insull was in charge of constructing what would become General Electric Corporation. In 1892, the directors of the Chicago Edison Company sent a telegram asking him to recommend someone to become president of their financially troubled company, which was one of twenty firms trying to supply electrical power to Chicago. He recommended himself. Insull demanded two things: a free hand and the right to buy two hundred fifty thousand dollars in company stock. The directors gave him the first, and Marshall Field lent him the two hundred fifty thousand dollars.

Insull immediately ordered the biggest generators ever built. He was the first to try a steam turbine in an electrical power plant. He then devised a billing system that combined fixed rates for service and adjustable rates for usage. This ultimately made his company profitable and was copied by everyone. Insull determined from the beginning that a utility company must be a monopoly to succeed. This ambition flew in the face of public opinion, which already was vehement about breaking up the oil, railroad, and mining trusts, which had made billionaires of the Rockefellers, Vanderbilts, and others. But Insull paid no attention. He immediately ran into the same City Council shakedown that Roger Smith had engineered with his fifty-year franchise to produce power for the city through the Ogden Gas Company, which existed only on paper. The scheme died when Sullivan and his colleagues learned that Insull had exclusive purchasing rights with all the manufacturers of electric generators. But Insull, as he did throughout his career, was always ready to pay for opportunity rather than make enemies. He paid Sullivan and his cronies $6 million for the exclusive franchise and in 1907 created Commonwealth Edison. Although his goal was to make customers of all 2 million Chicago residents, Insull realized the major users of electricity were the rails. When the elevated system teetered toward bankruptcy in 1911, Insull stepped in to save it and now controlled the major customer of his utility company. He took over the Chicago, Aurora, and Elgin Railroad; the North Shore; the Chicago, South Shore, and South Bend. In 1917 the city council was faced with another dilemma; Peoples Gas was going broke. They asked Insull to see what he could do. He added it to his collection in 1919.

Insull provided jobs and benefits to his employees and was among the first major Chicago business executives to employ blacks as clerks and repairmen. He also used his staff to sell stock to customers. Since his companies paid high dividends and cruised through the recession of the early 1920s, it was not a hard sell.

In the meantime, Insull built the first grid system that allowed excess power to be transferred between states, a system that existed for the rest of the century. He also convinced bankers that his empire should operate on a series of perpetual loans that never would be repaid, that the soaring profits of his companies would provide lenders with high interest, and that the total value of his firms would grow to be worth far more than the outstanding debts.

He formed holding companies such as Midwest West Utilities and Insull Utilities, and he continued to sell stock, which roared just like the twenties. From January 1929 to August 1929, Commonwealth Edison stock went from a price of $202 to $450 a share. Insull Utilities was improving its value at the rate of $7,000 a minute.

But Insull was increasing the empire's bond indebtedness at a faster rate. Bankers were only too happy to lend the millions he demanded to expand. The stock market's giddy rise drove the price of Insull stocks to heights that the value of the companies could not support. Shrewd investors and New York bankers, whom Insull had always refused to deal with, began buying controlling shares. In 1930, Cleveland financier Cyrus Eaton loomed to Insull as a potential raider. Insull borrowed $63 million to buy Eaton's shares in the Insull empire. Then stories broke that Insull had signed a $500,000 check to cover his brother's losses in the market. Charges of embezzlement rose. New York bankers demanded payment on the notes. On June 7, 1932, Insull, at age sixty-three, resigned as president of Edison, People's

Gas, and Public Service. He told reporters, "Well, gentlemen, here I am, after forty years, a man without a job."

Insull became for many the epitome of the monopolistic autocrat who had caused the Depression. The outcry for retribution against Insull was in reality the anger of the millions who were jobless and homeless and had lost their meager savings in the collapse of banks, many of whom were tied to the Insull investment empire. He fled to Europe in disgrace and was finally extradited from Greece to stand trial. He was acquitted in 1934 of all charges, and his pension of $21,500 a year was restored. That was all Samuel Insull had to show for being the most brilliant utility magnate of the century.

The man who Franklin Roosevelt denounced during his 1932 presidential campaign was also the man whose supply and grid systems were copied when FDR pushed through the popular Tennessee Valley Authority project in 1936. When the Rural Electrification Program was initiated it was mostly for the South and the West. The Midwest had no need of a federal program. Samuel Insull had already provided the power.

As for the myth of thousands who lost their life savings in Insull stock, they should have kept it. Commonwealth Edison never missed paying a dividend throughout the Depression, and the stock eventually nearly regained all its value.

Even in disgrace, Insull's accomplishments, the real and the alleged, had great ramifications for America. Shortly after his indictments in 1933, Congress passed several items of New Deal legislation, much of it in response to the Insull scandal: the TVA, the Public Utility Holding Act, and the Corporation Bankruptcy Act.

Insull and his wife, Gladys, moved permanently to Paris. He was spotted on a street one day by a *Chicago Tribune* reporter who inquired, "Are you Samuel Insull?"

"No, I'm not him. I'm somebody else," Insull said.

Insull died in 1938 of a heart attack in a Paris subway station. His body was unidentified for several hours, and the police report said the only thing in his pockets were seven francs (eighty-five cents) and a silk handkerchief with the initials "S.I."

4

THE SPIN DOCTOR: ALBERT LASKER

Not every Chicagoan who wielded great influence during the American Century made the country a better place. Unwittingly, but powerfully, Albert Lasker arguably turned more people into smokers than any other person, including the lords of the tobacco industry.

Ironically, and perhaps blissfully, Albert Lasker died of cancer before its direct links to cigarettes were made public in the famous surgeon general's report of the 1950s.

Equally ironic is that Albert Lasker became one of the most devout and philanthropic supporters of cancer research and medical science, establishing the prestigious research awards that bear his name.

And most ironic of all is that Albert Lasker became the richest, most successful advertising man of the first half century by trying to select products that he thought would make society a better and more pleasant place.

And to a great extent, he did.

Advertising had been around, like catalogs, since the printing press. It most likely began when some innkeeper painted a knife and fork on his door and grew in the 1800s to fill newspapers of the nineteenth century with some of the most preposterous and blatantly false claims for everything from patent medicine to Wild West shows.

Two companies that would become giant advertising firms, J. Walter Thompson and N. W. Ayers, were started in New York and Philadelphia, respectively, in the 1860s. In 1873, Daniel Lord and Ambrose

Thomas opened their shop, Lord and Thomas, in Chicago. These companies primarily served as space buyers, placing ads supplied by the growing army of retailers into newspapers. They bargained for rates and placement and relieved people like Marshall Field and Julius Rosenwald from these tedious chores.

In the 1890s, Lord and Thomas placed copy for a real estate development in Texas, but they never got paid because the company filed for bankruptcy. Lord and Thomas applied for a share of whatever assets were left but felt a Chicago firm was not going to have any success in Texas courts. However, the bankruptcy referee gave the advertisers a fair share of the remaining assets. Ambrose Thomas was grateful and told the referee, a prosperous Galveston, Texas, businessman named Morris Lasker, that he would forever be in his debt. In 1898, Lasker called in his marker. He asked Lord and Thomas if they would take on his eighteen-year-old son and teach him the advertising business. The young Lasker had, in his father's eye, been wasting his time as a fledgling sportswriter and was headed for a life of depravity among the ranks of newspapermen, who at the time were considered drunkards and liars.

Albert Lasker joined Lord and Thomas, and twelve years later he owned the firm. Lasker, with the help of two brilliant copywriters, revolutionized the advertising industry. The main thrust of advertising copy until Lasker came along was simply getting the company name or product out to the public. Lasker and John Kennedy created the definition of modern advertising, "Salesmanship in Print." Decades later, Lasker was among the first to transfer his creed to the new broadcasting industry. Lasker had great faith in the public's ability to read and desire to learn. Lord and Thomas ads had great detail, but they also had a gimmick. Lasker insisted that every ad demonstrate the reason why a consumer should buy the product. Lasker always found something different about a product that he could use as a sales tool and then ordered some creative soul to give it a name. When General Motors was trying to sell its Frigidaire refrigerators in the 1930s, Lasker demanded to know why the public should choose Frigidaire. He was told it was cheaper to run. A Lord and Thomas writer dreamed up the phrase "Meter Miser," and Frigidaire shortly outsold all its competitors.

One of his early accounts was the California orange industry. In the early 1900s California was overrun by orange groves, not strip malls, and there were so many oranges that growers were deliberately chopping down trees to prevent an even greater surplus. Lasker thought that deliberately killing trees was a shame and wondered how to create a market for the citrus surplus. He launched a national advertising campaign extolling the pleasures and virtues of orange juice, which no one had ever considered a beverage, let alone the drink that would accompany American breakfasts for a century.

In 1911 a Milwaukee company brought a green soap to Lasker and asked his help in promoting it. Why was it green, Lasker asked. Why was it called Palmolive? He was told the soap was a mix of palm and olive oil. Lasker created America's first beauty ad, "Keep That School Girl Complexion," and Palmolive was America's bestselling toilet soap for a half century.

One of Lasker's biggest clients was Quaker Oats. The oats were selling fine, but Quaker was having trouble with two new products called Wheat Berries and Puffed Berries. John Kennedy had by now retired, but Lasker's other brilliant sidekick, C. C. Hopkins, visited the Quaker plant where the grains were pressurized in a huge machine that looked like a cannon and puffed up to eight times their natural size. Puffed Wheat and Puffed Rice became "the grains that are shot from guns" and took their place on the table next to the orange juice.

Lasker figured out a way to explain delicately in copy exactly what a product developed by the Kimberly-Clark paper company was, and Kotex changed the sanitary hygiene of American women. He gained the wrath of textile manufacturers when he launched another Kimberly-Clark product by declaring it "the handkerchief you can throw away," and Kleenex became the most successful pocket tissue in the world.

Under Lasker, Lord and Thomas became the most successful agency in the country during the years before World War I. Their accounts included Armour and Swift, and various automakers, including Studebaker. A Lord and Thomas man figured out how to stamp the Sunkist name on oranges without bruising them, creating the citrus war between California and Florida. Lasker, born in 1880, was not even forty years old and was already a multimillionaire.

In 1923, Lasker decided to help the American Tobacco Company gain ground against two competitors who were outselling it by large margins with a new product, manufactured cigarettes. Before World War I, manufactured cigarettes were considered effeminate; men either chewed, rolled their own, or smoked cigars and pipes. It was also considered unladylike to smoke. But the war produced a huge demand for manufactured cigarettes, and R. J. Reynolds's Camels and Liggett and Myers's Chesterfields were the bestsellers. American Tobacco was getting nowhere with Lucky Strike.

Lasker determined that the way to build sales was to build the market, and the way to do that was to get women to smoke. He launched a campaign featuring European women, many of them opera stars and stage performers who were well known in America. They all acclaimed the pleasures of smoking. Cigarette sales grew, and candy manufacturers felt threatened and were planning an antismoking ad campaign. Lasker heard about it and decided to strike in advance, creating the single most successful slogan in American advertising history: "Reach for a Lucky instead of a sweet."

Sales of Lucky Strike grew more than 300 percent, from 80,000 cigarettes a day in 1923 when Lasker took charge to more than 150 million a day in 1926, becoming the market leader for the next two decades.

When radio was born, Lasker was there. Lord and Thomas sponsored the first enormously successful radio show, *Amos and Andy*, for its client Pepsodent, and when *Amos and Andy* began to lose listeners in the 1930s Lasker had Pepsodent sponsor a young comedian, Bob Hope. In the meantime he had become a part owner of the Chicago Cubs, eventually selling his interest to his close friend William Wrigley, and was instrumental in choosing Kenesaw Landis as baseball's first commissioner. He worked for Republican presidents and helped get nominations for Alf Landon and Wendell Wilkie, another close personal friend. He also served as a bag man, delivering $25,000 in hush money to one of Warren Harding's mistresses.

Albert Lasker had earned the astronomical amount of $40 million in advertising when he decided in 1942 to dissolve Lord and Thomas and turn his attention to health, science, Jewish affairs, and the arts. He turned over the firm's accounts to his top three aides, who formed

Foote, Cone, and Belding. Lasker, who by then was known as the "father of modern advertising," had trained other men who founded such successful firms as Benton and Bowles.

In that same year he created the Albert and Mary Lasker Foundation—he married his third wife, Mary Reinhardt, in 1940—which still awards major prizes in medical research.

Although he had lived most of his life in Glencoe and on an enormous estate in Lake Forest—Mill Pond Farm, which he donated to the University of Chicago in 1939—Lasker spent his final years in New York surrounded by his collection of modern art, which included priceless Picassos, Dalis, and anything that suited him.

He died in 1952 of cancer, a disease that science has made great strides in curing, and at least some of that credit goes to Albert Lasker, the same man who taught Americans how to smoke. Few men did more to change American social patterns and buying habits.

5

MOON TO EARTH, MOON TO EARTH: PAUL GALVIN

The business that Paul Galvin started seventy years ago was fairly basic. It involved someone talking and someone listening. Other people had founded that business with such things as telephones and radios. The tricky parts came when it was time for people in cars to listen to people on radios, for people in foxholes to talk to other foxholes, and for people on earth to hear astronauts on the moon.

That's what Motorola was all about. Talking and listening.

There are two Motorola stories. One is the story of Paul Galvin and the company that put music into automobiles, devised the Dick Tracy two-way radio, and supplied U.S. soldiers with the indispensable Walkie-Talkie. The other is the story of his son, Robert Galvin, who put beepers all over the world.

Paul Galvin's first business was in Harvard, Illinois, where he was born in 1895 and set up shop as a teenager selling popcorn and sandwiches. After a stint in the army in World War I, Galvin, by chance, got into the storage-battery business, manufacturing batteries that powered early radio sets. Before long, radios were built to run on alternating current available in any household. Galvin went broke a couple of times and staved off total failure by purchasing a bankrupt company that made battery-eliminators, a battery-charging device that enabled the dwindling number of battery-powered radios to operate on alternating current. But that was only a temporary salvation for Galvin Manufacturing Company, which Paul had started with his brother, Joe.

During a 1928 trip to New York, Galvin heard about two men on Long Island who were installing radios in cars, customizing each set for each auto and charging $240, almost as much as many cars cost.

Galvin decided to mass-produce car radios. While shaving at home one morning he was trying to think of a name that combined motion and radios. The Galvin Manufacturing Company became Motorola.

It was not a simple task. It took several years of tinkering and experimenting before Galvin came up with a radio that could be installed easily and worked. Many of the first models were impossible to hear over the sound of the car engine. The insulation on car roofs had to be torn apart to ground the antenna. The first models had separate batteries that had to be installed in the floor and avoid the muffler and transmission. Galvin spent a good deal of time seeking credit and loans. On one occasion his mechanics were installing a radio in the car of a banker who had just agreed to loan Galvin money. Only moments after the banker drove away from the factory at 847 West Harrison Street, Galvin employees raced outside to see where all the fire engines were going. Two blocks away the banker's car was in flames.

But Galvin persisted, and eventually Motorola became America's most popular car radio. He refused offers to make radios for Detroit's automakers, since he had already built up a national distribution scheme. It wasn't until after World War II when all cars were manufactured with radios that Motorola became a chief supplier to Detroit.

In the meantime, Galvin heard about an east-coast experiment with FM-band radio to provide two-way communication in police cars. In the early 1930s police experimented with convincing commercial stations to occasionally break into programming with reports of crimes. That worked until criminals learned to tune to the same stations and make their getaway as soon as they heard the broadcast.

In 1935 Motorola began making two-way radios that operated on a private frequency for police, and then taxicabs, and the company appeared to be on a permanent path to prosperity.

Then came World War II and more prosperity. Motorola developed the first battery-operated, hand-held two-way radio for use by the U.S. Army. It was called the Handie-Talkie. Later, the more powerful Walkie-Talkie was developed. At the end of the war, Paul Galvin moved toward consumer electronics, producing in 1948 a seven-inch television set that sold for less than two hundred dollars, half as much as the models developed by RCA, Admiral, Zenith, and others.

Like Julius Rosenwald and other successful entrepreneurs, he realized that volume rather than high pricing was the road to riches. He was a tyrant about lowering the production costs of all Motorola products. Bob Galvin recalled,

> I remember in the early 1950s, when Admiral came out with a $199.95 TV set and we had a model due to come out a few days later. I think ours cost $219.95. He asked me, "How are you going to handle Admiral's $199.95 TV set?" I think I responded by telling him our set had more features. "That's fine," he said, "but how are you going to handle Admiral's $199.95 TV set?" I told him our set was already priced at rock bottom. Then he said, "If you can't figure it out, let me know and I'll show you." By Monday of the next week, we figured out how to remove $20 in costs from our set and we had a $199.95 TV set.

Robert Galvin took over Motorola when his father died in 1959 and immediately pressed forward in the new semiconductor business, the transistors that replaced vacuum tubes and created a whole new product line of miniature radios and promised an electronic future that Paul Galvin never would have envisioned. That year Motorola acquired its first subsidiary, a supplier of hospital communication systems and transistorized hearing aids, which led Motorola to develop some of the first pagers. Under Robert Galvin's leadership, the company bailed out of the television business and went on to dominate the global wireless-communications market.

In the 1960s, Motorola developed the first analog cellular telephones and became the most profitable producer of pagers, which have beeped disturbingly in every American's ear ever since. The lunar explorers that visited the moon in the late 1960s were equipped with Motorola radios, beeping in space.

In 1988, Motorola became a national symbol of business success when it won the Malcolm Baldridge National Quality Award. The company became a model for other Fortune 500 companies, who sent emissaries to the Schaumburg headquarters to copy Motorola's business practices in search of the elusive 99.99947 percent errorless rate in production that Motorola called Six Sigma.

Robert Galvin stepped down as chief executive in 1986, and after three successors from outside the family, his son, Chris Galvin, took over the company in 1997.

By then, Motorola had lost its overwhelming edge in the cellular phone business to competitors who jumped ahead in digital advances. But the company remained the global leader in providing infrastructure in foreign countries and was rapidly expanding its base in China and other Asian countries. In 1995, Motorola had sales of $27 billion and with a market value of $40 billion was Chicago's number-one company.

And just as Paul Galvin did in 1928, Motorola continued counting on the future, investing hundreds of millions of dollars in its Iridium project, a constellation of sixty-six satellites that is expected to be operative by 1999 and will make it possible to send a page or make a cellular phone call from anywhere on earth.

Its anticipated revenues could be in the billions, but it's just Motorola's basic business—someone talking and someone else listening.

6

BUTTER TO BILLIONS:
LEO MELAMED

One theme that is consistent among the Chicagoans who made major contributions to the twentieth century is that so many of them came from somewhere else.

Nobody came as far as Leo Melamed.

Nothing grew as fast as the financial futures industry he launched at the Chicago Mercantile Exchange.

When Leo Melamed first joined the "Merc" in 1955, after graduating from John Marshall Law School and briefly practicing law, the exchange was trading just two agricultural futures contracts and facing collapse. The Merc, whose roots were in the Chicago Butter and Egg Board of the 1800s, was created in 1919, but by the late 1950s government price supports ended futures on butter and the Merc's business was in eggs and onions. In 1958, a scandal in the onion pits caused the federal government to ban onion futures trading. In the 1960s the Merc established futures trading on live cattle but was best known as the place that traded pork bellies (bacon). Radio announcers who paid no attention to any financial markets in those days often read the daily prices of pork bellies just because they thought it was such a funny name.

Then, two significant things changed the Merc: In 1969, Melamed was elected to his first term as exchange chairman. And in August 1971, Richard Nixon declared the United States would no longer back up the dollar with gold, which meant the value of the dollar would float on the world monetary market.

Economists understood this, and some, like Milton Friedman, had been urging such an action. Most Americans had no idea what it meant. The first indications were brought back when American tourists returned from Europe chagrined to discover that the dollar didn't buy as much as it once did.

Leo Melamed knew what was happening. He understood that if the dollar was worth 330 yen one day and worth only 310 yen six months later it was not much different than pork bellies. People would want to hedge their selling or purchasing power by investing in monetary futures. Leo Melamed and others—president of the Merc Everette B. Harris, other Merc members, and the economist Friedman—pushed to establish a financial futures exchange called the International Money Market.

Before the IMM opened in 1972, the Chicago Mercantile Exchange sold contracts whose value was counted in the millions. By 1990, the underlying value of all contracts traded at the Merc totaled $50 trillion dollars.

There was not that much money in the world when in 1939 Adolf Hitler invaded Poland. As Polish Jews, Isaac and Fayga Melamed and their seven-year-old son, Leo, were marked for extermination. The Melameds fled across Lithuania and into Russia, beginning a fifteen-month journey that would bring them safely to America. They rode the Trans-Siberian Railway from Moscow to Vladivostok.

"I remember the trip well," Melamed said in a *Chicago Tribune Magazine* article in 1992. "The trip took four weeks; my father taught me how to play chess; there was little food; and the whole time, the temperature hovered around 40 degrees below zero."

From Vladivostok, the Melameds made their way to Japan and in December 1940, a year before the attack on Pearl Harbor, set sail for America on the *Heian Maru*. They landed at Seattle, Washington, and traveled across another continent to reach New York, where the family remained a short time before moving to Chicago and settling in the Humboldt Park neighborhood.

Leo Melamed went to Roosevelt High School and the University of Illinois before attending law school and in a very brief time becoming one of the reformers trying to shove the Merc out of its indolence.

From his first election as chairman in 1969, Melamed remained leader of the Merc for more than twenty years in various positions: chairman of the IMM, chairman of the executive committee, special counsel to the board of governors, and whatever title he needed to push through all the new enterprises he envisioned to make Chicago the capital of the world's financial futures markets.

But it began with the IMM.

"The birth of financial futures was the convergence of three ideas going around in my head: The Merc needed to diversify its product line; I knew the Bretton Woods agreement [which pegged currency exchange rates to the dollar] was doomed; and I and a group of other young traders were looking for ways to make money, including speculating in certain foreign currencies we knew were vastly overvalued," he once explained. Melamed's plan to launch seven futures contracts based on the fluctuating value of seven different foreign currencies changed the course of modern investing throughout the world.

These currency futures paved the way for the successful marketing of a dizzying array of similar products at the Merc, the Chicago Board of Trade, and the Chicago Board Options Exchange. By the 1990s, these exchanges were trading futures and options on everything from Asian and American stock indexes to interest-rate swaps, Eurodollars, currency cross-rates, and Treasury bills, and their success transformed Chicago almost overnight into the risk-transfer capital of the world.

In those early years, Melamed traveled the world selling bankers and moneymen on the economic need of his financial futures market. It was heady stuff for the son of Polish immigrants who were both Yiddish teachers. Melamed has described himself as a "laborious perfectionist by nature and almost obsessive." Others say the man of small stature, intense drive, and gigantic ego generally gets his way, and this was no exception.

Financial futures trading opened new industries and changed the way market information was related to the public. The complexities of trading Treasury notes (interest rates inversely affect the sale price) and the addition of Standard & Poor's stocks lists created new avenues of data and led to the formation of cable television stations reporting financial data twenty-four hours a day to keep up with GLOBEX, a twenty-four-hour international trading service that Melamed was the driving force behind in 1989.

After twenty-one years of leading the Merc, Melamed stepped away from all his leadership posts, leaving the operation to one of his many protégés, Jack Sandner.

But Melamed apparently did not think his successors were doing the right things.

He hinted he was being frozen out of exchange policy decisions by his successor, Sandner. In 1997 he returned to power when the board of directors elected him permanent adviser to the board and its executive committee, a title, like so many he held, that belies the influence Melamed was given.

His continuing role at the Merc will probably require another biography and surely a final appraisal of his role in both Chicago business and worldwide investments. Until then this summation by the *Chicago Tribune*'s George Gunset will suffice:

> Head and shoulders above the few of his generation was Leo Melamed, perhaps the dominant figure in futures in the last half-century. One could make a case that he is the most significant individual in the industry in the last 100 years.

For many others, Leo Melamed is simply the "father of financial futures."

7

DOUBLE YOUR PLEASURE:
WILLIAM WRIGLEY

There is more than a metaphor about the massacre at the Alamo and the Chicago Cubs' century of defeat. In 1836, General Santa Ana brought more than four thousand soldiers from Mexico to slaughter 186 Texans defending a tiny mission at San Antonio. He also brought chicle.

Later, while living in exile in New Jersey, Santa Ana met an inventor named Thomas Adams, and the general generously asked if Adams would like to chew a little chicle, which is the boiled gum of the sapodilla tree. Adams tried it and decided he had found a substitute for rubber. When that didn't work he mixed up a batch of chicle in his kitchen and put it on sale at a local store. Chewing gum wasn't very popular in the nineteenth century. For one thing, almost every man smoked hand-rolled cigarettes, a pipe, or a cigar. It was also considered a vulgar habit, so women didn't try it. Almost no one chewed gum with any regularity until a young soap salesman in Chicago started giving it away.

The soap salesman was William Wrigley, one of the few men who virtually created a demand when none existed and then moved rapidly and creatively to fill the lion's share of that demand and leave behind a company that would dominate the industry he built for an entire century.

William Wrigley was one of the first businessmen to understand advertising and promotion.

One of the greatest promotions in American sales history came in 1915, when Wrigley collected every telephone book in the country and mailed four sticks of gum free to 1.5 million people. He did it again in 1919, even though the number of subscribers had climbed to 7 million.

During World War I some stores raised the price of Wrigley's gum. Wrigley was infuriated and after the war began a huge advertising campaign, "Five cents before the war, five cents during the war, five cents now." Since Wrigley was selling gum for five cents in 1914 and still selling it for five cents in 1954, it made some wonder how much profit there had been in it. Plenty. Wrigley was already making more than $8 million a year in 1920. William Wrigley Jr. Company sales totaled $1.85 billion in 1996.

William Wrigley was born in 1861 in Philadelphia and spent his boyhood working in his father's soap factory, but he quickly demonstrated his sales abilities. At age thirteen he left home to peddle soap in rural Pennsylvania and New York. In 1890, with a new wife and thirty-two dollars, he headed for Chicago and set up William Wrigley Jr. and Company. A partner had previously sold baking powder, which he persuaded Wrigley to add to the line. Wrigley believed in promotions and premiums. To help sell baking powder he included two sticks of chewing gum with the powder. In a few months, he noticed people began to ask if they could buy the gum without the powder. By 1893, the year of the great economic panic, Wrigley had bought the Zeno Manufacturing Company, which made the gum he gave away, and he was on the road, traveling across the Midwest, spending more than half the year away from his home. He promoted gum as though it were a miracle drug. He gave away counter scales and cash registers and display cases to stores that purchased large orders. He persuaded grocers and druggists and candy-store operators to put his gum on their cash registers where customers would notice it as they waited for their change. He designed a package for his gum, white with green arrows, and named it Spearmint. He created a second product that he called Juicyfruit. By 1910, Spearmint was the number-one selling chewing gum in the country. Juicyfruit was second.

In 1902 Wrigley paid a New York advertising firm the unheard of sum of $100,000 to promote his chewing gum. In 1907, another year of economic panic, he spent $250,000. By his death in 1932 he had spent $100 million on advertising, the most spent on any single product in America up to that time.

"Any fool can make chewing gum, the trick is to sell it," he often said.

By the 1920s, Wrigley had plants in foreign countries and all over America. Like other great business successes of his era, he understood the value of loyal employees and treated them generously. He was one of the first in the country to offer a five-day work week, and female employees were provided with free manicures and beauty parlor services.

And, by the 1920s, there wasn't much left for Wrigley to do but play. He had purchased in 1919 the controlling interest in the Chicago Cubs and turned his adoration from chewing gum to Wrigley Field, where he was always in attendance. He spent $5 million to purchase players for the Cubs, who actually won pennants in those days.

Wrigley also bought the Los Angeles Angels minor league team and its stadium, which also was named Wrigley Field. Off the southern California coast was an island called Catalina that had a town called Avalon. Wrigley bought everything but the town for $3 million in 1919 and began transforming it into a resort area. He had to import wild boars to rid the island of rattlesnakes, and then had to hire hunters to get rid of the boars.

In 1924 he built the terra-cotta clad Wrigley Building, one of Chicago's landmarks. He died in 1932 and, of course, never saw the baseball team he owned win a World Series.

8 ■

COLOR IT YELLOW:
JOHN HERTZ

John D. Hertz was a pretty tough guy. In the 1920s he bought a stretch of beach in Miami and convinced his closest friend, Albert Lasker, to build a place next door. Before they knew it a new neighbor had bought a strip of the beach. He was "Machine Gun Jack" McGurn. Hertz and Lasker demanded that the Chicago chief of police have McGurn extradited back to the city. Lasker thought they might be killed by McGurn's boss, Al Capone, but Capone wired a message saying there were no hard feelings.

John D. Hertz did not change America to the degree that the Krocs, Krafts, and his good friend Lasker did. But he was another one of the early twentieth-century innovators who knew a good idea when he saw one.

Hertz was born in 1879 in Ruttka in what later became Czecho-slovakia. His family immigrated to Chicago when he was five. He grew up on the hard West Side and ran away from home at eleven to sell newspapers at a time when a boy needed his fists to protect his street corner from his competitors. His father found him in a waifs' home, but Hertz took off again and drove a delivery wagon, then tried boxing, sportswriting for the *Chicago Record*, and managing boxers, including a couple of contenders, Benny Yanger and Jack O'Keefe, who made Hertz about ten thousand dollars. He became enthused about the new motorcars that were appearing on Chicago streets and became a demonstration driver for the Walden M. Shaw automobile agency, which sold Reo, American Berliet, and Premier automobiles.

He was earning twelve thousand dollars a year when he decided to purchase a share in a new French car company. Hertz took in a lot of cars as trade-ins, and he decided to put a few of them on the street as taxicabs, which were just being introduced in 1910. He started his company by offering a private service for the Chicago Athletic Association, and he quickly infuriated his competitors by cutting the exorbitant rates from $5 an hour and 70 cents a mile to $2.50 an hour and 20 cents a mile.

Hertz was convinced the taxi business had a big future. He went to Paris and noticed that the French taxis were much more economical, stripped of luxuries, and most importantly would pick up anyone who waved. In Chicago at that time, customers had to telephone in advance to order a taxi. Hertz returned and expanded his fleet, introducing curb pickups, and began to use only the most simple, low-maintenance vehicles. But his drivers kept getting into accidents, which cut profits. Hertz heard about a University of Chicago study that showed the most easily identifiable color was yellow.

In 1915 he opened the Yellow Cab Company, which also became a manufacturer of taxis. A few years later, a competitor, Morris Markin, heard about the same study, which showed that after yellow the most easily spotted colors were red and lime green, which became the pattern of his Checker Cab Company.

One reason for all the motor vehicle accidents in the early days of driving was that there were no traffic signals. Hertz installed the first traffic lights in Chicago on Michigan Avenue and Randolph Street. The city not only agreed to expand the system but paid Hertz the cost of his installation. His Yellow cabs were the first vehicles to have windshield wipers, which were operated at first by the driver turning a crank on the dashboard. Later Hertz installed motor-driven wipers. He also used the new balloon tire invented by Firestone to replace the thin, bicycle-type wheel used on Model Ts. He installed interior lights, the first fare meters, and heating.

Hertz made deals to build cabs for transit companies in New York, St. Louis, and other cities, and before long his Yellow cabs were seen in most American cities. By the early 1920s he was a millionaire and the Yellow Cab was an American icon.

That's when he recognized another good idea.

The idea belonged to Walter Jacobs, who in 1918 took a dozen banged-up Model T Fords, repaired them, and began renting them. In 1924, Hertz bought the company and named it the Hertz Drive-ur-Self system, which he licensed in other cities. By 1925 Hertz was operating offices all over America, which were recognized by the bright signs, in yellow, of course. Hertz also began building buses. In fifteen years, John Hertz had become a one-man transportation dynasty.

Another dynasty located in Detroit, General Motors, wanted a piece of the action and paid Hertz $16 million for his manufacturing company and the rental-car system. In 1953, GM divested itself of Hertz, which became a separate company.

By 1995 Hertz had offices in fifteen hundred cities and one hundred foreign countries.

In 1929, Hertz sold his Yellow Cab Company to Checker Cab, ending a bloody and deadly taxi war in Chicago. Checker had gone into business in 1922, but Hertz did everything he could to stop it from gaining a foothold. It is not certain that John Hertz ordered anybody hit, but they were still dredging parts of taxis out of the Chicago River in the 1950s, and some cabbies' bodies never were found. Morris Markin's home was bombed in 1923, and in 1928 Hertz's thousand-acre estate in Cary was set ablaze, killing eleven of his prized thoroughbred horses.

Horse racing became Hertz's fixation after he disposed of his transportation companies. Hertz, Laurance Armour of meatpacking fame, and lawyer Weymouth Kirkland were the first investors in the new Arlington Park racetrack built in 1928. Hertz was its executive secretary. He built one of America's great racing stables, Stoner Creek Farm, in Kentucky, and he owned the 1928 Kentucky Derby winner, Reigh Count, and the 1943 Triple Crown winner, Count Fleet.

In 1934, he became a partner in Lehman Brothers investment firm, where he remained until his death in 1961. The automobile, not John Hertz, changed twentieth-century America, but he made it more convenient and certainly more colorful.

9

PADDY AND ME:
JOSEPH KRAFT

No one ever saw John Wayne eating a cheese sandwich. In all the hundreds of western movies the hero never ate cheese, and neither did anyone else. There was always a scene in the general store where cowboys stocked up on beans, flour, bacon, and coffee. In *Shane*, the gunfighter buys a kid some candy. Either the hooker or the heroine is usually seen buying some material for a dress, and once in a while Butch Cassidy or the Sundance Kid bought a can of peaches. Yet, on the counters of most of those general stores sat a glass-covered wedge of cheese. Even in movies it was probably already beginning to smell. In the Old West and in turn-of-the-century America, hardly anyone ate cheese.

Cheese didn't stay fresh long, especially in the humid South or during the summer in Chicago. A lot of his friends thought thirty-year-old James Kraft was making a big mistake in 1904 when he left his home in Fort Erie, Ontario, and headed for Chicago with sixty-five dollars that he promptly invested in a wagon, fifty pounds of cheese, and a horse named Paddy.

"Two rolls and coffee for my own breakfast and a bag of oats for Paddy were all I had to show for my original outlay the second morning I was in Chicago," Kraft recalled years later. "At the end of the first year we were $3,000 in debt in spite of all the trotting Paddy did and all the sales I could make. In those days people didn't care much for cheese and that was easy to understand for American-made cheese of that day was an uncertain commodity. You bought it in chunks and no chunk was ever like another."

Kraft followed a tried business practice by attempting to expand his volume. He borrowed more money and bought another wagon and another horse. The second horse dropped dead, and then Paddy broke his leg.

But Kraft had developed a following among the grocers in the Austin neighborhood, where he and Paddy became a familiar sight. Instead of continuing to sell cheese in "chunks," Kraft began to package individual portions in glass jars and tinfoil packages, which kept the product fresh. Business got better. He convinced his four brothers to join him in 1907 to form J. L. Kraft and Brothers. He began to import European cheeses, and Chicago's large immigrant enclaves welcomed the memories of their homelands.

At the same time, Kraft kept experimenting in double boilers and copper kettles until in 1916 he patented a process of pasteurizing cheese that dramatically increased its shelf life.

He packed the cheese in four-ounce tins and quickly established a level of sales that was unprecedented. When America was preparing for World War I, the U.S. government bought millions of pounds of Kraft cheese for its soldiers. By 1923 Kraft's sales reached $22 million and cheese consumption in America had doubled.

The following year Kraft introduced Velveeta, one of its most profitable and successful products. In 1927, Kraft merged with Phenix Cheese Company of New York and acquired the immensely successful Philadelphia Cream Cheese. In 1930, Kraft sold out to National Dairy Products Corporation but remained as president of the Kraft subsidiary and continued to demonstrate his skills at marketing, adding new products such as Miracle Whip salad dressing. He also got the company involved in the early days of broadcasting, sponsoring the Kraft Music Hall first on radio and later on television.

He became an avid rock collector, and *Popular Mechanics* magazine described him as America's number-one "rock hound" and credited him with discovering American jade.

Kraft was born in a Mennonite family and was active in religious organizations all his life, becoming a deacon of the North Shore Baptist Church and a trustee of the Northern Baptist Theological Seminary. He credited most of his success to God's blessings and to his first partner, noting on the twenty-fifth anniversary of the company's founding, "Now, twenty-five years later when business deliveries are made by truck, airplane and railroad, I still consider Paddy one of the greatest assets of our business."

When he died in 1953 at age seventy-nine, Americans, even cowboys, were eating ten times as much cheese annually as they did when he and Paddy began trotting through the Austin neighborhood a half century earlier.

10

FOOT FETISH:
WILLIAM SCHOLL

Billy Scholl had a remarkable memory. He never forgot a foot.

Billy Scholl had a thing for feet even when he was a small kid. He never married, so it's possible to conclude he never found anyone with the perfect feet. He had the world's largest collection of shoes. But he made millions of feet feel better. And made millions of dollars.

William M. Scholl was born in 1882 on a farm near LaPorte, Indiana. He showed an early affinity for working with leather, making harnesses for the family horses, repairing boots and shoes for his parents and twelve siblings. At age thirteen, he was apprenticed to a local cobbler, and at the turn of the century he moved to Chicago to work as a salesman-cobbler in a shoe store. Scholl was quickly appalled at the condition of big-city feet: corns, bunions, hammertoes, fallen arches. Some of the problems were caused by shoe manufacturers, who didn't distinguish between left and right feet. Shoes were interchangeable. Billy Scholl was aghast. He hustled off to Illinois Medical College (Loyola University) and received his degree in 1904, but he never went into practice. Instead, he invented a leather arch support and went into business. The first of hundreds of patents he obtained, the support was called the "Foot-Eazer." Scholl also had a sales and promotion knack. When he called on shopkeepers, he would plop a skeleton of a human foot on the counter and begin explaining what evils could befall the delicate metatarsals unless huge quantities of the Foot-Eazer were placed in stock.

Soon, the arch support was joined by bunion pads and corn removers, callus files and foot powder, foot lotion and foot deodorant, corn salve and bunion salve, inserts for dress shoes and inserts for play shoes, and shoes themselves.

Scholl wrote several books on the health of feet and promoted stories about himself in newspapers, always providing some faddish tidbit such as recommending that people wear two pairs of shoes every day or that women's feet were in better shape than men's because housewives walked eight miles a day doing their chores.

In 1916, Scholl sponsored a Cinderella foot contest, and women throughout the country trudged into stores to have their feet measured on a Pedograph, a Scholl invention that evaluated the weight distribution of the foot.

Scholl's business thrived with virtually no competition. He opened more than one hundred retail stores, expanding to Canada and England before 1910. When he celebrated his fiftieth anniversary in business in 1954 he was selling corn remover in every nation of the world except communist China. He also invented the display racks that neatly stacked more than a dozen Scholl products on pegs and shelves and could be easily accommodated in any kind of store.

In 1908, he built a huge complex, a city block square, at Wells and Schiller to manufacture all his foot remedies. The factory was closed in 1981 and the building renovated for residential living. Scholl had homes in Long Beach, Indiana, and Palm Springs, California, but in Chicago he often worked seven days a week and lived in a single room (no private bath) at the Illinois Athletic Club.

He traveled considerably and was especially proud of his trips on the great dirigibles of the 1930s, the *Graf Zeppelin* and the *Hindenburg*.

In 1904, Scholl's company earned $815. He was still its president at his death in 1968, and the company then earned more than $600 million annually. Scholl was worth more than $6 million when he died at age 85. His company was sold in 1979 to Schering-Plugh Corporation of Madison, New Jersey.

But in the 1990s, in the heyday of Nikes and Reeboks, Dr. Scholl was still accommodating painful feet. The company announced in 1993 the introduction of a new patented slim insert for recreational shoes, aimed at the aging boomer generation whose march to unrivaled affluence inflicted the same number of corns and calluses that Billy Scholl found so alarming a century ago.

■ ■ ■ V

MEDIA'S
TOP TEN

Maybe it started with Terrible Tommy O'Connor. But Hilding Johnson is a big part of the story. Of course, there were the great publishers: Medill, Hearst, McCormick, Field, Knox, and Knight. Almost all of them wanted to be president at one time or another. There was Jake Lingle, the first newspaper reporter killed by the mob. Others have been killed for knowing too much. Jake merely wanted too much. There were the columnists, beginning with Finley Peter Dunne before the turn of the century and ending with Mike Royko, who died, too soon, before the turn of another century. Perhaps no band of journalists earned greater fame than the sportswriters: Ring Lardner, Irvin S. Cobb, Westbrook Pegler, John Carmichael, Warren Brown, Arch Ward, David Condon, Jerome Holtzman, Jack Griffin, Bill Gleason, Bob Verdi. There were the sports voices, Jack Brickhouse and Bob Elson and Jack Quinlan and Harry Caray. There was Kup. Always there was Kup. There were the critics: Sandburg, Hoke Norris, Herman Kogan, Claudia Cassidy, Vincent Sheehan, Dick Christiansen. There were the editors: James Keeley, Scott Beck, Walter Hovey, Henry Justin Smith, Clayton Kirkpatrick, Emmett Dedmon. There were the reporters: Buddy McHugh, Jack MacPhaul, Ed Lahey, Ray Brennan, Earl Aykroid, George Bliss, Lois Wille, Ray Coffee, Georgie Anne Geyer, Bob Wiedrich, and Norman Ross (*père et fils*). And there was Len O'Connor on politics and John Drummond on crime and Fahey Flynn and Floyd Kalber on forever.

Chicago helped invent early radio with WLS (World's Largest Store), owned by Sears, Roebuck, and WGN (World's Greatest Newspaper), owned by the *Tribune*. Despite its history of mayhem and murder it is a fair bet to say nothing that ever came from Chicago quite entertained the nation as much or as long as a radio show that began in 1928, *Amos and Andy*. There was Fibber McGee and Molly and Don McNeil's *Breakfast Club*, which began most of Middle America's day for two decades with the cheery "Good Morning, Breakfast Clubbers." There was Wally Phillips in the morning for twenty-five years and Milton Rosenberg at night for twenty-five years; in between, there was John Callaway.

There was pioneer Chicago television, where the omnipresent talk show of the 1990s was born with Dave Garroway and Studs Terkel. "Frontier television," said Terkel, who was there to watch the birth of Kukla, Fran and Ollie and Super Circus.

And there were reporters. Some of the best newspaper reporters who ever lived and worked during the decades in which newspapers were as essential to American lives as their freedoms. It was the newspapers that immigrants used for education in culture and language. It was newspapers that served their Jeffersonian mandate as the watchdogs of government. It was newspapers that entertained with fiction and comics and humor and commentary and most often with sensationalistic accounts of horrid crimes and lurid loves. It was newspapers that once appeared on Chicago streets almost hourly to provide some new glittering nugget of information about the rise of Al Capone and downfall of Samuel Insull, about the raid on a whorehouse or the birth of triplets. It was the newspapers and their reporters who conjured for America the image of "Front Page" journalism.

But the job of reporters is to record history, not make it. Despite their enormous contribution to the craft and lore of journalism, few of Chicago's most distinguished editors, writers, and broadcast commentators had much impact on the rest of the country. But some of them changed the way Americans thought, the way Americans received their information, the way Americans lived, and even the way they loved.

THE BUNNY:
HUGH HEFNER

In 1953, a movie called *The Moon Is Blue* was on the Catholic Church's forbidden list because the word *seduce* was used in it. Julius and Ethel Rosenberg were the first Americans executed for treason during peacetime. The poet Dylan Thomas and the politician Robert Taft died. Happily, so did Joseph Stalin. Maureen Connolly won the tennis grand slam, and Ben Hogan captured the Masters, U.S. Open, and British Open. Ernie Banks made his debut at Wrigley Field, and, in 1953, good girls didn't.

But some girls must have because the birth control pill was the latest rage, although no one talked about it above a whisper. Radios were just beginning to play amplified music called rock and roll sung by groups called the Crows and the Crew Cuts. America was still celebrating the twin triumphs of World War II and technology with dishwashers and televisions and saran wrap and high-fidelity music. Winston Churchill won the Nobel for literature and Ernest Hemingway won the Pulitzer. Things were pretty much as they always had been.

An Indiana University professor named Albert Kinsey explained why the pill was so popular in a study called "Sexual Behavior in the Human Female." It claimed that sometimes good girls did, and, while most people didn't believe it, some of them did it a lot. With a lot of different people.

One of the people who believed the Kinsey study, or at least hoped with all his heart it was true, was an ambitious circulation manager of an obscure magazine company. Each night he would sit at his kitchen table and dream of all the girls who did. He assumed most other men did the same thing. He also dreamed of being famous and rich and living in a mansion full of amply endowed young women and game rooms where the idle rich played pool and backgammon and watched movies in private screening rooms. He dreamed of lounging in silk pajamas like Cary Grant and drinking expensive scotch in fine crystal tumblers and listening to records from a collection of the world's finest jazz players. He thought this was what every other young man dreamed of, and he had an idea how they could achieve all this vicariously. They would simply buy the magazine he was creating on his kitchen table, the magazine he would launch with six hundred dollars of his money and six thousand dollars he borrowed. He had a name for the magazine that was simply his view of what he assumed every other man wanted to be.

Playboy.

In 1953, the first issue of *Playboy* hit the stands. It sold out and twenty-seven-year-old Hugh Hefner was on his way to the mansion, the hordes of busty women, the silk pajamas, the riches, and the fame. The scotch he left to his readers, but his refrigerator would always be full of Pepsi Cola.

The same generation of males who will always remember where they were the day Kennedy was shot cannot forget the first time they saw *Playboy*.

They usually saw it held sideways so the two-page vertical spread of the almost-nude "playmate" faced them. Marilyn Monroe was the first woman a lot of guys saw with a staple in her stomach.

Some five hundred stomachs and staples later, *Playboy* still is around. It has been passé for twenty-five years, but it is still slick and it still sells, although its circulation numbers are far diminished from its heyday of 8 million in the early 1960s. Hugh Hefner still is around, although he's far less the personification of hedonism than his playmate-a-week lifestyle once made him.

His success and the success of the magazine with the sophisticated bunny logo ultimately did him in. The sexual revolution he yearned for appeared in the 1970s. The "have fun, get rich" credo he espoused became Wall Street's war cry in the 1980s, and the technology of a trillion computer chips can turn any 1990s home into an electronic entertainment parlor that the young Hefner could have never imagined.

But no publisher, no editor, no cartoonist, no writer (Hefner was all of these), not in Chicago or anywhere else, can match Hefner's claim that he threw the biggest bomb in the greatest societal revolution in American history.

If Hefner did not singlehandedly start the sexual revolution, he was its Patrick Henry, Thomas Jefferson, and George Washington combined.

Robert Schmuhl, chairman of the American Studies Department at the University of Notre Dame and the author of several articles about the history of Chicago media, wrote:

> From the modest beginnings of launching a small magazine, Hugh Hefner helped set in motion not only the sexual revolution but also reactions to it, including the women's movement. With his "philosophy" and his emphasis on publishing the work of the world's top authors, Hefner made certain that *Playboy* was always more than a magazine with pictures that appealed to single men. What Hefner did in journalism changed America and had significant influence internationally.

Chicago Tribune columnist Bob Green once lumped the rather slouchy, shy Hefner with the volatile, magnetic Elvis Presley, claiming they had more influence on the second half of the American Century than anyone else:

> Every time you see a young woman walk down the street braless and in a thin-fabric blouse it is because of . . . Hefner. Every time you meet men and women who are openly living together outside of marriage . . . every time you see a person casually use an obscenity . . . every time you look in the newspaper and see the soaring divorce rate . . . every time you are upset by aggressively selfish and self-indulgent attitudes you see in so many of your neighbors, it is because of . . . Hefner.

Not long after Hefner published all-nude photographs of actress Jayne Mansfield he was hauled into court on obscenity charges by the city of Chicago. A now-forgotten psychologist testifying for the prosecution observed that Hefner was "a man trying to change the moral code of society because of feelings of guilt and inferiority."

He got it half right for sure.

So did Hefner. "If it feels good, do it," wiped out two hundred years of pretentious American manners. Hefner had some help, which he freely admitted. "I was the right guy in the right place at the right time," he often said.

America had copied Chicago as the city on the make. There was too much out there for the taking in the sixties, seventies, and eighties. "I'm OK, you're OK" was a loose translation of an old Chicago street axiom, "It ain't wrong if you don't get caught." Vietnam, which *Playboy* editorially opposed, and Watergate proved that presidents lied, and if the president lies everyone else is exempt from truth. Churches tried to get in touch with the new secular America but only relinquished much of the fire and brimstone that held congregations for centuries. Assassinations proved the futility of nobility. Open-heart surgery held the promise of longevity. Donald Trump was an American superstar. Lotteries flourished all over America, luring the poor with dreams of being interviewed on *Lifestyles of the Rich and Famous*.

But it began with *Playboy*.

Playboy began with Hugh Marston Hefner, who was born in Chicago in 1926 to Glenn and Grace Hefner, who raised him in a "middle-class, Protestant" household and sent him progressively to Sayre grade school, Steinmetz High School, and the University of Illinois, where he graduated in 1949 and like almost everybody in those days promptly married his high school sweetheart, Mildred Williams.

Hefner worked as a copywriter and at promotional jobs, including one at *Esquire* magazine that inspired him to tinker on his kitchen table with the rabbit wearing a tuxedo collar who would become the maître d' to the 1950s male appetite for stapled tummies.

The astonishing success of *Playboy* turned Hefner into a multimillionaire and launched a series of copycats such as *Penthouse* that ultimately ate into *Playboy*'s market share. But nothing could match the rabbit mystique, which in 1960 Hefner turned into a series of key clubs staffed by wannabe playmates attired in tights, rabbit ears, and cotton tails who promised the clientele everything but what the clientele wanted.

Hefner launched *Qui* magazine, a racier version of *Playboy*, which failed, and *Show Business Illustrated*, which he quickly sold after big losses. But the Playboy empire was far from faltering. Hefner lived in a sixty-nine-room mansion on Chicago's Gold Coast, not far, ironically, from the home of the Roman Catholic archbishop of Chicago. His parties were the stuff of 1960s myth and legend, and Hefner was rarely seen outside his enclave and rarely seen in anything but pajamas. The sexual freedom he preached in his monthly "Playboy Philosophy" columns was based on firsthand reporting. He supposedly dated every playmate and many, many more of the luscious young women who lived in dormitories built in the mansion. In 1968, he moved the Playboy myth to a Holmby Hills, California, retreat where the parties continued, and he began a ten-year, highly publicized relationship with Barbi Benton, then eighteen. "You're a nice guy," the teenager told Hef, "but I've never dated anyone over twenty-four." Hefner answered, "Neither have I." The legend grew.

Hefner, who had lived his fantasy as a playboy bachelor for thirty years since he divorced Mildred, finally remarried in 1989 to Kimberly Conrad, surrendering the most envied lifestyle any adolescent male could imagine. He had already surrendered running *Playboy*. Business had gone sour in the 1970s. Playboy Clubs lost their luster and disappeared. The most lucrative enterprise, casino gambling in Great Britain, came to a halt when the British government revoked Playboy's licenses.

In 1982, his daughter, Christie, became the president of Playboy Enterprises, Inc., and the company rebounded under a woman, which is delicious irony for such liberators as Betty Friedan and Gloria Steinem, who criticized it during its heyday for its unabashed chauvinism, rejoiced over what they called its irrelevance during the seventies, and prematurely declared it obsolete in the 1980s.

Under Christie Hefner, Playboy has navigated onto the Internet, where its early results indicate even more profits but where the visual reality will never match the artful imagination of stapled bellies. In 1998 Hefner and Kimberly announced a separation. The myth goes on.

2 ■

THE COLONEL:
ROBERT R. MCCORMICK

It is not certain that Colonel Robert R. McCormick hated anyone or anything, but for the first seventy years of the twentieth century the readers of the *Chicago Tribune* had a hard time believing that.

It appeared that the *Tribune* certainly hated Democrats. It was certain the *Tribune* hated internationalists and interventionists and, of course, liberals. The *Tribune* hated Woodrow Wilson's League of Nations in particular and Franklin D. Roosevelt in general. The *Tribune* had kind words for John Kennedy after he was shot and Harry Truman after he was dead. But the *Tribune's* approach to politics and government was never as partisan as its reputation. The *Tribune* didn't think much of Herbert Hoover, detested Thomas Dewey, and tended to ignore Dwight Eisenhower. Ike's secretary of state, John Foster Dulles, was an abomination. And, excepting Roosevelt, no one was more despised in *Tribune* columns than Republican Mayor William Hale Thompson.

For the first half of the twentieth century the *Tribune* didn't like England or anywhere else in Europe, with the possible exception of Germany in those rare years when it wasn't at war with the rest of the world. The *Tribune* definitely did not like Russia. The *Tribune* didn't like Henry Ford or New York City or the South. The *Tribune* did not like communists, socialists, activists, prohibitionists, or racists, although at times it may have sounded as though it did.

The *Tribune* did like Calvin Coolidge, Alf Landon, Robert Taft, Joseph McCarthy, and Barry Goldwater. The *Tribune* also liked Anton Cermak, Ed Kelly, and Richard J. Daley.

Similar things could have been said of many of America's great newspapers in the early part of the twentieth century. Almost all of them had, like the *Tribune*, been founded on strong political ideologies. Almost all of them dabbled in personal politics. Almost all of them, in the beginning, were ruled by autocratic figures who finally gave way to family or professional legatees more concerned with profits than passion.

The *Chicago Tribune* differed from its publishing peers because it did not simply support the Republican Party; it believed, with great cause, that it *was* the Republican Party. The *Tribune* used its powerful and loud editorial voice but violated the commonly accepted requirement of objectivity on its front pages. The *Tribune*'s owners also dabbled in personal politics. Its founder, Joseph Medill, was elected mayor after the great fire, and Robert McCormick began adult life as an alderman, president of the sanitary district, and on more than a few occasions considered the presidency albeit in a clearly whimsical fashion. But by the middle third of the twentieth century only the *Chicago Tribune* was ruled by an autocratic ideologue with both the power and inclination to use his newspaper as he believed his grandfather, Joseph Medill, would have wanted.

For the millions of Chicagoans and midwesterners who took parts of their daily *Chicago Tribune* with a grain of salt, the comfort for McCormick and his publishing heirs was that they took it. They took it because for most of the twentieth century the *Tribune* was the most complete newspaper in America. The *Tribune* had the best comics section, the widest sports coverage, the best color reproduction, the best magazine, the most interesting features, and, because it made the most money, could afford the widest distribution, the largest number of pages, the most reporters, and the most advertisements, which pleased its readers and its accountants.

But for most of the same twentieth century, there was very little about the *Tribune*'s view of politics and government that was as balanced as its color tones or its profit ledgers. And most of its readers knew it. Some of them, conservative, isolationist, and as Babbitt-like in their midwestern provincialism as the colonel, reveled in its attacks and disdain for anything that didn't match the McCormick spirit of patriotism. Others sighed and turned to the sports and features.

Robert R. "Bertie" McCormick was born in 1880, the second son of Sarah and Robert Hall McCormick, a cousin of Cyrus McCormick, whose manufacture of the reaper made him an American icon and one very rich Chicagoan. McCormick was sent off to prep school at Groton, studied at Harvard, and gravitated through a series of family squabbles and deaths to become one of the rulers of the *Tribune* in 1911. But he wasn't in total control. A firebrand editor named James Keeley really ran the newspaper, and McCormick shared with his cousin, Joseph Patterson, the rule of the business.

The early McCormick years were marked by some great journalistic accomplishments even as they were tainted by his growing reputation for bias. In 1912, the *Tribune* was threatened with a major and potentially deadly libel suit after disclosing that Republican boss George Horace Lorimer had bribed legislators to earn his U.S. Senate seat. Ultimately, after several scary months, the *Tribune* was vindicated when the Senate refused to seat Lorimer.

After both men served in World War I, Patterson came home and said he was going to start a tabloid newspaper in New York, which became for many decades the largest selling newspaper in America, the *New York Daily News*. Patterson had achieved the rank of captain, which he adopted for the rest of his life. Cousin Bertie, however, had become a colonel, a rank that he, too, kept for the rest of his life and that seemed to suit his role in 1919 as the sole proprietor and arbiter of the *Tribune*.

In 1920, the *Tribune* published the secret details of Woodrow Wilson's plans to create the League of Nations, creating a national backlash that ultimately doomed Wilson's hopes that America would join the organization. It was an act that Wilson's navy secretary, Franklin Roosevelt, said "broke the President's heart." Since Wilson died shortly after, Roosevelt wasn't speaking figuratively of his old Groton classmate, Bertie McCormick.

The *Tribune* under McCormick was fearless. On the eve of World War II only McCormick and a small band of equally dedicated isolationists were still arguing against any American involvement abroad. With Adolf Hitler's panzers freely roaming the French and Belgian countrysides it was not a popular position. Still, McCormick got FDR's secret military buildup plans and splashed them all over the *Tribune*'s front page, hoping to re-create his 1920 scoop that changed American opinion.

Roosevelt wanted to have him jailed, but cooler aides prevailed. In 1942, the *Tribune* again scooped the world by reporting that U.S. planes had won the Battle of Midway by breaking the Japanese secret "purple" code. This time no one tried to convince Roosevelt not to move against McCormick. The Justice Department convened grand juries to indict the *Tribune*. Several top editors were subpoenaed, but McCormick continued with his diatribes against Roosevelt and the investigation finally died of inertia, especially since the government couldn't determine what harm had been done. Although millions of Americans read the *Tribune* every day, obviously the Japanese government didn't, because the Japanese military never changed its code.

McCormick's national recognition was based on his perpetual and bitter feud with the White House, but he had been feuding with politicians long before Roosevelt took office, and his public battles won him respect from his peers as a publisher who adhered to the Jeffersonian concept that the press should be a "watchdog of government."

Until the peak of FDR's social experiments in the 1930s no one was more in the *Tribune* spotlight than William "Big Bill" Thompson, Chicago's earthy and embarrassing mayor from 1915 to 1923 and again from 1927 to 1931. Thompson, portrayed by the *Tribune* as a stooge of the Lorimer machine, was far more the Anglophile than McCormick. The *Tribune* attacked him repeatedly for what it believed was his pro-German position in World War I. The *Tribune* linked him to the Ku Klux Klan. Moreover, and with cause, the *Tribune* accused his administration of the most blatant graft and corruption. Thompson replied with libel suits totaling more than $11 million, an astonishing figure for 1918. Throughout the 1920s McCormick and Thompson waged a bitter personal war. Thompson thwarted McCormick's bid to have Governor Frank Lowden win the 1920 GOP presidential nomination, which went to Harding. That same year Thompson's crony Len Small was elected governor, giving McCormick yet another Republican for whom he exhibited great disdain with remarkably accurate instincts. Small would become the first of a sad and long line of Illinois governors to be indicted.

In 1923 the *Tribune* campaigned vigorously and defeated Thompson's reelection bid. Thompson extracted his revenge the following year by defeating the colonel's brother, U.S. Senator Medill McCormick, in the GOP primary. That Thompson lost the general election was not much solace for the McCormick clan. That he won reelection as mayor with the total support of Al Capone's gangland empire in 1927 was even more distasteful.

It was also embarrassing when it was revealed that McCormick had agreed to let his circulation boss, Max Annenberg, seek Capone's help in straightening out labor problems.

While McCormick was an adventurous journalist, he was not in the tradition of Pulitzer or Hearst, who invented ways to make their products more salable and more profitable. It was his cousin, Joe Patterson, who was the *Tribune*'s creative spirit. McCormick and Patterson shared the editorship of the *Tribune* before World War I. It was Patterson who launched the popular comics pages with the publication of the "Katzenjammer Kids." It was Patterson who conceived of special Sunday sections and women's sections. But it was the engineer in McCormick who became fascinated with the process of color printing and spurred the *Tribune* to experiment with color before any other newspaper in America. More than a publisher or an editor, McCormick was an entrepreneur who easily could be included among the most influential Chicago businessmen of the century. He spent the early 1920s roaming wild forests in Canada, which he bought and converted to newsprint farms that provided the *Tribune* with cheap newsprint for decades. He recognized the future of radio and its potential threat to the *Tribune*'s advertising dominance and bought an early station, which he renamed WGN. He experimented with everything, once considering whether newsprint could be made from cornstalks, a commodity in plentiful supply in Illinois.

When McCormick took full control of the *Tribune* after World War I there were ten other newspaper publishers in Chicago. He whipped them all and all those that would come later. At his death in 1955, only Marshall Field III remained in competition with the *Sun-Times* and *Daily News*.

And McCormick was eccentric in ways that only monarchs or despots could understand. His memos to various editors and reporters were enigmas. He once wrote to a foreign correspondent, "Fix Europe." He had a mechanical polo pony installed in the Tribune Tower. He once asked his personal pilots if they could build a barbecue grill in his private plane.

He made the cover of *Time* magazine in 1947 when the *Tribune* celebrated its 100th birthday.

Time did not notice when the *Tribune* celebrated its 150th birthday in 1997. It probably thought the Colonel was still there. Many people do.

3 ▓

OPRAH:
OPRAH WINFREY

As almost everyone knows, the Windy City got its nickname not from the arctic blasts that occasionally roar down the Michigan Avenue canyons but from the bombast of the town's leading citizens in promoting Chicago's future after the Great Fire. So it is fitting that some of the most successful talkers in the world have come from Chicago.

And the best of them have become good listeners.

The television talk show began in 1949 on the nineteenth floor of the Merchandise Mart when the National Broadcasting Company used a single camera, showed a bare studio stage with a ladder as the main prop, and let a radio disc jockey with a bow tie and horn-rimmed glasses begin talking.

His name was Dave Garroway, and the show, which aired at 9 P.M. on Sunday nights, was called *Garroway at Large*. In 1952, NBC whisked Garroway off to New York, teamed him with an adorable chimpanzee named J. Fred Muggs, and began the *Today* show, which is almost a half century old, has spawned hundreds of national and local competitors, and has evolved into a broader broadcasting phenomenon in which just about anyone can get to say what they want on television, cable, and radio. Channel surfing or punching car-radio buttons at any time of the night or day in America will prove that there is no problem finding people who want to talk.

The trick always has been to see how many people will listen.

Nearly fifty years after the Chicago school of television invented Garroway, the ultimate successor to all the talk show sensations—

from Arthur Godfrey and Jack Paar to Johnny Carson and Phil Don-ahue, from Garry Moore and Steve Allen to Barbara Walters and Arse-nio Hall—is a woman whose diets obsess more Americans than the Cold War did.

Oprah Winfrey is the most influential Chicagoan to appear on television during the century in which television became the most influential medium in the world.

More people have watched Oprah Winfrey since she started her show in 1985 than all the people who have watched all the other tele-vision talk shows over the same period of time.

If Oprah Winfrey promotes a book, it is immediately a bestseller.

If Oprah Winfrey tries a new diet, the manufacturer's stock rises.

If Oprah Winfrey declares war on child abuse, Congress intro-duces a bill.

If Oprah Winfrey interviews Michael Jackson, all of America watches.

If Oprah Winfrey invites the First Lady on her show, the First Man's approval ratings go up.

Nearly 15 million Americans watch Oprah every morning in every city everywhere. Some shows have drawn more than 20 million. If any Oprah fans miss it in the morning they can watch it later. The *Oprah* show's success prompted the network that syndicates it, ABC televi-sion, to offer it a second time each day in most of its major markets.

If financial success alone were an indication of national promi-nence, Oprah would be unchallenged. In 1997 she was on *Forbes* maga-zine's list of the wealthiest Americans with a fortune of $550 million. She was headed toward becoming the nation's first African American billionaire.

Unlike her predecessors or competitors, Winfrey has branched out into other areas of the media that enhance her prominence and influence. Winfrey is one of only three women in film and TV history to own a production studio. The others were Mary Pickford and Lucille Ball. Her studio, Harpo (Oprah spelled backward) Produc-tions was a $20 million investment and has produced many of the productions in which Winfrey has starred since her film debut in the 1986 movie *The Color Purple*, for which she won an Academy Award nomination.

She produced six movies for ABC under the logo "Oprah Winfrey Presents. . . ."

She owns condominiums everywhere, including her Chicago home, whose renovation cost millions. Her farm in Indiana, where she keeps horses she doesn't ride, was estimated to be worth $5 million, and she bought a Rocky Mountain chalet retreat at Telluride, Colorado, and Caribbean homes and continental homes.

"Girl! Look at you! You're not on the farm in Mississippi feeding those chickens no more!" Winfrey once remarked.

Winfrey did grow up on a Mississippi farm, but spent most of her childhood in Milwaukee and later attended high school in Nashville, Tennessee, before getting her show business start as Miss Black Tennessee while she was a student at Tennessee State University. The award led to a local television job and then to a stint cohosting a talk show in Baltimore.

The Chicago ABC affiliate, WLS-TV, hired her from an audition tape in 1984 to do its *AM Chicago* show, which had gone through a series of hosts—Steve Edwards, Charlie Rose, Rob Weller, Sandi Freeman—and was simply looking for another person to occupy the time slot that Phil Donahue dominated.

In the early 1980s, Donahue had become the number-one talk show host in the country. The talk show format had evolved from the Garroway brand of humor and wisdom. The father of television news, Edward R. Murrow, introduced the celebrity interview in his 1950s *Person to Person*, a title that evokes the now distant nondigital world when long-distance operators connected calls. There were also the venerable, elite, Sunday morning quizzes of politicians on *Meet the Press* and *Face the Nation*. And Jack Paar's *Tonight* show got a touch risqué. In the 1970s, Donahue mixed them all up. He would interview entertainers and politicians and ask the same kinds of questions, mostly serious but sometimes whimsical. A plethora of competitors appeared. While Donahue tried to maintain the dignity and authority of a host, others such as Morton Downey Jr. and Geraldo Rivera played the role of provocateurs. As the topics moved to discussions of once-taboo bedroom subjects, the inclusion of celebrities diminished. Anyone who had been raped or caught her husband sleeping with her best friend now qualified as a talk show guest.

In this new arena, Oprah became supreme. She was not an authority. She was not a foil. She was the perfect confidante, the best friend. She got down and dirty. She surprised even herself by blurting out to a guest discussing her sexual abuse as a child, "That happened to me, too."

In two years, Oprah had run Donahue out of Chicago and had claimed the top spot among talk shows. When she extended her contract in 1997 to run until the year 2000, she was still drawing 15 million listeners a day and had been number one for eleven years. She also had shrewdly become a part owner of her show, which made her extremely wealthy in only a few years.

Although she often mentioned giving up her daily grind, Oprah told her viewers, "I want to use television not only to entertain but to help people lead better lives. I realize now, more than ever, that the show is the best way to accomplish these goals."

Oprah ran her show like Pearl Bailey did "Hello Dolly," lots of hugging and kissing and touching, not only her guests but everyone in the audience. The *Oprah* show was an event.

Oprah was different from all of her predecessors. Oprah was one of us.

Her almost annual clashes with her weight, which fluctuated between 120 and 200 pounds, were not only the most talked about diets in America but indicate why Oprah was trusted and viewed as a buddy. She was not some remote icon, so beautiful or so sexy that she had to be envied. She was not some regal authority dispensing knowledge in sound bites. She was always looking for help, just like her audience. Oprah's ratings dipped 12 percent during the fall of 1997 when she was slim. An industry expert said, "When Oprah's heavier she's more approachable, more of a girl friend, less of an authority figure." During previous weight losses, Oprah's ratings also dipped, according to *Inside Media* magazine. "Then she put weight back on and the ratings returned."

Oprah, like Hugh Hefner and Colonel McCormick, was right for the time. Satellites and cable and instant coverage of anyone and anything has removed the mystique that once made celebrities aloof and their lives special and unattainable. America of the 1980s and 1990s was all about instant riches and anonymous successes. Any kid with a guitar could become a heavy-metal millionaire. Any kid with a computer could become Bill Gates. America was in a constant search for reassurances that its most rich and most famous were really just like everyone else. Oprah was and she said so.

"I've experienced what everyone else has experienced," Winfrey told the *Chicago Tribune*'s Cheryl Lavin in an interview. "I've had problems with my mother and with men for God's sake. I've stood by the phone afraid to run the water (for a bath) because I'd miss a call. I've been told, 'I'll call you tomorrow,' and then six days later I've held the phone, wondering what can I say that doesn't sound like, 'Why didn't you call?' I've felt terribly insecure about myself. I've had low self-esteem and no self-esteem. I've been there and so has everyone else. I'm just not afraid to admit it."

Winfrey has admitted having a relationship with a married man, admitted a long estrangement with her mother, and reveals details about her long ongoing relationship with Steadman Graham, including many wedding dates that always passed without a wedding. She has even publicly stated that she is not gay.

Edward R. Murrow never had to do that to get ratings. But then, neither Murrow nor anyone else who came after him ever had ratings like Oprah.

4

MR. BIG:
MIKE ROYKO

"Guess who I played golf with?" Mike Royko once asked a friend. "I'll give you a hint. 'The Tackle.' '*The* tackle.' "

The friend, who had often engaged with Royko on trivia about the great sports figures of their mutual childhood, replied, "Not Johnny Lujack?"

"Yeah, and he said it was an honor to meet me. He reads me all the time. Imagine Johnny Lujack thinking it was an honor to meet me?"

It was one of Royko's infrequent modest moments. Or, at least publicly modest. Under the gruff exterior, the growl, and the profane telephone bursts to dissatisfied readers, Royko was a shy, introverted, insecure, and troubled personality—the kind associated with great artists.

And that's what Royko was. He also was the most successful and most prominent newspaper columnist of the last half century.

For thirty-five years, beginning at the *Chicago Daily News*, then with the *Sun-Times*, and after 1983 with the *Chicago Tribune*, Mike Royko serenaded Chicago with its own love songs. He did it with irony, satire, conviction, reprimands, and humor. He was perfect for the role because he loved the city as much as anyone and understood it better than everyone.

He was the defender of the weak against the powerful and the small against the big. He understood what it was like to be weak, and he understood why the powerful enjoyed being big. Johnny Lujack would always be one of Royko's special heroes because Lujack had made "the tackle" in a 1946 Notre Dame–Army game that preserved a 0–0 tie. Although few people knew it, Royko had been sent to a military school after his parents separated. He was a lonely, confused thirteen-year-old being hazed by a group of cadets who had boasted all week that the highly favored Army would crush Notre Dame.

"It was the only time at that place that I was happy, when Lujack made the tackle," Royko said.

It might have been at that school that Royko first became incensed about unchecked authority, or even later during a stint in the air force. He would be fearless in his writings, with particular antipathy toward all the politicians and business leaders whose arrogance he publicly skewered. But he also understood how much they enjoyed their prominence. His closest friends were ordered to call him "Mr. Big."

If Mike Royko, who never told anyone he grew up being called "Mickey," was a complex and often confusing person to figure out, his columns never were. Five days a week for more than thirty years he poured out the most readable prose found in any American newspaper. Although his subject was usually Chicago, he was syndicated in more than five hundred newspapers, and readers throughout the country came to know his characters as well as they knew their own town leaders.

He handed out nicknames that became used nationally, such as Governor Moonbeam for California Governor Jerry Brown, Jesse Jetstream for Jesse Jackson, Mayor Bossy for Jane Byrne, and President Sneaky for Richard Nixon.

But the work that brought the most cheer to Chicago breakfast tables took place during the heyday of Mayor Richard J. Daley, who Royko alternately called the Great Dumpling, Da Mare, or Buddha. It was during the almost Kremlin-like atmosphere of the Daley regime that so much of the sleaze and corruption that Royko feasted upon took place. His book *Boss*, published with great success in 1971, depicted Daley on the cover as a Roman emperor, and the metaphor continued inside. Daley's sons were referred to by Royko as "Larry, Curly and Moe," which, to his credit, did not prevent Mayor Richard M. Daley from making a public declaration of sympathy after Royko's death in 1997.

Royko won a Pulitzer Prize in 1972 but always laughed about how he found out. "We were at a long lunch and when I got back home the cleaning lady was waiting for me. She pulled me aside and whispered, 'Your office called. You won the Nobel Prize.' "

If they gave that to newspapermen he would have won it, too.

Royko was born on the northwest side of Chicago in 1933. His father was Ukrainian and mother Polish. He lived above his father's tavern, and his most precious boyhood memories were of being allowed to take the tavern payoff down to the precinct sergeant.

Years later, it would inspire a column suggesting that the city's motto, *Urbs In Horto*, or City in a Garden, be changed to *Ubi est Mea?* or "Where's Mine?"

Royko began writing during a stint in the service and got his first professional job with the City News Bureau in 1956. He moved to the *Daily News* in 1959 and joined one of the best newspaper staffs of its time. One of his young colleagues then, Georgie Anne Geyer, nationally syndicated columnist and foreign correspondent, recalled, "You could look around the city room and see the most extraordinary talent blooming all about you: Ann Landers, Bill Mauldin, John Fischetti, Lois Wille, Bill Newman, George Weller, Peter Lisagor, Keyes Beech, Nicholas von Hoffman. It is not too much to say that we loved one another and that Mike, with his cute smile and wry and humorous ways, was the most loyal and precious of friends."

The *Daily News* would be an aggressive paper in covering the civil rights era, and Royko, with his unique perspective, was a key element of the paper's approach. When most Americans were castigating world champion Cassius Clay for changing his name to Muhammad Ali, Royko defended him and listed in his column all the show business celebrities who had changed their names.

One of his closest friends described Royko's ability to see things differently than others. "We were walking down a street and we noticed a man with an artificial leg. I said one leg's shorter than the other. Mike said, 'No, one leg's longer than the other.' "

Royko was quicker than everyone else. In the uproar over the tragic 1995 bombing of the federal building in Oklahoma City, commentators and talking heads were urging an all-out hunt for possible

Arab terrorists. Royko's column suggested such witch-hunts would be premature, since America had enough of its own crazies. As usual, he was right.

Royko could have gone to Washington to amplify his national forum, but he always turned down those opportunities, preferring to stay where he could watch his childhood idols, the Cubs, find new ways to lose. He never did have the kind of national impact that columnists such as Walter Lippman and even gossip mavens like Walter Winchell had in the days before television.

But in his era, he was simply the best. And that era is over. Newspaper readership continues to decline, and there is so much entertainment available that such once-cosmic events as the World Series go barely noticed. It is doubtful anyone will be able to raise a public outcry, influence an electorate, ridicule the most powerful, and defend the weak the way Royko did so well and for so long. He was not only the best. He was the last.

5

MISS LONELYHEART:
EPPIE LEDERER

The first column appeared on October 16, 1955, and began with a letter from a married man who enjoyed auto racing and had found a married woman with three children who enjoyed the same sports he did.

"Time wounds all heels—and you'll get yours," wrote Eppie Lederer, a thirty-seven-year-old Jewish housewife who had won a contest to write the "Ann Landers" advice column in the *Chicago Sun-Times* and who, according to the 1990 *Guinness Book of World Records*, was the most widely syndicated columnist in the world.

Her column appeared in more than twelve hundred newspapers worldwide, including those in such unexpected places as Bangkok, Guam, Mexico City, Korea, Tokyo, and Hong Kong. She was read by 90 million people daily. For more than forty years, her column appeared seven days a week.

The number-two spot would probably go to her twin sister, Abigail Van Buren, who began writing her advice column only nine months after Lederer began, spurring a rivalry that has often sliced into the relationship of the two women, who never spent a night apart from their birth on the Fourth of July 1918 until their double wedding at age twenty-one.

But "Dear Abby" will have to settle for being one of the most influential California media figures of the century, because she has never lived in Chicago, although her column has always appeared here.

Eppie Lederer, meanwhile, is a Chicago institution whose wise-cracking rebuttals and sincere advice to the writers of thirty-five

thousand letters have made her one of the most recognized and influential women in the world. She has made the list of most admired
women more than the late Princess Di and Hillary Clinton put together.
She has met every president since Truman and once stiffed the Pope.

Esther Pauline (E.P., hence "Eppie") and Pauline Esther "Popo"
Freidman were born in Sioux City, Iowa, during World War I. As
Ann Landers, Lederer has been giving out advice from the Cold War
to the Cold Peace. Her audience has been transformed from the traditional housewife to the sexual rebel, the feminist, the activist, and the
careerist.

She began by preaching the values of virginity above all else and
wound up defending homosexuality. She has launched the single
biggest letter-writing campaign to Congress in support of funds to
fight cancer and incurred the wrath of the National Rifle Association,
the Moral Majority, and every right-wing group that disagrees with
her pro-choice arguments.

Her critics called her writing improper and sophomoric. Her
readers loved it.

For two decades women in the most wretched of domestic situa-
tions were urged to seek counseling to save their marriages. After her
daughter's two divorces, she began advising "toss the bum out."

In one of the most widely read columns in newspaper history, she
shared the breakup of her thirty-six-year marriage with her readers:

> How did it happen that something so good for so long didn't
> last forever? The lady with all the answers does not know the
> answer to this one? . . . Not only has this been the most diffi-
> cult column I have ever written, but also it is the shortest. I
> apologize to my editors for not giving you your money's
> worth today. I ask that you not fill the space with other let-
> ters. Please leave it blank—as a memorial to one of the
> world's best marriages that didn't make it to the finish line.

Lederer treasured a box of consoling letters she received from
readers.

The advice column in newspapers began at the turn of the century, beginning with Emily Post's explanations of etiquette, which

were eagerly absorbed by the vast number of new immigrants anxious to learn the ways of their adopted society. The "yellow journalism" wars between Joseph Pulitzer and William Randolph Hearst spawned almost all the good and bad ideas that still exist in American newspapers. The first "sob sisters" turning up tales of women betrayed quickly developed into lovelorn columns, later dubbed by Nathaniel West's novel *Miss Lonelyhearts*.

The best of them for a half century was Dorothy Dix, who wrote until her death in 1951. Dix, too, was witty and sometimes irreverent for her times. Ann Landers was a fictional byline created by *Chicago Sun-Times* editor Milburn Akers, and the column was written by Ruth Crowley, a registered nurse who supplied some medical information along with solving *l'affaires d'amour*. When Crowley died in 1955, the *Sun-Times* auditioned twenty-eight people for the job.

Lederer was one of them. She has contended she won the spot by adopting from the start the technique that made her so successful. She did not read letters and dream up responses. She went to the experts. She always said that she called Justice William O. Douglas of the U.S. Supreme Court, who had been introduced to her by another friend, Senator Hubert Humphrey. Eppie Lederer, in time, would know every expert there was to know. Whether she used them or not, people trusted her advice.

In her early years, she dealt with a lot of questions about teens. Reading the collection she published in 1996, *Wake Up and Smell the Coffee*, stirs memories of a much more sedate sexual attitude. Mothers would write worrying about their son getting telephone calls from a girl. Girls would write that they had been caught necking on the front porch and were afraid their parents would never trust them again.

By the 1970s, those letters had disappeared. Discussions of living together, single parenting, and dealing with gay children and friends began to appear.

Ann Landers changed with the times, or at least Eppie Lederer did.

But it was not always the subject matter that counted, it was the instinct that Lederer had for what concerned people, what people talked about, and what they would be interested in reading. Not all the subjects were great social issues.

One of her most memorable queries dealt with whether people preferred toilet paper that hung back against the wall or rolled over the top. More than thirty thousand readers responded with various reasons for their choice.

There was also the occasional faux pas. Once she printed what she said was her favorite meat loaf recipe. With 60 or 70 million readers at the time, it was no surprise that someone would try it. The good news was that a lot of them did. The bad news was that it was terrible. Eppie said the recipe really came from her older sister.

A 1981 episode was a bit more serious. Editors at the Pontiac, Illinois, *News-Leader* accidentally discovered that several of the columns recently submitted by Ann Landers were almost exactly the same as those she had run during the 1960s. There was a lot of hemming and hawing, and some editors were outraged, not necessarily at the ethics, but at having to pay twice for the same material. Columnists from the beginning of time have rerun articles, but usually include a tag line notifying readers that the articles are reprints. Readers couldn't have cared less. All they wanted was what they have wanted for more than four decades: Ann Landers.

6

JIVE:
JOHN JOHNSON

Discussion of media figures and media influence in the twentieth century falls invariably into two categories, before and after television, a time span that almost exactly splits the century into two fifty-year segments.

Before television, newspapers were completely dominant in influencing public opinion. But, despite all their recent attempts to provide color and brevity, to be entertaining and fun-filled, newspapers are basically information vehicles that never could and never will appeal to audio or visual appetites.

Before television, there was another flourishing industry that filled, for its time, the visual and entertainment appetites of the public. Highly pictorial, celebrity-oriented weekly magazines could be found in almost every house in America and in every doctor's office or barbershop. Their names were *Colliers*, *Look*, the *Saturday Evening Post*, and *Life*. They are all gone now, although *Life* exists in a sporadic fashion.

From the start of the century through the 1950s these weeklies were the place where Americans turned for tidbits of gossip and interviews and, most importantly, stunning pictures of their idols, from Jean Harlow and Clark Gable to Elizabeth Taylor and Marilyn Monroe, from Babe Ruth to Ben Hogan, from Theodore Roosevelt to Dwight Eisenhower.

Or, at least, it was the place where white Americans looked.

With the exceptions of boxing legend Joe Louis, a spread on Shirley Temple with tap dancer Bill "Bojangles" Robinson hovering in the background, or an occasional crowd shot of Detroit autoworkers, the magazines were indeed full of every color but black.

The nation's newspapers, of course, didn't bother to cover black Americans as individuals. In the 1930s and 1940s one would have had to scan newspapers diligently to sort out news affecting the black population.

During the 1930s, John J. Johnson was working at a $6.25-a-week job editing a house organ for an insurance company. Among his tasks was to cull from newspapers items affecting blacks. Johnson decided a magazine serving this purpose would be widely accepted in the black community. In 1942, with a loan of five hundred dollars collateralized by his mother's furniture he started a weekly, *Negro Digest*. It was quickly grabbed up by blacks in big cities where Johnson was able to convince distributors it would sell.

When the newsprint shortage ended after World War II, Johnson brought out a weekly that typographically echoed *Life*.

"I was tired of reading crime stories about us," Johnson said. "You'd think we never got married, never ran successful businesses, or did anything normal. Before I started *Ebony* you'd never know that Negroes had beauty contests and had parties."

Ebony was a success from the start, growing from a circulation of ten thousand to five hundred thousand in its first decade. Johnson's first office was at 1820 South Michigan Avenue, a former mortuary that Johnson at first was unable to buy because when he approached the owner, he was told the building was no longer for sale. In 1949 he bought it anyway, through a white lawyer, Louis Wilson, who told the owner he represented a publishing firm in the East.

Johnson posed as a black custodian and dressed in work clothes to inspect the building. It was bought for fifty-two thousand dollars in trust so no one could identify the purchaser, and Johnson spent two hundred thousand dollars renovating it. Such masquerading wasn't unusual. In the 1950s when Johnson was traveling around the country, selling advertising and trying to find new distributors, he took along his circulation manager, J. Unis Pressley, who was so light-skinned that he could pass for white.

Pressley would register for a suite in hotels and order a meal for four or five. Johnson and other staffers then took a freight elevator to the room, pretending they worked at the hotel. "We'd eat a good meal, take a hot bath, sleep in a soft bed and sneak down the freight elevator the next morning," Johnson wrote in his autobiography, *Succeeding Against the Odds*.

"When we traveled in the South, Pressley would go into white cafes and buy food for the whole group."

It took Johnson six years to get Procter & Gamble to advertise in *Ebony* and ten years to sell ad space to Detroit automakers.

By the 1950s Johnson was expanding his publishing enterprises, which eventually would produce *Jet*, *Tan*, *Hue*, and other magazines for black readers. Johnson also owned an interest in *Ebony*'s main competitor of the 1990s, *Essence* magazine.

The magnitude of *Ebony*'s influence on American black people cannot be overestimated.

One *Ebony* editor recalled, "Fanny Lou Hammer, the civil rights leader, once came by our offices to say that, growing up in the Deep South, until she started seeing *Ebony*, she'd never known that some black people lived in nice houses, not just shacks."

Jesse Jackson, whose first job in Chicago was working in *Ebony* warehouses, has recalled how he was inspired by an *Ebony* layout of the 1950s on baseball pioneer Jackie Robinson. Jackson would wind up on *Ebony*'s cover as a presidential candidate in 1988 and have a constant presence during the civil rights turmoil of the 1960s and 1970s.

"I'll never forget those full-page pictures of Robinson and his wife living in Brooklyn, playing stickball in front of his house. There are those who use their light to shine among the people and I got that notion from that story in *Ebony*," Jackson added. "I feel very much like [Johnson] is a part of my family. He's an authentic legend."

Ebony was criticized by mainstream journalists for running only stories about successful blacks and rarely uncovering the nasty side of society, black or white. But *Ebony* was about black pride long before the civil rights movement.

"It made a lot of blacks feel they had something special that belonged to them," said Harvard psychiatrist Dr. Alvin Poussaint.

John H. Johnson was born in Arkansas City, Arkansas, in 1918 and moved to Chicago because there was no high school for blacks in the small town. His mother, Gertrude, worked as a servant and eventually went on public welfare during the Depression, but John Johnson excelled at DuSable High School, where he was class president in his junior and senior years. His valedictory speech impressed the owner of the Supreme Life Insurance Company of America, who gave Johnson a job and helped him get through college at Northwestern.

Johnson, whose firm ranked first or second in net revenue among black businesses for thirty years, also became chairman of the life insurance company where he first dreamed about a magazine for black Americans.

In 1996, Johnson was awarded a Presidential Medal of Freedom and the White House described him as the most influential African American publisher. Johnson had made his first visit to the White House in 1955, when he was invited by President Eisenhower, who already was aware of the impact of *Ebony* and *Jet* in the black community.

Ebony celebrated its fiftieth birthday in 1995, and with a circulation of 1.8 million remained not only the most dominant black-oriented publication in the country, but a survivor of a journalism tradition that television has virtually eliminated.

It is probably just as well that Johnson's choice for the magazine's name was overruled by his wife, Eunice, who picked "Ebony." Johnson wanted to call it "Jive."

7

SWEETHEART, GET ME REWRITE:
BEN HECHT

They finally got tired of waiting for Terrible Tommy O'Connor. They dismantled the gallows at the Cook County Jail in 1977, fifty-six years after O'Connor escaped from the old Cook County Jail and into immortality in the 1928 stage hit *The Front Page*, which created an image of Chicago journalism that is as enduring to the city's history as the St. Valentine's Day Massacre.

O'Connor, a thirty-one-year-old cop killer, jumped from a twenty-foot wall at the old jail behind the Criminal Courthouse at Dearborn and Hubbard and was never heard from again. The escape was only one of the real events and real people that Charles MacArthur and Ben Hecht used for their hit play, which has been made into at least six movie versions and is staged continuously in theaters everywhere.

MacArthur went on to become a successful playwright, but Hecht became one of the prodigious writers of the century, and his unaltering theme was the re-creation of the raucous, scheming, conniving world of Chicago journalism in which newsmen were relentless in their drinking, whoring, and unscrupulous search for the scoop.

Hecht was the best and worst of them. He never had to invent much.

Hecht was born in 1893 in New York City, the son of a Russian Jew who moved the family to Racine, Wisconsin. Hecht turned up in Chicago in 1910 and through an uncle got a job on the scandal-prone *Chicago Journal*. He became a "picture chaser" whose job was to cajole or steal photos or portraits of any noteworthy deceased person before any other paper could get one. He once recalled that the only portrait he could find of the deceased was hanging above the coffin. Hecht climbed on top of the coffin, removed the portrait, and fled.

He became the leading practitioner of never letting the facts interfere with a good story. He moved to the *Chicago Daily News* and wrote a column, "1,001 Afternoons in Chicago," that amazed readers with the stories he uncovered, many of them pure fiction, which Hecht was also writing in his spare time. His most outlandish tale concerned a fissure he found (or dug) in Lincoln Park that led to a column about the earthquake that had struck Chicago during the night.

After the Broadway success of *The Front Page*, Hecht moved to Hollywood, where he became its most prolific screenwriter, winning two Academy Awards and earning credits for *The Front Page*, *Scarface*, *Gunga Din*, *Notorious*, *His Girl Friday* (a remake of *The Front Page*), *The Outlaw*, *Wuthering Heights*, and *Stagecoach*, among many others. Film critic Pauline Kael once said Hecht had his name on half of the best movies ever produced.

He wrote ten novels but only his first, *Eric Dorn*, received critical acclaim. His best books, *Gaily, Gaily* and *A Child of the Century*, were colorful memoirs of Chicago, its people, its crimes, and its newspapers, and cemented his reputation as the city's minstrel.

He was always at his best dealing with real people and real things like Hilding "Hildy" Johnson, the venal protagonist of *The Front Page*, who was in fact a real reporter.

Johnson once cheated a condemned murderer out of his last two hundred dollars. The *Herald* and *Examiner* agreed to pay Carl Wanderer, who was convicted of murdering his wife in one of Chicago's most celebrated crimes of the era, for his life story. After giving the two hundred dollars to the doomed convict, Hildy persuaded him to play a few hands of gin rummy while Wanderer waited to be executed. By the time the hands were over, Johnson had the two hundred dollars back in his pocket. When Wanderer was asked if he had any last words he said, "Don't play rummy with Hildy Johnson. I think he cheats."

When he died in 1964 after concluding his career by hosting a television show in New York, Ben Hecht had written more than seventy movie scripts, twenty plays, and 250 short stories. But most of all he had created the defining image of Chicago newspapers, only another facet of a city whose crime, politics, and shady businesses made it the epitome of the American Century. And all the ethical mandates and doctrines of fairness that news organizations proclaim at the end of the century have not done much to change the fact that most Americans still think Hildy Johnson is somewhere out there calling the city desk and shouting, "Hello, Sweetheart, get me rewrite."

8 ▩

PAGE TWO:
PAUL HARVEY

Just as in art or architecture, some of the most influential Chicagoans of the century are not as significant in their own town as some other people.

In the seventy years of Chicago radio there have been thousands of voices that informed or awoke or kept people company during the day and all through the night. There were the early studio announcers who introduced the soaps and then the big bands. There were the early interviewers, Jack Eigen and others. Then they built expressways all over America, and every station needed a drive-time star. Wally Phillips was unparalleled. And there were Top 40 rock jocks. WLS's clear channel spun all over Middle America during late night in the 1950s, and Dick Biondi screamed into every state between the Alleghenies and the Rockies. There was the soothing Sid McCoy on WCFL and the sentimental Franklyn MacCormack on WGN. WGN's clear signal still carries a different late-night sound, the distinctly intellectual and sophisticated discussion of Milton Rosenberg.

But none of these and no other radio voice since KDKA went on the air in Pittsburgh in 1920 has been heard by more people in more places in America than Paul Harvey.

Each morning for fifty-five years Paul Harvey broadcast from Chicago to America. The routine varied, sometimes three times daily, sometimes twice; sometimes once on weekends, at other times, more often. Paul Harvey talked to 24 million people a day in the distinctive voice and style that was heard on fourteen hundred stations from Maine to Tijuana.

Chicago Tribune columnist Bob Greene wrote, "There are many professional musicians and actors who speak of Harvey's voice as if it were a musical instrument—or an entire orchestra. What he does with that voice—the way he can command an unseen audience's attention with a beat's hesitation, with an almost immeasurable shift in tone, with a quick drop in register—Harvey's voice is like a university in communications."

Harvey arrived in Chicago in 1942 in a 1938 Nash-Lafayette white coupe. He has been there ever since with his wife, Angel, who often gets a mention during his personalized commercials, which have dealt with everything from luxury automobiles to gadgets for removing chewing gum.

Harvey's politics were conservative, but it was his style, not his ideology, that was distinctive. He provided those items of news that he thought made a point, and being objective was not among his concerns. He talked to his audience rather than reported to them. He chuckled, questioned, made that instrument of a voice a tool for scoffing and ridiculing. And he brought both old-fashioned greetings and simple humor. A fixture of his broadcasts were daily anniversary greetings to those celebrating fifty, sixty, seventy years of matrimony, and happy birthdays to the elderly he celebrated as "ninety years young."

He had categories like "Don't Worry, Nothing's Going to Turn Out Right, Anyway," and he invariably made the news entertaining, even when the news was bad.

It is highly unlikely that there can be a single person in all of America who has never heard his familiar sign-off:

"Paul Harvey . . . . Good DAY."

9 ▪

MIDSUMMER'S DAY DREAM:
ARCH WARD

As with most things in Chicago, it started in city hall.

It was in early winter of 1933 when Mayor Ed Kelly called over the sports editor of the *Chicago Tribune* and asked Arch Ward if he couldn't cook up some sort of sports extravaganza to go along with the upcoming 1933 World's Fair. Ward, after all, was the guy who turned amateur boxing into one of the great Depression-era charity events, the Golden Gloves.

That's how baseball's classic all-star game was born.

That's how guys like Carl Hubbell got to strike out guys like Babe Ruth. That's how Stan Musial got to hit against Bob Feller and Ted Williams got to bat against Warren Spahn.

With the passing of the twentieth century, baseball's era as the national pastime is over. With the prospect of vast realignment, intraleague and interleague perversions, it is probably only a matter of time until the all-star game is discontinued. Everyone gets to play everybody. More significantly, the profusion of television coverage allows everybody to see everybody.

But that wasn't the way it was in the 1930s and into the 1950s. Only fans in places like New York, Chicago, and Philadelphia, where there had always been two teams, had the opportunity to see ballplayers from both leagues. In places like Pittsburgh, the only glimpse of someone like Ruth came in the final days of his career, when he was peddled like aging meat to the Boston Braves of the National League.

So Arch Ward marched out of Mayor Kelly's office and, using close friends like American League president Will Harridge, convinced the lords of baseball to play an all-star game in Chicago. They played it at Comiskey Park. Tickets were $1.65 and radio broadcast rights netted $5,175. Babe Ruth homered and the American League won 4–2.

Harridge doubted another such game would ever be played. "If it were an annual event it might sink to the level of an ordinary game," he said. But New York wanted whatever Chicago had, so in 1934 the all-stars went to the Polo Grounds, where Hubbell performed one of baseball's most memorable feats, consecutively striking out Ruth, Lou Gehrig, Jimmie Foxx, Al Simmons, and Joe Cronin.

Arch Ward's midsummer dream still is played.

Ward was a columnist, a reporter, and manager of a huge newspaper's sports staff, but at heart he was a promoter. A native of Irwin, Illinois, who had been Knute Rockne's first publicity man at Notre Dame, Ward was suspicious that the fledgling National Football League wasn't really capable of beating such collegiate giants as Rockne's 1930 undefeated champions. Ward thought the college kids would handle themselves respectably against the pros.

If one all-star game was a success, why not two?

In 1934, with the complete agreement of Chicago Bears owner George Halas, who was always looking for a big gate, *Chicago Tribune* charities staged the first College All-Star Game. Ward had to plead with Colonel McCormick to underwrite the expenses, but Ward, Halas, and McCormick were all smiles when eighty thousand turned out at Soldier Field to watch the NFL champion Bears and the first all-star squad battle to a scoreless tie.

The following year Ward proved he was more matchmaker than purist. The Bears lost the NFL title to the New York Giants but were invited back to face the collegians because Ward was afraid the Giants might not draw in Soldier Field. After that he played it straight.

The College All-Star Game lasted forty-two years until it was discontinued in 1976. No one had worried much about the possibility of future stars being injured until the NFL owners were paying those future stars millions of dollars in signing bonuses.

Arch Ward wasn't done changing the landscape of American sport. He turned down a $250,000 ten-year contract to become commissioner of the NFL in 1940 and a few years later founded his own league, the All American Conference. It was Ward who brought professional football to Los Angeles and San Francisco, and to Baltimore and Miami, even if they weren't ready for it yet.

He got his good friend Ben Lindheimer, owner of Arlington Park, to sponsor the Los Angeles Dons and tried to persuade Frank Leahy to leave Notre Dame to coach the AAC team in Cleveland. Leahy recommended that Ward get a guy named Paul Brown. Ward did, and one of sports' most storied franchises, the Cleveland Browns, was born until Baltimore kidnapped it in 1996.

Ward died of a heart attack at age fifty-eight in 1955 and was eulogized by the entire country, which had to be a first for a sportswriter.

Governor William Stratton of Illinois said, "The great loss of Arch Ward is shared by millions of Americans who know of his great contributions to the world of sports."

As a sportswriter, Arch Ward was no Grantland Rice or Red Smith. As a reporter he was no slouch. Among his scoops was the first interview with Eugenio Pacelli after that obscure Italian cardinal was named Pope Pius XII. But as an innovator he created some of the great spectacles of midcentury sport that stirred imaginations, triggered tavern arguments, and brought reality to the fantasy leagues that once existed only in little boys' minds.

HEY-HEY:
JACK BRICKHOUSE

"Any team can have a bad century," said Jack Brickhouse, who insisted he was not the author of the statement that summarizes the most futile adventure in all of sport, the Chicago Cubs.

"Jack Brickhouse has seen more bad baseball than anyone alive," Steve Daley once wrote in the *Chicago Tribune*.

Although Harry Caray, a legend in his own right, was the voice of the Cubs from 1982 through 1997, Brickhouse will always be the voice of Chicago sports for much of the century. He arrived fresh from Peoria in 1940, and for the next four decades he was everywhere the Goodyear blimp wanted to be.

Brickhouse broadcast the Cubs for nearly thirty-five years, the White Sox for twenty, the Bears for twenty-four; he covered political conventions from 1944 to 1968 and squeezed in an interview with Pope Paul VI. He broadcast the Rose Bowl and the Prep Bowl and something called the Corn Bowl. He was the voice all America heard in the 1954 World Series when Willie Mays made his miraculous catch. He was the voice on the first nationally televised All-Star game at Comiskey Park in 1950, which Red Schoendienst won for the National League with a dramatic fourteenth-inning homer.

From 1948 to 1956 most Americans watching television thought Chicago was mostly the home of athletes named Gypsy Joe and Gorgeous George and a guy named Brickhouse who appeared several times a week from Marigold Arena and other places where wrestling mania dominated television.

If anyone in broadcasting ever personified the "I never had a bad day" spirit it was Brickhouse, and good cheer was his specialty and always was through six thousand baseball games in which his game-concluding "Oh, brother," was far more familiar than his triumphant, "Now for the happy totals."

But Brickhouse was more than simply a sports voice. Broadcasting on powerful WGN, he spewed the spirit of Chicago throughout the Midwest. He painted images of ivy-walled Wrigley Field and the hapless Cubs for millions of Americans who had never been there. His excitement at a Bears–Green Bay game sent chills through listeners as though they were in frigid Wrigley Field instead of their living rooms.

"One time in 1954 I did three shows on three networks in twenty-four hours," he wrote in his autobiography. "First I broadcast the final game of the World Series, in Cleveland. Then back to Chicago for a wrestling show at night. Then I took the train to Green Bay for the Bears game the next day."

Brickhouse grew up in Peoria and got a part-time radio job after finishing fifth in a six-man audition contest. He was never at a loss for words except when the great actor John Barrymore passed through Peoria and stopped for a brief interview. Brickhouse, who had only seen Barrymore in movies, innocently asked, "Did you ever think of going on the stage?"

It was not the only gaffe that Brickhouse laughed about. As time ran out in the 1957 Prep Bowl contest between Mendel and Calumet, Brickhouse observed, "You simply couldn't ask for a more appropriate score because neither of these great high school teams deserve to lose." On the next play Mendel completed a forty-one-yard touchdown pass to win 6–0.

For twenty-four years Brickhouse and gossip columnist Irv Kupcinet teamed up to do the Chicago Bears' games. Their play-by-play became a favorite parody of comics and tavern talk. Brickhouse would make a statement, and Kup, who was probably busy talking to Bob Hope or Carol Channing, would echo, "Dat's right, Jack."

Once, comedian Tom Dreesen introduced Brickhouse by saying, "Do you know tens of thousands of people grew up not knowing anything about football because they listened to Jack Brickhouse and Irv Kupcinet broadcasting the Bears?"

Brickhouse always had a comeback. "Our broadcasts were sold out every year."

For nearly four decades he was the goggle-eyed perennial in the Cubs broadcasting booth, first on WGN radio and later TV. He seldom saw an Ernie Banks homer he didn't go wild about, no matter how often the Cubs blew a late-inning lead. Banks's five hundredth still rated as his biggest thrill.

A million kids grew up with "Hey-hey!" ringing in their ears.

Brickhouse came to Chicago in 1940 to cover the Cubs and Sox for WGN, where he also covered Big Ten football. He did Notre Dame football for WJJD in 1946, the same year he took a sabbatical to New York to cover the baseball Giants. He was back in Chicago doing the Cub games for WBKB-TV and returned forever to WGN in 1948.

Brickhouse was in the service the year that the Cubs won their only pennant of his lifetime. Hey-hey!

VI

LAW'S
TOP TEN

▪ ▪ ▪ LAW

There is absolutely no historical evidence that a lawyer was the first person to arrive at the scene of the Fort Dearborn massacre.

But it didn't take them long to discover Chicago.

When Chicago became a city in 1837 there were four thousand people, one newspaper, one church, and seventeen law firms. They multiplied.

By 1860 there were three thousand lawyers in Chicago, and they already were dabbling in real estate and politics, a marriage that continued through the twentieth century, making many millionaires and a considerable number of convicts.

When Chicago became America's center of commerce, manufacturing, and transportation in the nineteenth century, it was through the enterprise and vision of men like McCormick, Medill, Pullman, Ogden, Field, Palmer, Sears, and Ward. They all had lawyers. Even carpetbaggers like Abraham Lincoln of Springfield managed to get a piece of the McCormick pie and bankrolled his political career fighting the battles of the Illinois Central Railroad.

It was a lawyer, Norman Judd, who was instrumental in engineering Lincoln's nomination for the presidency.

Nearly one hundred years later it was another lawyer, Jake Arvey, who engineered Adlai Stevenson's nomination for the presidency.

And in 1960 it was another lawyer who contributed mightily to John Kennedy's election, although Richard J. Daley never spent a day in court in his life, except under subpoena.

In 1866, Norman Williams and John Thompson, two of the city's five hundred lawyers, formed a partnership. They represented the Chicago, Alton, and St. Louis Railroad and George Pullman, and the Western Union Company. Five years later one of their good friends, Edward Isham, formed a partnership with Robert Todd Lincoln, the son of the late president. In 1892 one of Williams and Thompson's bright young lawyers left the firm to join Isham's, which then became Isham, Lincoln, and Beale, one of the nation's most respected firms until its demise in the 1980s.

In 1893, William Sidley joined the Williams-Thompson firm and stayed there for sixty years. In 1914 he hired young Edwin Austin, and he stayed there for sixty years. Sidley and Austin has almost been around as long as the city itself and has had something to do with just about everyone and everything that has made Chicago big and rich.

But such powerhouse firms, including Winston and Strawn and the megamix of the 1980s, Baker and McKenzie, do not always wield national influence. Howard Trienens, the chairman of Sidley and Austin from 1975 to 1993, played a huge role in the dissolution of the AT&T monopoly that created the Baby Bells and ushered in a new era of telephone service for the nation, but the courts, not Trienens, were the driving force behind those changes. Few of the men whose names identify the great law firms were legal pathfinders.

Some of the most nationally famous Chicago lawyers were not necessarily pathfinders. In the late 1960s and early 1970s many people must have thought the only lawyer in Chicago was Albert Jenner. As counsel for the Warren Commission, a member of the President's Commission on the Causes and Prevention of Violence, and minority counsel to the House Judiciary Committee during the Watergate hearings, Jenner was constantly bobbing up and down on the nation's front pages. Thomas Reynolds, who made Winston and Strawn a powerhouse firm during his reign as chairman, said Jenner's greatest contribution to American law was the pro bono (free counsel) division he inaugurated at his firm, Jenner and Block. Reynolds said many other firms in America emulated Jenner's innovation. Another Chicagoan who popped up in a major congressional investigation was Richard Phelan, who served as special prosecutor investigating House Speaker James Wright. Later Phelan ran successfully for president of the Cook County Board and unsuccessfully for governor.

If excellence, celebrity, and wealth were the criteria, no Chicago lawyer of the last half century would be more influential than Philip J. Corboy, who has been one of the most successful personal-injury lawyers in the nation and the very best in Chicago. Corboy won more $1 million civil suits than just about anybody, was a master at courtroom theater, and in the eyes of many peers he had no peer in delivering winning closing arguments. The only case he ever lost was eventually won on appeal. He consistently ranked near the top of the highest-paid lawyers in the nation. His firm, Corboy and Demetrio, was a finishing school for personal-injury lawyers and just about every first rate P.I. lawyer in Chicago apprenticed there or formed partnerships with people who did.

In the last two decades of the century Chicago women lawyers have risen to great prominence. Susan Getzendanner became the only female federal judge in the nation when she was appointed by President Carter to sit on the U.S. District Court in Chicago. Ann B. Williams was the first black female judge to join that court in 1985. Carol Bellows was the first woman elected president of the Illinois Bar Association in 1980.

Perhaps no woman lawyer from Chicago was as significant as Jewel LaFontant, the first black woman graduated from the University of Chicago Law School. LaFontant later became an assistant U.S. attorney for the northern district of Illinois, U.S. representative to the United Nations, and was appointed by President Nixon in 1975 as the first woman deputy solicitor general in the Justice Department. Other influential African-American lawyers in Chicago include James Parsons, the first black to serve on the federal bench in the United States, and George Leighton, who also was named to the U.S. District Court.

Chicago has produced some brilliant judges. And some who were not.

Otto Kerner was not. Otto Kerner was a bright young lawyer when he married the daughter of assassinated mayor Anton Cermak. He rose in Democratic Party circles to win appointment to the U.S. attorney's office, to be elected twice governor of Illinois, and ultimately to be chosen to the august appeals court. In between, he chaired the famous presidential commission on violence in America in 1968 and served with distinction in the U.S. Army, rising to the rank of brigadier general. In between, he also accepted gifts of lucrative stock from Chicago racetrack owners seeking favors from the governor's office. In 1973 he was convicted of mail fraud and perjury.

Ironically, his prosecutor, James R. Thompson, considered a gifted lawyer and teacher who many viewed as a future Supreme Court candidate, decided to emulate the object of his most famous conviction. He ran for governor and served a record fourteen years.

In between, there was Dan Walker, Naval Academy graduate, corporate lawyer, and governor of Illinois from 1972 to 1976. Thompson made his transition from politics back to law by becoming the head of Winston and Strawn. Walker followed Otto Kerner to prison on fraud charges stemming from what the government said was the bilking of a savings and loan company.

It would be complimentary to Chicago if Kerner and Walker were the exceptions and Thompson were the rule. But far more Chicago lawyer-politicians have ended up in the slammer than sitting atop the citadels of legal influence and power.

Being a city of thieves, it is only natural that criminal lawyers would multiply as rapidly in Chicago as bagmen. There were the mob lawyers, like Thomas Nash, and the union lawyers, like Maury Walsh. There were the four Bs of the post–World War II era, Melvin Barsky, Charles Bellows, George Bieber, and Harry Busch, who dominated criminal court proceedings from the 1940s to the 1960s. Barnabas Sears earned a national reputation as a defense counsel in the 1960s. George Cotsirillos was one of the best in the nation during the 1970s but did almost all his work here. Eugene Pincham and Earl Neal were among the best of the 1970s. In the 1980s and 1990s, there was Patrick Tuite, Dan Webb, David Stetler . . . But none of these gained the national celebrity or influence to rival Louis Nizer or Samuel Liebowitz in New York, or Edward Bennett Williams in Washington, D.C. (who defended Otto Kerner), and such later national figures as F. Lee Bailey, Percy Foreman, Gerry Spence, and Harvard gadfly Alan Dershowitz.

But that does not detract from the city's legal history.

Chicago, after all, had the single greatest lawyer of the American Century.

THE GREAT DEFENDER:
CLARENCE DARROW

The most publicized trials of the modern era demand that juries understand DNA testing, complex blood-group matches, high-tech weaponry, explosive devices, pathology reports, and a gaggle of highly paid lawyers who rely on computer-selected juries and extensive investigative staffs. Once upon a time juries were spared all that expertise. Instead they heard closing arguments like this:

> I speak for the poor, for the weak, for the weary, for that long line of men who, in darkness and despair, have borne the labors of the human race. . . . Out on the broad prairies where men toil with their hands, out on the wide ocean where men are tossed and buffeted on the waves, through our mills and factories and down deep under the earth, thousands of men and women and children—men who labor, men who suffer, women and children weary with care and toil—these men and these women and these children will kneel tonight and ask God to guide your hearts.

The jury acquitted.

It usually did when Clarence Darrow rose for the defense.

In this particular case Darrow's closing argument lasted twelve hours and convinced twelve men from Idaho that William "Big Bill" Haywood, a leading radical, was innocent of planning the bombing murder of former Idaho Governor Frank Steuenberg, who had brutally suppressed a miners' strike several years earlier.

The 1907 acquittal of Haywood was a great victory in the early days of the American labor movement and was viewed as a bitter defeat for big business, which was accustomed to having the government and the courts protect their monopolies and their dismal treatment of workers.

It was only one more trial in a career of causes for Darrow. No other lawyer in American history has been involved in so many cases of legal and social significance. Darrow's career as the nation's most celebrated and scorned lawyer spanned four decades from the 1890s to the 1930s. He fought for labor and the rights of workers, fought against capital punishment and Prohibition, and believed fervently in the right of free expression.

He is remembered as the greatest criminal lawyer of all time, but Darrow loved causes and only rarely cared about criminals. Darrow said he hated mankind, but loved people. A strident agnostic, he hated religions but enjoyed priests. He hated spinach and most forms of food that weren't steak and potatoes. He loved women and hated marriage. He married twice. He saved hundreds of men from the death penalty but refused to represent con man "Yellow Kid" Weil because he was a repeat offender. He took many cases for free and spent much of life fretting about money.

Darrow was born on April 18, 1857, near Kinsman, Ohio. He attended Allegheny College and the University of Michigan briefly before being admitted to the Ohio bar in 1878.

As the 1800s drew to a close, no industry in America was as powerful as the railroads. The Vanderbilts, Harrimans, James J. Hill, and their imitators were the most influential lobby in the nation. They determined whether towns would live or die, whether Americans would get food or go to work. They were the linchpins of an economic dynasty that included the Carnegie-Frick steel combines, the Rockefeller oil monopoly, and the McCormick farm machinery cartel. These were the robber barons, who were merciless in their resistance to sharing any of the massive wealth they derived from the nation's resources with the men who labored for them. The fledgling labor movements of the period were treated as anarchy. Strikers were beaten, killed, blackballed.

Clarence Darrow arrived in Chicago shortly after seven men convicted of the 1886 Haymarket bombing were sentenced to death. He immediately joined the futile effort to win amnesty for the alleged anarchists. Three of the men were hanged, and Darrow's often-repeated regret was that he had not come to Chicago earlier and been involved in the original trial. Despite his efforts in the Haymarket case he was appointed a city corporation counsel, and his work soon won him a prestigious appointment as general counsel of the Chicago and North Western Railway.

Darrow was staving off lawsuits and profitably settling claims for the railway when Eugene V. Debs, president of the American Railway Company, called a strike against the Pullman Company in 1893. For the first time in American history, federal troops were sent in to defend the company and break a strike. The federal government issued an injunction. Debs defied it. Conspiracy and contempt charges were filed against Debs.

The general counsel of the Chicago and North Western Railway quit his job and set about keeping Debs out of jail. Darrow's defense of the conspiracy charges forced the government to drop its case midway through the trial. But the judge nevertheless sentenced Debs to six months in prison for contempt. Darrow was bitter over the government's role in siding against workingmen, and he never relinquished that cause above all others in his storied career.

It almost sent him to prison.

Although still despised by big business and big government, the labor movement had made strides in the immigrant conclaves of the eastern big cities. The bastion of antiunionism was the Far West, where General Harrison Gary Otis and his *Los Angeles Times* railed passionately against liberals, progressives, and anything or anyone that stood in his path to great wealth and a half-century dominance of the lush southern California basin.

It came with a shock but no surprise that on October 1, 1910, his *Los Angeles Times* plant was demolished by a bomb that killed twenty people. It was also no surprise that a pair of labor-activist brothers,

James and John McNamara of Indianapolis, were indicted for the crime and extradited, probably illegally, from Indiana to California to stand trial. It was also no surprise that the American labor movement raised two hundred fifty thousand dollars for their defense and demanded that Darrow take the case.

Darrow refused at first. He estimated it would take two years to resolve the case, and he was fifty-three years old and wanted to remain in Chicago and meet with his friends and lecture. Samuel Gompers, the dominant labor figure in America, said if he refused the case he would "go down as a traitor to the great cause you have so faithfully championed and defended." Darrow went to Los Angeles. But the trial did not take two years. On its first day, December 1, 1911, the McNamaras pleaded guilty. One was sentenced to life, the other fifteen years.

But Darrow would not get back to Chicago for another year. The Los Angeles establishment was not through with him. Darrow was arrested on charges of bribing the jury in the McNamara case. An investigator that Darrow had hired was caught passing money to one of the impaneled jurors and implicated Darrow. In August 1912, Darrow addressed his own jury. "I am on trial because I have been a lover of the poor, a friend of the oppressed, because I have stood for labor all these years and have brought down upon my head the wrath of criminal interests in this country." The jury returned in thirty minutes with a verdict of not guilty, although there is great reason to believe that if Darrow hadn't directly ordered payoffs to probable jurors he implicitly sanctioned it in his belief that when you are fighting big business moral law is a more demanding mistress than legal statutes.

Darrow returned to a chilly welcome in Chicago. The *Chicago Tribune*, which predictably always despised him for his support of the Haymarket bombers and Debs, publicly doubted his innocence. Hearst's *Herald-Examiner* was mad at him for accepting fees from both sides in a dispute involving the newspaper. He was ready to forsake law and make a full-time career as a lecturer, where his ability to go on at length without notes as he did in all his famous arguments drew huge crowds to hear his discourses on Voltaire and Russian literature.

But in 1915 the excursion liner *Eastland* capsized in the Chicago River at Clark Street, where it berthed, while loading hundreds of people for a day cruise. There were 812 deaths and a public outrage that finally focused on the ship's chief engineer, John Erickson, who was charged with negligence. Darrow, again sensing that society's worst characteristics—anger, frustration, and revenge—were behind the charges, agreed to take the case. Erickson was acquitted.

Darrow spent the years after World War I defending many of the radicals caught up in the "red" hunts spawned by the Espionage Act of 1917 and the Sedition Act of 1918, under which more than two thousand people, including writers, educators, and clergymen, had been jailed for objecting to American involvement in the war.

The persecution of communists was also in full swing. In one case Darrow defended William Bross Lloyd, a shirttail relative of the *Tribune* McCormicks, and sixteen other "communists" for conducting open meetings in Chicago. They were sent to jail for a year, but no one forgot Darrow's summation:

> You can only protect your liberties in this world by protecting the other man's freedom. You can only be free if I am free. . . . I know that the nation that is not watchful of its liberty will lose it. I know that the individual that will not stand for his rights will have no rights.

Darrow was in his sixties when his most dreaded fear, Prohibition, became the law of the land. He lectured all over America against what he accurately perceived would be a social experiment in disaster, leading to lawlessness and, worse, abrogating the individual rights of man. The 1920s were full of lawlessness, but the most sensational crime of all had nothing to do with Prohibition. It had everything to do with Darrow.

Clarence Darrow was sixty-seven years old when at 2 A.M. one spring morning he was awakened in his Hyde Park apartment by two men promising him a million dollars to save a pair of boys from the hangman. The "boys" were Richard Loeb and Nathan Leopold, who had just confessed to the "thrill" killing of fourteen-year-old Bobby Franks. Darrow took the case because he was aghast at the thought of the state executing two people who he thought were both deranged and thoroughly unlikable.

In his argument he made it clear that he thought they should be sentenced to jail with no chance of parole. It is unlikely Darrow would have ever voted to free Nathan Leopold, who finally was released from prison after thirty-five years.

In that first "crime of the century" trial Darrow again spent twelve hours arguing in mitigation to save the lives of two young men who everyone wanted to hang. When he finished there were tears seen on the cheeks of the trial judge, who ultimately spared their lives. But Darrow's words were not as impressive as his argument that temporary insanity should be allowed as a mitigating factor in sentencing. It was the first time such a defense had been used to save anyone from the scaffold, and it became a major factor in capital punishment cases for the rest of the century.

It seemed that there surely was nothing left for Darrow to prove. Once again he vowed his courtroom days were over, that he would spend his remaining years writing and lecturing. But the following year, another "trial of the century" loomed.

In Dayton, Tennessee, a schoolteacher named John Thomas Scopes, twenty-four, had agreed to become a test case for the American Civil Liberties Union, which was in an uproar over a spate of recent fundamentalist legislation sweeping America's Bible Belt. The Tennessee legislature had passed a bill making it a crime to teach Darwin's evolution theory, which "denied the story of man as taught in the Bible."

The guiding spirit behind such laws was the aging William Jennings Bryan, thrice defeated presidential candidate, spearhead of the populist movement, and self-proclaimed "Great Commoner," who would personally prosecute Scopes.

The temptation was too much for Darrow.

In what has become the climactic moment of films and stage plays, Darrow dissected Bryan's naive adherence to the biblical metaphor, trapping the aging orator by asking where Cain found a wife if Bryan insisted, as Genesis relates, that Adam, Eve, Cain, and Abel were the only people on earth. The cross-examination continued bitterly. Bryan dissembled. Bryan was beaten. Scopes was convicted, as Darrow and the ACLU hoped. But the case was of far more social significance. At the time, America was truly schizophrenic. Half of

America was merrily ignoring the Volstead Act and indulging in the hedonistic outrages of the Roaring Twenties. Half of it was clinging to Puritan values and trust in the punitive vengeance of the Almighty. Half of it didn't care what anyone did, and the other half wanted to punish everyone who did anything.

It was a fitting climax to Darrow's career that while he hardly could have been said to be on the side of the angels, he was on the side of individual liberties, where he had spent the most successful, most influential, and most dramatic career of any lawyer in the century.

2

THE NEGOTIATOR:
ARTHUR GOLDBERG

One day in 1962, two precinct captains who happened to have jobs that only required them to hang around city hall were discussing the latest political gossip. One said, "Did you hear? Kennedy made Art Goldberg a judge." The other replied, "Who's his committeeman?"

Arthur Goldberg never needed any committeeman to get him a job. But he could have used some advice on keeping one. Goldberg grew up in the Maxwell Street neighborhood, where Jake Arvey shepherded bright young Jewish boys into all sorts of promising positions under the auspices of the Cook County Democratic Party, but Arthur Goldberg didn't need Jake Arvey, either. Throughout his long, varied, and notable career Goldberg never was considered either a fixture or a fix of Chicago City Hall. But he made career choices that often mirrored the bizarre decisions of Chicago pols who regularly gave up seats in Congress to run for alderman or abandoned the state legislature to get on the sanitary district board.

Goldberg was only the third person in U.S. history to give up his seat on the Supreme Court to take another job, accepting the post of U.S. ambassador to the United Nations, where he spent three futile years trying to convince Lyndon Johnson to get out of Vietnam.

It may have been the only job at which Goldberg didn't succeed.

Arthur Goldberg rarely appeared in a courtroom, and he never stayed in one place too long, but wherever he went and whatever he did the United States of America changed. The plainspoken Goldberg was not a lush courtroom orator in the mold of Darrow. Nor did he win celebrity in sensational, highly publicized cases. But he was arguably the best negotiator in the country at a time when big labor won equal footing with big business.

Goldberg was born in 1908 on the West Side. He was the youngest of nine children born to a Russian immigrant couple who lived near the Baltimore and Ohio station so they could welcome other Jews escaping the Czar's hussars. Goldberg's earliest memories were of helping his father hitch up a blind horse to a cart and begin selling produce in the Maxwell Street market. His most pleasant boyhood memories were of being taken to the old ballpark on Polk Street where the Cubs were losing regularly even before they moved into beautiful Wrigley Field. In his seventies, Goldberg still rued the only disappointments of his life, Vietnam and the Cubs.

Goldberg graduated from Harrison High School in 1924, attended Crane College, and was admitted to Northwestern University's law school, where he graduated at age twenty-one with a peerless academic record. He opened a law practice and in 1936 was approached by Joseph Germano of the fledgling Steelworkers Organizing Committee. "We need a lawyer but we don't have any money," said Germano, who later rose to be a confidante of Richard J. Daley and a powerful force in Illinois Democratic politics. Goldberg replied, "I'll take the job and when your organization is able, I'll submit a bill."

The bill was paid in full in 1948 when Goldberg, now general counsel of the United Steel Workers, was offered the post of chief lawyer for the Congress of Industrial Organizations. From there he made his mark on the nation.

Goldberg was the key figure in settling nationwide strikes in 1949, 1951, 1956, and 1959, and he wrote the agreements for the first pension plans between the unions and the big steelmakers, which were copied by every other labor union in America. He was the critical behind-the-scenes diplomat in the merger between the CIO and the American Federation of Labor and became a close friend and adviser to George Meany, who headed the unified labor force for more than twenty years. Goldberg also fought against communists in the labor movement. He made an enemy of Teamster boss Jimmy Hoffa when he led the battle to expel the corrupt truckers' union from the AFL-CIO. He made an even better friend in Robert Kennedy, who was the counsel to the Senate committee ruthlessly investigating the Teamsters.

That relationship led to Goldberg's influence in obtaining labor support for John Kennedy's 1960 campaign and his support of Lyndon Johnson as Kennedy's running mate despite labor's wariness of the Texan, who rarely supported labor issues during his days as Senate majority leader.

After Kennedy's election, he immediately named Goldberg as his secretary of labor.

Two years later, Felix Frankfurter resigned from the U.S. Supreme Court because of ailing health and Arthur Goldberg got the "Jewish seat," which also had been held by Louis Brandeis and Benjamin Cardozo. Kennedy said that Goldberg's "scholarly approach to the law combined with his deep understanding of our economic and political systems will make him a valuable member of the court."

He was the first Chicagoan of the century to sit on the highest court in the land.

In one of Goldberg's most famous decisions he held that the Connecticut anti–birth control law was an unconstitutional infringement of the right of privacy for married couples, a decision that paved the way to the landmark 1973 ruling in *Roe v. Wade*, which made abortion legal.

Goldberg also wrote the opinion in the *Escobedo v. Illinois* case, which invalidated any conviction based on a confession made after police had denied a suspect the right to see a lawyer. It was the forerunner of the Miranda case, which threw out all convictions unless suspects were warned of their right to counsel and their right to remain silent.

Then, Lyndon Johnson came calling. An old Goldberg idol, Adlai Stevenson, had died suddenly, and the post of ambassador to the United Nations was vacant at a time when Johnson was trying to round up world support for his failing war in Vietnam. "You're the best negotiator in the world and the country needs you," Johnson told Goldberg.

"I leave the court with great sadness and great regret. I have no illusions that peace can be achieved rapidly. But I have every confidence that it is going to be possible to inch forward to it, inch by agonizing inch," Goldberg said.

He had no way of knowing that at every inch of the way Johnson would turn his back on any peace initiatives that did not give him the military victory he could claim to salvage his presidency and lift the burden of being the only president who ever lost a war.

There were some successes. When fighting broke out in 1965 between India and Pakistan, Goldberg was credited with bringing about the cease-fire after intense discussions with both sides. He was a principal figure in getting the Russians to agree to an international treaty banning weapons of mass destruction in outer space. But his repeated proposals for a unilateral halt to the bombing in North Vietnam were rejected by Johnson. After three years of frustration, Goldberg resigned the UN job and looked for a new challenge.

In 1970 he was persuaded by New York Democrats to run against incumbent Republican Governor Nelson Rockefeller, who was thought to be vulnerable in seeking a fourth term. Goldberg, always a striking figure with his sheet-white sculptured hair and trademark horn-rimmed glasses, proved he was a far more persuasive speaker in back rooms and judicial chambers than at county fairs and on television talk shows. He was trounced.

In an interview shortly before his death in 1986, Goldberg was asked for the thousandth time why he gave up a lifetime job on the Supreme Court.

"I did it out of vanity. I didn't want to. I know it sounds corny, but I did it because our country was in terrible danger. I thought I could persuade Johnson to get the hell out of Vietnam. I couldn't understand what we were doing there."

It was the only negotiation he ever lost.

3 ▨

THE LONE RANGER:
JOHN PAUL STEVENS

When Arthur Goldberg left the Supreme Court in 1965, he left a group of men who had done more to change American society in the midcentury than anyone else. The Court led by Earl Warren would in the fifteen years of his leadership author some of the most important and controversial rulings in its history. It began in 1954 with the *Brown v. Topeka* case, which ended forever the "separate but equal" doctrine and ushered in the civil rights era. It gave the American press expansive freedoms in the *New York Times v. Sullivan* ruling in 1962, and it put a temporary halt in 1967 to capital punishment, giving some posthumous redemption to the legacy of Clarence Darrow.

Richard Nixon's election pointed the Court in another direction. His appointee as chief justice, Warren Burger, tried mightily in the next seventeen years to remedy what Nixon and the growing number of American conservatives viewed as an era of unguided liberalism with far too much concern for the rights of individuals, the rights of the poor, and the rights of the accused. But even as Nixon added two more of his own choices, Harry Blackmun and Lewis Powell, the Court he thought he and Burger could control ruled in 1971 to allow the publication of the Pentagon Papers and in 1973 to make abortion legal in its historic *Roe v. Wade* decision. From Brown to Roe, the Supreme Court had cobbled a remarkable list of decisions that changed the roles of minorities and women and created a framework for the society that would leave the twentieth century far different than it began.

By the time John Paul Stevens got to the Supreme Court in 1975, the era of great decisions had passed. But Burger and his successor, William Rehnquist, continued their efforts to try and erode the laws that their sponsor, Nixon, abhorred. Stevens was appointed by Gerald Ford, who assumed he had picked a sound midwestern conservative to join the majority that was reexamining the moratorium on the death penalty, affirmative action, obscenity, school prayer, and other issues that Ronald Reagan already was raising from the California governor's mansion.

As so often has happened on the Supreme Court, it didn't turn out that way.

John Paul Stevens, of the Stevens Hotel (Conrad Hilton) family, graduate of the University of Chicago Lab School, Phi Beta Kappa at the University of Chicago, Northwestern University Law School graduate, antitrust wizard, Nixon appointee to the 7th Circuit Court of Appeals, was a maverick.

Stevens, who was fifty-five when he joined the Court, was considered a centrist and a conservative, a likely supporter for the conservative majority of Burger, Rehnquist, Potter Stewart, Powell, Blackmun, and Byron White, who, although a John Kennedy appointee, had become a regular member of the majority bloc.

Stevens was also seen as a possible swing voter on some social issues.

The unassuming Chicagoan who wore a bow tie and flew his own small airplane had his own ideas. About everything.

He found himself aligned with the Court's liberals, William Brennan and Thurgood Marshall, on voting rights, free speech, separation of church and state, and, always, the death penalty. In his first term he was caught between factions in Burger's attempt to push through a resurrection of the death penalty that would have allowed states to apply few of the safeguards the Court had earlier demanded. He was a key force in defining the new law that went into effect in 1977 with the execution of Gary Gilmore, but he was vigilant of possible excesses and stopped just short of opposing capital punishment for any reason.

In March 1995, Stevens asked judges across the nation to consider whether the execution of a longtime death row inmate falls under the cruel and unusual punishment provision of the Eighth Amendment.

In February 1995, Stevens wrote an impassioned dissent as the Court refused, 8–1, to rein in Alabama judges' power to impose death sentences for convicted murderers after juries recommended life in prison as the proper punishment. Stevens accused the Court of "casting a cloud over the legitimacy of our capital-sentencing jurisprudence." He wrote, "The absence of any rudder on a judge's free-floating power to negate the community's will, in my judgment, renders Alabama's capital sentencing scheme fundamentally unfair and results in cruel and unusual punishment."

From the beginning his independence made him a critical vote in many cases. His quiet and unassuming manner did not hide his keen legal mind. Although he rarely resorted to the testy or hostile questioning sometimes employed by some of his colleagues, it often was Stevens's questions that exposed the most telling weakness of a lawyer's arguments.

He authored an important 1982 decision involving the National Association for the Advancement of Colored People in which the Court ruled that economic boycotts are protected by the First Amendment's free-speech guarantee. Stevens also spoke for the Court in a series of important search-and-seizure cases. In one, the Court ruled that police needed an arrest warrant before entering someone's home to arrest him. In another the Court said police who have probable cause to believe a car contains illegal materials can search the whole car, and all containers within it, without a warrant.

When in 1978 the Court ruled that the Federal Communications Commission could ban the broadcast of "indecent" words even if they were not legally obscene, Stevens's majority opinion said, "We simply hold that when the commission finds that a pig has entered the parlor, the exercise of its regulatory power does not depend on proof that the pig is obscene."

In dissenting from a 1976 decision in which the Court's majority ruled that disability benefit plans that exclude pregnancy benefits do not discriminate based on sex, Stevens decided to explain the birds and the bees.

"By definition, such a rule discriminates on account of sex for it is the capacity to become pregnant which primarily differentiates the female from the male," he wrote.

But he had inconsistencies. In *Justices and Presidents*, Henry J. Abraham noted that from 1978 to 1984 Stevens voted against four racial preferences for minority-group members. In 1986 and 1987 he switched sides and joined the liberal side on five similar cases, only to flip again in 1989, joining the conservatives in holding unconstitutional a set-aside requirement for minority-owned firms.

Burger called him a "wild card." Professor Bradley Cannon, writer and longtime observer of the Supreme Court, said, "John Paul Stevens is in effect the Lone Ranger of the Supreme Court, championing justice in a cloud of opinions . . . one whose effectiveness is very much limited by numbers and circumstance."

Cannon summed up the major criticism of Stevens's twenty-plus years on the Court: he was expected to be a far more forceful leader rather than the cornerstone of the center.

The historic periods of the Court have been marked by their extremes, the presence of such liberals as Brandeis or William Douglas and such conservatives as Felix Frankfurter often driving the Court toward decisions that had far-reaching impact on America. Rarely has the center driven the landmark decisions. In the case of the Court since Warren, however, it has been the center that has held firm to many of the decisions that shaped America in the last three decades, allowing only small corrections to suit political demands, but holding a course that gives Americans a smooth ride.

The Lone Ranger in the middle was John Paul Stevens.

4 ◼

THE SCHOLAR:
EDWARD LEVI

When John Paul Stevens arrived in Washington in 1975, another brilliant, bow-tied lawyer was already making waves.

Edward Hirsch Levi was the attorney general of the United States, the only Chicagoan of the century to hold the nation's chief law-enforcement office, which traditionally had far less to do with enforcing the law than enhancing the political power and status of the president.

The politicizing of the office in this century began with Mitchell Palmer, who was Woodrow Wilson's ambitious attorney general. At the end of World War I, with the nation furtively looking in alleys and in schoolrooms for radicals, Palmer virtually ignored every civil rights law on the book and arrested thousands of Americans who had opposed the war, sympathized with the revolutionaries in Russia, or dabbled in socialist thought. Very few of them were fortunate enough to have Clarence Darrow keep them out of jail.

The office turned professional during the Roosevelt and Truman years, but Dwight Eisenhower placed his political strategist, Herbert Brownell, in the job and John Kennedy turned the job into a political weapon with the appointment of his brother Robert. But Richard Nixon's appointment of campaign chief John Mitchell escalated the politics and the ultimate degradation of the post. Mitchell not only used the office to go after supposed Nixon enemies, but turned it into the criminal brain trust that led to Watergate.

When Gerald Ford succeeded Nixon and declared that the "long national nightmare had ended," he knew he had to fix the office where most of those horrible dreams began. He needed an apolitical man of unquestioned integrity and unabashed legal brilliance.

Edward H. Levi, the president of the University of Chicago, was his man.

Levi, who was fifty-three in 1974 when he accepted the attorney general's job, was recognized as a great university leader. He was also regarded as a thinker, not a politician, an assessment that proved accurate during his two years in Washington and one that eventually nettled the partisans who first hailed his appointment.

Levi was not even so much a Chicagoan as he was a creature of the University of Chicago. He began his education in kindergarten at the university's lab school and remained there for his undergraduate and law degrees. He escaped briefly to Yale to obtain a doctorate and joined the University of Chicago faculty in 1936. He served from 1940 to 1945 as an assistant attorney general, working on antitrust litigation under Thurman Arnold, the New Deal's trustbuster. When he returned to the university in 1945 he was named professor of law. Five years later he became dean of the law school. In 1962 he was named provost, and in 1968 he became the eighth president of the school.

Levi appeared as a Mr. Peepers, a scholarly, slender, balding man, imposing and unapproachable. "He operates on a very high level of thinking. I didn't think his feet touched the ground," said his colleague at the law school Philip Kurland, who also authored the most famous two-line description of Levi: "It is often said of Edward that he is cold and calculating. He is warm and calculating." As a teacher he was ruthless in demanding excellence. "There was venom in his antitrust course," one student said, recalling Levi's scathing attacks on students' ignorance.

He quickly raised the law school's reputation by making admission standards high. He ensured the quality of the school's graduates by imposing tough grading.

"He did it in a very rough, hard way. He flunked me out," said one student who became a Levi friend.

Following his trust-busting years he became regarded as the nation's top legal authority in that field, and despite his New Deal experiences he called for more moderate measures than a total assault on big monopolies. Even as he headed the university he engaged in controversial issues of law. In a famous 1968 speech he ruffled many feathers by criticizing politically motivated prosecutors, the imposition of fines set without regard for the defendant's ability to pay, and the inadequate and abusive practices of police in urban areas; and he advocated a restoration of the maxim that "justice delayed is justice denied."

These were not the sentiments that many Republicans wanted in an attorney general, and many conservatives were wary of Ford's selection.

Levi would give them good reason to be wary.

After appraising the disaster he inherited from Nixon's four attorneys general in two years (Mitchell was indicted, Richard Kleindienst and Elliot Richardson were fired, and William Saxbe resigned), Levi decided that the FBI was the problem.

He began by snitching on all the abuses carried out by J. Edgar Hoover, telling a congressional committee about all the files Hoover kept privately on public officials and celebrities, and he vowed no FBI director would have that kind of power again. He transferred it to the attorney general's office.

He was urged to fire the FBI director, Clarence Kelley, and urged to retain him. Levi retained him. He caught criticism for allowing a special prosecutor to look into allegations that President Ford had violated campaign funding laws in his 1972 congressional reelection. He was criticized for setting tone while ignoring substance. "He has provided no leadership in antitrust matters, in civil rights or in the criminal division," one critic said.

What Levi did was impose guidelines to curb the FBI abuses in domestic security and civil disorder. The cavalier wiretapping of possible political enemies was stopped. The surveillances of dissidents stopped. Conservatives moaned that Levi was destroying the FBI. Liberals said he had not gone far enough.

Levi's two years as attorney general did not produce a miracle in the Justice Department, but it did what Gerald Ford had hoped. It restored the integrity of an executive arm that had become a criminal weapon.

Levi returned in 1977 to the University of Chicago, where he remained as president emeritus and law professor.

Levi had said that the Justice Department should have a mood of "high morale, firm belief and particular objectives—the line between that and unfairness is a very easy line to cross."

Edward Levi drew that line strongly. It lasted for a dozen years. In 1988, Ronald Reagan's attorney general, Edwin Meese, resigned after widespread reports of financial and political conflict of interest.

5

FREEDOM OF THE PRESS:
WEYMOUTH KIRKLAND

In 1927 the owner of a Minneapolis weekly that printed all sorts of outrageous rumors was restrained by the courts from publishing a story calling the local prosecutor a crook. Jacob Near appealed the ruling to the Minnesota Supreme Court, which upheld the restraining order. Newspapers had always been free to publish with the knowledge that if they were wrong they could be sued for libel. The Minnesota court's ruling threatened to endanger newspapers' freedoms under the First Amendment.

The problem was that the aggrieved party was Near, a rather scurrilous, irresponsible rabble-rouser and, most likely, what he wanted to publish probably wasn't true. What was unlikely was that his champion would be the ubiquitous Colonel Robert R. McCormick, who certainly would have despised Near's politics and his practice of journalism. But like Voltaire, the colonel was ready to defend Near's right to print it. McCormick spent years and thousands of dollars fighting Near's battle to the Supreme Court. More accurately, McCormick spent the money. Weymouth Kirkland fought the battle.

Kirkland, a native of Michigan, moved to Chicago in 1892, was graduated from the Kent College of Law in 1901, and went into private practice. In 1914 he joined the firm of Shepard, McCormick, and Thomason, which had been founded by the colonel in 1908 and in which McCormick remained an active partner until he resigned in 1920 to work full-time on making the *Tribune* the "World's Greatest Newspaper."

Along that path he called auto tycoon Henry Ford an anarchist and called Chicago Mayor William H. Thompson a liar, a crook, a scoundrel, a buffoon, and whatever else he could think of that was not too profane to put in his newspaper. And every time he did it he called Weymouth Kirkland to defend his right to do it.

Kirkland defended the colonel in the three-month 1919 libel suit filed by Henry Ford, who the colonel maligned for stating that if any of Ford's workers left their jobs to go with their national guard units during the Mexican border skirmish of 1916 they would be fired. Kirkland established in that case the right of the newspaper to "fair comment," a precedent that editorial writers and columnists took refuge in for the remainder of the century. Kirkland lost. The jury awarded Ford six cents in damages and six cents in costs.

Next, Kirkland defended the colonel in the landmark *City of Chicago v. Tribune* case in 1920. The mayor sued the *Tribune* for stating that Thompson's fiscal policies bankrupted the city. Kirkland argued that British law implied in the Constitution protected newspapers from any libel on government. He won, and this case became an important precedent forty years later when the Supreme Court ruled in the *New York Times v. Sullivan* case that no public official could sue successfully for libel unless he could prove "knowing, reckless disregard of the truth." It was that ruling that allowed newspapers to pursue such stories as Watergate. It also ushered in an era of relentless public and personal attacks on public officials at all levels of American government.

It took Kirkland four years to get the Near case to the U.S. Supreme Court, but in 1931 Chief Justice Charles Evans Hughes ruled that prior restraint of publication was specifically forbidden by the Constitution, one of the most important First Amendment rulings in American history. It was the argument that the *New York Times* used when the Nixon Administration tried vainly to halt publication of the Pentagon Papers in 1971.

Kirkland remained with the firm ultimately known as Kirkland and Ellis for fifty years until his death in 1965, but his place as one of America's premier defenders of First Amendment rights had been taken by a protégé several years before. Weymouth Kirkland was revered. Don Reuben was feared.

Don Reuben was not always feared. He began simply as a brilliant student at Northwestern's law school and was recruited by Kirkland's partner, Howard Ellis. He quickly joined the team that represented the firm's most important account, the *Tribune*, and he became its sole counsel for legal and corporate work in 1956 at age twenty-seven. From there Reuben went on to represent the most visible Chicago institutions: the archdiocese, the Chicago Bears, Standard Oil, the Board of Trade, and thirteen thousand depositors of the bankrupt City Savings & Loan Association, for whom he recovered $20 million, arguing in a landmark case that the State of Illinois could not invoke "sovereign immunity" when it should have been protecting the assets of the depositors.

Reuben's first major defense of a libel suit against the *Tribune* came when the newspaper mistakenly called a psychologist the owner of a brothel. He wrote a critical brief supporting the *New York Times* case against Sullivan, and the nation's preeminent First Amendment lawyer of the era, Floyd Abrams, called him a "most intelligent" defender of press freedoms.

Consumer advocate Ralph Nader had a different view. "No lawyer in any other city is as powerful or feared as Don Reuben is in Chicago."

Reuben undoubtedly preferred the second description.

6

NOBODY:
ABNER MIKVA

Only a handful of lawyers who have gone into politics in Chicago have risen to become influential Americans. Of those few who have been successful in politics, even fewer have distinguished themselves in the judiciary. Most of the great jurists Chicago has supplied the nation have been with few exceptions free of the stain of political office.

The Chicagoan who most successfully combined politics and the law was a maverick Democrat, liberal congressman, member of the nation's second highest court, and counsel to the White House. A guy who Mayor Daley always called "Mifka."

Abner Mikva is the only Chicagoan who excelled in all three branches of federal government. His political career in the state legislature and in Congress does not match the ideological greatness of one idol, Paul Douglas. His judicial career stopped just short of equaling the heights reached by his mentor and law partner, Arthur Goldberg. His days as chief counsel to President Clinton were not marked by either a presidential or constitutional crisis that put him in headlines. Yet no other Chicago lawyer ever proved so versatile in so many fields, especially when Abner Mikva was the original guy that nobody wanted.

The late Chicago political historian Milton Rakove made Mikva one of the city's Democratic icons by choosing a book title based on the response young Mikva received when he first tried to enter politics by asking the Democratic committeeman of the 8th Ward for a job.

"We don't want nobody nobody sent," was the reply and the ultimate book title.

The rest of the conversation included, "We don't want nobody from the University of Chicago and we don't want nobody who don't want no job."

Thoroughly rebuked, young Mikva continued to campaign for Douglas and Adlai Stevenson, who were elected, respectively, to the U.S. Senate and the governor's office in 1948. In 1956 he won a spot in the state legislature as a liberal from Hyde Park and forged a ten-year record of integrity, teaming with other Democratic mavericks such as future senator Paul Simon and future judge Anthony Scariano to wage a usually futile but fun-filled battle against the entrenched machine stooges. In 1966, Mikva ran for Congress against one of the city's great hacks, Barrett O'Hara, and lost. But he returned in 1968 and defeated O'Hara. Again nobody wanted Mikva, not even the Democrats he represented. So in the 1971 remap, Mayor Richard J. Daley moved Mikva from the security of the South Side city district to the uncertainties of a sprawling North Shore district where Republicans had been going to Congress since Lincoln's administration. Mikva moved his family to Evanston, but in 1972 he learned again that he was not wanted. He lost the congressional race in the national Democratic debacle. But he came back to win again in 1974, 1976, and 1978.

In Congress he was a visceral extension of Douglas, serving as the liberal conscience for all those issues Douglas had raised. Mikva was for gun control, against the Vietnam war, for full financial disclosure by congressmen, for lower defense budgets, for higher education spending. It was only natural that he was a prime target of the National Rifle Association and other conservative groups.

In 1979, President Carter appointed Mikva to the U.S. Court of Appeals in Washington, D.C., often considered second in rank only to the Supreme Court since it hears nearly all the federal government lawsuits before they reach the highest court. It is also a court that has served as a feeding ground to the Supreme Court.

But again it looked for a time like Mikva wasn't wanted. The National Rifle Association mounted what Mikva later said was a $1 million campaign to scuttle his nomination. The NRA failed but delayed Mikva's arrival to the court for several months before he was confirmed by the Senate 58–31. Still, conservative Senator James McClure of Idaho sued in the U.S. Supreme Court to toss Mikva off the court. It was not until November 1981 that the high court found in favor of Mikva.

In the meantime, Mikva already had written two opinions supporting the First Amendment's freedom of speech provision. He later joined to bar the Bush administration from enforcing rules restricting family planning clinics from telling patients about the availability of abortion. In 1990 he ruled that the military's existing policy of excluding anyone who acknowledges being homosexual was unconstitutional.

Mikva's opinion dripped acid as he noted that a sailor caught in a homosexual act can remain in the service if he can convince his superiors that it was an aberration—that he is actually heterosexual. But a sailor who admits he is gay will be dismissed even if he has been perfectly celibate.

In 1990, Mikva stepped up to chief judge of the appeals court, and many speculated about the possibility of him moving up to the Supreme Court. But by the time a Democratic president took office Mikva, then sixty-seven, was considered too old and probably too liberal for Bill Clinton.

Instead, Clinton offered him the chance to complete the federal hat trick, a spot in the executive branch as White House counsel. Mikva accepted in 1994 and spent a year denying there were any illegal activities in the White House concerning a plethora of charges against the Clintons: Whitewater, Travelgate, the Vince Foster suicide, campaign funds shenanigans. He quit, saying it was a young man's game, a year later, fortunately escaping the Monica Lewinsky debacle.

He returned to teach at the University of Chicago, where he had graduated from law school in 1948 and where, after nearly forty years in public service, he could chuckle at being the nobody that nobody wanted.

7

MR. P.I.:
JAMES DOOLEY

When James Dooley began practicing law in 1939, the field of personal injury was the bottom feeder of the law profession. There was little chance for an individual to sue a big corporation or a wealthy manufacturer for injuries incurred on the job or caused by a major corporation. Public employees such as firemen and policemen were never entitled to file civil suits because of injuries suffered on the job. Product liability didn't exist. Caveat emptor was the law of the land.

Even in cases where people were struck by automobiles or injured by railroads, settlements were usually bestowed by the big corporations, because few people could afford the costly legal battles of taking on big business. And when individuals did win, the awards were paltry. Loss of a limb might bring five thousand dollars. Awards based on the lifetime earning capabilities of injured persons were never considered.

Jim Dooley changed all that, becoming a multimillionaire and the most nationally influential trial lawyer in Chicago history after Clarence Darrow.

Dooley's passion for defending plaintiffs against the establishment rooted from the death of his father when Dooley was fourteen. His father died of a burst appendix after a doctor delayed his surgery. "He died of malpractice," Dooley often told friends bitterly.

His most successful protégé, Philip Corboy, once considered leaving Dooley's firm to take a lucrative job with a railroad defending personal-injury suits. Dooley urged him to reject the offer: "You are not philosophically or emotionally attuned to work for the railroad. You could not possibly represent big business or corporate interests. You're Irish like I am and so you're philosophically, intellectually and emotionally antagonistic to big business," Corboy told the *Chicago Sun-Times* when Dooley died.

In the 1940s, when Dooley was exempted from the draft because he suffered from epilepsy, he began his campaign to change the personal-injury field. He formed legal associations that began lobbying state legislatures in Illinois and nearby midwestern states. He organized informational campaigns and newsletters detailing breakthroughs in state law.

The case that resulted in nationwide publicity and set a new precedent for product liability came in 1969 and involved a woman who had been blinded when she opened a can of Drano. Dooley asked for the then unheard-of sum of $1 million for Mrs. Frances Moore of Oak Lawn. Dooley brought a parade of chemists to the witness stand, testifying that the Drackett Products Company of Cincinnati, Ohio, was liable because moisture had leaked into the can and caused a reaction between the lye and aluminum particles that produced the explosion.

The jury awarded Mrs. Moore $930,000, the largest product liability award ever given in the country. As always in Dooley's historic cases, the defendants appealed. As usual, the Illinois Supreme Court ruled in favor of Dooley.

Whenever Dooley tried a case it seemed to break new ground, as in *Dini v. Naiditch*. Dooley sued to collect for a fireman who had suffered severe burns and facial deforming. The late Leonard Ring, a lawyer and one of Dooley's closest friends, once recalled, "In those days you couldn't recover for a fireman. It was considered an assumed risk. But Jim got $235,000, which was a tremendous amount. But, more important, he turned the law around so that a fireman can recover damages if the owner of the property is negligent and contributes to the cause of the fire."

In another case, *Nelson v. Union Wire*, Dooley found a way for an employee who was injured in the course of his job to recover damages, even though he could not sue his employer under the state Workmen's Compensation Law. The employee was hurt when an elevator fell at a construction job. Dooley sued the insurance company that carried the workmen's compensation insurance. Dooley argued that the insurance company had assumed the responsibility to inspect the site and should have known it was unsafe. Dooley collected $1 million for the worker.

Again, he had changed the law.

Dooley grew up on the West Side and got both his undergraduate and law degrees at Loyola University.

In the courtroom, he was not theatrical. He never wasted words. He presented facts. He would never have made the kind of dramatic, sociological appeals that Darrow mastered. He was always prepared and a great student of the law. At one time or another he was president of the International Academy of Trial Lawyers, the Law Science Academy of America, the National Association of Claimants' Compensation Attorneys, and the Plaintiff's Trial Lawyers Association of Illinois, the latter two of which he was instrumental in establishing.

In 1976, Dooley sought a new challenge. He went to Mayor Richard J. Daley and asked to be endorsed for the Illinois Supreme Court. Daley, characteristically, offered encouragement and then, equally characteristically, slated a close friend and former law partner for the post.

Dooley stepped totally out of character. He mounted an independent campaign and paid the regal sum of two hundred thousand dollars to a firm handling political media. Dooley's friends were shocked. Although he was a millionaire many times over (at his death in 1978 his estate was worth $13 million), he was a notorious tightwad. He bought everything wholesale, walked rather than take taxis, bought mail-order suits, and persuaded friends to let him sleep in their hotel rooms.

But he was serious about being a judge, and he upset the Democratic organization in the 1976 primary and was elected to the court. Friends kidded him about taking a pay cut, but Dooley said he enjoyed being a judge so much that he didn't mind the loss of income.

Shortly before his death of a heart attack at age sixty-three, Dooley wrote a dissent of a court decision, saying, "Today, we have buried a great body of law."

It would have made a fitting epitaph for James Dooley.

8

MR. WASTELAND:
NEWTON MINOW

Television's most famous lawyer was not Perry Mason.

Newton Minow would rather be remembered for other things than the "vast wasteland," his terse 1961 description of television programming that elevated him atop all the other stars of John Kennedy's New Frontier.

He has spent nearly forty years doing other things, although his guardianship of television programming, particularly the children's shows that drive him to despair, has never wavered. It is as though he will always be chairman emeritus of the Federal Communications Commission.

For many Americans, he was the *only* chairman of the FCC.

If Don Reuben was once the most influential lawyer in Chicago, then Newton Minow was the most connected lawyer in Chicago. Minow was seemingly tied to everything or everyone of any importance or value in the last forty years.

He was hardly out of Northwestern Law School, first in his class, when he joined the staff of Governor Adlai Stevenson, who he worked for vigorously in two presidential campaigns and, later, in Stevenson's law firm. In 1960, he tried to persuade Stevenson not to embarrass himself by seeking a third Democratic nomination, which was already sewed up for John Kennedy. He tried to resolve the dilemma while driving the future president to a meeting with Stevenson. "I suggested he make Stevenson his secretary of state. He just stared at me. They really didn't like each other." Stevenson was not made secretary of state. Minow was made chairman of the FCC at age thirty-five.

Minow later surprised Mayor Richard J. Daley by declining any of the mayor's cajoling that he run for senator or governor. "I told him I'd like to be a delegate to the Democratic convention."

Minow grew up in Milwaukee, where his boyhood friend was Abner Mikva. He is related by marriage to Arthur Goldberg. He is a good friend of Richard Posner and Edward Levi. Justice John Paul Stevens was a law school classmate. Sandor Vanocur, who covered the Kennedy White House for NBC, was his college roommate. When he helped merge his old firm—Leibman, Williams, Bennett, Baird & Minow—into Sidley and Austin in 1972, the key negotiator and future chairman of the firm was Howard Trienens, who Minow had clerked with for Chief Justice Fred M. Vinson at the Supreme Court.

Minow was the first Jewish member of the Notre Dame Board of Trustees and served there thirty years. He was made a lifetime trustee of Northwestern, where he also taught law. He served on the board of CBS for years, questioning why they did what they did. "I once asked the news director why they were going to broadcast predictions of who won the elections before the polls closed. I didn't think it was right."

Minow would not place himself on a list of lawyers who significantly influenced American life in the twentieth century. "If I changed anything, I helped change the media."

Besides his famous declaration about television, Minow was the spearhead behind congressional approval to launch the first communications satellite in the early 1960s, the development that ultimately paved the way for CNN and instant transmission of history. The satellite allowed the entire world to watch Boris Yeltsin climb on a tank during the failed 1990 Soviet coup. It allowed Americans to watch Polaris missiles hitting doorways in Baghdad and allowed the rest of the world to watch Michael Jordan play.

More important, perhaps, was his thrust to create educational-television funding:

When I got to Washington I learned that there were only two educational television stations in the country, Chicago and

Boston. We passed a bill funding education television and converted a commercial station in New York to education. That was the beginning. Now every major city in America has an educational station. I am proud of that.

Minow, however, knows he will never escape his famous two words.

"My daughters tell me that the epitaph on my tombstone will be, 'On to a vaster wasteland.' "

9 ▮

THE PROFESSOR:
RICHARD POSNER

Except for John Paul Stevens, no sitting federal judge in Chicago in this century has become more of a significant legal figure than Richard Posner.

Posner is not a household name, but he might be the most influential legal scholar, writer, and jurist of the last quarter century. He is certainly one of the most innovative and controversial. He has been called a menace and a genius, an enemy of civil rights, a defender of government rights, and the foremost advocate of the "law and economics" theory pioneered at the University of Chicago Law School, where Posner taught for thirteen years before Ronald Reagan appointed him to the 7th U.S. Circuit Court of Appeals in 1981.

The theories that economic principles should be applied to law came out of the "legal realism" movement of the late 1920s and flourished at the University of Chicago during the 1930s and later when Edward Levi was dean of the law school. Both George Stigler and Ronald Coase, who is considered the intellectual godfather of the movement, won Nobel prizes in economics and had a great influence on Posner, who in the 1970s became the leading exponent of the movement with his book *The Economic Analysis of Law*, which argued that free-market and economic efficiency principles can and should be applied to every legal issue from antitrust cases to whether Jewish children should be allowed to wear yarmulkes during interscholastic sporting events.

His critics revel in recalling that Posner once theorized that it would be more economically efficient if babies were sold in the marketplace rather than placed for adoption by regulated agencies.

Posner was born in New York City in 1939, the son of a lawyer and a schoolteacher. He once wrote that he drifted into law because he "didn't have any strong pull in some other direction." He received an undergraduate degree from Yale in 1959 and a law degree from Harvard in 1962. After Harvard, Posner was a law clerk for U.S. Supreme Court Justice William Brennan, then held a series of government positions in Washington during the Lyndon Johnson administration. Brennan reportedly once said that Posner and Supreme Court Justice William O. Douglas were the only true geniuses he ever encountered. Interestingly, Douglas was one of the radicals of the "legal realism" movement.

Posner has never become the conservative Satan liberals feared when he was first appointed by Reagan. He has established a reputation as an excellent jurist and, as the court's chief judge since 1993, an administrator. He is the most prolific opinion writer in the 7th Circuit in addition to authoring more than twenty books and more than one hundred journal articles.

"He still embraces economics (and social science generally) as valuable tools for judges and lawyers, but to his fundamental principles of analysis he has added liberalism of the sort practiced by John Stuart Mill and pragmatism as practiced by Oliver Wendell Holmes Jr. and John Dewey," wrote Stephen B. Presser, professor of legal history at Northwestern University, in 1995.

Commenting on Posner's twentieth book, Presser said, "There is still enough of the old Posner in *Overcoming Law* to delight his fans and enrage his foes, including an abundance of unexpected and possibly brilliant—although possibly merely weird or wrong—observations: 'Social welfare might increase if the IQ's of all tax lawyers could be reduced by 10 percent.' 'We know that the framers of the Constitution tried to design a government that could be operated by moral and intellectual mediocrities.' He is self-consciously politically incorrect about some matters of race and gender while at the same time boldly contemptuous of some attempts to regulate sexual behavior.

He even gives a qualified endorsement to the legalization of homosexual marriage."

He was the foremost judicial advocate of Reagan and Bush administration economic practices, and, however much Posner's economic theories irk liberals, the failure of anticapitalist societies in the Soviet Union and Asia in the 1980s and 1990s reinforced many of his free-market theories.

After nearly twenty years on the bench there is little to argue with the assessment made of him by John Donohue, a law professor at Northwestern University, in 1987: "He has thought more about issues of jurisprudence and judicial administration than any other judge in the country. He's one of the great geniuses of the 20th Century. He's influential in the following sense: Everybody reads what he says."

THE DEAN:
JOHN WIGMORE

Since the advent of the televised courtroom millions of Americans have become schooled in trial procedures, watching intently as Johnnie Cochran produces a glove that is too small for O. J. Simpson's hand, judging for themselves whether the death of an infant in Massachusetts was caused by accident or the brutal act of a teenage au pair.

Those same Americans watch *Court TV, Nightline, Dateline*, Larry King, and Geraldo Rivera's nightly parade of modern legal geniuses discussing and debating evidence. Very few of them have ever heard of John Henry Wigmore.

Yet, for almost the entire century, every trial in America followed the rules of evidence written in 1904 by Wigmore, who served fifty years on the faculty at the Northwestern University Law School and was its dean from 1901 until 1929.

Wigmore was the preeminent legal scholar in America for the first half of the twentieth century. He was the authority on almost every facet of law, consulted by the courts on many major issues, and the scholar who influenced every law school faculty.

He wrote forty-two books, compiled seven casebooks, edited and provided translations for thirty other volumes, and contributed a great number of articles and book reviews to various legal journals. He did it without a staff of researchers.

But his legacy is *Treatise on Evidence*, every word of which he wrote out in longhand. It was originally published in 1904 and expanded by him to ten volumes in the final edition, which appeared in 1940. It is generally regarded as one of the greatest law books in any language.

Wigmore was born in 1863 in San Francisco, and attended Harvard and the University of Wisconsin before joining the Northwestern faculty in 1893, where he remained until his death in 1943 at age eighty.

Wigmore clearly deserved the title of "America's first legal scholar," which was conferred upon him when he was awarded the American Bar Association's gold medal. But he was not a refugee hidden in the halls of academia along the lakefront.

He attacked the Chicago judicial system and was a rabid opponent of Prohibition, which he declared "a huge mistake, imposed upon us by a fanatic minority who overawed timid politicians." Wigmore was speaking from firsthand knowledge, since his Evanston home was only a few blocks from the headquarters of the Women's Christian Temperance Union, which spearheaded the ban on alcohol.

In the wake of the 1930s financial disaster caused by Samuel Insull's utility-stock schemes, Wigmore took the unpopular side. He wrote an opinion that Insull had broken no laws, and the court ultimately agreed with him. He wrote the national draft law in 1917 and served on the judge advocate general's staff, attaining the rank of colonel.

In 1931 he condemned as "Scrooge-like" Evanston's plan to tax nonresidents using its beaches. In the late 1930s he led the legal community's attacks on Franklin Roosevelt's attempts to pack the Supreme Court.

On his retirement as dean in 1929, Chief Justice William Howard Taft, the former president, called him "one of the outstanding contributors to the science of law in our time."

On the one-hundredth anniversary of Wigmore's birth in 1963, a former student and then Supreme Court justice, Arthur Goldberg, described Wigmore as a conservative in social and economic values but a great liberal in matters of law. "His liberalism was shown by the fact that he was a great believer that no precedent can sanction injustice."

His name means virtually nothing to most Americans today, but his work has influenced the judicial system perhaps more than any other individual in the century.

■ ■ ■ ■ VII

PERFORMING ARTS'
TOP TEN

Chicago, of all places, is proof that art is eternal.

By century's end the raucous, violent age of machine guns no longer painted the city's image. In the twilight of political activism the legends of ghost voters and patronage armies faded in the glare of television commercials that replaced and doomed the precinct captains. They butchered the last hog at about the same time it still was safe to steal a vote. The steel mills that drew the Poles, the Slovenians, the Croats, and the Bohemians were long ago replaced by open-hearth furnaces in Korea.

Marshall Field's hasn't been owned by a Marshall Field for thirty years.

Basketball is too new. Sears is too old.

But the music never has stopped.

From the day in 1891 that Theodore Thomas agreed to create a symphony to keep Chicagoans out of the whorehouses after dark, the city lusted for dominance in culture the way its merchant princes hungered for riches and its politicians craved power. The riches have vanished and the power is illusory.

The sound of Chicago is the sound of the world. After the Chicago Symphony's conquest of Europe on its 1971 tour Chicagoans abroad were not asked about Al Capone anymore. The Chicago Symphony is older than the century and more highly regarded, too.

The music the world hears every day on CD, radio, and television grew up in Chicago. It may have started in New Orleans or, before that, in an African village, but Chicago is where they created jazz and swing and blues and everything else that everyone hears or plays. Chicago was where the great Creole and black musicians moved to develop their music. It was where young white musicians of the twenties like Bix Beiderbecke and Hoagy Carmichael first heard the sounds of jazz and turned it into "Star Dust." It was the place that moved the blues from smoky, small rooms to auditoriums and outdoor concert arenas. It was in Chicago that Sonny Blount became Sun Ra, the most avant-garde jazz musician of his age, and where Dr. Thomas Dorsey invented gospel.

It was opera, beginning in 1910 with the traditional "Aida," and the sultry Mary Garden in *Salome*. It barely survived until Samuel Insull built his grand opera palace on the river. It died along with Insull's career in the Depression and was given birth again in the 1950s by Carol Fox. At century's end, the Chicago Lyric Opera is one of the finest in the world, the venue where Maria Callas made her American debut and Pavarotti has canceled enough appearances to almost justify the early century skeptics who said Chicago would never support opera.

Had Chicago given the world its symphony and its jazz it would have been enough. But there was more culture than the first pioneers and pimps ever dreamed.

It was Hull House that staged the first American productions of plays by Galsworthy and Ibsen, and it was the Fine Arts Building where in 1912 Maurice Browne opened the ninety-one-seat Chicago Little Theater, which began the country's "little theater" movement. From *Front Page* and Kenneth Sawyer Goodman, whose early death led to the creation of a major playhouse named in his honor, to David Mamet's terse, stark phrasing, Chicago has been a vital force in American theater. It was in Chicago in the 1960s and 1970s where off-Broadway was reborn, spurring a theatrical resurgence across America. Richard Christiansen, the *Chicago Tribune* and *Chicago Daily News* critic whose role in that renaissance cannot be understated, has argued that Mamet is certainly one of Chicago's most influential artists of the century.

"I don't think there is a young playwright today in America who has not been influenced by the language and mannerisms of David

Mamet," Christiansen said. "In his early plays, *American Buffalo* and *Glengarry Glen Ross*, Mamet followed [Samuel] Beckett and [Harold] Pinter but he created an Americanization of the short, terse statement followed by the significant pause. Mamet has become a role model and his plays are popular in Europe and Asia."

There were Chicago sculptors, Lorado Taft and Richard Hunt, the first black sculptor to achieve an international reputation. There were painters such as Ed Paschke and Roger Brown who led the Chicago school of imagists, which flourished over the century's last four decades and influenced artists throughout the world.

The first movie production company in America started here in 1910. Chicago could claim Orson Welles, arguably the most influential filmmaker of the century, as its own since some of his earliest works were done in Woodstock. Walt Disney went to school here before inventing Mickey Mouse in Hollywood. The greatest showman of the 1920s, Florenz Ziegfeld, grew up on the West Side and got his start promoting a strongman at the 1893 World's Fair before heading to New York and his famous Follies.

From Waukegan's Jack Benny to Wheaton's tragic John Belushi, Chicago gave the world comedy, and the stars who created the *Saturday Night Live* laughter as well as the Seinfelds of the nineties owe much of their tradition to Second City, the seedbed of improv comedy after it was opened in 1959 by Paul Sills and Bernie Sahlins and where Mike Nichols and Elaine May invented a modern satire. More than any other subject in this book, it is conjectural as to which artists Chicago can claim because of birth or impact. Again, applying H. L. Mencken's reasoning about literature, it seems safe to include those artists who got their start in Chicago or "passed through there in the days when he was young and tender."

In August of 1922, one of those young and tender men arrived in Chicago. Before he departed seven years later he changed music forever in America, and in the world.

SATCHMO:
LOUIS ARMSTRONG

It is not even debatable that of all the Chicaogans who have left their mark on this century and the world the one certain genius among them was Louis Armstrong.

It can be argued that Louis Armstrong was not the most influential Chicagoan of the twentieth century, but he would do in a pinch.

Armstrong had to be a genius. There is no other explanation behind the story of the New Orleans–born cornet player who invented jazz as it was played in the 1920s and as it developed into swing, metamorphosed with the blues, and was thriving at the end of the century with variations that echoed the improvisations he began at the Lincoln Gardens cabaret in 1922. When Armstrong showed up on Chicago's South Side, he left behind in New Orleans his mother, Mayann, who had supported him by working the brothels of Story-ville, and a wife, Daisy, who worked the same rooms. He had no formal musical training, beginning as a bugle player in a waifs' home, where the police had tossed him when he was thirteen. He knew some of the early jazz innovators, such as King Oliver and Kid Ory, and he learned a little about the technique of the cornet while he played for a few years on excursion steamboats that paddled the Mississippi, where Armstrong was happy to work because of the free lunches that bloated the rather small man with the mouth that looked like a piano keyboard.

Lil Hardin, the piano player in King Oliver's band, which had offered Armstrong a spot in Chicago, remembers her first glance at

Armstrong, who later would make her his second wife. "Everything he had on was too small for him. His atrocious tie was dangling down over his protruding stomach and to top it off he had a hairdo that called for bangs. All the musicians called him Little Louis and he weighed 226 pounds."

Then he blew his horn.

When he died a half century later, the *New York Times* called him the "root source of all jazz." On behalf of the nation, Richard Nixon called him the "architect of a unique American art form."

Only days before his death, Armstrong summed up his career in the syntax that the whole world recognized and loved: "There ain't going to be no more cats in this music game that long."

And it was a game to Armstrong. He never used the word *artist* or even the word *jazz*. To him it was music and entertainment. When in later years he mostly held his trumpet by his side while singing pop songs in the voice once described as "a piece of sandpaper calling its mate," critics complained he had wasted his genius. But all Armstrong cared about was applause. His popularity endured whether he was inventing melodies that no one had ever heard before or endlessly repeating "Hello Dolly" for audiences in Asia, Africa, Europe, and wherever else he was invited to perform.

The *New York Times* described an Armstrong performance: "The man radiated a jollity that was infectious. Onstage he would bend back his stocky frame, point his trumpet to the heavens and joyfully blast out the high C's. When he sang he fairly bubbled with pleasure. And as he swabbed away at the perspiration stirred up by his exertions, Satchmo grinned his famous toothy smile so incandescently that it seemed to light up the auditorium." Historian and Armstrong biographer James Lincoln Collier explained the worldwide adoration: "You could warm your hands in front of Louis Armstrong. You could not be unhappy when he was singing."

"Before Louis Armstrong came to Chicago," said *Chicago Tribune* arts critic Howard Reich, "there was only a music called New Orleans music. It was folk, it was rough and mostly improvised by musicians who couldn't read music. Overnight, Armstrong changed all that. No one could hit such high notes, no one had his technique, no one could swing like Louis Armstrong."

Armstrong began swinging in Joe "King" Oliver's Creole Jazz Band at the Lincoln Gardens at 31st Street and Cottage Grove Avenue. By March of 1923, Oliver, Armstrong, and the Creole Jazz Band had begun making records for the Gennett label in Richmond, Indiana, and these would ignite the still-emerging world of jazz. The rounded, golden tone that Armstrong brought to "Chimes Blues" (his first recorded solo) announced the arrival of a young cornetist already more proficient, more inventive, and more distinctive than his boss, King Oliver.

Armstrong immediately began an affair with Lil Hardin and divorced his first wife, Daisy Parker, who Armstrong said "wouldn't give up her line of work." Hardin, who came from a middle-class black family and had attended Fisk University, felt that Oliver had hired Armstrong to keep him under wraps. Hardin wrote in her memoir, *Satchmo and Me*, that she would hear her husband whistling in the house and inventing beautiful music, and she asked him why he didn't play like that. Eventually Hardin, who Armstrong married in 1924, convinced him to break away from Oliver.

Armstrong packed up his instrument and headed to New York City for a job in Fletcher Henderson's band, which was still playing the dated and stodgy dance forms that remained popular in New York. "Chicago was hot," Reich said. "In New York they still were playing quadrilles." In New York, Armstrong tried his revolutionary "scat singing," which embarrassed Henderson as too "down home." After a year, Armstrong returned to Chicago, where his new venue, the Dreamland Cafe, put up a sign, The World's Greatest Trumpet Player.

Now Armstrong began to flex his musical muscle. He made a series of records between 1925 and 1927 with two groups, the Hot Five and Hot Seven, which changed jazz. The tunes, "Potato Head Blues," "West End Blues," and the frolicking "Strutting with Some Barbecue," contained solos of unprecedented brilliance that eclipsed forever the standard ensemble playing. It didn't happen in New Orleans and it didn't happen in New York. Reich noted,

> Only in Chicago—its night life driven by such brilliant players as Oliver, [Earl] Hines, clarinetist Johnny Dodds, drummer Baby Dodds, banjoist Johnny St. Cyr, singer Chippie Hill

and trombonist Kid Ory—could Armstrong find so rich a setting in which to flourish. Only in Chicago—its rambunctious, freewheeling, anything-goes clubs run by mobsters (such as Al Capone) who loved both jazz and Satchmo—would the atmosphere be ripe for such musical experimentation. And only in Chicago—with its numerous publishing houses, record labels, national radio broadcasts and so on—could Armstrong launch his revolution nationwide.

The cuts with the Hot Five and the Hot Seven represented the critical and vital contributions of Louis Armstrong to American music. Jazz historians would say the rest of his career was an anticlimax, that it was the years in Chicago between 1925 and 1929 that established the new art of jazz, once and for all, as a timeless and important one.

Armstrong moved again to New York in 1929, then to California to make movies, and began his frequent trips to Europe, where blacks often found life less restrictive. Even when he was acknowledged as the world's greatest jazz musician, Armstrong recalled touring through the South and being forced to find sleeping quarters in private homes, since he was not allowed to stay in hotels. In Europe, black men could be seen with white women without a lynch mob forming. On a 1933 tour Armstrong played for King George V, unaware of the protocol that performers were not supposed to address royalty. Before the start of a hot trumpet number, Armstrong announced, "This one's for you, Rex." It was a London newsman, incorrectly hearing the pronunciation of Armstrong's boyhood nickname, "Satchelmouth," who christened him "Satchmo." On a visit to Italy in the 1950s Armstrong and his fourth wife, Lucille, had an audience with Pope Pius XII, who inquired if they had any children. Armstrong replied, "No, Pops, but we're still wailing."

Armstrong, who never paid much attention to names, called everyone "Pops" or "Daddy," which is ironic since the man who his mother said was his father never paid him any attention at all. Willie Armstrong had left his wife when Louis was an infant, and only later when he needed a full-time babysitter for children he had with a second wife did he bring Louis to his home, briefly. Armstrong was raised by his grandmother while his mother lived with prostitutes. "Whether my mother did any hustling, I can't say," Armstrong recalled. "If she did, she kept it out of my sight."

Armstrong was born on July 4, but whether it was in 1900 as he claimed, or a few years earlier or later, no one knew for certain. After his stay in the waifs' home (for firing a pistol in the street), he worked as a junk man and delivered coal while begging every bandleader in New Orleans to let him sit in. He did many things to stay alive. "I was foolin' around with some tough ones," he recalled before his death. "Get paid a little money, and make a beeline for one of them gambling houses. Two hours, man, and I was a broke cat, broker than the Ten Commandments. Needed money so bad I even tried pimping—but my first client got jealous of me and we got to fussing about it and she stabbed me in the shoulder. Them was wild times."

Armstrong fell out of favor during the swing era, when the stylized bands of Benny Goodman, Glenn Miller, the Dorsey Brothers, and others became the rage with their comprehensive, distinctive sounds and their featuring of various soloists. It might have been that Armstrong was content to replay the songs that had made him famous, but some biographers believed he was unwilling to lead a band that would showcase anyone but himself. Although Armstrong had a most cheerful public persona, he was intensely territorial about his stature as the world's finest jazz musician. On more than one occasion he backed down from promised dual appearances with other jazz notables such as Coleman Hawkins.

By the end of World War II the swing era was dying, and the hot trend in records was the male vocalist. Although Bing Crosby had been "the crooner" for years, it was the sudden celebrity of young Frank Sinatra that created the popularity of the balladeer. Armstrong fit right in and soon was back in the public limelight with such vocal hits as "Blueberry Hill," "A Kiss to Build a Dream On," and "Mack the Knife."

He appeared on network television throughout the 1950s and 1960s, although militant blacks criticized his earthy speech and his manner of rolling his eyes and grinning. They accused him of persisting in the stereotypical characteristics of the shuffling, lazy black man. He did speak out when Arkansas Governor Orval Faubus blocked black children from integrating the schools in 1957 and after the brutal Selma, Alabama, march in 1965. After leaving for Chicago, Armstrong did not go back home to perform in New Orleans for more than forty years, refusing to play in a state with segregation laws. He finally made a triumphant return after the passage of the 1965 Civil Rights Act.

He died in his home in Queens, New York, on July 7, 1971. A quarter of a century later his importance was even more clear.

Howard Reich said, "Louis Armstrong gave jazz a face and a charisma. If Armstrong had not come to Chicago in the 1920s the music we now call jazz might not have taken place. It would be something else. Without him, it would not be the same thing."

2

HALIE:
MAHALIA JACKSON

There were two Mahalia Jacksons, and both of them belong right up there with Louis Armstrong.

One Mahalia was the soul of gospel music. She was the star, the face of gospel, just as Armstrong was the face of jazz. The other Mahalia was the sound of the civil rights movement.

The big fat lady with the big fat voice resonated throughout America when she stood by Martin Luther King at the Lincoln Memorial in 1963 and shouted to two hundred thousand black people, "I been 'buked and I been scorned; I'm gonna tell my Lord when I get home just how long you been treating me wrong."

It was a nation that Mahalia Jackson was rebuking for its treatment of her people, treatment that she also had endured despite twenty years of celebrity among white audiences and on mainline television shows. Most of white America had never heard gospel music until Mahalia. Most of white America had never heard "We Shall Overcome" until Mahalia sang what became the most powerful and pervasive social plaint of the second half of the century.

"Halie" Jackson, like Louis Armstrong, was from New Orleans, where she lived near the high levee that keeps the Mississippi River from boiling all over the city. She was raised by a matriarchal aunt after her mother died when she was five. Her early life as an uneducated laundress and child care servant was wound deeply into the church, where her aunt would lead the family two or three times a week and all day Sunday.

It was in the church that Mahalia's rich contralto first burst loose with traditional hymns. And it was on early crank-up phonographs that she heard smuggled records of Bessie Smith singing the blues, the laments that decent colored people like her Aunt Duke forbid in the house. Mahalia Jackson never would sing the blues, although in later years Louis Armstrong, Duke Ellington, and just about everyone pleaded with her to enter show business. "Any Negro can sing the blues," she scoffed.

But while she always dedicated her singing to praise of the Lord, she never forgot the sound of Bessie Smith.

In 1928 Jackson moved with another aunt to Chicago's South Side, where the sounds of Armstrong and Jelly Roll Morton and Earl "Fatha" Hines were pouring out of the black enclave. She worked as a hotel maid, ironed shirts, watched children, and joined the Greater Salem Baptist Church, where she quickly became a soloist.

As with any great artist, or for that matter almost anyone who achieves greatness, there is always that combination of skill and timing. Just when Mahalia Jackson was belting out her church solos, Dr. Thomas Dorsey was only a few blocks away writing a new kind of church music.

Dorsey had once been a jazz musician. As "Georgia Tom" he accompanied the great Bessie Smith for many years. But after his wife died in childbirth, Dorsey turned to a religious life and began composing church music. But just like Mahalia, with all her nontheological faith, he could not escape the sound of the blues, and the music he wrote was filled with laments and wails and swing. "I wanted to get the feeling and the moans and the blues into the songs," he once told the *Chicago Tribune*. "Before that, they would sing 'Spiri-tu-al-fellow-ship-of-the-Jor-dan land.' Jubilee songs. Wasn't nothing to them. But then I turned those blues moans on, modified some of the stuff from way back in the jazz era, bashed it up and smoothed it in. It had that beat, that rhythm. And people were wild about it."

And Mahalia began to sing it. Dorsey's biggest hit, "Precious Lord," became one of the staples of her performances, and she joined Pilgrim Baptist Church, where she was surrounded by such other gospel greats at Clara Ward and the Barrett Sisters.

Her first record, "God Gonna Separate the Wheat from the Tares," was cut in 1934, but the swinging sound of gospel was still not accepted among the middle-class black churches. Gospel grew because there was a vacuum. The Depression had forced the closing of many of the jazz clubs and nightspots. Many of the great musicians of the 1920s were without work, and even the most successful, like Armstrong, resorted to European tours to make money.

For a decade Jackson crisscrossed the South and Midwest, often driving alone to Detroit or St. Louis or any town where a church group wanted to see the majestic, towering woman who shook her hips and her whole body, and whose internal exhilaration burst forth in her voice as her combs flew from her hair and her throat spewed the sounds of black faith in God. She regularly traveled across the country to the annual National Baptist Convention, and regularly was refused admittance to hotels and restaurants, eating cold cuts in cold cars, indignities that later made her one of the first and most fervent supporters of King and the civil rights crusade.

She made some money and she got to be somewhat of a miser, stacking thousands of dollars in her suitcase among the underwear. She also sent money back to New Orleans to support a host of cousins. She married Isaac Hockenhall, a chemist, in 1931, but Hockenhall was an inveterate horse player who she divorced in 1943, although they remained friends all her life.

In 1946, Mahalia cut a record for Apollo called "Move on Up a Little Higher." It sold 2 million copies, an unheard-of number for a black artist selling mostly in the black community. The hits continued throughout the 1940s. Studs Terkel began playing her records on his radio show, and Chicagoans were the first whites in America to hear the big black woman singing the glory of God.

In 1950 she appeared on *The Ed Sullivan Show*, although that and all her subsequent television appearances were far more placid and sedate than the style Mahalia delivered in person. Despite her many refusals and fears, a concert was scheduled for October 4, 1950, in Carnegie Hall. It was a raging success, and she made repeat appearances there for years. In the 1950s she also toured Europe and the Middle East. She was particularly popular in Israel. Although she never broke a pledge to God that she would never appear in a theater, she was flexible enough to join Duke Ellington's band in a performance at the Newport Jazz Festival during the 1950s.

In Chicago, she opened a florist shop and a beauty parlor and despite her largesse to relatives was a shrewd businesswoman and became a millionaire. She bought a home in 1952 in a white neighborhood of the South Side. Shots were fired at her house, but eventually the acts of violence disappeared. So did her white neighbors, who began selling their homes. In a few short years Jackson was living in an all black neighborhood again.

In the 1950s Jackson was signed by WBBM to do a local television show, with Studs Terkel as the off-camera host. Station officials were apprehensive about Terkel because he was, during the red witch-hunt era, listed as one of those radicals who signed petitions outrageously supporting world peace and civil rights. But Mahalia, who insisted that Terkel had discovered her, also insisted he be a part of the show, which ran twice a week. When Jackson asked why the show wasn't broadcast nationally, she suffered another indignity. A television show with a black star wouldn't get any sponsors in the South, she was told. "Halie" Jackson didn't have much education, but she couldn't figure out why if her records sold all over the South and white people cheered her all over the South she wouldn't get any sponsors. But she never did.

She often sang at the Ebenezer Baptist Church in Atlanta, where the pastor was the Reverend Martin Luther King Sr. When she heard about King Jr.'s crusade in Montgomery she became the focal point of fund-raising. The Reverend Ralph D. Abernathy and King had visited her in Chicago to ask her help, and Jackson organized many concerts and enlisted the help of other black entertainers to support the movement in the 1950s and 1960s, spreading the sound and the spirit of "We Shall Overcome" through America's black communities.

In 1964 Jackson married for a second time, to Sigmund "Minters" Galloway, and that union also ended in a divorce shortly before her death in 1972. She had no children, but she had millions of admirers. More than fifty thousand people attended her funeral.

She made the kind of gospel music that thrived into the 1990s with the work of the Winans Family, the Barrett Sisters, Albertina Walker, and Pops Staples.

"Without Mahalia Jackson there would have been no Aretha Franklin. Without Mahalia Jackson there would be no Grammies for gospel. Gospel music would not be the thriving industry it is today," said Howard Reich.

More important, it thrives in churches across Chicago and around the world.

3

SIR GEORG:
GEORG SOLTI

When Georg Solti arrived in Chicago in 1969 he thought the place was rather sleepy. He saw the magnificent architecture, which had become run down, and he thought the city in some ways had turned inward, isolated from the rest of the world. He couldn't have known that the lowered chins and grim faces were only mourning the collapse of the 1969 Cubs.

In a matter of months Solti would watch a new architectural renaissance. The city that didn't have direct flights to Europe suddenly became the center of global trading in financial futures, and banks from Tokyo to Tel Aviv opened Chicago branches. Flights from O'Hare flew direct to every capital of the world. The Cubs continued to make faces grim. Solti couldn't have known that unlike the other places he lived—Budapest, Paris, Munich, London—the civic pride of Chicago revolved only around the Cubs, the White Sox, and the Bears. Chicagoans knew they had an art institute, but few of them cared about the Impressionist wonders stored there. Chicagoans knew there was an opera, but they didn't know anybody who went to it. Chicagoans knew there was a symphony, but no one could stop in at the corner saloon and argue the earned run average of an oboe player.

When Georg Solti left Chicago twenty-two years later, he was a civic treasure. Only the Super Bowl Bears of 1985 had been given a bigger ticker tape parade than the one they threw for Solti after his triumphant European tour in 1971. "It was just like the Super Bowl," recalled *Chicago Tribune* critic Richard Christiansen. "For an orchestra!"

Solti, who enjoyed the same megalomaniac characteristics of other great conductors, had stunned a 1977 news conference by declaring the city should build a statue of him. Solti's statue was erected in 1986.

By then he and the Chicago Symphony Orchestra were considered national treasures. The *New York Times* would write during his final concerts, "The central figure of the Solti-Chicago success was the sheer stunning quality of the playing, which few other groups could rival. For many listeners, there suddenly seemed something new under the sun: an orchestra that could grasp those huge, complex works whole and, with remarkably sustained virtuosity and power, render them as gleaming monolithic unities, seemingly perfect in every detail and cumulatively overwhelming."

Solti wouldn't have liked the modifiers.

"They [the symphony] need me—I don't need them," he announced on accepting the CSO position.

"The Chicago Symphony does not play bad concerts. We are playing good or very good concerts. We have had many very good concerts. What I love about this orchestra is that they never play badly for anyone, even a guest conductor they hate. When I am 5,000 miles away, I know they are keeping my standard. Their professional pride is unique," Solti said in his memoirs.

And modest to end, he told the *Tribune* in 1995, "I don't think this orchestra has ever been better than it is now."

Solti was born in Budapest in 1912, began playing the piano at age six, and was enrolled in the Franz Liszt Academy at age thirteen. He joined the coaching staff of the Budapest Opera when he was only eighteen. In 1937 he studied at the Salzburg Festival, where he was an assistant to Arturo Toscanini. Because he was Jewish, Solti was forced to flee Nazi persecution after the outbreak of World War II in 1939. He went to Zurich, Switzerland. In 1942 he won the Geneva International Piano Competition, and in 1946 he became the musical director of the Bavarian State Opera in Munich. He directed the Frankfurt Opera for eight years until 1960, when he accepted the directorship of the Royal Opera at Covent Garden. Ever modest, he declared it would become the finest opera in the world. The British press dubbed him the "Prussian of Covent Garden" for his autocratic manner. Solti demurred, "I wasn't commanding people, but rather encouraging them to seek improvement." Whether the Royal Opera became the greatest in the world is debatable, but there was little question that he raised its standard, for which in 1972 he was made a knight of the British Empire.

Between 1958 and 1965 he completed his acclaimed recordings of the Ring cycle. By 1969 he already was acclaimed for his music and his slashing style on the podium, which one biographer, William Barry Furlong, described as like "a spastic stork, bending and rearing convulsively, elbows pumping, knees popping, torso laboring until it seems almost as if he is going to tear the music from himself in a Dionysian frenzy."

In Chicago, in less lofty terms, he was known as the Fastest Baton in the West.

By the end of the 1960s Solti was searching for new worlds and had his eye on the Orchestre de Paris, which was seeking a new conductor after the departure of Herbert Von Karajan, the only conductor of the age that Solti sometimes considered an equal.

At the same time the Chicago Symphony was seeking a replacement for conductor Jean Martinon, whose eight-year reign was marked by indifference, low morale, uninspired performances in New York, and the acid criticism of *Chicago Tribune* critic Claudia Cassidy, who, though near the end of her powerful tenure, waged a war for Martinon's dismissal.

Unlike the Cubs, Sox, and Bears, the CSO that Solti took over in 1969 was not in total disarray or perennially last in its field. Ever since its founding in 1891 by Theodore Thomas, the CSO was considered an outstanding orchestra. Yet the CSO was never considered an equal to its rivals in New York and Philadelphia.

"The orchestra still had its supporters and benefactors, but as far as the city was concerned, it was rather like a beloved but neglected piece of old furniture," Solti recalled.

The main reason for this, Solti decided, was that like much of Chicago, the CSO had remained provincial. The orchestra rarely toured. Solti began raising money for a European trip. He also imposed his own style on the CSO, which *Tribune* music critic John von Rhein recalled:

When Solti made music, he turned into a man possessed, lunging at the orchestra with a ferocity and dynamism punctuated by the famous "Solti snap"—a precise marking of the beat that signaled his complete control of every detail of the score's unfolding. That style was not universally admired. Some critics and musicians found his musicmaking clinical, lacking in warmth and spontaneity. Still, there was no denying he got orchestras to give him everything he wanted.

By 1970, the Solti CSO had begun its conquest of New York City with a celebrated performance of Mahler's Fifth Symphony. In years to come, the appearances of Solti and the CSO in New York were always one of the season's hottest tickets. In 1971 came the orchestra's first European tour, with a triumphant parade down State Street upon its return.

Solti led the CSO on nine overseas trips: five to Europe, including a Russian stop; three to Japan; and one to Australia for the country's bicentennial celebration in 1988. A banner greeted the CSO at the airport: Sydney has waited 200 years to welcome Solti and the Chicago Symphony!

Solti made the cover of *Time* magazine and continued collecting the Grammy Awards that would number thirty-two at his death, more than any other performer, classical or pop.

Solti died of a heart attack in 1997. His pairing with the CSO was clearly accepted as one of the great orchestral combinations of the century, in the same company as Toscanini and the NBC Orchestra, Leopold Stokowski and the Philadelphia Symphony.

Von Rhein noted, "All his life, Solti seemed driven by a single desire: to make an indelible, unmistakable impact upon the symphonic and operatic music of our time. He succeeded, perhaps better than the far-from-modest maestro ever would have imagined."

But the greatness of the CSO was not his alone.

4

A GIANT:
FRITZ REINER

There is not only the question of whether Fritz Reiner made a greater contribution to America than Georg Solti, but also how much of a role he played in bringing the Chicago Symphony to the level where Solti could exploit it and expand its reputation. Although Solti spent twenty-two years with the CSO compared to Reiner's single decade, Reiner was a formidable presence on the American orchestral scene before his arrival in Chicago, while Solti's pre-Chicago reputation was based on his European performance.

To make comparisons even more difficult, both of them were from Budapest. Both of them were Jewish, although Reiner converted to Catholicism.

Both of them were demanding, arrogant, and brilliant.

But Reiner was the greater tyrant and the greater lover—at least his amorous ways made great adventure in the usually sedate world of classical music. And many would say Reiner was the greater conductor.

The *New York Times* called him one of the "giants of American podiums" and lamented that the city had only a fleeting chance to take his full measure.

His trademark was the "vest pocket" baton stroke. He used a large baton but made very little motion with it. The beat was so tiny that it could be seen only by the musicians. With rare exception, one hand and an occasional stiff arm movement were all he ever used to command an orchestra to do his bidding. That and his awful glare peering from hooded eyes. His countenance was often compared to that of a hunting falcon, and he loomed at times like a vampire on the hunt.

He was born in 1888 and played the piano at an early age. By nine he could play a Wagnerian overture from memory. He graduated from the Budapest Royal Academy of Music in 1908, where he studied under composer Béla Bartók. He worked in opera houses in Europe, during which time he divorced his first wife and married Berta Gardini, with whom he had been conducting a rather open affair. From 1914 to 1921, he was in command of the Royal Opera at Dresden.

In 1922, he accepted the position of conductor of the Cincinnati Symphony, where he stayed for nine seasons under the patronage of a Taft family doyen who tolerated his martinet style until his dalliance with an actress became a public scandal. Reiner divorced Berta, with whom he had two daughters, and married the actress, Carlotta Irwin. Fifty years later, a musician who played under Reiner in Ohio spoke unforgivingly of his "sadism," but said in the next breath that he was the greatest conductor, including Toscanini, he had ever played for. Reiner was renowned for ridiculing his musicians, forcing even the most inexperienced to play solo passages during rehearsal so he could criticize them in front of their colleagues. When possible, he fired musicians who did not meet his standards, and to the musicians this seemed an arbitrary punishment, since no one could truly meet his standards. One of the most publicized accounts of his sadism and sarcasm occurred with the CSO, when Ray Still was a new member in the second oboe chair and angrily responded to a Reiner tongue-lashing by declaring he was not an amateur and had played in Baltimore. "With the Orioles, no doubt," Reiner replied.

In 1931, Reiner went to the Curtis Institute in Philadelphia for a ten-year term as orchestral and conducting professor. Then he resuscitated the Pittsburgh Symphony from 1938 to 1948 and spent five years at the Metropolitan Opera, where he occasionally made guest appearances conducting Toscanini's NBC Orchestra or the New York Philharmonic.

In 1953, the CSO was in a shambles. Under Theodore Thomas from its founding in 1905 and with Frederick Stock at the baton for the next thirty-seven years, the CSO was a successful orchestra content to be judged of high quality but not as high as the showcase symphonies in Boston, New York, and Philadelphia. After Stock's death in 1942, four conductors came and went with little distinction other than the chaos and bitterness they left behind. It was a legacy that would stalk Reiner as well.

But from the moment he arrived in 1953 the CSO began an upward spiral that resulted in a national reputation during the 1950s surpassed only by Eugene Ormandy and his orchestra in Philadelphia. Reiner had been an advocate of recording symphony music from his early days in Cincinnati, and his enthusiasm for recording coupled with his brilliant direction produced works that stamped the CSO as one of the world's great orchestras.

John von Rhein wrote that thirty years after Reiner's death it was time to "acknowledge the fact that, although Georg Solti drew the credit for making the world sit up and pay attention to our orchestra, it really was Reiner's Chicago Symphony the world was admiring. He had taken over a demoralized band and, within weeks, rubbed away years of tarnish and restored internal pride. Within just a few seasons, Chicago had a world-class orchestra. And this was the ensemble Jean Martinon preserved for five seasons and Solti inherited in 1969."

But Reiner was never able to bring the CSO to the world-class status Solti claimed, primarily because of his refusal to travel. Not until a two-week eastward swing in the early autumn of 1958 did awestruck audiences in Boston, New York, Philadelphia, and Washington hear firsthand what Fritz Reiner had created in Chicago. But it was the only eastern tour the CSO made under Reiner. A planned tour of Europe in 1959 was canceled, and Reiner was blamed. In 1960, he suffered a circulatory ailment six days before the start of the new season. He was already seventy-one, and as Roger Dettmer, the critic who covered the symphony for *Chicago's American*, noted, "He ate richly, smoked heavily and never walked where he could ride."

Sadly, his days in Chicago ended with the same kind of jealousies and territorial battling that had marked the CSO's management since Stock's death twenty years earlier. In the middle was the redoubtable Claudia Cassidy, angry at everyone involved, including Reiner, who resigned as conductor in 1962 and was given a final one-year contract as musical director for the 1963 season. He was not even asked his thoughts about a successor. He read of Jean Martinon's appointment in the *New York Times*.

A few months later, in November 1963, Reiner died of pneumonia in New York's Mount Sinai Hospital at age seventy-four.

The *New York Times* said, "As a musical intellect, as an incomparable technician, as the possessor of an ear virtually unparalleled in his field, Fritz Reiner held a unique spot in 20th Century musical life and thought."

5

SWING, SWING, SWING:
BENNY GOODMAN

The date was January 16, 1938. The city was New York. The place was Carnegie Hall. Nothing in American music was quite like that night.

There had been historic and seminal events in American music, such as Louis Armstrong's Hot Fives recordings, but they took place in studios, and the impact of what happened took weeks and sometimes years to appreciate. There were certainly dozens of late-night jam sessions on Chicago's South Side that linked Armstrong with Earl Hines and Jelly Roll Morton and with countless other jazz immortals, but only a few people were there to hear them, and no one recorded or wrote about them. There would be in the future such scenes as swooning girls mobbing Sinatra at the Paramount, Elvis Presley's national television debut on Ed Sullivan's show, and millions of American kids screaming at the arrival of the Beatles.

But Benny Goodman's show at Carnegie Hall in January 1938 was the spontaneous event that canonized one of the most popular and enduring forms of American music. It was called swing, and Goodman was its king.

The single-microphone recording of that concert remained the number-one selling jazz album for a half century. The raucous finale, beginning with drummer Gene Krupa's soft tom-tom beat and descending into a series of choruses followed by Goodman's clarinet solo and Jess Stacy's soft piano, was the apex of swing. In less than a decade swing would be gone. The bands of Glenn Miller, the Dorsey Brothers, Artie Shaw, and those of all the Goodman sidemen—

Krupa, Harry James, Lionel Hampton, and Teddy Wilson—would disappear as fragile American tastes switched to listening rather than dancing and the metamorphosis of post–World War II America created suburbs where people disappeared after dark. The dance halls and nightclubs closed. The bandstands were empty.

But from 1935, when he built his band, until 1945 no musician was more popular, more highly paid, and more influential than Benny Goodman.

Benny Goodman was not a creator like Armstrong or a composer like Duke Ellington. He was, arguably, the best clarinet player of his era and, perhaps, before and since.

Benny Goodman's legacy, however, is not based on his playing alone. He was the face of swing just as Armstrong was the face of jazz and Mahalia Jackson the face of gospel.

Benny Goodman was one of twelve children raised by David and Dora Goodman, who left the pogroms of Russia for the sweatshops on the West Side of Chicago. Goodman's father worked in the stockyards and in garment shops and eventually was given a newsstand at Madison and California by his children. Dora did little else but raise the children she bore almost yearly. Goodman recalled in his autobiography that breakfast was always coffee and rolls. "There wasn't money for milk," and he also remembered there were times when "there was nothing at all to eat, nothing."

But David Goodman wanted his children to be educated. When Benny was twelve his father enrolled him and two older brothers in music classes at the Kehala Jacob synagogue. Goodman said he was given the clarinet because it was the smallest instrument and he was the smallest child. The Goodman boys moved on to Hull House, which had a more accomplished youth band. He was introduced to jazz when his brother, Louis, brought home a record by clarinetist Ted Lewis. Goodman quickly learned to emulate the recording, and Louis Goodman convinced the manager of a local vaudeville house to put his kid brother onstage as a novelty act. Unpaid for that performance, Goodman was called back in a few weeks and received five dollars, his first professional payday.

Goodman began to take lessons from Chicago Symphony clarinetist Franz Schoepp, who probably donated his time to Hull House.

Others in the class included two of the finest clarinetists in jazz, Jimmy Noone and Buster Bailey. It was in these classes that Goodman synthesized in his mind the techniques of classical music with the free-flowing lyricism of jazz and conceived his unfailing belief that swing and harmony were inseparable.

In 1925, Goodman quit Harrison High School, where one of his classmates was Arthur Goldberg, and took a job at age sixteen with Ben Pollack's band. He cut his first record with the band in 1926. He showed at an early age the disdain with which he held almost all other musicians by abruptly quitting Pollack and going to work with Red Nichols and the Five Pennies, where he also quit. Goodman moved to New York, where he found steady work in theater orchestras and on radio shows.

In 1934 Goodman was offered a chance to form his own band for a new nightclub being opened by Broadway impresario Billy Rose. The club closed after a year, but Goodman's big break came when his band was selected as one of three to play on a nationally broadcast radio program, *Let's Dance*.

In 1935, Goodman took the band on a tour, which was a mixed success. The brand of swing they performed fell flat when they were booked into a Denver dance hall that charged customers by the dance. The owner wanted songs that lasted no longer than a minute, and he wanted the dreary sweet stuff that enticed his customers to fork out another dime. He listened to Goodman's band swing and fired them.

The band's final stop on the tour was at the Palomar in Los Angeles, where the band's swing records had been selling well. Goodman, frightened at the prospect of another irate owner's wrath, began to play the syrupy stuff, but there was no reaction from the crowd. Finally, one of the band members, perhaps Krupa or trumpet star Bunny Berrigan, convinced Goodman to play swing. The audience went wild. The band's next show was in Chicago's Congress Hotel, where Goodman wondered if swing would be as popular in the decorum of a hotel as it was in a California dance pavilion filled with teenagers. It was.

It was also in Chicago that Benny Goodman became the first to put blacks into a white orchestra in America. He brought pianist Teddy Wilson in to join with him and Krupa as part of the trio that he broke out of the big band during his performances. Later, he formed the Benny Goodman Quartet by adding Lionel Hampton on vibes. Although Wilson and Hampton often had to sleep in Negro hotels and eat in different restaurants from other band members, the public rapidly accepted the integration of a major band. Some, such as Hampton, credited Goodman with opening the way for Jackie Robinson to integrate baseball. That may have been an overstatement, but in the late 1930s the big bands drew fans with the same fervor as sports and most Americans knew not only the names of the bandleaders but the first, second, and third trumpet players.

In 1937, Goodman sold out the Paramount Theater in New York as twenty-one thousand people attended the first day's five shows. A year later it was Carnegie Hall and immortality.

Goodman continued to form bands during World War II and later tried halfheartedly to capture the sound of the new bebop. Then he turned to classical music and made several successful recordings, but his reign as the king of swing was a memory. In 1962 he put together remnants of his old band and made a tour to Russia sponsored by the State Department. The reissues of his recordings continued to sell.

Benny Goodman died in 1986 at the age of seventy-seven, but he remains an icon of American music.

■ 6

THE INVENTOR OF JAZZ:
JELLY ROLL MORTON

The tragedy that shortened the lives of some of America's greatest jazz performers usually had to do with drugs and booze. Bix Beiderbecke drank himself to death. Billie Holiday and Charlie Parker overdosed. The list could fill pages. But the pathetic demise, the depreciation of his work, and the untimely death of Jelly Roll Morton was basically due to his big mouth.

Jelly Roll Morton was arrogant and pompous, flashed a diamond in his incisor, and when times were good splashed them all over his vests and shirts. He was a loner and enjoyed little camaraderie with the great jazzmen of his age. Louis Armstrong once recalled him as that "boy who went to California in the early days." He did not dedicate his life to his music. He preferred hustling pool. He promoted boxing matches. He ran a hotel and a dance hall. He opened a tailor shop. He performed in blackface in minstrel shows and he worked for a music publisher. In his spare time, he was a pimp.

He infuriated fellow musicians by claiming that he had invented jazz. And he shortened his span of popularity by refusing to play anything but the laid-back music of the New Orleans bordellos, where he first began to play and write some of the jazz compositions that would move the music from the realm of dancing, listening, and marching to the form of art.

"Jelly Roll Morton proved jazz could be an art," said Howard Reich. "He was the first person to write out jazz music note for note the same way Beethoven wrote symphonies and Chopin wrote piano sonatas. It had never been done before. Jelly Roll Morton was Duke Ellington's hero. Without Jelly Roll Morton there would be no 'Black, Brown and Beige,' and all the great pieces Ellington wrote. There would be no Wynton Marsalis's 'Blood in the Fields,' which won the Pulitzer Prize in 1997."

For nearly forty years after his death in 1941, Jelly Roll Morton was remembered mostly for being a foppish character who wrote such jazz greats as "Alabama Bound," "Milenburg Joys," "The Pearls," and the "King Porter Stomp" (which Benny Goodman appropriated as his own), and then spent the rest of his life telling everyone how important he had been. His most outrageous and embarrassing moments came in 1938, after the *Ripley's Believe It or Not* radio show labeled W. C. Handy as the originator of jazz and blues.

Morton wrote to *Downbeat* magazine, "It is evidently known, beyond contradiction, that New Orleans is the cradle of jazz and I, myself, happened to be the creator in 1902."

At the time, Morton was in musical exile, playing in a worn-out Washington club where his audience fortunately included Alan Lomax, the curator of the Library of Congress archives of American folk song. Lomax recorded Morton playing his music, as well as his imitations of just about every New Orleans jazz figure along with a running commentary on his life and his music. Lomax's book *Mister Jelly Roll* became one of the most important pieces of jazz history and literature.

Despite his outlandish claims, it is now clear that Morton, like Armstrong, was a seminal figure in jazz.

When "Jelly Roll said that he wrote his first jazz tunes in 1902, or that he used scat-singing as far back as 1907, there is not only no proof to the contrary, but Jelly's own considerable accomplishments in themselves provide reasonable substantiation," wrote jazz historian Gunther Schuller.

Jelly Roll Morton, who was born Ferdinand LeMenthe, began playing piano in the "sporting houses" of New Orleans's Storyville crib district at the turn of the century. He was a Creole—"My folks was all Frenchmans"—and from the beginning kept aloof from the African American offspring of slaves, who he regarded as beneath him socially and musically. Morton began playing all sorts of instruments as a child, moving from the harmonica to the guitar and finally the piano, in which he was given lessons and, unlike many of his contemporaries, was able to read music and understand the notations.

Morton's pomposity may have been raised a notch by his status as a piano "professor" in white sporting houses, where he earned one dollar a night and big tips. Piano players enjoyed a special status over horn blowers such as Buddy Bolden, who set the standard for Joe Oliver and Louis Armstrong. At any rate, Morton didn't associate much with his jazz compatriots.

Morton left New Orleans and tried New York, then California, where he was the first to introduce the New Orleans style of jazz to the West Coast, and finally wound up in Chicago in 1922. Work was plentiful, but Morton never could achieve the kind of bandleader status of Oliver or Jimmy Noone. But he did produce a set of recordings that competed with Louis Armstrong's "Hot Fives" as the most influential in American jazz. Morton's recordings with his Red Hot Peppers epitomized what New Orleans music, as perfected and played in Chicago, was all about. The delicate balance between composition and improvisation, the undeniable sense of swing—these elements pervaded pieces such as "Black Bottom Stomp" and established Morton as the preeminent jazz composer.

Morton moved to New York in 1929, but his career was in an irreversible free fall. The big bands were in and the small groups were out. Harlem musicians ridiculed him. He lost his recording contract with Victor. During the Depression he worked in pit orchestras. He left his wife, Mabel, nearly destitute and moved to Washington, where he worked for "coffee and cakes." Finally in 1940, he drove to California in his Lincoln while towing his Cadillac. He had asthma and probably a variety of other circulatory problems. Lomax details the pitiful notes he wrote to Mabel in New York, enclosing five or ten dollars when he had it. He died in the summer of 1941. Kid Ory and Papa Mutt Carey were two of the pallbearers. Duke Ellington was appearing at the Mayan Theater in Los Angeles but didn't attend the funeral.

In 1997 Jelly Roll Morton was inducted into the Rock and Roll Hall of Fame, which may be stretching things just as Jelly did in claiming that he invented jazz. But as the first full-fledged composer of jazz his influence and reputation are immeasurable.

7 ▪

ROLLIN' STONE:
MUDDY WATERS

The sound was only heard, Muddy Waters told biographer James Rooney, in an area of about one hundred miles surrounding Clarksdale, Mississippi. "It seems funny, but Texas is a different sound from Mississippi. Mississippi and Louisiana are close to together, then over in Alabama and Georgia it's a whole lot different. Well, that Delta sound is the one I brought to Chicago."

The sound was blues. Not the languid, lamenting blues that came out of New Orleans but one with a hard rhythm accentuated by a slow, deep beat and the Muddy Waters voice, which combined range, depth, and subtlety in an inimitable fashion to blend with his guitar and the drums and harmonica that accompanied him.

And then he added amplification and it became Chicago blues, one of the most influential forms of music in the last half century. *Chicago Tribune* arts critic Howard Reich said,

> When Muddy Waters came up from the Mississippi Delta as part of the great black migration, he was no longer playing at fish fries and small parties. He began in dance halls and clubs and an acoustic guitar couldn't be heard over all the noise and occasional fights. He switched to an electric guitar and the blues became big city music. He led the whole blues revolution that has carried through the 1980s and 1990s. Everybody loves the blues today. They may not be hearing the authentic

blues that Muddy Waters wrote back in the Forties, but it's blues.

The evolution of music from Muddy Waters touches almost everything today. He was the first electric bandleader to tour England in the late 1950s during the folk-music craze, repelling most white audiences as he did in America. But young musicians such as Mick Jagger and Keith Richards began to emulate him, and when they formed their band they named it after a Muddy Waters song, "Rollin' Stone." Bob Dylan's rock song "Like a Rolling Stone" and the rock newspaper *Rolling Stone* also took their names from Muddy's original composition.

By the 1970s several major rock guitarists—Eric Clapton, Jimmy Page, and Johnny Winter, to name a few—credited Waters for their musical interpretation.

But no one could sound like Muddy Waters. "They say my blues is the hardest blues in the world to play," he said in a 1978 interview. His blues sounded simple, but it was so wrapped in decades of Negro music from the Delta that unless someone had heard Robert Johnson or played with Son House, studied the recordings of Memphis Minnie and Blind Lemon Jefferson—as Waters had—his sound was impossible to replicate.

Muddy Waters began making musical sounds at age three, playing harmonica at his grandmother's home on a plantation near Clarksdale. He was born McKinley Morganfield, but his grandmother named him Muddy because he was always playing in the mud. Childhood playmates called him "Muddy Waters." By his early teens he was playing the harmonica and guitar at country picnics, and in his twenties he was leading his own band. Jazz and blues historian Alan Lomax recorded Waters in 1941 for the Library of Congress, and after hearing the records, Waters decided to head north and see if he could make any recordings that would sell.

In 1944 he began playing the electric guitar and, with Jimmy Rogers on second guitar, Little Walter on harmonica, and Baby Face Leroy on drums, became one of the most popular blues attractions in the black clubs. Then another of those fortuitous pairings that mark American musical history occurred. Waters signed with a record company called Aristocrat, which was shortly renamed after its owners, Leonard and Phil Chess. Chess Records became the foremost distributor of music that would revolutionize blues and inaugurate rhythm and blues and modern rock, distributing such artists as Chuck Berry, Bo Diddley, and Howlin' Wolf. Its leading artist in the early 1950s was Muddy Waters. Willie Dixon was the Chess musical director, and he persuaded Waters to try some of the songs he had written; one of them was the classic "Hoochie Coochie Man."

Waters began touring in the 1950s, still working black clubs, but his trip to Europe won him recognition, and he was invited to play his blues at Carnegie Hall in 1959. In 1960 he appeared at the Newport Jazz Festival, where he performed his big hit "Got My Mojo Working."

Although black artists had broken through in the rock-and-roll 1950s, Waters didn't. Biographer James Rooney wrote, "Muddy Waters' music was too rough, too real and solid, to get swept into the national frenzy. He didn't try to change his music. It was the only music he could play."

During the 1970s Waters achieved the recognition other musicians had been according him for decades. He won six Grammy Awards and was featured in a film. He never earned the six-figure concert fees that lesser musicians picked up nightly, but his later recordings, never as vivid and original as his earlier work with Chess, sold better than anything he had done. He lived in suburban Westmont and in 1978 declared, "This is the best point of my life." Waters, who died in 1983 at the age of sixty-eight, made "Chicago blues" an indelible part of the American sound.

8

THE KING:
NAT COLE

The early 1950s were the last dominant period of the record in American music. Portable phonograph players and 45s with their fat spindles could be found in the home of every teenager in the country. The record store was a weekly if not daily ritual for American youth. Radio was struggling with its identity after the advent of television and had not yet become a total music environment. Although musicians would become millionaires throughout the century with the sale of cassettes and then compact discs, those sales were heavily influenced by the celebrity of television performances and the rejuvenation of live appearances at outdoor and indoor concert arenas. In the early 1950s, it was simply the record that drove star status. The age of the crooner had wiped out the popularity of big bands. Although the popularity of the male singer began in the 1930s with Bing Crosby, it exploded during the World War II years with the social phenomenon of Frank Sinatra and the bobby-soxers. But as the 1950s approached, Crosby's easy baritone was getting tedious and Sinatra's career was in remission. A new group of various Italian Americans, Perry Como, Frankie Laine, Tony Bennett, and Vic Damone, was rising in the record charts. But the most enduring and in many ways most unique voice of the era belonged to the son of a Chicago minister who coincidentally was one of the best jazz pianists in the world, Nat "King" Cole.

Jazz purists still flinch at the mention of his name. They never forgave Cole, who was *Esquire* magazine's top jazz pianist of 1946, for his apostasy in shifting to pop singing. But while the music of other jazz greats who surpassed anything Cole could ever have achieved is listened to at the end of the millennium only as an academic or exotic experience, the ballads Cole sang are still used in new movies and his voice flows through almost every nostalgic re-creation of the fifties.

Nat Cole's music haunts a generation, which is fitting since "haunting" was quite a favorite description of his hits "Nature Boy" and "Mona Lisa." Cole's voice also was described as velvet, satin, husky, hoarse, furry, and sugarcoated.

Although a latter day balladeer, Johnny Mathis, could ape the sound, no one could match the rhythm and the precise phrasing that was Cole's trademark. He never tried to capture the sound of most black vocalists, who customarily mimicked the sounds of the instruments backing them, for instance, slurring like a trombone. Undoubtedly, the most distinctive part of Cole's appeal was that as a vocalist he approached a song as a pianist, which is how he started.

He was Nathaniel Adams Coles when he was born in 1919 in Montgomery, Alabama, and moved to Chicago at age four when his father became minister of the True Light Baptist Church. He began playing the church organ as a child and formed his first band, the Rogues of Rhythm, while attending Wendell Phillips High School. He cut his first record for Decca in 1936, accompanying his brother, Eddie, on bass. His style already was evocative of Earl Hines, who had been a South Side musical legend during Cole's boyhood. After finishing high school Cole joined a traveling company of the revue *Shuffle Along*. When the show went broke in Long Beach, California, he fed himself by playing solo piano in "practically every beer joint in Los Angeles, never making more than five dollars a night."

The owner of the Swanee Inn urged Cole to form a trio in 1937. He hired guitarist Oscar Moore and bassist Wesley Prince, dropped the *s* from his name, and they became the King Cole Trio. It was this format—piano, guitar, bass—that became the standard small group that filled nightclubs in America until the heyday of rock in the 1960s. Oscar Peterson, who virtually lived at Chicago's London House during the 1950s and 1960s, along with Art Tatum and Horace Silver, were disciples of both Cole's piano style and his trio format.

In reviewing a reissue of the trio's recordings in 1992, *Chicago Tribune* editor Jack Fuller, who doubled as jazz critic, wrote, "The cool ease of his style, which reflected and was reflected in his perfect vocal phrasing, managed to make some of the abstract harmonic discoveries of the emerging bebop revolution accessible to large audiences." Cole never grew to the heights in jazz that many were predicting for him after a tipsy patron demanded one night that he sing. Cole sang "Sweet Lorraine," and kept on singing. The trio cut a record for the fledgling Capitol label in 1943. It was "Straighten Up and Fly Right," a novelty tune that Cole had written in 1937 and later sold for fifty dollars, so that when it became a big hit he got nothing.

In 1946, he added strings to an arrangement of a new song written by Mel Torme, "The Christmas Song." Then came "Nature Boy," and Nat Cole was on the way to selling 50 million records before his death from lung cancer at age forty-five in 1965.

Aesthetically, his last hits, "Rambling Rose" and "Those Lazy-Hazy-Crazy Days of Summer," were not in the same league with "Route 66" or "I Love You for Sentimental Reasons," but in a business that is as fickle as public taste, he remained on top for twenty-five years.

He also broke down racist walls that were as high in the 1950s as they had been a generation earlier. His was the first Negro jazz group to have a sponsored network radio show. In 1956 he became the first Negro to have his own weekly television show, on NBC. Cole was allowed to do little but play, sing, introduce his mandatory white guest, and say good night. After sixty-four weeks the show was canceled because the network could not find a national sponsor for a show starring a black man.

"There is a lot more integration in the actual life of the United States than you will find on television," he once said. "I notice they always have integration in the prison scenes on television."

When he and his second wife, Maria, moved into a sixty-five thousand dollar home in the Hancock Park section of Los Angeles in 1950, they would awake in the morning and find signs posted on the lawn reading, NIGGER HEAVEN and GET OUT! A lawyer for some of his neighbors told Cole, "We don't want undesirable people coming here." Cole replied, "Neither do I."

In 1956 at the Municipal Auditorium in Birmingham, Alabama, six white men rushed the stage and attacked Cole in the middle of a performance. He was only slightly injured but canceled an Atlanta appearance and never performed in the South again. Cole, like Armstrong and other black musical celebrities, was never strident enough for the militant blacks of the 1950s, but he was a life member of the NAACP and gave thousands of dollars to civil rights groups.

Some might dispute Cole's inclusion on a list of Chicago figures, but unlike Walt Disney, who needed Hollywood's motion picture factories to achieve his unique influence, or Jack Benny, whose career was built on the radio networks, Cole was clearly a Chicago product. His voice was his own, his phrasing nurtured by singing in his father's church. The unique rhythm and harmony in his voice came from growing up on the South Side, where jazz great Eddie Condon once declared, "You could throw a horn in the air at 35th and Calumet and it would blow itself."

Hardly a day or certainly a week goes by that someone somewhere on radio or television or in the movies isn't playing "Unforgettable," which is fitting for Nat "King" Cole.

9

PRIMA BALLERINA:
RUTH PAGE

When Ruth Page took her final pirouette Chicago arts critic Richard Christiansen wrote, "For more than 70 years she had been a constant factor in dance circles, a legendary figure who was always there, and the dance world without her was unimaginable."

For much of the century, for Chicago and the Midwest, without Ruth Page the dance world would not have existed. As a dancer and choreographer, Ruth Page was one of the pioneers of ballet in America. In the 1930s, with partner Bentley Stone, she created *Frankie and Johnny*, one of her most enduring ballet achievements, inspired by the barroom ballad of love, betrayal, and revenge. She was also known for *Hear Ye, Hear Ye*, a 1934 ballet with a score by Aaron Copland, and *Billy Sunday*, a 1948 dance production derived from the life of the evangelist who was memorialized in "Chicago" ("the town that Billy Sunday could not shut down").

"She was the first to do contemporary folk ballet, which was quite fresh and novel at the time," Christiansen said. "She was, as a choreographer, one of the best story tellers in dance. She loved story ballet, *Nutcracker, Romeo and Juliet*."

It was Ruth Page who arranged the American debut of Rudolf Nureyev after he fled the Soviet Union in 1962. Her role in American dance, if not dominant, was more varied and spanned a greater period than any other figure in ballet.

She performed with Anna Pavlova's classical ballet, with Sergey Diaghilev's avant-garde Ballets Russes, and with German expressionist moderns.

She danced in opera houses around the world and performed at the coronation of Emperor Hirohito in 1928. She danced in Moscow in 1930.

Page was born in Indianapolis in 1899. She was taken at age five to see Pavlova's company perform, and she recalled in 1977, "After my mother took me to see Pavlova in Indianapolis, I never wanted to be anything but a dancer and a choreographer." Her parents encouraged the young girl's interest in dance and invited Pavlova to be a guest in their home, which led to Page's brief tour with the great Russian ballerina in 1914.

Page first appeared in Chicago in 1919, with the Chicago Grand Opera Company in a production of Russian dancer Adolph Bolm's *The Birthday of Infanta*. She continued on for several years as première danseuse with Bolm's Ballet Intime company.

During a tour in Chicago, Page met a young lawyer, Thomas Fisher, whom she married in 1925, when she also became première danseuse and ballet mistress of the Ravinia Opera Company. She continued to dance for Bolm and Chicago Allied Arts and then formed the Page-Stone Ballet Company, which toured the United States for nearly a decade and was the first American ballet company to tour South America. It was the first of her many unsuccessful efforts to create an enduring ballet company in Chicago.

In 1928, Page danced the role of Terpeschore in the world premiere of Stravinsky's *Apollo*, months before George Balanchine created his version.

"If you watch the old films of her, she was a firecracker as a dancer, engaging and vivacious," Christiansen said.

When Rudolf Nureyev made his first American appearance on stage in 1962, following his defection from the Kirov Ballet to the West, he chose to dance the grand pas de deux from *Don Quixote* as a guest artist with the Ruth Page Chicago Opera Ballet at the Brooklyn Academy of Music. He later appeared at the Civic Opera House. To Page's sorrow, none of the troupes she founded lasted, and Ballet Chicago, which she began in 1974 with generous funding, foundered amid internal disputes over repertory and leadership and closed in 1978.

In 1965 she staged a production of *The Nutcracker* that continued until 1997 as an annual Christmas event.

Until she was eighty-seven, Page took a dance class every day, even though she had not performed publicly since the early 1950s.

She founded the Ruth Page Foundation School of Dance, which after her death at ninety-two continued to draw more than four hundred children and adult students regularly. In her lifetime Ruth Page choreographed more than one hundred ballets and danced in thousands. But, as Christiansen wrote at her death, "In the end, however, Page's greatest gift to the ages may have been herself."

10

FAN-TASTIC
SALLY RAND

When the 1933 "Century of Progress" World's Fair opened during the bleakest days of the Depression, its sponsors hoped millions of Americans would come to be uplifted by the promises of scientific advances: automobiles with glistening chrome and luxury interiors, kitchens with modern appliances, and bathrooms that seemed like spaceships to many Americans still using outdoor plumbing. And millions of Americans did come to the Century of Progress.

They came to see Sally Rand.

At century's end there is nothing novel or, for the most part, even interesting about performers taking their clothes off. Cable television offers nudity in movies throughout the day. Topless dancing has been part of Las Vegas, and elsewhere, for four decades. Nudity in the theater is common. Nudity is boring.

But in the 1930s movie stars weren't allowed to embrace lying down. The sight of a man's bare chest was risqué. This was an America whose moralist traditions had just given the nation a dozen years of Prohibition. There were of course bawdy burlesque houses and private clubs where, then as now, all sorts of perversity could pass for entertainment. But Sally Rand was more than a stripper. She actually rescued the provocative dance from striptease joints and made its derivative forms respectable for legitimate theater.

Helen Gould Beck was born in 1904 in Missouri and went into show business as a teenage chorus girl in Kansas City. She later joined a vaudeville company featuring Eddie Cantor and George Jessel and began taking singing, acting, and dancing lessons, hoping to break into silent films. Rand said her stage name was chosen by Hollywood director Cecil B. DeMille from a Rand McNally atlas on his desk.

After working briefly as an acrobat with the Ringling Brothers circus, Rand formed a dance troupe and was a regular in Chicago speakeasies prior to the 1933 World's Fair. She said it was some moth-eaten ostrich feathers she saw in a costume shop that inspired her to create the fan dance, which, in turn, created a nationwide sensation.

She got a job at the fair's "Streets of Paris" concession after staging a stunt as Lady Godiva, riding through the concession with fake long tresses covering some of her. When Rand danced to the strains of DeBussy's "Clair de Lune" she twirled the fans, giving the audience only the briefest glances of her naked body, but it was enough to bring the Chicago police, who arrested her for indecency.

In an early landmark ruling on obscenity, Judge Joseph B. David denied the city's request for an injunction to stop the fan dance. "Some people would like to put pants on horses," the judge remarked. "This court holds no brief for the prurient or ignorant. Let them walk out if they wish. If you ask me, they are just a lot of boobs come to see a woman wiggle with a fan." The judge concluded that the Constitution also protects the rights of boobs.

Rand continued her dance and earned five thousand dollars a week during the fair's peak. She continued earning top dollar, dancing until a 1978 heart condition ended the fan dance, which she said she had changed "not a whit, not a step, not a feather" since she shocked the country forty-five years earlier.

In the 1930s, when her popularity was at its crest, she made repeated appearances before civic groups on behalf of various causes such as the antifascist forces in the Spanish Civil War. She was married three times and had one son, who she raised in Glendora, California, where the woman who once shocked the nation was president of the PTA.

■ ■ ■ VIII

LITERATURE'S
TOP TEN

In 1917, H. L. Mencken pronounced loftily that Chicago was the literary capital of the world. Almost everything Mencken pronounced was not only lofty but accepted by that certain segment of America that considered itself thoughtful if not quite intellectual. Chicago, of course, never questioned anyone or anything that equaled its own remarkable view of itself.

There probably never was a literary capital of America during the twentieth century that rivaled the New England renaissance of the 1850s, which produced Emerson, Hawthorne, Longfellow, etc. But Chicago can surely claim that it influenced some of the great American writers of the century, who in turn influenced almost everyone else. With the exception of Faulkner and his southern offspring as a separate class, almost every notable writer of the first half of the century had some relationship with Chicago.

Sinclair Lewis only drank here, but his portraits of midwestern provincialism were inspired by Edgar Lee Masters and Sherwood Anderson, who wrote *Spoon River Anthology* and *Winesburg, Ohio*, respectively, while they lived in Chicago after its lusty turn of the century. Edna Ferber's Pulitzer Prize novel, *So Big*, was written in Chicago, and the climax of *Showboat* was set here. Some of F. Scott Fitzgerald's most haunting passages almost mystically describe his train rides through Chicago, which he imagined as a geographical and metaphorical link between St. Paul and the glittering East, where neither he nor Jay Gatsby ever escaped their midwestern awe of the very rich.

Others came to Chicago only to jeer, but A. J. Liebling, the incomparable press critic and boxing aficionado, is most memorable for sneering, "Second City."

Of the writers that can be clearly identified with Chicago, there are several categories. Some of them were born in Chicago. Many of them moved to Chicago. Some of them passed through briefly. Many of them wrote about Chicago when they were here. Others wrote about Chicago after they departed. Some never wrote about Chicago at all, but their writing was influenced by what they saw, what they learned, and what they did and felt in Chicago.

Mostly, they were influenced by Chicago itself. Literary scholars have argued that Chicago's consuming passion with making money created one of the great themes of twentieth-century American literature. Chicago, as the cosmopolitan and libertine "painted lady," was an oasis of creative freedom in a wheat-topped sea of Heartland provincialism and Protestant morality. Chicago was the rail center that merged the immigrants of Europe with the gold seekers of the frontier, the pseudocontinental culture of the East with the manifest destiny of the West, the hogs and cattle of the Great Plains with the supper tables of America. It had whorehouses and churches and saloons and theaters and gamblers and pimps and some of the richest men in America. There were scoundrels in every category.

It was all new, and it would take new forms of literature to tell its story.

Scholars debate whether the many authors who made Chicago famous (or were made famous by Chicago) created the naturalist or realist or modernist or humanist or determinist form of American literature. In retrospect, it might be labeled urban literature.

What was real and modern about so much of the work by Chicago writers was its social themes, its discoveries of commonplace life and death and simple existence in the new metropolis of the twentieth century. It is no accident that the first realist city novel was about Chicago or the first muckraking novel was set in the stockyards, or that the first books about the nouveau-riche capitalists were about men who manipulated the grain markets, men who dreamed of giant monopolies in transportation and electric power with no remorse for the consumers, or men who used up everything but the oink, including their workers.

This was not simply new fiction. It was the new America, and it was born in Chicago. It was not by mistake that Chicago writers explored the ethnic traditions of the Irish, Poles, and Jews. This was what Chicago gave them.

From Theodore Dreiser's *Sister Carrie* to Saul Bellow's *Herzog*, Chicago provided literary innovation and experiment in the American Century. Its writers seldom stayed here. They did not win every Pulitzer or Nobel Prize, but they copped more than their share. Some of them inarguably rank at the top of American literature, while the work of others receives revisionist reviews. Carl Sandburg's "Chicago" is eternal, but modern critics do not rate him as much of a poet. Some historians believe Hemingway was the father of most current literature; others claim he had no more style than a competent second-grader. Dreiser's writing was clumsy and his books are not what current critics would call "page-turners." James T. Farrell's Studs Lonigan books are just too repetitious for moderns.

What writers can Chicago truly claim? Willa Cather wrote here, but her great books depicted the Nebraska frontier. Hemingway wrote of wars and bullfights and courage and only mentioned Chicago as a place where one of his heroes got gonorrhea during a cab ride in Lincoln Park. Dreiser moved to New York to write his Chicago novels. Richard Wright moved to New York and then Paris. Nelson Algren spent his final years in New Jersey. Saul Bellow wrote as much in New York as in Chicago and finally, at age seventy-eight, moved to Boston.

What makes them Chicago authors? From Dreiser to Bellow there is the physical quality of Chicago. Both men, and Farrell and Algren as well, brought realism with their descriptions of the city and the streets and the people. But there was another quality, the city on the make, the city of the hustle, the conniving, cynical side of twentieth-century America, just as evident in Hemingway and just as powerful in Wright, that is the authentic Chicago literary legacy.

Certainly no American city is better depicted in twentieth-century literature. "What other American city do you get such a geographic sense of from its writers?" noted John Blades, a longtime *Chicago Tribune* book editor and critic. "Chicago's writers made it a city of neighborhoods." Farrell's South Side and Algren's Division Street, Mr. Dooley's Archer Avenue saloon, and Bellow's forays into

Humboldt Park provided a sense of Chicago that was unique in American literature.

And the hookers and gamblers and traders and immigrants and housewives and fathers and bankers and professors and junkies and politicians and peddlers and cops and killers gave to America a glittering array of literature produced by a gathering of writers unmatched by any other city and few countries.

PAPA:
ERNEST HEMINGWAY

There are only two questions to resolve in ranking the Chicago writers who had the greatest influence on the American Century: Does Ernest Hemingway, who wrote of wars in Europe and bullfights in Spain and lions in Africa, qualify as a Chicago literary figure because he was born and grew up in Oak Park? And if he qualifies, was his impact greater than that of anyone else?

The answers are yes and yes.

Chicago's literary history is so rich that one could demand Theodore Dreiser occupy the top position for his pioneering urban novel *Sister Carrie*. Or Richard Wright, whose *Native Son* arguably opened the door to the civil rights movement in 1950s America. Certainly Bellow's body of work, recognized by a Nobel Prize in 1976, provided the most cerebral explorations of human interaction.

But if Hemingway is a Chicago writer, he has to be on top. Where, of course, Papa always viewed himself.

Hemingway was born in 1897 in Oak Park, separated by a boulevard and a culture from the saloons and bawdy houses of neighboring Chicago. He was raised with the same bourgeois Middle Western attitudes of self-reliance and preordination that produced so many of Chicago's great figures, as well as its literary rebels. The same disdain for complacent society that marked the modernist vision of Sherwood Anderson and Sinclair Lewis was embodied in Hemingway. There was also the love affair with naturalism, the bonds between the rich soil and the cold streams, and the prosperity of the American Heartland still stronger at the turn of the century than any fascination with the technology bursting loose all over Chicago.

Hemingway's intellectual rebellion against his parents—the domineering matriarch and his ultimately suicidal father—was also a rebellion against social traditions as much as Upton Sinclair's indictment of meatpackers and Dreiser's dissection of corrupt corporations. Chicago writers, the youthful Hemingway among them, were in the swirl of a new social experiment.

"Chicago was a battleground," the critic Alfred Kazin wrote. "And thanks to both Jane Addams's Hull House and the rise of social-science investigation at the new University of Chicago, Chicago also became—for novelists at the university like Robert Herrick, poets like William Vaughan Moody, liberals like Robert Morse Lovett, pioneer theoreticians of the leisure class like Thorstein Veblen, philosophers like George Herbert Mead and John Dewey—a prime social specimen and social laboratory."

The old rugged individualism that served as a catechism in the farmhouses of the Middle West and the neighborhoods of Chicago was being tested by the largest swarm of immigration in American history. Old values were being cast aside. The language of America was changing.

It changed most of all in 1926 with the publication of *The Sun Also Rises*, Hemingway's novel dealing with disillusioned expatriates in post–World War I France and Spain. The novel was written in the sparse sentences, clipped dialogue, and spare descriptions that became Hemingway's distinctive style. It was praised for being technically and thematically innovative. Some say it is the only Hemingway novel still worth reading.

"A lot of Hemingway doesn't hold up," John Blades judged. "The line is one good book and a lot of good short stories. The rest is marginal. What he did write changed the language."

That was enough. For the next seventy-five years, the majority of writers in America wrote like Hemingway. Everyone wrote like Hemingway. Movies began to sound like Hemingway. Letters from friends sounded like Hemingway. People talked the way Hemingway wrote dialogue, which was only fair since people had always talked that way, but until Hemingway no writer had written dialogue the way people actually spoke.

His biographer, Carlos Baker, stated, "He was an epoch making stylist with a highly original talent who spawned imitators by the score and dealt, almost single-handed, a permanent blow against the affected, the namby-pamby, the pretentious, and the false."

It sounds like an advertisement for the Chicago school of literature. Hemingway did not spend much of his adult life in Chicago. He lived for a while on the 1300 block of North Clark Street, where he courted his first wife, Hadley Richardson, a St. Louis native who had come to Chicago to visit friends when she met Hemingway. After their marriage, using her small trust fund, they set sail for Paris with letters of introduction to the American literary colony living there. The letters were written by Sherwood Anderson, whose style influenced Hemingway, although Hemingway steadfastly refused to ever give Anderson credit. What he did give him before embarking on the Paris adventure was all the canned food he and Hadley had left behind. Anderson was grateful.

In Paris, Hemingway fell under the spell of Gertrude Stein, who also was preaching a new clarity in literature and had published several works. He met Scott Fitzgerald, who was writing *The Great Gatsby*, and began a study of the French impressionists, whose painting styles influenced his writing.

After *The Sun Also Rises*, Hemingway began work on a novel based on his experiences as an ambulance driver in Italy in World War I. It was the bittersweet love story of an American, Frederic Henry, and a British nurse, Catherine Barkley. He called it *A Farewell to Arms*, and a movie version of it is made about every ten years or so, or so it seems. The book was based on Hemingway's infatuation with a nurse, Agnes von Kurowsky, who was not in love with Hemingway. But in his first two novels, Hemingway had created two nonheroic heroes, Jake Barnes and Frederic Henry, who both very much resembled Hemingway.

Hemingway was also Nick Adams in the stories of his Michigan summers, the "Battler" and "Big Two Hearted River" (which even the harshest of critics still praise). He was Harry in "The Snows of Kilimanjaro," which, with "The Short Happy Life of Francis Macomber," are the major trophies of his safari years, and which created for a generation the exotic romance of the great white hunter. And Hemingway was Robert Jordan, the American who went to Spain to blow up a bridge in *For Whom the Bell Tolls*, which was published in 1940.

Hemingway wrote dozens of short stories and several more novels, winning a Pulitzer Prize in 1953 for *The Old Man and the Sea*. He was awarded the Nobel Prize in 1954.

In the 1960s and 1970s, there was a broad reassessment of Hemingway, a common occurrence in American literature. Herman Melville was buried for a century before "Billy Budd" was rediscovered.

Influential critics such as Leslie Fiedler and Dwight McDonald dismissed nearly all of Hemingway's novels, admitting some value in *The Sun Also Rises* and most of his short stories. Glendy Culligan wrote in the *Washington Post*, "Hemingway was finally surpassed by his own imitators." Malcolm Cowley responded, "I wonder what books by which imitators she had in mind."

Malcolm Cowley, in his memoirs, *And I Worked at the Writer's Trade*, supposed that many critics were getting even for Hemingway's persona, which contributed to his enormous celebrity status as much if not more than his writing. Hemingway worked very hard at writing and at playing.

He left Oak Park as a teenager to find newspaper work in Kansas City, volunteered as an ambulance driver in World War I and was wounded in Italy, shot the bravest lions and the biggest water buffalo, killed the big fish that swam in the sea, braved the dangers of the Spanish Civil War, survived plane crashes and gun accidents, married four women and slept with many more, and surely either outdrank or outlived all the imitators whose writing careers were cut short by drinking, living in Key West, or hunting in Africa.

Hemingway always claimed he did the things he did for the experience, so he could write truly about danger and death. Alfred Kazin guessed he did it because he liked to fight, shoot, and fish, and live on the edge. That made him more newsworthy than most of his books. Hemingway was a celebrity like no other American writer had been or would be again. Rock stars, news anchormen, ballplayers, lawyers, and billionaires have far surpassed writers in the galaxy of American public prominence.

The criticism that devastated Hemingway most occurred while he was still alive. His rival, William Faulkner, who won the Nobel Prize four years before Hemingway, was asked by a reporter his thoughts on Hemingway.

> I thought that he found out early what he could do and stayed inside of that. He never did try to get outside the boundary of what he really could do and risk failure. He did what he really could do marvelously well, first rate, but to me that is not success but failure . . . failure to me is the best. To try something you can't do, because it's too much but still to try it and fail, then try it again. That to me is success.

Hemingway believed Faulkner had called him a coward. The strongest conviction of Hemingway's life was to test again and again his own ability to face danger bravely, not fearlessly, for without fear there was no danger, no possibility of being a coward.

This was how he worked out his definition of courage—grace under pressure—the ability to face the great challenges of life and behave properly. It was something his father, who had shot himself, failed to achieve.

On July 3, 1960, in his cabin at Ketchum, Idaho, Ernest Hemingway, convinced he no longer could face the challenges of life, also shot himself.

Whether few or many of his works will be cherished in the next century is uncertain, but Hemingway's value to twentieth-century literature is secure.

Alfred Kazin, in *An American Procession*, wrote, "He put life back on the page, made us see, feel and taste the gift of life in its unalloyed and irreducible reality. . . . To read Hemingway was always to feel more alive."

2

MR. HERZOG:
SAUL BELLOW

Saul Bellow may not have had either the influence on other writers or the macho persona that Ernest Hemingway flashed across his half of the American Century, but from the moment Moses Herzog began composing letters to himself in Bellow's 1964 novel it was clear who was the dominant American writer of the last half century.

Bellow is the antithesis of Hemingway by choice. Hemingway belonged to the Midwest tradition, whose ancestry had gloried in its American purity. Bellow is the leader of the immigrants, particularly first-generation American Jews. Hemingway cleaved himself from the nineteenth-century stylists, eliminating excesses of language and extensive explanations of characters and plotlines. Bellow put it all back, but with a command of twentieth-century language. Hemingway wanted it simple. Bellow sounds simple, but his quest for universal solutions to human conflicts are as complex as the burden he imposed on himself.

Bellow was born in 1915, in Lachine, Quebec where his parents had emigrated from St. Petersburg on the eve of the Russian revolution. In 1924, his father, Abraham, a tailor, moved the family to Chicago, where Bellow attended public grammar schools and Tuley High School. Saul attended the University of Chicago, where he developed his lifelong disdain for academic interpretations and directions about literature. He quit and graduated from Northwestern University in 1937 with a degree in anthropology, a career he considered only briefly.

Bellow taught literature at a small women's college, where his syllabus included *A Farewell to Arms*. During the final years of the Depression he wrote biographies and book reviews for the Federal Writers' Project. During the 1940s he produced his earliest novels—*Dangling Man* (1944) and *The Victim* (1947). Critics made immediate comparisons with Kafka, Sartre, and Camus.

Bellow's first works established him as one of the writers moving away from the modernist tradition of Hemingway, Fitzgerald, Faulkner, John Dos Passos, John Steinbeck, and others of the 1920s and 1930s preoccupied with new social and economic upheavals and the unsettling consequences of both capitalism and communism.

Bellow and his peers were looking at something far more complex, a world recently exposed to the horrors of the Holocaust and the bomb, and a surge of corporate capitalistic success that threatened to destroy individuality. The social concerns of the modernist writers were about class and privilege and exploitation. But it was the threat of David Riesman's "lonely crowd" and William Whyte's "organization man" that molded what critics described as postmodernist writing.

With the publication in 1953 of *The Adventures of Augie March*, Bellow became the premier member of a group that included fellow Chicagoan Nelson Algren and a crowd of Jewish writers: Lionel Trilling, Norman Mailer, Bernard Malamud, and, by the early 1960s, Philip Roth, who like Bellow attended the University of Chicago and who used Hyde Park as a setting for stories and his novel *Letting Go*.

Augie March was not only the story of a Chicago Jew seeking adventure and refusing to be cast as one of the faceless "lonely crowd," it was a vivid description of Chicago's squalor and prosperity, updating the fictional tours taken earlier by Dreiser in *Sister Carrie* and Farrell in the "Studs Lonigan" trilogy.

Augie March was perhaps the most amiable version of Bellow who, like Hemingway, like almost all authors, appears in one form or another in all his antiheroes and heroes. Bellow and his peers and successors of the late twentieth century are far more demanding of a reader than the early writers of the 1920s and 1930s. They are not, as critics observe, easily digestible. And the characters are not necessarily endearing.

As Bellow himself once told the *Paris Review*, "I got very tired of the solemnity of complaint. Obliged to choose between complaint and comedy, I choose comedy as more energetic, wiser and manlier. This is really one reason why I dislike my own early novels. I find them plaintive, sometimes querulous."

Bellow's next work, *Henderson the Rain King*, the story of an "organization man" millionaire who treks off to Africa to find his identity, was published in 1959 and, as is the fate of all authors great and small, was chewed over by critics.

But *Herzog*, published in 1964, was a great critical and commercial success. Much of *Herzog* was written in Tivoli, New York, where Bellow had bought a farm home with an inheritance from his father. Herzog appears as a history professor whose wife has an affair with his best friend and divorces him, causing Herzog to begin a mad, often hysterical, and hilarious correspondence with friends and public figures discoursing on the great issues of the time and for that matter, all time.

Bellow never boasted publicly, as did Hemingway, about taking on the great writers of the past, but with *Herzog* he had. In 1975, *Humboldt's Gift* brought one of those Pulitzers that novelists win as consolation prizes because the board failed to recognize an earlier great work. The Pulitzer board did not award the prize in 1964, which should have gone to *Herzog*. Faulkner was handed a Pulitzer in 1961 for his mediocre *A Fable* after some of his masterpieces of the 1930s had been passed over. Hemingway's *The Old Man and the Sea* was another example of better late than never.

Not that *Humboldt* wasn't worthy. Almost anything Bellow wrote from the 1940s through the 1970s was worth some kind of a prize. He collected three National Book Awards, but the year after *Humboldt* he joined the elite when he won the Nobel Prize. There was little left to conquer, but Bellow's quest continued with *The Dean's December* (1982), *More Die of Heartbreak* (1987), *A Theft* (1989), and *The Bellarosa Connection* (1989).

Bellow taught variously at Princeton, Bard College, Minnesota, and in 1962, returned to the University of Chicago, where he remained until 1993. Then, at seventy-eight, he fell prey to the old Chicago writers' syndrome and left for Boston, where he currently lives.

Bellow married four times, and his Nobel money financed both a lengthy legal fight and a divorce settlement. In a 1985 piece published in the *Chicago Tribune*, Alfred Kazin described meeting him:

> Bellow took himself seriously, in a way that most novelists of the city streets never could. He was the hero of his books, he was their only hero, he was his own hero. In 1942, when I met Bellow—of course in New York—I was astonished by his sense of destiny. He had not yet published a novel. But he was the first writer of my generation who talked of Lawrence and Joyce, Hemingway and Fitzgerald, not as books in the library but as fellow operators in the same business. As I walked him across Brooklyn Bridge and around my favorite streets overlooking the port of New York, his observations transformed my own city to me. He had the gift of making you see the most trivial event in the street because he happened to be there. At the same time he seemed to be measuring the hidden strength of all things in the universe. Over and over again in his fiction the central observer would dwell on the physical hardiness of other people, the thickness of their skins, the strength in their hands, the force of their chests. This was the Chicago note over and over again: The world around us is pure grit.

3 ◼

THE TRAILBLAZER:
THEODORE DREISER

No American writer of stature was ever as generally ignored during his lifetime as Theodore Dreiser. Except for one brief flurry of fortune and fame in the 1920s, Dreiser was neither praised for his trailbreaking early works nor acclaimed in his declining years as a great pioneer in the art of the novel.

The Nobel Prize that he should have won went to Sinclair Lewis, whom Dreiser despised. When he died, most people thought he already was dead. In his native Indiana, he was, if not reviled, certainly far less revered than his older brother, who wrote the 1890s hit, "On the Banks of the Wabash." For two generations after his death he was largely unread except in English departments, where he was studied by literary geographers who trace the explorations of prose from Dante to Doonesbury.

And, as Dreiser whined his entire life, that's not fair. Dreiser's works are no longer readable for aesthetic pleasure or escapist enjoyment. But he is one of the few artists of the century of whom it can be said that he changed everything that came before him and influenced everyone who came after him.

And he thwarted the aspirations of every writer who ever joined in the massive and elusive quest to create the Great American Novel. He wrote two of them.

Dreiser's biographer, W. A. Swanberg, wrote that he was the victim of the most notorious publishing blunder in American history when *Sister Carrie* was tossed into obscurity by its publisher, Double-day and Company, in 1900. Doubleday accepted the book, then got cold feet over its immorality and gloomy realism. Dreiser claimed for years that Doubleday kept all the copies in a cellar and never sold one. Actually, 1,000 copies were printed, 456 were sold, and Dreiser received $68.50 in royalties.

Dreiser later purchased the printing plates, and *Carrie* went through a score of editions through the century, preserving what critics and scholars agree was the first modern naturalist novel. What frightened and angered fin de siècle readers and moralists was the story of Carrie Meeber, a character loosely based on one of Dreiser's sisters, who, finding herself penniless in Chicago becomes the mistress of two men, one an embezzler, and claws to a career as a leading musical comedy star. Readers were outraged that the sluttish Carrie emerges triumphant.

Dreiser's disappointment over *Carrie* sent him into a period of depression and illness while he supported himself as a magazine editor and prolific article writer. He was helped greatly by his older brother, Paul, the composer who had earned a great deal of money on his songs, including the tinny "My Gal Sal," written to honor a Terre Haute madam. Dreiser's next novel, *Jennie Gerhardt* (1911), was also condemned because, like *Carrie*, it was a story of unconventional sexual relationships. Critics and public alike objected to Dreiser's view of people as victims of blind forces and their own uncontrolled passions. He then wrote two books based on the life of Charles Yerkes, who tried to monopolize Chicago's transit system in the 1890s. *The Financier* in 1912 and *The Titan* two years later were better received, but Dreiser was not recognized until H. L. Mencken proclaimed him America's greatest writer in 1917.

Sister Carrie displayed Dreiser's fascination with Chicago and became the first novel that dissected the city as its growth and passions raged in the 1890s. The Yerkes-based books offered a remarkable view of how the city worked, how the upper levels of society, commerce, and finance influenced the lives of the lowliest immigrants. The Yerkes character remarks in *The Financier* that "Chicago is a good place to make money," as clairvoyant a sentence as anyone could write at any time, then and now.

But America's greatest living writer didn't write much else of value until 1925. After years of researching notorious murders, Dreiser found the one that encapsulated his belief that the individual is trapped by his own desires for sex, fame, and fortune (as Dreiser himself was), that society further lures the individual to seek whatever pleasures are available and to take the boldest steps to acquire them.

Nothing seemed more appropriate than the case of Chester Gillette, a drifter who suddenly found himself rising in the shirt-factory business in upstate New York. He had his eye on courting the daughter of the factory owner, except he had already had his hands on a company seamstress, Grace Brown. When Gillette learned Brown was pregnant, he took her boating on a lake and beat her savagely with a tennis racquet and tossed her body into the deep water. Later he confessed and was executed in 1908.

For Dreiser, Chester Gillette became Clyde Griffiths, the most tragic figure of *An American Tragedy*. It was a smash bestseller, the book Dreiser had hoped for all his life, which began with his birth in 1871 in Terre Haute, Indiana, the twelfth child of an impoverished, devoutly Catholic, aloof German immigrant. The combination of poverty and rectitude instilled in Dreiser his hunger for fame and fortune and a rebellion against morality whose rewards he found unsatisfying and humbling.

Dreiser left his Indiana home at sixteen and headed for Chicago, the city that so amazed him he would chronicle its sights and smells in all his early works. He worked on newspapers in Chicago and St. Louis before heading to New York in 1894, where he wrote *Sister Carrie*.

Dreiser grew up to be a somewhat unlikable person, homely, parsimonious, self-absorbed, and petulant. But he possessed a charm that women found endearing, which was fortunate for him, because he found almost every woman irresistible. He was married to Sarah White for forty years and separated for thirty, only occasionally sending her money but using his matrimonial state to avoid permanent relations with the horde of women he attracted. He, like others, flirted with communism in the 1930s. He visited Russia, where his vivid portrayals of the decadence of American society had made him a hero, and he fought with publishers, moviemakers, and friends until he had none.

The critic Joseph Epstein wrote, "Tormented by a childhood dreary almost beyond imagining, later in his life he was not above tormenting others: women, editors, publishers, the most faithful of friends. His many personal problems were not so much interesting as repulsive, many of them had to do with sex."

He once wrote Mencken, according to W. A. Swanberg, promising him five thousand dollars of the Nobel Prize money if Mencken would launch a campaign for him. He offered a few more dollars for Mencken to spread to other possible proponents. Despite his huge income after *An American Tragedy* he seldom visited or helped his siblings, many of whom had helped him through his various illnesses and love affairs. He was, at age thirty-eight, smitten with a seventeen-year-old whose mother, a close personal friend, had to whisk the adolescent off to South Carolina, then to England, to keep her from Dreiser's sexual demands. In his last years, he lived in California churning out the huge, overwritten novels he had always composed. Two novels, *The Bulwark* (1946) and *The Stoic* (1947), were published after his death in Hollywood, California, on December 28, 1945. In 1983, the University of Pennsylvania, the repository of his papers and multitude of letters, published *An Amateur Laborer*, which Dreiser wrote in 1904 describing his crack-up after the commercial failure of *Sister Carrie*.

Although Dreiser, with his characteristic paranoia, had turned viciously on him, Mencken was always steadfast in his declaration of Dreiser's true worth as the father of naturalism and realism. But being Mencken, he did not shy away from an evaluation of Dreiser's style that is as valuable and accurate today as when it was written in 1917:

> Such is the art of writing as Dreiser understands it and practices it—an endless piling up of minutiae, an almost ferocious tracking down of ions, electrons and molecules, an unshakable determination to tell it all. One is amazed by the mole-like diligence of the man, and no less by his exasperating disregard for the case of his readers. A Dreiser novel . . . demands attention for almost a week, and uses up the faculties for a month.

Dreiser began the naturalist-realist literary renaissance in Chicago. He was the pathfinder for Masters, Sandburg, Anderson, Dos Passos, Faulkner, Hemingway, Farrell, Algren, and the entire generation of writers who flourished in the 1920s and 1930s. While his impact on the public did not rival that of some of his literary progeny, he was utterly uncompromising in his creation of a new form of art.

4

NATIVE SON:
RICHARD WRIGHT

During the time Richard Wright was growing up in poverty as the oldest son of a sharecropper, about five hundred blacks were lynched in Mississippi. That averaged about one every two weeks. Some of them were women.

"Richard Wright came from hell," begins the biography by Margaret Walker of the man who became not only the nation's foremost black writer but one of the handful of great literary figures of the twentieth century.

Richard Wright actually came from a crossroads hamlet near Natchez, Mississippi, where he was born in 1908. Young Wright's childhood was generally one of poverty, frustration, and despair. When he was five his father left the family, and when he was not yet ten, his mother became paralyzed. He was sent to live with relatives.

Wright's boyhood left the sensitive child scarred with the tyranny of racism. He would spend his life trying to erase the memories of being treated as a nonhuman. Racist stereotypes in Mississippi depicted blacks as nothing more than menial laborers with little ambition, low intelligence, huge sexual proclivities, and a latent desire to violate white women. Wright's boyhood came during the era of Senator Theodore Bilbo, who, first as governor and later in Washington, became the epitome of southern racism and segregation and the author of a book, *Separation or Mongrelization*. He pledged to "send all 'nigras' back to Africa" and fretted that "many good white men have stooped to 'nigra' women, for which sin God forgives us." He did not mention that he was one of them.

As a boy, Wright had paid little attention to schooling but was a compulsive reader, consuming mysteries and adventure stories, moving on to Mark Twain's Huck Finn and Tom Sawyer, then to the contemporary writings of Dreiser, Hemingway, and Faulkner before fastening on Dostoevsky as an idol.

Unable to tolerate the racial box in which he had been born, Wright, at nineteen, headed for Chicago, where Negroes had been migrating since the end of World War I and lived in a safer, if not necessarily more tolerant, environment. In Chicago, he found work as a busboy in a cafe, a porter, a day laborer, an insurance debt collector, and a substitute worker in the post office. The post office job was, in the Depression of the 1930s, about the best job a black in Chicago could have, and one so many of them kept that by the 1950s almost every postal employee in the city was black. During one period when he was out of work, Wright joined the Communist Party, which was advocating in its many revolutionary facets the freedom of blacks throughout the world. In 1936, Wright got a job with the Federal Writers' Project, an offshoot of the WPA. His 1938 collection of stories, *Uncle Tom's Children*, with graphic descriptions of lynching, won a Story prize. Next, Wright headed where all Chicago writers go to write about Chicago—New York.

Wright was working on a novel that he hoped would reveal to American society how the exploitation of the Negro was responsible for the most violent acts imaginable. Influenced by Dreiser's technique of using reporting as the basis for a novel, he incorporated in his book the story of Robert Nixon, a Chicago Negro who was tried and convicted of raping and killing five women. Chicago newspapers were little better than their southern counterparts, often describing the defendant as a "baboon," which Wright also put into his book, which he called *Native Son*.

The year 1940 was a good one for Adolf Hitler and American literature. Hemingway published *For Whom the Bell Tolls,* Carson McCullers wrote *The Heart Is a Lonely Hunter*, Walter Van Tilburg Clark wrote *The Ox-Bow Incident*, and Thomas Wolfe published *You Can't Go Home Again*.

The most provocative book of the year was *Native Son*.

"The day *Native Son* appeared, American culture was changed forever," wrote critic Irving Howe. "It made impossible a repetition of the old lies. . . . It brought into the open the fear and violence that crippled and may yet destroy our culture."

Wright's protagonist, Bigger Thomas, is reared in a Chicago slum and led by his environment into a world of crime. He is patronized by 1930s left-wing idealists who are the friends of his employer's daughter, who he accidentally murders. In his ensuing flight, he irrationally kills his own girlfriend before he is captured and sentenced to death.

The violence of *Native Son* was stark and pictured with brutal realism what it meant to be black in a white society. His style placed Wright with the naturalists of the earlier part of the century. The book also was a great financial success.

In less than six weeks after its publication, *Native Son* had sold 250,000 copies. It was reviewed with praise and disgust everywhere. It was picked as a Book of the Month Club selection, the first time a book by a black writer had been listed. It remained on bestseller lists for months. It was adapted for the stage in 1941 and had a successful run on Broadway.

Wright's first marriage—to a ballet dancer—ended in divorce. In 1941 he married Ellen Poplar of New York City, and they had two daughters. Wright became increasingly disillusioned with the Communist Party and finally left it. In 1945 he published *Black Boy*, an autobiography. It confirmed him as a major American writer.

His discontent with American society persisted. As a youth he had experienced not only hardship but vicious racial prejudice as well, and as a man he continued to encounter it. In 1946 he and his white wife left the United States to live in Paris.

Wright wrote several novels during the next fourteen years, but they were of little consequence compared with *Native Son* or *Black Boy*. On November 28, 1960, he died in Paris of a heart attack.

Although every author suffers through generational reassessments and periods of disfavor, *Native Son* has had no revisionary abatement. What dissident critics said in 1940 may still be true. The naturalism that was left behind by Bellow and the writers of the 1980s and 1990s does not diminish Wright as it has Dos Passos, Dreiser, Anderson, and many others. If Wright had written nothing but *Native Son*, he would have achieved with one book almost as much as the greatest literary figures achieved with many.

There were some, however, who achieved it with only a few lines.

5

HOG BUTCHER:
CARL SANDBURG

At almost any time during and after his life Carl Sandburg was one of America's best-loved and least-read poets.

After his death in 1967, one critic said if there were a Mount Rushmore for poets Sandburg would be there along with Walt Whitman, Edgar Allen Poe, and Emily Dickinson. Another critic called his work "sentimental rubbish."

Robert Frost called Sandburg a "fraud," and Sandburg thought Frost even worse.

Sandburg wrote many poems, and his notable six-volume life of Abraham Lincoln won him a Pulitzer Prize and the disgust of historians who considered much of the work a fable. Every American who has bothered to get through most of high school has at least a fleeting memory of a teacher standing at the front of the class intoning:

> The fog comes
> on little cat feet.
> It sits looking
> over harbor and city
> on silent haunches
> and then moves on.

Cat lovers seem to remember that verse better than others.

But with the sole exception of a single phrase, "Fog" is what most people remember reading when asked about Sandburg.

Carl Sandburg was born Charlie Sandburg in Galesburg, Illinois, in 1878. His father was a Swedish railroad worker who had changed his name from Danielsson. His father earned six dollars a week and allowed himself one cigar on Saturday night. Even after Sandburg became famous and wealthy, he was known to accept an expensive cigar and clip it into three pieces to prolong the luxury. Part of the myth that he cultured along with his shock of stark white hair (his rival, Robert Frost, affected the same "do") was his love for common things, which made his poetry unique. He always turned down invitations to upscale restaurants by insisting he preferred the common stews and meat loaf specials at restaurants under the "El" tracks. His friends knew he was cheap.

But few literary figures knew the America of their times as well as Sandburg. He began driving a milk wagon at fourteen, swept out barbershops, worked for a tinsmith, and cut ice in the winter. He was an itinerant farmworker in Kansas and Nebraska, washed dishes in Omaha and Denver, worked on a railroad in Missouri, and in a wheat field in Minnesota. At age twenty, he enlisted in the army and was sent to Puerto Rico for the Spanish-American War. He had hopped freight trains all over the Middle West, and just as he guarded his money he hoarded the lyrics of the folk songs that he was to sing so robustly in later years.

It was during these years he began to compose the poems exalting the steelworker, the farmer, the man who worked, as Sandburg did, with rough, gnarled hands. In 1907 he became an organizer for the Social Democratic Party of Wisconsin and then labor editor of the *Milwaukee Journal*. In 1908 he married Lillian Steichen, the sister of famed photographer Edward Steichen. During the 1930s, Steichen spent a great deal of time taking photographs of Sandburg looking thoughtful and, probably to Sandburg, omniscient. Sandburg dashed off a biography of Steichen.

He moved to Chicago in 1912 and became an editorial writer and later a literary critic for the *Chicago Daily News*. In 1914 he published "Chicago." The poem made him a celebrity and prompted a book, *Chicago Poems*, which included "Fog." In 1916, he published another collection, *Cornhuskers*, which also received several prizes. In 1926, *Abra-*

ham Lincoln, the Prairie Years appeared; it was followed the next year by Abraham Lincoln, which was a Book of the Month Club selection. The story of Lincoln's boyhood, Abraham Lincoln Grows Up, was published in 1928.

The Sandburgs, who had lived at 4646 North Hermitage in Chicago, moved to Maywood and then Elmhurst, where most of his Lincoln writing was done. In 1932, like any self-respecting Chicago author, he left the city. He bought a farmhouse in Herbert, Michigan, where he wrote the four-volume Abraham Lincoln and the War Years, which won the 1940 Pulitzer.

In 1945 Sandburg moved to Flat Rock, North Carolina, where he spent more than twenty years in residence as a guitar-strumming, folksinging national icon, gathering awards at a pace equal to Frost as each continued for a half century their claim as America's poet laureate.

Sandburg's poetry was considered avant-garde for a few days in the century's second decade. But its lack of rhythm, use of slang, and choice of topics offended both romantics and true modernists. He was quickly regarded as a traditionalist after the appearance of T. S. Eliot and Ezra Pound. Sandburg's poetry, jumbled in rhythm, allowed words rather than meter to convey his feelings. There was no subtlety. In short, readers could understand him.

Despite the critics, another poetry collection, Complete Poems, won the 1951 Pulitzer, although this could have been another of the Pulitzer board's consolation awards. When Hemingway accepted his Nobel in 1954 he said it should have gone to Sandburg. John Steinbeck said to Sandburg, "All of us could have learned from you and a lot of us did."

Kenan Heise, Chicago historian and the author of fifteen books, said, "Sandburg was remarkable for always re-inventing himself. He wasn't a fraud but he could change. In the 1920s he was pessimistic about the American people, then in the Depression, it's, 'The People, Yes!' When they stopped reading his poetry he became a historian."

If Sandburg's poetry—with the exception of a few classic lines— is mostly unread at the turn of the twenty-first century, it will not lessen his stature as America's minstrel, the first poet of the working man. His peers, Pound and Eliot, may be more lasting, but no writer in America or any other place ever created such an enduring, precise, and prescient vision of a city:

> Hog Butcher for the World,
> Tool Maker, Stacker of Wheat,
>
> . . . .
>
> City of the Big Shoulders

6

THE MUCKRAKER:
UPTON SINCLAIR

Upton Sinclair was not into literature, but he influenced the lives of Americans in a more basic way than any other writer of this or the previous century.

Upton Sinclair was a crank, a rabble-rouser, a reformer, a prohibitionist, a socialist, a pamphleteer, a politician, a feminist, a womanizer, a dreamer, a self-promoter, a publisher, and the prolific author of more than ninety books in ninety years.

Sinclair was born in Baltimore, schooled in New York, worked in Canada, and spent most of his life in California, where he ran for governor, senator, and various other things as a candidate of either the Socialist or Democratic Party.

He arrived in Chicago for the first time on September 20, 1904, and was gone by the end of October that year. But he is one of Chicago's great literary figures because his novel *The Jungle* exposed the stockyards and meatpacking industry, the throbbing heart that made Chicago the great crossroads of America, the "hog butcher of the world," and was the cornerstone of the great industrial metropolis that grew in the twentieth century.

The Jungle was published in 1906 and immediately became the most widely quoted book in America. It was reprinted in seventeen languages. Winston Churchill gave it a two-part review in London. It was, in literary terms, melodramatic, sentimental, and written with little concern for prose purity. In social terms, it was dynamite.

The Jungle told the story of Jurgis Rudkus, who comes to Chicago to work in the packing plants, where he is quickly victimized by real estate frauds and plant supervisors. His wife is forced into prostitution, his daughter is forced to accept the sexual advances of Rudkus's worst enemy, and his son drowns in a mud puddle. The book revealed how the packing plants operated, which no number of denials could disprove. Hogs with cholera and cattle with tuberculosis were routinely slaughtered and sold to the public, and workers toiled in the most unsafe and unsanitary conditions imaginable.

J. Ogden Armour and the other meatpacking barons set out to denounce the book, but no less a figure than President Theodore Roosevelt (who had eaten rancid tinned beef before charging up San Juan Hill) believed the stories and launched the investigation that led to the Pure Food and Drug Act in 1906.

That should have been accomplishment enough for Sinclair, but he spent the next sixty years attacking just about every form of social injustice he uncovered, and he uncovered many of them, sometimes less real than imagined, but always with a fierce determination to change the world into what he wanted it to be, not what it was.

Along the way he advocated free love and even tried it in his first marriage to Meta Fuller, but their candid discussions of her numerous infidelities proved too much a test for his libertine pretenses. He divorced her in 1912 and married Mary Craig Kilbourne, with whom he had conducted an affair before his divorce and who had at least one abortion before their marriage. After her death he took a third wife at age eighty-three. The bride was seventy-nine, and Sinclair declared publicly that their sex life was satisfactory.

In between romances he was churning out social tracts disguised as novels, attacking the morals of a society created by great fortunes in *Metropolis* (1908), the Colorado mining strike in *King Coal* (1917), the oil trust in *Oil* (1927), the newspaper industry in *The Brass Check* (1919), the profitable clergy in *The Profits of Religion* (1918), the Sacco-Vanzetti verdict in *Boston* (1928), and on and on.

He wrote eleven "Lanny Buddy" novels from 1940 to 1953. One of them, *Dragon's Teeth*, won the Pulitzer Prize in 1943. Sinclair never pretended his writing was art. His words and stories were merely weapons in his battle for social change.

He learned from Theodore Dreiser how authors can be exploited by publishers who want to restrict their sales out of fear of social retaliation, poor judgment, or stupidity. In 1916, he bought back all the lithographic plates of his novels and began publishing on his own, increasing the wealth he received as the author.

He never stopped being a busybody, albeit an ebullient and cheerful one. During the battle for the Pure Food and Drug Act he deluged Theodore Roosevelt with so many telegrams and instructions that the president pleaded with Sinclair's publisher, Frank Doubleday, to "Tell Sinclair to go home and let me run the country for a while."

Sinclair decided in 1910 that California would be his home. But he found the politicians running the state no more receptive to his ideas than the Wall Street bankers, the oil and coal magnates, or the meatpackers. So he ran for Congress and the U.S. Senate on the Socialist ticket. In 1934, in the wake of Franklin Roosevelt's overwhelming triumph, and with Republicans everywhere in disrepute, Sinclair declared himself a candidate for the Democratic nomination for governor. He upset the party regular, George Creed, and became the center of the most fascinating political battle in America that year.

His slogan was EPIC (End Poverty in California), and his platform contained all his socialist ideas, but they didn't seem so radical in a state filled with jobless migrants and dominated by a handful of families who controlled the railroads and the real estate and the newspapers, which uniformly predicted Armageddon if Sinclair were elected. Actually, the one that predicted Armageddon was the *New York Times*, but it did so by way of explaining the way the California establishment looked at it.

Sinclair's bid for governor brought on the first political use of advertising men, highly paid by the Hollywood studio chieftains and Harry Chandler, publisher of the *Los Angeles Times*, who was most vindictive and most frightened of Sinclair. The ad men began to use techniques that later, when refined, would turn up in the campaigns of Richard Nixon and Ronald Reagan, and subsequently every American politician. One trick was to hire the dingiest derelicts in Los Angeles and send them into middle-class communities wearing signboards that read, Vote for Upton Sinclair.

Sinclair lost in a three-way race but might have won if the Progressive Party candidate had dropped out. He also might have won had

FDR followed through with a pledge to support the Democratic candidate. But FDR was already planning his second presidential campaign, and Democrat or not, Upton Sinclair was a bit too far-out.

Still, it was Sinclair's strength in California that many believe prompted Roosevelt to push for Social Security in 1936, a program that was the keystone of Sinclair's EPIC. In 1934, *Literary Digest* polled newspapers as to the most influential men in the world. Roosevelt came in first, followed by Adolf Hitler, then Benito Mussolini. Sinclair was fourth.

Leon Harris, who wrote *Upton Sinclair: American Rebel*, may have given Sinclair too much credit for affecting social change in America, but if he overstated his case it was not by much:

> When Sinclair became an important writer . . . there was no minimum wage, no maximum working hours, no employer liability for accidents, no right to bargain collectively, no strong unions . . . no rights for women, no education permitted on birth control or venereal disease, no health insurance or social security or unemployment compensation, and no supervision of banks or stock exchanges or insurance companies. These are only a few of the areas in which Sinclair's propaganda helped to bring about reform.

Sinclair died at age ninety in a New Jersey nursing home. In one of his final interviews he spoke of a new project. "The race problem is of dreadful importance to the country, probably the most urgent thing we have to do at this time."

The year was 1968.

7

THE MAN WITH A GOLDEN PEN:
NELSON ALGREN

Nelson Algren was the culmination of realism in the Chicago school of literature. He walked the streets, talked to the pimps, hookers, addicts, and gamblers. He lived in dives, hopped freights, did jail time, slept with prostitutes, cheated, lied, and robbed.

Algren was a better reporter than James Farrell. He was tougher than Dreiser and Hemingway. Sometimes the poetry of his prose matched Fitzgerald. But most of all, Algren struck that haunting, unattainable note of truth.

Maybe it was because he was a compulsive gambler that the universal truth was so obvious in a simple line like, "Never play cards with a guy named Doc." Or, maybe it was because his dialogue was always real, because he rarely used what he hadn't heard mumbled by one of his downtrodden, underbelly-of-society characters.

Nelson Algren's most powerful novel, *The Man with a Golden Arm*, won him acclaim and the first National Book Award for fiction in 1950. But he gave new lyrical power to the myth and reality of Chicago, updating Sandburg with his prose poem "Chicago: City on the Make."

> "Watch out for yourself" is still the word. "What can I do for you?" still means "What can you do for me?" and that's supposed to make this the most American of cities.
>
> It used to be a writer's town and it's always been a fighter's town.

Most native of American cities, where the chrome-colored convertible cuts through traffic ahead of the Polish peddler's pushcart. And the long, low-lighted parlor-cars stroke past in a single, even yellow flow.

Nelson Algren Abraham was born in Detroit in 1909 and died in Sag Harbor on New York's Long Island in 1981. From 1911 to 1974 he lived in Chicago, making him the most loyal of Chicago's men of letters, even though he eventually was driven off by the city's benign neglect.

Algren's sympathies for the underdogs may have begun as early as 1920, when his family moved from the South Side to the northwest side. He once explained to a *Chicago Tribune* writer, "Do you know what it's like being a White Sox fan when everybody else on the block roots for the Cubs? It's like being a Moslem moving into a Jewish neighborhood."

Somehow, Algren survived and went to the University of Illinois, where he departed in 1931 armed with a license to practice journalism. It was the Depression, and there were no jobs open on either big-city newspapers or small-city newspapers. Algren zigzagged across the Southwest, hopping freights, living on day-labor wages, sleeping in open parks in New Orleans and cheap brothels when he found them. He stole a typewriter from a college in Alpine, Texas, and was sentenced to two years in the penitentiary. But the jails were so full that Algren was released with the promise he would not return. He later would observe that if he had been black he'd have been locked up.

Back in Chicago, he published his first novel, *Somebody in Boots*, based on his experiences drifting through the South. Soon he became infatuated with the Communist Party, which he probably joined during the late 1930s. His first Chicago book, *Never Come Morning* (1942), was about a Polish-American hoodlum, Bruno "Lefty" Bicek, who dreams of a better life as a prizefighter. Algren's lifelong love of boxing and the skill with which he wrote about it made him a rising star, especially to those writers with similar affinities, such as Hemingway and Budd Schulberg, the author of *The Harder They Fall*.

Schulberg would later write that when Algren died he left a "hole in American letters so big that it can never be filled, because like the straight right hand of the fighter he could describe better than any of us—there never was a writer like him . . . who was his own man, an absolute original, both in his writing style and his self-abnegating grungy lifestyle."

Algren was grungy. He dressed like a slob and spent his days at the racetrack, his nights at poker games or in the arms of a variety of women he loved, married, or simply slept with over the years, including his wives, Amanda and Betty, several journalists, countless prostitutes of various races and ethnic origins, actress Geraldine Page, and French writer Simone de Beauvoir, who felt compelled to chronicle their long affair and make it one of the most celebrated of the century.

Algren's final novel, *Walk on the Wild Side*, a Depression-era tale of sex and sin in New Orleans, came out in 1956 and was a disappointment to critics who yearned for the reality of *Golden Arm*. It was Algren's last novel. He spent his last twenty-five years doing various magazine pieces, and mostly lectured, taught, or wrote for money. His early successes had not brought him great financial success. He got only a few thousand dollars for the rights to the movie of *Man with a Golden Arm*, which made millions for its producer and a full-fledged cinema star of Frank Sinatra.

Algren was openly bitter about his place in the literary world, believing, rightly, that the eastern establishment never gave him proper respect and instead chose Bellow as the literary star of the Cold War age. "When it comes to technical skill and literary manipulation I couldn't touch Bellow or [John] Updike. But I'm a more enduring writer. I'm more in touch with real life."

Chicago Tribune book editor John Blades agrees that Algren was underrated in his lifetime and thinks he will endure. "I think we will see a big Algren revival. When you reread Algren it still holds up. It's still very good fifty years later."

Although he was far more faithful to Chicago than to any of the women in his life, Algren finally moved to New Jersey in 1974. It was only a few years after a Chicago magazine held a literary symposium and invited such writers as Alberto Moravia, Jean Shepherd, Arthur C. Clarke, and Calvin Trillin. Algren was not on the guest list.

"Never did a writer do more for a city and never did a city repay him more meagerly," Algren said in 1977. "I was treated like a nonperson there."

He did not live for the final insult. For the last twenty years, city hall has been taken with changing names of streets to honor celebrities. It began with Martin Luther King Drive, but the practice is so common that dozens of streets bear the names of aldermen, sewer commissioners, sportscasters, and newspaper columnists. After Algren's death, the city council passed a resolution changing Evergreen Street, where he lived overlooking Wicker Park, to Algren Street. So many residents complained that they changed it back.

8

OUR MISS BROOKS:
GWENDOLYN BROOKS

Gwendolyn Brooks had none of the characteristics that seemed common to most of the writers grouped with her in this section. She never left Chicago. Except for the first month of her life, when she had no choice, she always lived there. She wrote about Chicago, no other place. She did not trade in spouses with regularity. She did not spend a lifetime haggling with publishers over royalties or finagling to win monetary awards. None of her poems were made into movies.

Gwendolyn Brooks never made news. Except for the annual awards she made for twenty-five years to children's poetry and an occasional notice of her readings, she was almost obscure by the standards of most great writers. Her last best work was published in the 1960s, although she was always available to compose a special verse for such events as Chicago's 150th birthday.

Gwendolyn Brooks is a certified part of American literary history. She was the first black to receive a Pulitzer Prize, winning in 1950 for her collection *Annie Allen*.

When a *Chicago Tribune* photographer arrived at her house in 1950 after the Pulitzer, Brooks was sitting in the dark, hoping he would not need to use electricity to take his pictures. She and her husband, Henry Blakely, had not been able to pay the bill.

When she won her first of three Midwestern Writers poetry awards, she had not been invited to attend the ceremonies. A few days later an editor trudged up a long flight of stairs to the kitchenette apartment at 623 East 63rd Street to deliver the award. "She said she was shocked to discover I was a Negro."

Two years later, she was in attendance when it was announced that she had won her third Midwestern Writers award. She sat still. Finally, Paul Engle, who headed the Creative Writing Department at the University of Iowa, said, "Gwendolyn, you'd better come up here or I'll give the prize to someone else."

Brooks recalled, "I'll never forget the gasps that went through the audience. Remember, things were different then, and Negroes just didn't win prizes of that sort."

Gwendolyn Brooks was born on June 7, 1917, in Topeka, Kansas. Her mother had come home to Topeka from Chicago to give birth to her child. When Gwendolyn was one month old, the family returned to Chicago. Encouraged by her parents, Gwendolyn began to write poetry at about age seven. When she was in her early teens, her poem "Eventide" appeared in a well-known magazine of the time, *American Childhood*. She continued to write poetry while attending Englewood High School. More than seventy-five of her poems were printed in the *Chicago Defender*. In 1934, she entered Wilson Junior College, where she majored in literature. She worked for a time as a receptionist and then became publicity director for the local chapter of the NAACP, where she met her future husband, also an aspiring poet. They were married in 1939 and had a son and daughter.

Gwendolyn Brooks's first book of poems, *A Street in Bronzeville*, was published in 1945.

The poems were praised for their lyricism and wit, and critics were quick to separate her race from her work. The largest section in the book was a sequence about a soldier called "Gay Chaps at the Bar." These pieces are still considered her finest work. One critic noted, "And finest of all, they can be read for what they are and not, as the publishers want us to believe, as Negro poems. For they should no more be called Negro poetry than the poems of Robert Frost should be called white poetry."

Her first major work earned her two Guggenheim Fellowships in 1946 and 1947. *Annie Allen*, a ballad of Chicago black life, was published in 1949. This was followed by *The Bean Eaters* (1960) and *Selected Poems* (1963).

One of her more poignant pieces describes a mother trying, but failing, to explain why a department-store Santa Claus had ignored a small black child.

Paul Engle, a staunch admirer, wrote, "She marvelously balances between the merely savage and the merely sentimental. Her eye is candid, as aware of the gay sun as it is of malevolent midnight." Her early work was praised for both its social content and lyrical structure, although she never was out on the edge. One critic wrote that before the civil rights turbulence of the 1960s she balanced Western influences and black culture, a shrewd anatomy of white behavior and explorations of the black experience. But in her later work, the "irony turns to iron."

If there was a bitterness in Brooks's works, it appeared more sad than strident. She wrote the "Ballad of Emmett Till" to commemorate the 1959 lynching of a fifteen-year-old Chicago boy who was visiting family in Mississippi when a white mob unjustly judged and executed him for talking to a white woman. In her 1962 autobiographical collection, *Report from Part One*, Brooks wrote of a "new note that would become a scream, an intensifying fury." She wrote, "There is indeed a new black today. He is different from any the world has known. He's a tall-walker. Almost firm. By many of his brothers he is not understood. And he is understood by no white. Not the wise white; not the schooled white; not the kind white." Her next collections, *In the Mecca* (1968), *Riot* (1969), *Family Pictures* (1970), and *Aloneness* (1971), were more militant in tone, but continued to dwell on the daily existence of blacks.

Brooks lectured and taught at Northeastern Illinois, Columbia College, and Elmhurst College. She was poet laureate of Illinois for thirty years. Her only predecessor was Carl Sandburg.

9 ▪

STUDS:
JAMES T. FARRELL

The perfect time for any boy to read *Studs Lonigan* is "on the verge of fifteen," the exact age of the tragic antihero at the beginning of James T. Farrell's classic trilogy depicting the self-destruction of a South Side Chicago youth in the 1920s.

Although the suggestive sex and graphic immorality of Studs caused Farrell to be labeled a sensational and shocking writer in the 1930s, the profanity and sexuality is tame, almost nonexistent, by modern standards. Still, for three generations of youths discovering the adult novel, nothing was more tantalizing than studying the cover of the paperback Studs with a cigarette curled on his lip, standing in the glow of a streetlight and staring up at a promising woman waiting on the "El" platform.

At fifteen, Studs (and his adolescent audience) has passed the early rituals of postpubescence and eagerly anticipates the fame and women and riches that adulthood promises. What Studs found was poverty, social decay, and an environment that doomed him.

That was the theme that stamped Farrell as another of the great Chicago naturalist writers, and it was the theme that, sadly, he repeated again and again and again in fifty-two novels spanning nearly fifty years. His great flaw was that he always included everything. Nothing Farrell ever wrote was bad, but nothing else was ever as good as the Lonigan trilogy. Beyond its raw realism and exploration of the lower working class, it was the great Chicago novel up to its time, advancing and surpassing the realism of Dreiser in its feel for the city bursting with its mix of rich and poor, hope and hopelessness.

Farrell's critics called him a reporter and a verbal photographer. But those were the strengths of "Studs Lonigan," published in 1932, when movies were still one-reelers shot on a Sunset Boulevard back lot and the miracles of television and live satellite coverage were more remote than trips to other planets. Books provoked the American imagination. No one painted a more real picture of Chicago in the 1920s than Farrell. In *Judgment Day*, the third book of the Lonigan trilogy, Studs, nearing despair, travels to the Loop to meet a girl, and no reader had to visit Chicago to know what it was like:

> He halted on the opposite side of Van Buren Street to look at the ordered rows of black and tan oxfords in the window of Hassel's shoe store. . . . At Jackson Boulevard . . . he walked by the Great Northern Hotel, stopping to study a news photograph of Lindbergh. . . . At Madison Street, he halted to permit the passage of a west-bound surface car, reading above a window in the center of the car: Madison & Western. He had hardly ever been on the West Side and he wondered about it. . . . He turned the corner on to Randolph, the Loop noises bursting upon him with a sudden increase of volume, the elevated trains from Lake Street, the clanging of a street-car gong on Dearborn. . . . He heard the jazz band of a nearby, second-floor, Chinese dine-and-dance restaurant. . . .

Farrell was born in 1904 on Chicago's South Side. After elementary school he attended St. Cyril's, now Mount Carmel, where he lettered in baseball and football. He attended the University of Chicago, where an English teacher looked at a four-page essay and told him he should expand the story to a novel. Between working at the same kind of odd, dead-end jobs that Studs had tried, Farrell ultimately did write the book. It was *Young Lonigan*, which was followed by *The Young Manhood of Studs Lonigan* in 1934 and *Judgment Day* in 1935. The books were combined into a trilogy by the Book of the Month Club in 1937.

One critic labeled the Lonigan works "the most considerable con-tribution of proletarian fiction that has yet been made in this country." Others called the book stenographic sociology.

Farrell next embarked on a series of "Danny O'Neill" books that were very much like the Lonigan books. By the 1960s and 1970s his nov-els sold poorly and his reputation declined. If he was remembered for anything but Studs, it was his controversial politics.

Like most writers of the Depression he was part of the Marxist movement, except Farrell was a vehement anti-Stalinist and devout follower of Leon Trotsky. This put him at odds with many others, including fellow Chicagoans Richard Wright and Nelson Algren.

Farrell, too, deserted Chicago for New York after the Lonigan suc-cess and lived there until his death of a heart attack at age seventy-five. Algren, writing in the *Chicago Tribune* on Farrell's death, said, "Farrell lacked the tension of Hemingway. He lacked the poetry of Fitzgerald and the profundity of Faulkner. He had no style at all. But he lasted . . . Studs Lonigan afforded an impact which, 50 years later, they still feel."

Chicago has owned so many great writers that Farrell could easily be omitted from the top ranks. But Studs Lonigan, the tragic middle brother of American literature, tucked somewhere between Huck Finn and Holden Caulfield, will always belong there.

POETRY:
HARRIET MONROE

In 1893, a thirty-three-year-old Chicago woman published a poem as an ode to the Columbian Exposition. The verse was reprinted verbatim in the *New York World* with no credit for the author. The author sued the newspaper and in 1894 was awarded five thousand dollars in the first case of copyright infringement in America.

The letter instructing her lawyer to file suit was undoubtedly more important for future American writers and poets than any of the verse Harriet Monroe had ever composed.

But it was not her most important contribution to Chicago literature.

Harriet Monroe was the founder and editor of the only successful literary magazine in the history of Chicago, a city whose successes in almost any other commercial endeavor embarrassingly has ignored or beaten down just about every effort at quality publishing. For all its wealth of literary figures, for all the millions of words written about the city, Chicago has never been able to even approach New York as the publishing center of America.

But Harriet Monroe's *Poetry* magazine has survived.

Harriet Monroe was born on December 23, 1860, in Chicago. Her father was a well-known attorney. She attended Dearborn Seminary in Chicago and completed her schooling at the Visitation Convent in Washington, D.C., in 1879. After graduation Monroe earned her living doing newspaper work as an art and drama critic and by contributing to magazines. She became the theater critic for the *Chicago*

Tribune in 1888 and mingled with the creative upper crust of Chicago as well as the many literary visitors to the city, which even then fascinated writers from all over the world. Encouraged by such authors as Robert Louis Stevenson and William Dean Howells, she published *Valeria and Other Poems.*

As a poet, Harriet Monroe knew that other poets had little chance to become known and earn money. Few books by living poets were published, and magazines bought poetry mainly to fill leftover space. She decided to start her own poetry magazine, knowing such a publication with a small circulation would never be profitable. Using the connections of her family and her own circle of friends, she approached Chicago's aristocracy—which, then as now, meant the people with money. She convinced one hundred people to pledge fifty dollars annually for five years. The McCormicks, Palmers, Burnhams, and Pullmans were initial donors.

The first issue of *Poetry: A Magazine of Verse* appeared on September 23, 1912, and had a press run of one thousand, which sold quickly, prompting another printing of one thousand. The *Chicago Tribune* was skeptical, noting that such a publication was attempting to be successful in "the most commercial city of the age."

A Philadelphia newspaper dubbed the debut, "Poetry in Porkopolis."

Monroe became the magazine's first editor. As its motto she chose a line from Walt Whitman: "To have great poets there must be great audiences too." *Poetry* published the work of nearly every notable modern American and British poet. Some well-known poems that first appeared in the magazine include Joyce Kilmer's "Trees" and Vachel Lindsay's "Congo."

Monroe was not necessarily avant-garde. She was far more comfortable with Sandburg than Eliot. But in 1911, while traveling on an around-the-world trip, she was introduced in London to Ezra Pound, who gave her a book of his poems, which she thought had a wonderfully "strange and beautiful rhythm." She recruited Pound as her European editor, and he urged her to publish Eliot as well as D. H. Lawrence, William Butler Yeats, and Rabindranath Tagore.

Poetry magazine has survived for nearly ninety years and has been the home of James Joyce, Marianne Moore, Wallace Stevens, Robinson Jeffers, Gwendolyn Brooks, and William Carlos Williams, among others.

Harriet Monroe remained the editor of *Poetry* for twenty-two years before leaving the post to continue her lifelong fascination with travel. She attended a writer's conference in Buenos Aires in 1935 and decided to extend her trip with a train ride across the pampas and into the Andes Mountains to Santiago, Chile. Then she boarded a cruise ship bound for Peru, where she disembarked to visit Inca ruins. At Arequipa, Peru, at an altitude of 7,500 feet, the seventy-five-year-old patroness of poets became light-headed, suffered a fall, went into a coma, and died.

It could be argued that there are some great Chicago writers rather than Harriet Monroe who should be included in this book with Sandburg, Algren, Farrell, and the rest. There are. But there is no one who matches Harriet Monroe's ability to endure for the sake of art in a city that only endures for the sake of money.

■ ■ ■ IX

ARCHITECTURE'S
TOP TEN

Chicago's first architect was Jacques Marquette. Near the Damen Avenue bridge over the south branch of the Chicago River, the young Jesuit priest built the first structure of the Chicago school of architecture to survive the bitter winter of 1673. The tiny log cabin fulfilled many of the dictums that Chicago architects would set forth for the world in the centuries to follow.

The cabin was deliberately built very small to retain what little heat the fire gave, an early adherence to Louis Sullivan's famous "Form follows function."

The frame was simply logs stacked on each other and held together by mud and clay, what Mies van der Rohe would later proclaim as "Less is more."

The cabin was barely visible in the wilderness along the Chicago River, predating Frank Lloyd Wright's creation of structures that retained the harmony and physical association of the landscape.

Almost exactly three centuries later, and a few miles to the north of Marquette's shack, the world's tallest building rose on the banks of that same sluggish stream. In between, and even after, some of the world's greatest architects decorated Chicago with an array of structures that changed every home, school, office building, hotel, museum, prison, and fast-food stand in the world.

Chicago may always be parodied for its lawless and violent history. It may always be remembered as the last citadel of corrupt but efficient machine politics. It will always be envied for its lakefront and admired for its enterprise. No city had better brothels or more of them. No city had more thieves running its biggest companies and serving in its highest offices. Chicago's legacy of the twentieth century is one of great men and great fortunes and great ideas.

But its undisputed national treasure is its architecture.

It is as easy at the turn of the twenty-first century to stumble upon a national landmark in Chicago as it was to trip over a hooker at the turn of the last century.

People who have never been to Chicago know exactly how the Sears Tower looks as it rises a fourth of a mile into the sky. It doesn't matter that someone in Malaysia built bigger antennas. And what else could the massive structure with the crossed Xs be but Big John? Perhaps no building in modern America has been photographed more than the twin corncobs of Marina City. Perhaps no building is more of a shrine to twentieth-century architecture than John Wellborn Root's Rookery.

There is the Board of Trade with its marvelous art deco crown, and the NBC building's 1990s salute to the art deco age. There is 333 North Michigan, the city's first setback skyscraper. There is 333 Wacker, a 1990 creation that fits as perfectly with the Chicago River as did Father Marquette's cabin.

There is the Wrigley Building with its stunning terra-cotta facing that is unlike any other building anywhere. And across from it is the Tribune Tower, the result of an architectural design competition that spawned an entire new school of skyscraper design between the two great wars.

Even the mistakes are marvelous: Helmut Jahn's "Starship Chicago," the futuristic State of Illinois Building that no one liked but which functions exactly as a public building should; Harry Weese's Metropolitan Correction Center, the prettiest prison in the world, and Weese's Marriott Hotel on Michigan Avenue, immortalized by the late *Chicago Tribune* architecture critic Paul Gapp as "a touch of crass."

In 1885, a Civil War major named William Le Baron Jenney built the Home Insurance Building at LaSalle and Adams Streets. If it was not the first steel-frame skyscraper, it was generally credited with giving birth to the modern skyscraper. But Chicago architecture did not start with Jenney.

It actually started with the great fire that leveled the city and left Chicago a virgin landscape for the design geniuses that came from everywhere to try out their ideas. Chicago historically knew what to do with any kind of virgin. In a matter of decades they had rebuilt the city and created a new brand of architecture that would be emulated all over the world.

Tracing the lineage of Chicago architecture is like reading Genesis. Jenney begat Sullivan and Roche and Holabird. Sullivan begat Wright, who begat Mies. Holabird and Roche and Burnham and Root begat Holabird and Root, which begat Holabird, Root, and Burgee. Burnham begat Graham, Anderson, Probst, and White, which begat C. F. Murphy, which begat Murphy and Jahn. Dwight Perkins begat Lawrence Perkins, which begat Perkins and Will. Skidmore begat Owings, who begat Merrill, who begat Graham and Kahn and Netsch and Smith. Stanley Tigerman begat himself.

Some were imitators, some were visionaries. Bertrand Goldberg once asked Mies, "Am I to look forward to copying you all my life?"

"Isn't that enough?" Mies replied.

LESS IS A LOT:
LUDWIG MIES VAN DER ROHE

A first-time visitor to Chicago took the elevator to the top of the Sears Tower, stood at the Michigan Avenue bridge admiring the Wrigley Building, and rubbed several of the historic stones patched to the street-level wall of Tribune Tower. When urged to take special notice of the aging twenty-six-story apartment buildings overlooking the Oak Street beach he remarked, "They don't look very special. They look like buildings all over the world."

That is the glory and curse of Ludwig Mies van der Rohe.

When Mies designed the two towers at 860–880 Lake Shore Drive in 1951, they didn't look at all like buildings all over the world. They looked like some of the sketches for sparse, glass and steel skyscrapers that he first concocted in the early 1920s, when he worked at the Bauhaus in his native Germany. They echoed the "less is more" credo he unveiled for the world with his Barcelona Pavilion in 1929. But they looked like little else in Chicago, whose historic buildings had passed through several waves of design from the fortress foundations of the Monadnock and Rookery to the historical ornamentation of Louis Sullivan, from the open-space "prairie school" of Frank Lloyd Wright to the odd but appealing stylistic mixtures of the Wrigley and Tribune structures.

Mies's glass boxes glowed on the lakefront at night like lanterns. In the next three decades Mies and his imitators would fill the cities of the world with these skin-and-bones, black-and-gray glass rectangles.

They were built to live in, to work in, to study in, to shop in, and to house art and literature. They were indistinguishable, critics said. They were impersonal. By the end of the century they were everywhere.

The problem was that unless they were built by Mies they did not always have the stoic beauty, the infinite precision, the complete attention to every detail from color to doorknobs that Mies gave his greatest works. Some of the best buildings in the world owe their structural and aesthetic heritage to Mies.

So do some of the worst.

The critics and the postmodernists who parodied his maxim by declaring "less is a bore" never cast a disparaging word about the Seagram Building he designed in 1958 in Manhattan, which may end the century acknowledged as the most beautiful skyscraper in the world.

It was the only building he ever designed in New York. It was also his first office building, although there is little to distinguish the purpose of a Mies high-rise. Whether for work or for living, they look the same. He designed more than thirty buildings for Chicago, including the Federal Center complex with its grace note of an Alexander Calder stabile eating the plaza.

His disciples did the rest, turning out such clean-lined and muscular showpieces as the Inland Steel, Equitable, Daley Civic Center, and CNA Buildings, as well as the McCormick Place convention hall with its steel-trussed roof and vast open space and the curving beauty of Lake Point Tower, which traced its glass sculpture to Mies's first experiments.

They adapted new technology and some structural twists to create the giant monoliths of Sears and John Hancock, which Mies did not live to see. But if he had he would not have said much. If he had not been the most influential architect of the century he would have been the most quoted, for his conversation was as lean as his designs, and the few bon mots he tossed to the masses became a catechism for architects and city planners.

"Don't talk. Build" was a favorite expression. When a student complained that his rigorous demands for precision stifled her self-expression, he produced a tablet and told her to write her name. When she finished he said, "Now work."

The taciturn Teutonic visage that has hovered over American urban landscapes for a half century was as understated as his buildings. But he was not modest.

He was not even Mies.

Ludwig Mies was born in Aachen, Germany, in 1886, the son of a stonecutter who put young Ludwig to work as a mason before he completed high school. He quickly developed his skill as a draftsman and in 1905 moved to Berlin. From 1908 to 1911 he worked in the office of Peter Behrens, a leading architect whose other pupils included Le Corbusier and Walter Gropius, the founder of the Bauhaus school of design, which Mies later headed.

It was during these years that he changed his name, taking his mother's maiden name as a surname and dropping Ludwig. His fame took care of van der Rohe. He became simply Mies.

Mies built roads as an engineer in the German army in World War I and then returned to Berlin, where in the 1920s he experimented with designs for glass-walled skyscrapers and concrete office buildings with glass commanding more space than the structural material. His youthful work as a stonemason lingered in his adoration for such materials as brick and marble, and he used them in his dramatic Barcelona Pavilion, which his mentor, Behrens, called the most beautiful building of the century. Unfortunately, not many people saw it. The Pavilion was dismantled after only seven months and returned in parcels to Germany, where it was destroyed during a World War II air raid. In 1986 a replica was built in Barcelona.

For the Pavilion, Mies also designed the leather and metal seat that became the world-famous Barcelona chair.

Mies, like most great artists or great people in any field, was fairly oblivious to the world around him except as how it translated to his work. When the Nazis came to power in Germany in the 1930s, Mies tried to work with them, foreseeing a new era of prosperity and the possibility to finally build something from all his theoretical designs. But the Nazis were Wagnerian in all things, including their view of architecture. As Gropius and others had before him, Mies headed for America.

If Mies's work reflected a certain lack of warmth, so did his love life. He married Adele Bruhn in 1913, had three children, and separated from her in 1921. They never divorced and never again lived together, freeing Mies for his many brief liaisons.

One of his extended romances was with German fashion designer Lilly Reich, who he took up with in 1925 and who remained his constant companion for thirteen years before he left Germany for good.

He formed a close relationship with Lora Marx that lasted from 1940 until his death. Lora liked to drink as much as Mies, whose only joys other than designing seemed to be Dunhill cigars and dry martinis.

One of his painful relationships involved Edith Farnsworth, a wealthy Chicago doctor who commissioned him to do the house that became one of the most architecturally celebrated residences in the world, even though the Fox River's flooding threatens to smash through its vast glass panels. Mies eventually had to sue Farnsworth to get the money he claimed was owed him from the house. As *Chicago Tribune* architecture critic Blair Kamen observed, "She thought the architect came with the house."

When Mies arrived in America he was offered a job at Chicago's Armour Institute that paid eight thousand dollars a year and gave him a free hand to build a new campus. The centerpiece was his most famous low-rise structure, Crown Hall, which occupied a space half the size of a football field without a single interior partition and was designed to meet any future needs of its occupants. It was hailed as innovative but suffers in historical perspective.

Paul Gapp, the late Pulitzer Prize–winning architectural critic of the *Chicago Tribune*, once wrote, "It is a risky thing to claim that Mies ever designed a 'bad' building, yet his work was flawed in some respects. Mies' devotion to flowing interior spaces sometimes defied common sense. Crown Hall, whatever its beauty and flexibility, is not much of a space for learning. Farnsworth House near Plano, Ill., is a splendid residence if you never walk around in the buff and don't mind sweltering airlessness in the summertime."

While at Illinois Institute of Technology (IIT), where he remained until he was unceremoniously booted out in 1958, he began the designs for the 860–880 Lake Shore Drive buildings, which changed cities forever.

He opened his own firm, which built the federal buildings that opened the shadowy south Loop and began the design for One IBM

Plaza overlooking the Chicago River, which was finished after his death in 1969 at age eighty-three.

Mies was as sparse as his buildings. He never had anything bad to say about other architects. He never said anything good, either. Asked his thoughts on the legacy of great architecture in Chicago, Mies said he knew nothing about it. "You see, I never walk. I always take taxis back and forth to work. I rarely see the city."

Actually, Mies preferred to dodge a question rather than be insulting. He despised the patching of historical bric-a-brac to new buildings and particularly disliked Louis Sullivan's ornamentation.

Philip Johnson, who has been as influential as anyone in charting the various courses of American architecture in the twentieth century, was an early admirer of Mies and coined the term *international style*, of which Mies was the unchallenged master. But Johnson found him trying.

"He was only interesting after four or five martinis," Johnson said. "He was such a Puritan. He was such a difficult man. So convinced about being good and truthful and honest."

Mies would have ignored him and simply muttered in his heavy German accent, "God is in the details."

So was Mies.

2

THE LOVER:
FRANK LLOYD WRIGHT

Frank Lloyd Wright would have become famous if he had been a grocer. He would have found a way.

In July 1928 the *Chicago Tribune* reported, "For Sale: One romantic, rambling, famous picturesque home on a hill with 190 acres of farm and park, known as a 'love nest,' murder scene, fire scene, raid scene and showplace."

At any time during the remainder of the century the sentence would have included the words "a Frank Lloyd Wright home." But in 1928 just about every reader of the *Tribune* knew it was *the* Frank Lloyd Wright home, Taliesin, near his birthplace in Spring Green, Wisconsin.

At the time of the proposed sale, Frank Lloyd Wright was the most famous architect in the world and one of its most flamboyant showmen. His masterpiece Imperial Hotel in Tokyo had just survived the worst earthquake ever to hit the Japanese capital. He was a prolific author on every phase of building, and his early homes, Charnley House and Winslow House, were already being declared landmarks. He was sixty but was involved anew in one of the romantic trysts that kept his name in headlines even when he wasn't designing some of the most spectacular homes in America.

Wright had three wives, a mysteriously murdered mistress, and countless other women in his life. He fathered seven children and left a legacy of architecture that made him a household name to people who never heard of Le Corbusier or Mies.

The "love nest" became famous in 1913 when Wright walked out on his wife, Catherine, and their six children, leaving them the famous Oak Park home where tourists flock in the 1990s. He scooted off to Taliesin, the showpiece of the low and sloped roof, angled rooms, and wide overhangs harmonizing with the landscape that were the trademarks of the Prairie House he conceived of shortly after the turn of the century and that ultimately impacted the design of every house in America.

With him was Mamah Borthwick, the wife of a close friend, and her two children. Trailing them were reporters from Chicago and Milwaukee. Wright's destruction of two marriages and the subsequent divorce travails were news. The love nest was front page.

It became even bigger news in August 1914. Wright was in his Chicago office working rapidly to finish his Midway Gardens project, an indoor-outdoor pleasure dome on Chicago's South Side that blended with his ideas for the Imperial Hotel in Tokyo (both have been demolished).

At Taliesin, Mamah, her two children, and several employees were having lunch when a servant, Julian Carlton, splashed gasoline throughout the famous structure, set it afire, and went on an ax rampage, killing Mamah, her children, and four other men. Carlton died in prison a few months later of a hunger strike. Taliesin had burned to the ground. Wright later rebuilt it, but not nearly as fast as he rebuilt his love life. He shortly began a long affair with Miriam Noel, who he made his second wife in 1923. A few years later he dropped Miriam in favor of a young Montenegro native, Olgivanna Lazovich, who bore Wright's seventh child, Iovanna, in 1925, while he still was married to Noel. There ensued a great public comedy, with private detectives hired by Noel hounding Wright and Olgivanna, charges that Wright violated the Mann Act by taking Olgivanna across state lines for sexual purposes, an FBI chase, Wright arrested and released, and finally a divorce from Noel that necessitated the selling of Taliesin, which resulted in the *Tribune* story.

And Frank Lloyd Wright still had thirty more years to live.

Wright was born in 1869 in Richland Center, Wisconsin, the son of a Unitarian preacher and mother who had planned for him to be an architect even before his birth. He attended the University of Wisconsin in 1884 for a course in engineering, but quit and moved to Chicago in 1887 to work with the architect J. L. Silsbee, soon shifting to Louis H. Sullivan's firm.

He was fired by Sullivan in 1893 for taking private commissions and did not speak to his mentor for many years, although he later publicly decried the decline of Sullivan's status as one of the great architectural innovators and gave the destitute Sullivan money until his death.

During the next eight years Wright developed the "prairie school" of architecture which gave homes a "sense of shelter and a sense of space," mixing new technologies with an appreciation of the landscape that became America's indigenous style.

Wright announced his prairie style in a 1901 *Ladies' Home Journal* article, calling it a "city man's country house on the prairie." In the early 1900s Wright brought his prairie style to bloom with such masterpieces as the Willits, Robie, Fricke, Dana, and Heurtley Houses. By 1910, Wright had designed some sixty prairie-style houses in Illinois alone. By the end of the century there were few states unmarked by a Wright house.

The prairie house hugged the ground in wide horizontal fashion, with large eaves, casement windows, and interiors that set rooms off at angles and eliminated the series of boxes that most houses contained. Wright also designed new furniture to blend in with his houses, and he claimed to have designed the first wall-hung toilet, which changed plumbing installation and repair.

It was after this rush of creation that Wright embarked on the series of romances and tragedies that almost ended his career. After the divorce from Noel and his subsequent marriage to Olgivanna, Wright, virtually bankrupt, lectured and wrote exhaustively, including his autobiography. The Depression made it difficult for all architects to find work, and Wright concentrated on turning Taliesin into a teaching center and drew sketches for model cities.

His zenith as America's foremost architect was considered over.

In 1932, approaching seventy, the man in the broad-brimmed slouch hat swirled his trademark cape, flourished his silver-tipped cane, which had always been an affectation, and burst forth with another spurt of creativity.

In Connellsville, Pennsylvania, Wright designed Falling Water, a house cantilevered magnificently over a waterfall. In Racine, Wisconsin, Wright created a much-honored office and research complex for the Johnson Wax Company that was done in the modern style and has been described as literally floating through the air.

In the Herbert Jacobs residence in Madison, Wisconsin, Wright included prefabrication, radiant heating, and many of the design ingredients that were used in suburban housing during the great post–World War II building boom.

He had experimented with decorated concrete blocks for the Arizona Biltmore Hotel in Phoenix in the late 1920s. He conceived the idea of carports, and in 1957 he proposed a mile-high skyscraper that was to be built in Chicago. He remained incredibly active until his death in 1959.

His familiar white mane and black ensemble were never far from the front pages. He called public housing an "evil thing" and said the government had no business in housing. In his last years he designed some of his boldest works, including the controversial Guggenheim Museum in New York City, which clashed fearfully with its surroundings. Some of the latter works that bear his name probably had little of his input.

Unlike Mies, Wright had no vast school of disciples. His ideas and concepts were not so constant as the "international style" he abhorred. He did take Mies under his wing when the German arrived in America, inviting him to Taliesin for a visit. But if there was any doubt where Wright felt Mies belonged in the pantheon of architectural greatness, he dispelled it at a 1938 dinner in Chicago. After introducing the German as "my Mies," he and his entourage strolled out of the building without waiting for Mies to speak or be praised.

Paul Gapp of the *Chicago Tribune* defined Wright's greatness:

The work of other great architects challenges orthodox description, but none more strongly. Wright's ability to render three-dimensional experiences on a two-dimensional sheet of drafting paper was awesome—not unlike a Beethoven or a

Mozart hearing an orchestra in his head while jotting notes on a staff.

How many architectural giants can America be said to have had in the 20th century? Three, I think: Ludwig Mies van der Rohe, Louis Sullivan, and Frank Lloyd Wright. And of these, it is easy to say that Wright was the greatest of all.

3

FORM FOLLOWS FUNCTION:
LOUIS SULLIVAN

Most of Louis Sullivan's best work was done in the nineteenth century, but he was the definitive American architect, whose philosophy
on verticality influenced the world's skyline. He has been described as
the first true American architect and is most memorable for his
encompassing axiom, "Form follows function," even if most people
who know the phrase don't know who said it, and if most architects
who slavishly followed it didn't quite understand what is meant.

In comparison with Mies van der Rohe's aloof arrogance and
Frank Lloyd Wright's flamboyant self-promotion, Sullivan was a rather
cranky character with little flair but a lot of mystery. He was driven to
depressions that left him alcoholic, penniless, unappreciated at his
death, and neglected by historians for much of this century.

His last twenty years were spent building small midwestern banks
and writing on architecture, which he believed was an art, not a science. He considered himself a poet, not a philosopher. He took up
boxing and spent much of his life living in men's clubs. He may have
been homosexual. He may have been dominated by his art. His only
liaison with a woman was an apparently disastrous marriage that lasted
less than a decade. His biographer, Robert Twombly, was rather
amazed that Sullivan expressed such relief when his wife left him for
the man she had been sleeping with during their marriage. "Now I can
get back to work," Sullivan told friends.

He shared with other giants of design a huge ego and a fierce
demand to do exactly what he wanted, often losing lucrative contracts

by his haughty treatment of the people who were paying the bills. Mies and Wright could be haughty as well, but they tempered their pomposity for the sake of building something and earning something. Sullivan often decided if it wasn't his way it was no way.

From the 1880s to the turn of the century, it usually was his way.

Sullivan was born in Boston in 1856, attended the Massachusetts Institute of Technology for a year, and in 1873 moved to Chicago, where he found work in the office of William Le Baron Jenny. He spent a year in Paris studying at the Ecole des Beaux Arts, the leading architectural school in Europe, and several years in Chicago working as a draftsman on many of the buildings constructed in the boom that followed the Great Fire.

In 1879 he met Dankmar Adler, and they formed a partnership in 1881 that would produce more than one hundred buildings over the next fourteen years, including several of the most famous in world architecture.

Sullivan was the first architect to conceive that buildings must reflect the people who live in them. He wrote, "Nothing more clearly reflects the status and tendencies of a people than its buildings. They are the emanation of a people; they visualize for us the soul of our people." That was what Sullivan meant by "function," not simply whatever tangible or material purpose was intended for a structure.

The first great building by Adler and Sullivan was the Auditorium Building, whose theater, refurbished many times, still glitters with opulence today. Completed in 1889, the ten-story limestone and granite building with its seventeen-story tower was one of Sullivan's designs that did not burst with the ornamentation for which he would become famous and controversial.

Sullivan's most important building came next. He received a contract to build a skyscraper in St. Louis. He had great experience with the steel frame developed by Jenney, but he wanted to give a visual expression to tall buildings that was lacking in the heavy, fortresslike appearance of such Chicago landmarks as the Monadnock.

He mulled over the problem and finally showed his young draftsman, Frank Lloyd Wright, his conception of a building that would be "every inch, proud and soaring."

Another Sullivan biographer, Willard Cooley, quoted Wright's reaction: "This was the great Louis Sullivan moment. The skyscraper as a new thing beneath the sun . . . with virtue, individuality, beauty all its own, as the tall building was born."

The design was the Wainwright Building in St. Louis, which still stands and is considered one of the nation's great architectural landmarks.

The recurrent curse of architects, an economic panic, hit the nation in 1893, and Adler split the partnership to take a position with a continuing retainer. A permanent rift occurred after Sullivan, in a pique, left Adler's name off a design both men had prepared. They never spoke again, and Adler died in 1900.

The 1893 Columbian Exposition was a great disappointment for Sullivan. He thought it would be a great opportunity to advance his new theories, but the theme was neoclassical, and the Great White City was created under the direction of Daniel Burnham. Sullivan's contribution was the Transportation Building, which he splashed with all sorts of greens and golds to contrast with the other white structures. No one liked it.

Sullivan's bitterness over the exposition, which he believed for the rest of his life contributed to the decline of his stature, was not understated. "The damage wrought by the World's Fair," he wrote, "will last for a half century from its date, if not longer." Many historians later agreed with him.

But he had one masterpiece in his future. He received a contract from the Schlesinger & Mayer department store to erect a building at State and Madison. This structure perfectly mirrors his dictum of "Form follows function." He conceived the store as a theater displaying merchandise, and he managed to combine the soaring verticality he pioneered in the Wainwright Building with a sense of horizontality to capture the essence of State Street, a design couplet that has fascinated and challenged architects ever since.

He wrapped the building, which was sold to Carson, Pirie, and Scott, in cast-iron ornamentation in a mixture of geometric and floral patterns, leaving a landmark that was the epitome of Sullivan's work as a designer of architectural ornamentation. Sullivan's style of ornamentation later fell into great disfavor when the international style forged by Mies came to dominate building design.

Over the century, critics have debated Sullivan's work, mostly agreeing that it is difficult to evaluate. In the 1930s, Henry Russell Hitchcock and Philip Johnson, of New York's critical establishment, declared that Sullivan "produced one original building, the Wainwright, which he then just repeated." Lewis Mumford, the great critic and social commentator, argued that Sullivan's work comprised the cornerstone of organic architecture. Mumford called Sullivan the first truly "American" architect.

Although Sullivan's writings, including his life story, *Autobiography of an Idea*, are classics on architecture, he was often obtuse and verbose. Frank Lloyd Wright once proclaimed that Sullivan "may have been ridiculous when he wrote but was miraculous when he drew."

The debate on Sullivan's ornamentation gave rise to theories of his homosexuality. Critics have wondered if the ornamentation at the top of his skyscrapers represented a feminine form dominating the male physical aspect, or vice versa. Biographer Twombly speculated that Sullivan's problems with clients and obtaining contracts during his declining years may have resulted from rumors or suggestions about his sexual orientation, but it seems clear that most of his problems were caused by his own petulance.

Sullivan, flawed, bitter, drunk, and broke, spent his last days in a seedy hotel on Cottage Grove Avenue. His death commanded only a sparse obituary in the *Chicago Tribune*. More tragic were the deaths of great buildings he created—the Chicago Stock Exchange, the Garrick Theater (Schiller Building), and dozens of others—demolished so unthinkingly that Pauline Saliga, then associate curator of the Art Institute of Chicago's department of architecture, said in 1986, "Chicago has lost more great buildings than many cities ever had."

To the city's shame, for most of the century, it also lost Louis Sullivan.

4 ▦

MAKE NO SMALL PLANS: DANIEL BURNHAM

It seems every great architect turned a great phrase. "Make no small plans" made Daniel Burnham the most often-quoted architect in Chicago, especially around city hall, where the aldermen and bagmen thought it applied to money.

That wouldn't have shocked Burnham, who once aspired for a career in the legislature and who also might have said, "Form follows cash," or "Less is not as good as more."

Daniel Burnham was a very rich man even before the 1909 Chicago Plan, which is famous for his admonition about little plans. Burnham authored the plan but he didn't inspire it. After that he got richer.

Burnham was neither an architectural pioneer or a genius. He was a hustler. It is not certain that Sullivan or Wright would have achieved greatness had they tried their new ideas in a city less open to experiment and excitement than Chicago. But it might have happened. On the other hand, Burnham and Chicago fit like a judge and a bribe.

"If . . . Burnham had lived anywhere except in the city of Chicago he would not have the architectural reputation he now enjoys. He was an organizer and merchant of work often designed by others. He enjoyed the greatest success of the Chicago architects, but he did so by increasingly turning against what they stood for," the late critic Carl Condit wrote in 1964.

Burnham was the Chicago school's first architectural entrepreneur. If Burnham didn't have the vision to see buildings "proud and soaring" or homes harmonizing with their landscape, he did understand that a design without a client was just a piece of paper. He spent far more time wining and dining prospective clients than contemplating buildings floating in space, but that allowed his partners the creative room to conceive the list of landmark structures that bear Burnham's name.

Daniel Burnham was never intended to be a genius. He barely finished at Central High School in Chicago, where his parents had moved in 1854 from Henderson, New York. He was rejected by Harvard and Yale and trooped off to the Nevada silver fields, where he went broke. He turned his eye to politics but lost an election for the state senate. One of his only skills, besides being a hale fellow, was drawing. His father found him a draftman's slot in the firm of Carter, Drake, and Wright, where he met John Wellborn Root and formed a partnership that helped revolutionize downtown Chicago.

Despite his lack of a formal education in architecture, Burnham was at ease behind a drafting table. And if he did not personally conceive the details of grand designs, he gave his more creative colleagues all the exhortation and support they needed while he played his role as expert administrator and promoter.

It was Root who was the principal designer of the Rookery, the Monadnock, the Montauk, the Masonic Temple, and such smaller Chicago gems as St. Gabriel's Church. With those Chicago buildings alone, the names of Burnham and Root took on formidable significance, and by the early 1880s they were designing buildings in other cities as well.

Burnham and Root were put in charge of laying out the World's Columbian Exposition of 1893. Root died of pneumonia in January 1891, but Burnham pushed on by adding Charles Atwood to his team as the fair's chief architect. Although Louis Sullivan was devastated by Burnham's decision to fawn to the eastern establishment and opt for a neoclassical theme, Atwood distinguished himself with the Fine Arts Building, a large-scale neoclassical triumph that survives as the Museum of Science and Industry.

It was Atwood who designed the glassy, steel-framed Reliance Building at 32 North State Street. The Reliance bridged the muscular Chicago style and the international style of the 1920s and is the best-known landmark carrying Burnham's name. Shortly after its completion in 1895, Atwood, who had secretly become a hopeless drug addict, died, leaving Burnham in search of more worlds to conquer and more politicians to meet.

He took many trips and became interested in creating greater beauty and order in American cities, comparing their haphazard growth with the harmony found in European cities. He got himself named chairman of a national commission to redevelop Washington, D.C., and subsequently became the preeminent national city planner, creating guides for Cleveland, San Francisco, and the Philippine cities of Manila and Baguio.

"He is vastly underrated as an architect and city planner," said *Chicago Tribune* critic Blair Kamen. "He was more influential than any other city planner of the twentieth century."

He was also getting richer. He was Chicago's busiest architect during the first decade of the twentieth century, thriving while his contemporary Sullivan was drowning in gin. Burnham expanded his firm with offices in New York and San Francisco and hired as his top associates Ernest Graham, Pierce Anderson, Edward Probst, and H. J. White.

He became one of Chicago's leading citizens and gourmands, his wallet, international reputation, and waistline swelling in equal proportions. He became a major benefactor of the Chicago Symphony and was the unanimous choice to devise Chicago's plan for the future.

By 1910, Burnham's architecture firm had become the largest in the world, building skyscrapers, department stores, banks, railroad stations, and other major structures in New York, San Francisco, Detroit, Cleveland, Pittsburgh, Boston, Washington, D.C., and London, England.

Burnham ran architecture as a business, something his clients—all businessmen—appreciated, and if he caved in to quirky demands that violated the principles that Root and Sullivan cherished, the checks never bounced. After Burnham died in 1912, the architects who inherited his practice formed the immensely profitable firm of Graham, Anderson, Probst, and White. Their lucrative work included the Merchandise Mart, the Wrigley Building, and Chicago's main post office.

Burnham and his wife were on a European trip in 1912 when the architect suddenly fell ill in Heidelberg, Germany. He died on June 1 of colitis, made acute by food poisoning and by the diabetes he had suffered for many years. He was sixty-eight.

On the seventy-fifth anniversary of his death, the late Paul Gapp of the *Chicago Tribune* wrote:

> Architecture is an art, a science and a business. Burnham's grasp of all three was firm, pragmatic and occasionally inspired. He personally turned out no single structure that assured him a place in history—no Robie House, no Auditorium Theater, no Board of Trade Building. But he was a whole architect who disdained no aspect of his profession. And by excelling at it in so complete and exuberant a manner, he became one of its giants.

5 ▩

THREE BLIND MIES:
SKIDMORE, OWINGS, AND MERRILL

The myth may be that Daniel Burnham's dream was to create a Paris of Chicago's lakefront, but the great architectural entrepreneur was really fantasizing about Skidmore, Owings, and Merrill.

Louis Skidmore could have been Daniel Burnham's clone. Skidmore, one of many Chicago architects struggling during the Depression, secured the job as chief designer of the 1933 Century of Progress exposition and used it as a launching pad for the firm that later would be known as SOM. It was exactly the formula Burnham had used in overseeing the 1893 fair. Like Burnham, Skidmore was more a pitchman and organizer than an architectural visionary. Like Burnham, Skidmore and his partner, Nathaniel Owings, who was his second-in-command at the Century of Progress, enjoyed moving in political circles and became favorites of Chicago mayors Edward Kelly and Martin Kennelly. The firm was formed in 1937 with John Merrill, and there was little business during the Depression. But SOM's political connections came through at the start of World War II when they won the massive federal contract to build Oak Ridge, Tennessee, a community of seventy-five thousand people who would work on the atomic bomb project.

After the war, SOM landed the multimillion-dollar contract to build the huge military base on the island of Okinawa.

By the 1950s, SOM was ready to rebuild America. It did. By the 1970s there were few places anywhere that did not have the SOM look, the unfailing international style done with consistency and a respect for detail that Mies demanded. And most of the young geniuses in SOM were such unfaltering Miesian disciples that the firm often was referred to as "Three Blind Mies."

The SOM stamp on buildings often shrouded the great individual talents of their designers, but Skidmore and Owings, much like Burnham, were far more interested in commissions than being ranked with the Sullivans and Wrights. The team approach to architecture created petty bickering and jealousies and confusion about who was responsible for what; senior designers grabbed credit for their praiseworthy buildings and remained silent about the lackluster productions.

But the list of SOM designers was as impressive as some of the American landmarks they created.

The nineteen-story Inland, built in 1958, was the first high-rise designed by Bruce Graham, who was SOM's "team captain" from the 1960s until his retirement in 1989, a period that spanned the peaks and valleys of SOM's world influence and saw Graham become one of America's most influential designers. Graham was born in Bogota, Colombia, in 1925 and joined SOM in 1949 after graduating from the University of Pennsylvania. Chicago architect Stanley Tigerman's introduction to Graham's 1989 book of his work depicts Graham as a tough, arrogant fellow who often ran roughshod over his colleagues. "Few, if any, are perceived to be his equal."

Paul Gapp of the *Chicago Tribune*, who was often critical of such Graham works as the Chicago Board of Options Exchange, praised him for giving the "lean, crisp modernist look a Chicago-style muscularity expressing the structural framework of his buildings."

Graham was captain of the team that built Chicago's biggest architectural icons, the John Hancock Building and the Sears Tower.

"'Big John' is Chicago's Eiffel Tower, one might say, and will be regarded as a singular feat of construction long after most skyscrapers have been forgotten," Gapp wrote about the Michigan Avenue giant that was completed in 1970. Gapp didn't care as much for the Sears Tower, which he thought harsh and intimidating, but said "the Chicago-style power of the building as an engineering achievement cannot be denied and will long guarantee its importance even if its world's-tallest record is toppled some day." (It was topped by thirty-three feet in 1997 by the twin Petronas Towers in Kuala Lumpur, Malaysia.)

But Graham was not singularly responsible for these "proud, soar-ing" behemoths. Much of the credit went to two other SOM visionaries.

Fazlur Khan, who died in 1982, was one of the world's foremost structural engineers and a central figure in post–World War II Ameri-can architectural technology. The native of Bangladesh joined SOM shortly after graduating from the University of Illinois in 1955 and developed a tubular framing system to support tall buildings. It was the innovation that made Big John, the Sears Tower, and their counter-parts all over Asia possible.

Use of the rigid tubular frames reduced the size, weight, and cost of the elements that support a building and also minimized interior columns that normally clutter interior space. While accepting Gra-ham's collaboration, Gapp wrote, "It was Khan's engineering that gave those structures their visually powerful forms, expressive of the frameworks that support them. Khan's engineering strides were among the most important of the century."

There was also Myron Goldsmith, who worked for one dollar an hour helping Mies on the landmark high-rises at 860 and 889 North Lake Shore Drive in the late 1940s and then joined SOM, where he played a key role in developing the steel and concrete framing systems that enabled the building of the X-braced John Hancock Building. Goldsmith, who died in 1996, also built the sleek rapid-transit stations of the Dan Ryan and Kennedy Expressways.

There was the maverick, Walter Netsch, the son of a meatpacker at Armour & Company, who went to MIT, served in the Army Corps of Engineers, and in 1947 joined SOM, where he stayed thirty-two years and designed two of the most controversial projects the firm ever handled. His University of Illinois–Chicago Circle campus was widely criticized, and the soaring aluminum-clad chapel he designed for the Air Force Academy went far beyond the orthodox architecture of the time.

Another senior partner at SOM, William Hartman, at Mayor Richard Daley's behest, convinced Pablo Picasso to create the sculp-ture that has adorned the Daley Center Plaza since 1967.

As architectural attitudes shifted in the 1970s and 1980s, Skid-more's stature as the world's foremost architectural firm was threat-ened. A new style, known as postmodernism, rejected the austere forms of Mies and embraced a more eclectic brand of architecture. It sought to relate skyscrapers to their urban surroundings more sympathetically than the often-forbidding steel-and-glass boxes that had become Skidmore's forte.

The 1990s recession sent architecture reeling but forced SOM to look abroad, and by 1997 foreign ventures provided more than half its revenues, including a hefty piece of change for the 1,380-foot Jin Mao Building in Shanghai, China, which was scheduled for completion in 1998 and would be the world's fourth-tallest building.

The firm's 1990s superstar was Adrian Smith, who was credited for the NBC Building, which was praised as the most handsome masonry-clad skyscraper built in Chicago since the 1930s and assures that SOM will continue into the next century as a formidable force in American architecture.

6 ▦

CORNCOBS:
BERTRAND GOLDBERG

For SOM, architectural greatness equated to volume. For Bertrand Goldberg, it was one building and one idea.

The building was Marina City, the five-building complex on the Chicago River whose twin towers adorn postcards, maps, and the scrapbooks of a million tourists. Marina City has been described as twin corncobs, grain elevators, flower petals, and steam radiators.

To William McFetridge, who sponsored the project, it meant jobs.

For "Bud" Goldberg, it was the rebirth of the inner city.

For Goldberg, a Mies disciple who rarely built anything that Mies would have designed, Marina City was a pioneering effort to put people back in the city after dark. While Mies and SOM were building massive steel and glass houses where people would work, it was Goldberg, more than any other architect of America's 1950s, who was obsessed with keeping people in the city.

Marina City was the first "city within a city" complete with shopping, entertainment, parking, and pie-wedge apartments that were affordable. It also was the first effort at refurbishing the dingy banks of the Chicago River, upon which nothing had been built for people to live in since Jacques Marquette's cabin. Marina City even had boat slips.

"Marina City will survive close scholarly appraisal well into the next century as a superb example of architectural plasticity as well as a multiple-use facility reflecting Goldberg's concerns about urban amenities," Paul Gapp of the *Tribune* commented in 1991 when he ranked Marina City among Chicago's ten most significant postwar buildings.

"We are still trying to find out what we can design that will invite people to form community," Goldberg said in a 1994 *Tribune* interview. "We can't force them to form communities, but we can invite them. . . . Urban areas must find ways to restore community, otherwise urbanism itself is at peril. . . . It has come to be my belief that what the city has to do is provide enormous freedom and opportunity for expressing freedom for life and living patterns. The city is not a storage place for people."

Goldberg grew up in Hyde Park, went to local private schools, and proceeded to Harvard and then Germany's famous Bauhaus school of design. He studied there with such giants as Mies and painters Wassily Kandinsky and Josef Albers, and knew Paul Klee. He left Germany in 1933 as the Nazis came to power. Returning to Chicago, he was greatly influenced by the 1933 Century of Progress exposition and its art moderne motif, and he began to distance himself from Mies and the international style.

His fascination with discovering ways for people to live in high-density cities was evidenced by his 1940 design of the Stanfab prefabricated bathroom.

Marina City, which he began to design in the late 1950s, marked his defining moment. With middle-class families fleeing the city for the suburbs, Mr. Goldberg teamed with a special client, William McFetridge, who headed a union of elevator operators and building janitors. The union's membership was bound to suffer if downtown Chicago emptied out.

Marina City articulated Goldberg's view that the denser a city is the better, because only with a critical mass of people in proximity can society provide itself efficiently with such services as transportation and public safety.

Not everyone shared his vision, and Goldberg's attempt to broaden the scope of Marina City's plan with a network of high-rise towers to house forty thousand people in what he called River City was rejected in the 1970s as too dense by city planners.

As with many architects, he was criticized for many of his other buildings that used the same cylindrical forms as Marina City: the

Raymond Hilliard Homes public housing development; the Prentice Women's Hospital in Chicago; and hospitals in Tacoma, Washington, Milwaukee, Boston, Phoenix, and the Elgin State Hospital in Elgin.

A 1985 book published by the Paris Art Center, *Goldberg: On the City*, described Marina City as the first mixed-use downtown complex in the United States to include housing. A West Coast architecture critic called him "Chicago's great poet of urban community."

On his death in 1997 at age eighty-six, *Tribune* architecture critic Blair Kamen wrote simply, "Goldberg's significance transcended architecture. In the 1950s, when there was widespread pessimism about the future of cities as places to live, Goldberg posed a vital alternative."

7

HOLABIRDS AND ROOTS:
JOHN HOLABIRD AND JOHN ROOT JR.

There have been Holabirds and Roots designing buildings longer than any other firm in Chicago's illustrious architectural history, although it took nearly fifty years for the two families to get together and the combination of Holabird and Root has never been quite as famous as their first-generation forebears.

"Holabird and Root is greatly underrated," said the *Tribune*'s Blair Kamen. "Their work in the 1920s was a tremendous influence on all of American architecture."

The first Holabird and the first Root are seminal figures in the Chicago school of architecture. William Holabird and Martin Roche both joined the firm of William Le Baron Jenney in 1875 and met Louis Sullivan, who had been working there for two years. Holabird and Roche formed a partnership in 1882 that lasted until Roche's death in 1927. During that period they prodigiously designed seventy-two downtown buildings, including their first success, the Tacoma, and their masterpiece, the Marquette, which still stands at 140 South Dearborn. Their next most impressive work, the sleek Republic Building, was, sadly, razed in 1961.

While Holabird and Roche were extending the design of the steel-skeleton skyscraper, John Wellborn Root was working with Daniel Burnham, creating two chunks of history, the Monadnock and the Rookery, before his death at age forty-one in 1891, leaving a four-year-old namesake.

In 1909, John Wellborn Root Jr., following in his father's footsteps, was a student at the Ecole des Beaux Arts in Paris, where he met John A. Holabird, a West Point graduate also following in his father's path. Young Root, the visionary, and young Holabird, the engineer, became friends, and both went to work in the firm of Holabird and Roche. They became the senior partners after the death of William Holabird in 1923, and when Martin Roche died in 1927 the firm's name was changed to Holabird and Root, which it has remained, with shifting additions and deletions, for the rest of the century.

Kamen's contention that Holabird and Root have been underrated is based not only on what they did but that it would have been hard, if not impossible, to do anything that surpassed the stone and steel legacies of their fathers.

But they tried.

In the midst of the Roaring Twenties, while Al Capone was sweeping down gangland enemies and Red Grange was sweeping through the Michigan line, the art moderne and art deco craze was sweeping America. No one was more emphatically successful in merging the new with the old than Holabird and Root.

In 1928 they built, on the spot where Fort Dearborn had stood more than a century earlier, the 333 North Michigan Avenue building, a thirty-five-story limestone tower marked by the setbacks that became their trademark in the final years before the Depression halted all American building. The critic Carl Condit called the structure, which was greatly influenced by Eliel Saarinen's second-place sketches in the Tribune Tower contest, "aristocratic." The building's top floors housed the Tavern Club, whose breezy murals, pastels, and airy lighting differed vastly from any other men's bastion of its age.

At almost the same time, Holabird and Root were working on the Palmolive Building, now 910 North Michigan Avenue, again using setbacks as the keystone for the thirty-seven-story modernistic building fronted by projecting bays and topped with a 150-foot-tall light beacon that was Chicago's most distinctive landmark for three decades. Initially named the Lindbergh Beacon, it was called the Palmolive Beacon after the hero aviator failed to appear in Chicago for its dedication.

Holabird and Root were among the pioneers in the use of exterior lighting on big-city buildings. Besides the Palmolive, the 221

North LaSalle building at LaSalle and Wacker was brilliantly illumi-
nated. This was another soaring aristocrat formed by two twenty-story
towers serving as arms for a recessed forty-one-story monolith over a
courtyard.

Holabird and Root's Chicago Daily News Building, now Two
Riverside Plaza, was the first Chicago structure erected on air rights
above railroad tracks when it was finished in 1929, its block-long plaza
sitting over the western edge of the south branch of the Chicago
River across from its new neighbor, the thronelike Civic Opera House
built in 1929 by Graham, Anderson, Probst, and White.

Holabird and Root's final two buildings before the Depression
were the Michigan Square Building, an eight-story office and retail
center surrounding a three-story atrium done in marble and chrome
called Diana Court, and their tour de force Chicago Board of Trade
Building. The Michigan Square Building at Michigan and Ohio was
torn down in 1973 and replaced by Paul Gapp's biggest nightmare, the
Marriott Hotel.

But the Board of Trade Building at the foot of LaSalle Street continues to tower over the city's financial district with its thirty-one-foot
statue of Ceres, Roman goddess of agriculture, sitting atop its pyra-
mid roof overlooking the twenty-four-story postmodern addition that
Helmut Jahn deftly added in 1980. The Board of Trade's three-story
lobby in glass, chrome, and marble continued the art deco effect created with similar materials in the Riverside Plaza, 333 North Michigan
building, and Palmolive Building, in which extensive grillwork, bas-
relief doors and walls, and terrazzo floors were other Holabird and
Root signatures.

Holabird and Root moved comfortably through the Depression
years, adding Joseph Burgee as a partner until 1948 and continuing to
thrive for the remainder of the century. But it is the remarkably
enduring edifices of their art moderne period that—unlike bathtub
gin and the Charleston—remain as stunning visual reminders of the
Roaring Twenties.

8

THE LITTLE SCHOOLHOUSE:
PERKINS AND WILL

In 1940, Lawrence Perkins and Phil Will, former classmates at Cor-
nell, were building houses on the North Shore, their five-year-old
architectural firm just emerging from the construction slump of the
Depression. They bid on a contract to do an elementary school in
Winnetka. The school district wanted a building that did not look like
all the other structures that were built for adults to house children.
They wanted a schoolhouse that fit with the progressive philosophy of
education.

Perkins and Will joined with Finnish star Eliel Saarinen to create a
long, low building with skylights, walls of windows, and child-sized
interior design. It was the Crow Island School, one of the most celebrated landmarks of twentieth-century architecture and the forerunner for thousands of schools all across America.

While many Americans will never live in a Frank Lloyd Wright
house or work in a Mies van der Rohe building, almost everyone under
fifty has gone to school in a building that resembles Crow Island.

The school is considered one of the most famous small buildings
in America. In 1956, an *Architectural Record* poll placed it as the twelfth
most significant building in the previous one hundred years of American architecture, and the first among schools. In 1971, Perkins and
Will's firm received the 25-Year Medal from the American Institute of
Architects for the lasting importance of the school's design.

When Lawrence Perkins died in 1997 at age ninety, his son, Brad-
ford, a New York architect, recalled how his father, a towering figure

at six-foot-three, was an incongruous sight as he sat among Winnetka second-graders, watching how classes were taught so the Crow Island School design could respond to human needs.

It was the first school to be zoned by pupil age groups, with groupings of classrooms that gave it a new and more child-friendly scale than its predecessors. With a distinctive clock tower that served as a reminder of the school's civic identity, Crow Island was hailed as a prototype for the modern American school and became one of the most influential school buildings in the nation.

Each classroom has its own restroom, with fixtures scaled to the height of children, and its own workroom. Every classroom has two walls of windows, its own exit to the outside, storage "cubbies" under the long rows of window seats, and a carpeted gathering area for stories and discussions.

The auditorium has child-sized seats, smaller in the front and gradually getting bigger toward the back. Light switches, door handles, and railings throughout the building are all at child height. Little "spots of fun"—ceramic sculptures of animals and historic figures done by Lillian Saarinen, wife of architect, Eero—dot the walls inside and out.

Chicago's great architectural critic Carl W. Condit wrote, "It marked the beginning of a triumphant career for Perkins and Will, whose rapidly expanding firm became the leading school architects of metropolitan Chicago and eventually of the United States."

By the middle 1950s, the firm, then known as Perkins, Wheeler, and Will, was the leader in the school-design field; by 1960, it had finished 372 school projects in twenty-four states. Some of the Chicago-area schools it designed were Evanston Township High School in Evanston and Glenbrook North High School in Northbrook.

Their success was no accident.

Perkins was the son of Dwight Perkins, who had gone to work with Burnham and Root in 1888 and eventually formed the firm of Perkins and Hamilton. "Perkins was the architect who set the standard for scholastic building in Chicago," said Condit. Perkins was appointed chief architect for the Chicago Board of Education in 1905 and designed forty schools, including what Condit considered his masterpiece, Carl Schurz High School at Milwaukee and Addison.

Perkins and Will did not only design schools. The firm collaborated in the late 1960s with C. F. Murphy on the First National Bank Building, with its sweeping base and sunken plaza. In the 1980s and 1990s the star at Perkins and Will was Ralph Johnson, the creative force in the dramatic Morton International Building at 100 North Riverside Plaza with the world's tallest clock, and the International Terminal at O'Hare International Airport.

The Morton clock rises 550 feet above the sidewalk and is listed in the *Guinness Book of World Records*. Crow Island School also has a clock tower. It is about 500 feet lower than the one on the Morton Building, which only proves that size isn't everything when it comes to changing the world.

9

STARSHIP HELMUT:
HELMUT JAHN

If Daniel Burnham were alive today he'd want to be SOM. If Frank Lloyd Wright were alive today he'd want to be Helmut Jahn.

Helmut Jahn also might not have minded being Frank Lloyd Wright. Jahn burst on the American architectural scene in the 1970s with his design of the Kemper Arena in Kansas City, Missouri, and no one minded when its roof collapsed in a thunderstorm. Since then he has built some of the most dramatic and innovative buildings in the world. Not all of them are good, but everybody talks about them, which is something Wright would have liked.

While other architects are of the IBM school or the artsy-tweedy set, Jahn was strictly jet-set. Draped in expensive Italian designer suits, Jahn skied Aspen and the Alps, raced sailboats, and whizzed about in chic autos such as a Porsche 911. The German-born Jahn became one of Chicago's very few "beautiful people" during the 1980s while he was creating buildings that differed very much from the "floating in space" effect mastered by Wright.

The space in Jahn's buildings was all inside.

His most controversial work, the State of Illinois Building, appeared in 1985 and was dubbed "Starship Chicago," its glass facade sloping like a launching pad, with hues of blue, red, salmon, and silver at a time when few architects dared put color on the exterior of what were supposed to be stately buildings.

The colors, Jahn explained, were reflective of optimism. It has been a very optimistic America since then, with Jahn's color schemes being imitated everywhere.

Paul Gapp of the *Tribune* called the State of Illinois center the "most spectacular building ever constructed in the Loop," but he didn't like much of the exterior, which at once tried to echo and clash with its more sedate neighbors across Randolph Street—the classic, granite-based city hall and Jacques Brownson's soaring rust monolith, the Daley Civic Center.

The interior was a different matter. "What we did not have in Chicago until Jahn designed the center was a contemporary vertical space of such splendid and theatrical dimensions. Tall, broad, soaring, full of interactive light and color that yield a rich complexity of changing images as you walk at any level of the center or ride in one of the exposed glass elevators," Gapp wrote.

Another nickname that greeted the oddly dressed Loop new-comer was "Thompson's Folly," named after Governor James Thompson, who had selected Jahn to design the building.

Only two years after "Starship Chicago," a massive collection of Jahn's works appeared by Paris art dealer Ante Glibota, a startling tribute for someone who was then only forty-seven years old. Glibota characterized Jahn as one of the architects "having glorious revenge on the eve of the new millennium." He labeled him a "romantic modernist," a tag that has stuck, and "the unchallenged master of American architecture today."

Others preferred an earlier nickname, "Flash Gordon."

Helmut Jahn left Germany at the age of twenty-five to study at IIT under Mies disciples Fazlur Khan and Myron Goldsmith. He took it for about three months and then departed, turning up at C. F. Murphy and Associates, "palace" builder to His Excellency, Richard J. Daley. Murphy had built the first post–World War II high-rise in Chicago, the Prudential Building, as well as the Civic Center. In 1967, Gene Summers headed Murphy's design function and was in charge of rebuilding McCormick Place after the fire. Constructing such a large convention hall required an innovative design for the stresses, and young Jahn came up with it. By 1973 he had taken Summers's place as Murphy's design director, and by the 1980s he owned the firm.

His first high-rise was the Xerox Center at Dearborn and Monroe, whose rounded corner paid tribute to Sullivan's design of the Carson, Pirie, and Scott grand entrance a few blocks away. The building had historical touches and modernistic lines. It did not look like a Miesian production, nor did it signal Jahn's future excesses. He became a superstar in the 1980 building boom.

Jahn's productions became widely anticipated, like a new line by Dior or a new movie by Spielberg. When he completed the United Airlines Terminal at O'Hare, it drew raves. The grandly scaled barrel-vaulted spaces and exposed piping and white-painted steel girders recaptured the drama and romance of travel once symbolized by high-ceilinged railroad terminals. His futuristic lighting and pastels glowing in the connecting tunnel speak to modern high technology.

And Jahn looked the part. *Chicago Tribune* columnist Eric Zorn described his "Prince Valiant hair cut," and reporters of the social scene gave him top billing at parties and charity affairs. He expanded his work internationally, accepting several commissions in his native Germany, including the 845-foot Messeturm in Frankfurt, Europe's tallest office building.

Jahn was never pleased with the wags who looked at his futuristic buildings and nicknamed him after the 1930s comic-book space hero. But in 1997 in England, his sailing team won the Admiral's Cup, one of the world's premier sailboat-racing events. It was the first victory by an American team in twenty-eight years.

Jahn's boat was named *Flash Gordon*.

10

REBELS WITH A CAUSE:
STANLEY TIGERMAN, ET AL.

Stanley Tigerman once built a phallic symbol that looked like a house and a garage that looked like a car. Tigerman has been an innovator, a rebel, a traditionalist, a scold, and over forty years moved from l'enfant terrible to éminence grise and back again. The critic Paul Gapp called him the "clown prince" of Chicago architecture. Another critic, Blair Kamen, called him its "King of Zing." He also was the ringleader of the Chicago Seven, a group of architects who in the 1970s challenged then-current dogma and demanded a more inclusive architecture for both traditionalists and unorthodox modernists. It stirred the postmodernist movement, whose results were, like Tigerman's moods, very good and very bad.

Tigerman kicked off the rebel era in 1976 by poking fun at an exhibition of Chicago architecture that was mostly a tribute to Mies and excluded virtually all other Chicago architects whose brilliance captivated Tigerman. He joined with Laurence Booth, Stuart Cohen, and Benjamin Weese to stage a counterexhibition that opened simultaneously with the "100 years of Chicago Architecture" show, which had originated in Munich. The four rebels quickly became the Chicago Seven with the addition of Thomas H. Beeby, James Ingo Freed, and James Nagle. Helmut Jahn and Cynthia Weese later joined the alliance. The group's work in the 1980s made them a major force in Chicago architecture, which in turn made them a major voice everywhere.

Nearly twenty years later, in 1993, Tigerman was at it again, producing an exhibition that virtually attacked the city's political, business, and city leaders for their timidity about bold projects such as the scuttled 1992 World's Fair, a new sports stadium, or a new airport. The center-piece of the exhibit was a photo of the late Mayor Richard J. Daley, a pointed reminder of a time in Chicago when things got done. Tigerman was particularly upset about the opportunities lost by the inability of politicians to finance the fair, pointing out that the highly successful 1933 Century of Progress fair was held in the midst of the Depression, only a year after Chicago could not afford to pay its schoolteachers.

Tigerman didn't just insult and infuriate. He did build, and so did his compatriots. In 1985, Paul Gapp labeled him one of the city's and the nation's most important architects, particularly praising his Illinois Regional Library for the Blind and Physically Handicapped at 1055 West Roosevelt Road and the whimsical Anti-Cruelty Society head-quarters at LaSalle Street and Grand Avenue.

One of his best projects outside of Chicago was the Knoll Inter-national showroom building in Houston, where Gapp applauded, "Tigerman created an oasis of beauty on an ugly and difficult site."

Thomas Beeby carried the Chicago Seven philosophy to the biggest city architectural controversy of the 1980s with his neoclassi-cal design for the Harold Washington Library, something that looks like a Henry Richardson classic of the 1880s, with large green owls perched on its rooftop corners.

Freed, who was one of Mies's successors as dean of the IIT archi-tectural school, moved off to New York, where he did the award-winning design for the United States Memorial Holocaust Museum in Washington, D.C., in which he built bridges and towers reminiscent of concentration camps to create a powerful emotional theme.

Booth and Nagle, who worked for Tigerman, formed their own firm, which lasted for a few years, in 1970. Booth designed the Grace Episcopal Church at 637 South Dearborn Street in 1985 and worked on the rehabilitation of Navy Pier. Nagle led the 1986 transformation of 20 North Michigan Avenue, the old John M. Smyth Company furni-ture store, taking a building with little architectural merit and revamping it into a handsome addition for a street lined with the works of America's greatest architects—all of them from Chicago.

■ ■ ■ X

POTPOURRI

■ ■ ■ POTPOURRI

Some Chicagoans were so superior in their fields of endeavor that they made it impossible for their peers to even approach their impact on American life. The categories already listed were a useful device in forcing the selection of only a few individuals out of the many who were considered in such areas as business, sports, media, architecture, and entertainment. But there were all kinds of Chicagoans who do not fall neatly into categories. Most of them excelled so well that to create a ranking system would have been artificial. There were just not enough Nobel Peace Prize winners to make up a category. There were not enough great religious leaders to pick ten. There was only one saint.

In previous chapters the ranking device was intended not only to establish a subjective hierarchy of importance but to cull the lists. Rightly or wrongly, senators like the dedicated Alan Dixon, Adlai Stevenson III, Paul Simon, Charles Percy, and Carol Mosely-Braun did not make it. Neither did businessmen like Oscar Mayer or Arthur Andersen or A. C. Nielsen. Local media legends like Irv Kupcinet or Wally Phillips didn't make it. Not even the gifted Walter Payton, the ferocious Dick Butkus, or basketball's first big man, George Mikan, qualified.

The previous parts of this book were designed to discuss as many of the most memorable and significant Chicagoans as possible.

There could have been a discussion of inventors. Chicagoans invented such odd things as the envelope with a window, the lava lamp, the pinball machine. George Stephens filled America's patios with the Weber grill. There could have been a discussion of aviation. The first plane to carry mail took off from Chicago piloted by an unknown barnstormer named Charles Lindbergh. Bessie Coleman was the first black woman who held a pilot's license. Octave Chanute was experimenting with gliders on the Indiana Dunes before the Wright Brothers got to Kitty Hawk. There were doctors such as Daniel Hale Williams and philosophers such as Thorsten Veblen.

The focus of the previous parts of this book has been on the people who made the great American institutions, from the National Football League to McDonald's. If this was a discussion of institutions, it would be simple to declare that the University of Chicago with its seventy-odd Nobel Prizes had as much if not more impact on the twentieth century than any other institution in Chicago or anywhere else in America.

Although it is not a category in the sense of professional definition, the final listing has a consistent theme, one that Chicago is as notable for as any other of its hallmarks. The people listed in this part cared about people. And while this final grouping may be the most subjective of all, its format remains consistent with the previous lists. It's certainly possible, more likely probable, that more than one of the people in this group could be considered the most important and influential Chicagoan of all.

The first was a woman.

HULL HOUSE:
JANE ADDAMS

In 1889 Chicagoans such as the McCormicks and Swifts were manning the barricades of their nouveau riche wealth and privilege while hundreds of thousands of swarthy and swarming foreigners filled their labor shops. The Haymarket riot was three years old and the Pullman strike was three years hence. The Chicago establishment was too busy building dynasties and a most remarkable city to fret over sweatshops and infant deaths. In 1889, the glorious Auditorium Theater opened with both the president and vice president of the United States in attendance. The Adler and Sullivan masterpiece was proclaimed the finest theater venue in the world. In 1889, John Hertz ran away from his West Side home to peddle penny newspapers. In 1889 Chicago's Irish hated the Italians, who hated the Jews, who hated the Poles, who hated the Germans, who hated everybody. In between their ethnic dislikes they were overworked and underfed, lived in conditions that bordered between unhealthy and disgraceful, and died almost as fast as they reproduced.

In 1889 two women set out to do something about it. They rented a run-down mansion at the corner of Halsted and Polk Streets and in their clean clothes and starched collars began inviting the immigrants of Chicago to bring them their troubles. They opened the first day-care center, the first kindergarten, and the first free clinic. They created arts programs to teach sewing and social programs where people who spoke no English could discover a common ground without producing knives. They called it all Hull House.

In 1889 Jane Addams was twenty-nine years old, a product of a well-to-do Quaker family in Cedarville, near Freeport in northwestern Illinois. Her biographers say she was smallish and attractive, although the most famous photographs depict her in middle age as a stout, matronly figure with a stern visage, which she had acquired in changing American attitudes toward the needy and changing the needy's attitude toward themselves. In her autobiography she called herself an "ugly duckling." Perhaps that is why she spent all her life working for society's "ugly ducklings."

Addams had visited London in 1885 and marveled at Toynbee Hall, a settlement house in the Whitechapel slums. She and her lifelong companion, Ellen Gates Starr, modeled Hull House after Toynbee Hall. It eventually grew to encompass thirteen buildings, Chicago's first playground, and a summer camp near Lake Geneva, Wisconsin. Addams and Starr used their own money to support Hull House, although they charged a nickel for day care if any of the women sweating in the fabric shops could afford it. Addams believed fervently that even in poverty there should be time for play and recreation. Her youth in a bucolic farm setting spurred her efforts to create green-space playgrounds for children when most Chicagoans, including their parents, believed they should be working. Hull House sponsored courses in languages, literature, music, painting, history, mathematics, elocution, dancing, and wood carving. To give immigrants, mostly uneducated, a sense of their traditions, she created a labor museum to depict how the skills of spinning and weaving began. One of her early converts was Sidney Hillman, who by 1940 was the head of the garment workers and the most powerful labor leader in America.

Her music courses gave Benny Goodman and Art Hodes their opportunity to become jazz legends. Her parlor was visited regularly by John Dewey, the father of progressive education, and Clarence Darrow, who was Addams's soul mate in almost every social endeavor from the founding of America's first juvenile court system to pacifist opposition to World War I. The Little Theater groups she sponsored were among the nation's first, and the Chicago theater success of the 1980s and 1990s can trace its beginnings to Hull House. Almost any institution anywhere that is concerned with the plight and rights of the lower class can trace its beginnings to Hull House. No one was turned away at Hull House. Princes and paupers were welcome. The prime minister of Great Britain visited. Blacks newly arrived from southern poverty usually found their only signs of Chicago kindness on Halsted Street. All this, despite being located in a neighborhood that journalist Lincoln Steffens described as "first in violence, deepest in dirt, loud, lawless, unlovely, ill-smelling, criminally wide open, commercially brazen, socially thoughtless and raw."

Addams fought against the indiscriminate sale of milk, which often carried tuberculosis and thus quickly killed nursing infants. She became so infuriated at the corrupt ward politics that she got herself made a garbage inspector to clean up what was then the 19th Ward. She later got "clouted" out of the job. She ran an opposition candidate against the city council's most formidable alderman, Johnny Powers, but failed to oust the confidante of Bathhouse John and Hinky Dink. She fought for the eight-hour day and workers' compensation for the many injuries that occurred in the packing plants and at railroad yards. She sponsored research to discover the causes of poverty and crime.

In the first decade of the twentieth century she was at the forefront of every social movement. She was the president of the National Conference of Charities and Corrections. She headed the Women's International Peace Party from 1915 until 1929 and visited the crowned heads of Europe to try and dissuade them from starting World War I. She was an advocate of the National Association for the Advancement of Colored People and the keynote speaker at almost every women's suffrage rally.

She became the first woman to address a major political convention, offering a seconding speech in 1912 for Theodore Roosevelt at the Progressive Party gathering. She later became a staunch advocate of Wisconsin's Robert LaFollette and his unsuccessful third-party efforts to capture the presidency.

After World War I she continued her work for peace at international gatherings in Zurich in 1919, in Vienna in 1921, in The Hague in 1924, in Dublin in 1926, and in Prague in 1929. She had urged liberal peace terms for Germany and started food programs for hungry children in war-torn Europe. She argued for total disarmament. The *Chicago Tribune*, always suspicious of anyone that worried about the good health of Europe, noted, "Addams Favors Reds."

She was against drinking, but thought it was fine for women to smoke, and despite her rather frumpy apparel she applauded the flapper look of the 1920s.

In 1931 she was awarded the Nobel Peace Prize for her international efforts to stave off war. She gave the prize money to Hull House.

She was given honorary degrees by Yale, Chicago, and Wisconsin, among other schools. She was called "the greatest woman internationalist," the "mother of social service," and the "first citizen of Chicago." The world mourned when she died of stomach cancer in 1935.

In 1993, the Sienna Research Institute in New York, in cooperation with the National Women's Hall of Fame, ranked Eleanor Roosevelt and Jane Addams as the two most influential women in America in the twentieth century.

None of the awards could measure what Jane Addams meant to tens of thousands who found at Hull House what jazz pianist Art Hodes described in his autobiography:

So much to do at Hull House. You could play basketball, go to gym, or theater. Occasionally I'd pass Jane Addams. I can still remember the sight of her; in a way she reminded me of my mother, sort of short, buxom, filled out, gray hair and the warmest eyes. This woman had taken a part of a city block and carved out a bit of humane living for I don't know how many thousands of kids.

2

LUNCH, EVERYBODY:
ENRICO FERMI

Enrico Fermi so revered lunch he might have been mistaken for an alderman. In fact, Enrico Fermi was never mistaken for anyone in Chicago. He was never recognized. The man who may have changed the twentieth century more than any other person was virtually invisible in Chicago.

He lived in Chicago for twelve years. He headed a premier research institute at the University of Chicago. He died in Chicago. From the time he arrived here in 1942 until his death in 1954, virtually nothing was ever said in Chicago about Enrico Fermi. Quite a bit was said in scientific circles throughout the world. The *New York Times*, more worldly than the provincial *Chicago Tribune* of the 1950s, buried Fermi on the front page with companion stories and laudatory quotes. The *Chicago Tribune*'s farewell was on the obituary page, the kind the *Trib* usually reserved for retired generals and Republican congressmen.

The *Tribune* did note in passing that Fermi was "known as the architect of the atomic bomb."

The *Trib* undoubtedly would have been more interested if he had been the architect of its publisher's mansion.

But the *Tribune* couldn't be blamed too much for ignoring Fermi during the years of World War II. His whereabouts and his work was the best-kept secret of the U.S. government.

From 1942 until his death, Fermi usually had lunch at the University of Chicago's Quadrangle Club, or at home, first on Ellis Avenue and later at 5327 University Avenue. For a while in 1944 and 1945 he had lunch at P.O. Box 1663, Santa Fe, New Mexico, the code name for the nuclear bomb plant at Los Alamos, New Mexico. In November of 1938 he had lunch in Stockholm, Sweden, where he was awarded the Nobel Prize in physics for his discovery that the bombardment of uranium with neutrons led to atomic fission.

Fermi began his incredible life and passion for lunch in Rome, where he was born in 1901, the son of a ranking civil servant who educated his extraordinarily bright son in private schools and at the University of Pisa, where he earned undergraduate and advanced degrees. Fermi studied abroad in Germany and the Netherlands, where the great theoretical physicists were located in the 1920s and where he would meet many of the men who later would help him build the bomb. Fermi became professor of theoretical physics at the University of Rome in 1926 and remained there until fascist dictator Benito Mussolini began mimicking his Axis friend Adolf Hitler's anti-Semitic philosophy. Fermi, whose wife, Laura, was Jewish, was already under official scrutiny for the scientific community's resistance to Mussolini's dictatorial overtures. The announcement of his Nobel award was ignored by Mussolini and the state-controlled Italian news media. But Fermi was given permission to travel with his wife and their two children to Stockholm to accept the award. Once in Sweden, Fermi informed Italian authorities he was going to take a temporary teaching assignment in America, and the family arrived in New York in January 1939. Fermi joined the physics department of Columbia University, where he and other exiles learned that German physicists had achieved nuclear fission.

In March 1939, Fermi tried to interest the Navy Department in the possibility of building an "atomic bomb." The navy wasn't interested. The exiled scientists, many of them Jewish, knew that Nazi Germany was pressing ahead with such a project. They enlisted the most famous scientist-exile of all, Albert Einstein, to write the letter to Franklin Roosevelt that launched the Manhattan Project.

Fermi now began working on what he called a "pile," where he hoped to achieve the first self-sustaining chain reaction that would free nuclear energy. Eventually he hoped to control the accelerating speed of the reaction and produce a monstrous explosion.

In 1942, the government moved the Manhattan Project to the University of Chicago. In a squash court under the west stands of now-abandoned Stagg Field—where the university no longer played football—Fermi began to construct the pile that would become the first atomic furnace, the first nuclear reactor.

For weeks he charted the construction of the pile made of graphite surrounding a core of uranium that weighed six tons. Neutrons bombarding the uranium would ultimately reach a critical stage that would produce a chain reaction. Controlling the speed of the bombardment were cadmium rods that acted as neutron deflectors. By removing one or more of a series of cadmium rods, Fermi could control the exact moment of criticality. No one really knew what would happen. Fermi was certain there was no danger of a nuclear explosion that would decimate the university or any part of Chicago. He was not certain about a smaller blast. As the scientists added more graphite and uranium to the pile on the night of December 1, 1942, Fermi went to bed after extracting a promise that no one would start the reaction until his return.

On the morning of December 2, the test continued. Fermi measured each reaction as the cadmium rod was slowly withdrawn an inch at a time. In Cambridge, Massachusetts, James B. Conant, president of Harvard University and FDR's appointee to head the Manhattan Project, waited anxiously by his telephone. In Chicago, the greatest physics talent assembled in America waited nervously as the small, balding Italian flipped the windows of his slide rule and ordered the rod removed just a little bit more. The pile did not become critical. Fermi looked at the clock and said, "Let's go to lunch."

When Fermi returned from lunch the test continued, and at 3:20 P.M., the pile went critical and the nuclear age was born.

Dr. Arthur Compton telephoned Conant with an impromptu code: "Jim, you will be interested to know that the Italian navigator has landed in the new world."

"Were the natives friendly?" Conant asked.

"Everybody landed safe and happy."

By late 1944, the government had built Los Alamos in the high New Mexico desert as the atomic bomb laboratory under the direction of J. Robert Oppenheimer. The Fermi family moved in under the code name "Eugene Farmer" and met old friends such as "Nick Baker," who was the great Danish physicist Niels Bohr, and new friends such as Klaus Fuchs, who would later betray England's nuclear secrets to Russia, and Edward Telling, the leading proponent of the hydrogen bomb.

After the first atomic bomb was tested on July 16, 1945, many of Fermi's colleagues urged him to join them in demanding a test demonstration be held before dropping a bomb on Japan. Fermi sided with Oppenheimer in arguing that the Japanese might not surrender after a test and, worse, such a test could fail. There was also the problem of obtaining enough uranium. New President Harry Truman was in no mood to listen to scientists forecasting the doom of mankind when his generals had told him up to five hundred thousand Americans would become casualties if Japan had to be invaded.

On August 6 and August 9, 1945 two atomic bombs were dropped for the only time in the twentieth century. They brought to an end the most devastating global armed conflict in civilized history.

Fermi returned to Chicago and became head of the university's Institute for Nuclear Studies, where he remained the rest of his life. Only twelve days before his death from stomach cancer in 1954 he was the recipient of a special twenty-five thousand dollar award given by the Atomic Energy Commission.

As the millennium approaches there will be countless arguments as to the significance of many individuals who left huge footprints on the twentieth century. There undoubtedly will be those who say none were bigger than those of Albert Einstein, whose theories led the way to nuclear energy and the exploration of space. Enrico Fermi was not Albert Einstein, but he wasn't far behind.

3

ALL IN THE GAME:
CHARLES DAWES

It would not be much of a surprise to suggest that either Jane Addams or Enrico Fermi could have been the most influential Chicagoan of the century. Most people would be shocked if a nomination were offered for Charley Dawes. Charles Gates Dawes is one of those people who fit into the story that begins, "A woman had two sons. One joined the navy to see the world. The other became vice president and was never heard from again."

Charles Gates Dawes was the vice president of the United States between 1925 and 1929, the only Chicagoan who ever served in that post and, arguably, the only person who ever gave the office any distinction. What other vice president won a Nobel Peace Prize?

No Chicagoan and few other Americans ever held as many responsible and coveted positions as Dawes—lawyer, banker, utility magnate, author, composer, industrialist, statesman, soldier, diplomat—and vice president.

Charles Dawes also bankrolled the 1933 World's Fair, kept Europe at peace between Germany's irritating habit of starting world wars, went on the biggest European shopping spree of any American in history, and paid very little attention to suggestions that he run for president.

One of the most famous political phrases in American history was Calvin Coolidge's terse, "I do not choose to run." When Silent Cal said that in 1927 almost every Republican assumed his vice president, Dawes, would take up the GOP mantle. But Dawes, among all his other virtues, was a loyal fellow and deferred to the longtime ambitions of his friend and fellow Illinoisan Governor Frank Lowden, who had been denied the 1920 nomination that the boys in the smoke-filled room handed to Warren Harding. But while Dawes was shilling for Lowden, whose time had passed, the energetic Herbert Hoover swept away the GOP nomination. It might have been a far different world if Charley Dawes wasn't so loyal.

Dawes was born in Marietta, Ohio, a few months after the Civil War ended in 1865. He attended Marietta College and attended law school in Cincinnati, where his passing grades were approved by another Buckeye with a national future, William Howard Taft. He traveled to the frontier to seek his fortune in 1887, hanging his law shingle in Lincoln, Nebraska, where he prospered and made two lifelong friends. One of them was a young congressman named William Jennings Bryan. Another was a frustrated army lieutenant named John B. Pershing.

Although Lincoln was a growing town, it wasn't growing fast enough for Charley Dawes, who like almost everyone else in America had visited Chicago for the 1893 World's Fair and fell in love with the city. He moved his wife, Caro, and their two children to Chicago in 1895. He had already made money in land investments in Nebraska, and now he purchased the Northwestern Gas Light and Coke Company of Evanston, which later became People's Gas Light and Coke Company of Chicago. Dawes was going to be a rich young man.

Dawes's father had been a one-term Republican congressman from Ohio, and Charley Dawes had already met several presidents when in 1896 he managed the Illinois campaign of another Ohioan, William McKinley, whose victory led to almost four decades of government service for Dawes. His first Washington job was as Controller of the Currency, and from 1897 until 1902 he collected for taxpayers more than $25 million from banks that failed during the 1893 panic.

He returned home certain that he would be chosen by the legislature as U.S. senator, but he ran afoul of the William Lorimer machine, which later was discredited by Colonel McCormick's *Chicago Tribune*. Dawes vowed to never again enter a political race, which may have been another reason for his reluctance to seek the presidency in 1928.

Instead, fresh from his financial job in Washington, he organized the Central Trust Company of Illinois, which became the Central

Republic Bank and Trust Company, known for the first three decades of the century as the "Dawes Bank."

When America entered World War I Dawes prevailed on his old friend, now General John "Black Jack" Pershing, for a commission as lieutenant colonel of the 9th Engineers, which was the first army unit to sail for Europe. After a few months of building railroads, Dawes was given the job of purchasing all army materials in Europe. Pershing needed ships to carry troops, not material. Dawes spent $100 million in the next six months and persuaded both England and France to join his efforts on what became the Allied Supply Board. Dawes was promoted to general and remained in France until 1919, liquidating the army surplus of more than $100 million.

In 1921, Warren Harding offered Dawes the cabinet spot of treasury secretary, but Dawes declined. He wanted and got the newly created post of director of the Bureau of the Budget, where in his first year of consolidating all appropriation bills he reduced federal spending by $1.7 billion from the previous year.

In 1923, war seemed ready to break out again in Europe. Inflation had made German marks worthless, yet Germany's World War I conquerors, England and France, were demanding billions in reparations. Dawes gave the allied governments a plan in 1924 to stabilize German marks with loans of $800 million and mortgages of $15 billion on German railroads and industries. He tied this to a reparations payment program that would work. The French pulled their troops back from the Rhine. England accepted the Dawes Plan and the European neighbors managed to go another fifteen years before beginning to kill each other again.

In 1925, Dawes was given the Nobel Prize for his peacekeeping.

He would have been ballyhooed for president in 1924 if Harding had lived and not sought a second term. But Harding died, and the new incumbent, Coolidge, was the unanimous GOP nominee. He picked Dawes as his running mate.

After Hoover's election four years later, Dawes was named ambassador to Great Britain, where he played a critical role in disarmament talks that reduced the size of the British, American, and Japanese navies and stalled the eventual Japanese encroachment into Manchuria.

But in 1932, with America in the midst of the Depression, Hoover called Dawes back in America to head the Reconstruction Finance Corporation (RFC), Hoover's last-gasp effort to save the banks. Dawes used $2 billion to bail out banks before he resigned to save his own.

Only weeks after his resignation, the RFC loaned $90 million to save Central Republic Bank, which resulted in the only public criticism in Dawes's career. The loan was a useless gesture, since a year later Roosevelt closed all the banks. Central Republic was restructured as City National Bank, and Dawes ultimately paid more than $1 million out of his pocket to repay the debts. He remained chairman of the bank until his death at age eighty-five in 1951.

The only other embarrassment in Dawes's illustrious career was his music. He played the piano and flute, although he had no formal training. And he composed songs. One of them was called "Melody in A Major," which he wrote in 1911 and which was published by one of the many professional musicians he befriended. The tune was played in different arrangements for different groups throughout the country. Whenever Dawes appeared for a speech or political rally the band invariably struck up "Melody in A Major," which always embarrassed him.

Only a few years after his death, lyrics were put to the tune with a modern arrangement and it made the Top 40 charts as "It's All in the Game."

4

THE FIRST RED HAT:
GEORGE MUNDELEIN

On May 18, 1937, the Roman Catholic Church in America became the American Catholic Church. After a century of insecurity and inferiority, the church of immigrant America became the church of righteous America. The long dominance of the Protestant sects who founded the country and maintained a suspicious scrutiny over the Catholics and their vowed allegiance to the Vatican was no longer exclusive.

It happened when George Mundelein, the authoritarian archbishop of Chicago, the son of a German immigrant, the consummate financial genius who invented modern church finances, decided it was time somebody said something about Adolf Hitler.

In 1937, most of the world was trying desperately not to do anything that might cause the megalomaniac Nazi leader to ignite another world conflagration. Hitler had taken Austria. He had started his catastrophic persecution of Jews. And he was arresting Catholic priests.

Mundelein, who had been appointed Chicago's first cardinal in 1924, made his regular appearance before the diocesan clergy and emotionally urged support for the Pope's formal protests against Germany. As an aside he referred to Hitler as "an Austrian paper hanger and a poor one at that I am told."

The remarks were reported around the world, and Nazi Germany was infuriated. Protests were made to the Vatican. The German ambassador protested to the U.S. secretary of state. Pope Pius XI was forced to script an apology for the uproar, not for the sentiment. In one brief phrase, Mundelein became a political figure, an international figure, something Roman Catholic prelates in America had avoided conscientiously for a century.

But Mundelein was more than that. He had already become a political figure for his unswerving support of the New Deal and his warnings against the spread of atheistic communism, especially in the Spanish Civil War. He had gained national renown as a liberal for his defense of labor unions in the turbulent 1930s. And he was celebrated for his courage in attacking Father Charles Coughlin's anti-Semitic radio ramblings. He was perceived by Americans as a confidante of Franklin D. Roosevelt, the first Catholic bishop to have formed such a relationship with an American president. It didn't matter if Mundelein was being used by Roosevelt as the president used almost everyone. It only mattered that Roosevelt had made a personal visit to Mundelein in Chicago, had invited him several times to the White House, and used him as an emissary to the Vatican. Not until John Kennedy's election in 1960 elevated a Catholic to the White House was there a Catholic considered more influential than George Cardinal Mundelein.

George Mundelein was an old hand at banquets when he arrived for his first civic dinner in Chicago a few days after he was appointed archbishop in 1916, so he wisely skipped the soup. But hundreds of other diners getting their first glimpse of the new archbishop were not so wise. The soup had been poisoned. Three people died and scores of others were taken to hospitals. An anarchist, and there were plenty of them around in 1916, claimed credit for the deaths but was never caught.

When Mundelein, at age forty-three, was named the youngest archbishop in America, the Catholic Church was very much a suspect institution, particularly in the Midwest and rural South, where the Ku Klux Klan was vehemently anti-Papist. Catholic prelates walked a narrow line to avoid involvement in any activities that might appear to threaten the sacrosanct separation of church and state prescribed in the Constitution.

Equally difficult for the young archbishop was the pressure from Rome, where the popes thought the American church was far too secular and far too poor.

George Mundelein changed all that. He became the most successful banker ever to run a diocese or, as some critics believed, the most successful priest to ever build a bank. He believed in pomp and pomposity. He was not beloved or saintly. He mixed politics and money and came up with power. Chicago and Mundelein were a perfect match.

Mundelein was born in Brooklyn in 1872, the son of a German immigrant. He attended a seminary in Pennsylvania, was sent to study in Rome, and returned after his ordination to become secretary to the bishop of Brooklyn. He rose to the rank of auxiliary bishop by 1915, when he was appointed archbishop of the Chicago diocese, one still considered a missionary district by the Vatican, which probably thought Pottawattomies still roamed Michigan Avenue.

When Mundelein arrived in Chicago, he took over a totally disorganized diocese that had been fractionalized by ethnic squabbling and a series of weak bishops. Priests wandered from parish to parish at whim. Pastors kept no books and gave the diocese whatever share of the collections they felt necessary. There was no uniformity to the curriculum in Catholic schools or the liturgical schedules in the churches.

Mundelein's first goal was to raise cash. He stopped all the individual building by pastors. He banned priests from attending theaters on the grounds that it might appear immoral. He banned midnight mass on Christmas Eve, for he feared parishioners would show up drunk and be held in scorn by non-Catholics. He instituted a schedule of masses for every church in the diocese so that the families moving from one area to another would feel some conformity. He prepared a three-year series of sermon topics that priests could only deviate from on church holidays. The rest of the time they delivered sermons Mundelein wanted his congregations to hear.

Most of all he set quotas for fund-raising. He began slowly, but in time his pastors found that the modest annual goals were constantly being gouged by special assessments of 10 or 15 percent. Rome quickly took notice when the Peter's Pence collection taken annually by every church in the world to support the Vatican first doubled, then tripled in Chicago. Mundelein was sending the Pope more money than any other diocese in the world.

He also vowed to rid the diocese of the transient priests, many of whom owed their loyalties to the ethnic followings in the Slavic, Polish, and German communities. He courted the few wealthy Catholics of the time and bought one thousand acres of land near Libertyville to build a model seminary to produce Chicago priests. Eventually he spent $10 million to build St. Mary's of the Lake Seminary, which by 1930 was producing more than half the diocesan priests. His pastors called him the "Dutch Master" behind his back. If he heard about it, the pastor was relieved.

In 1924 he was named cardinal, the first American prelate west of the Alleghenies to receive the red hat. As he was the youngest arch-bishop in 1916, he was also the youngest member of the College of Cardinals.

He limited his early political affairs to protecting the church's tax-free status and trying to prevent the government from intervening in charitable works, which he and clergymen of all denominations believed was their bailiwick and also the avenue that generated money. He hobnobbed with the Insulls, Rosenwalds, Wrigleys, and other corporate giants of Chicago. When he needed a particularly influential law firm to fend off a tax suit, he dumped the diocese's regular lawyer and signed on with the firm formerly headed by Colonel Robert R. McCormick. The two men became amiable acquaintances but never close allies.

In 1926, Mundelein hosted the International Eucharistic Congress, with dozens of cardinals in flaming red visiting America and Mundelein's private preserve at St. Mary's of the Lake. The inevitable boosterism of Chicago allayed any concerns about a Papist invasion. McCormick's *Tribune* delighted in the extravaganza, which brought six hundred thousand visitors to the city. There were not even any gangland murders that week.

By the Depression, Mundelein began to shake off the political conservatism that immunized the American Catholic hierarchy. While other bishops in New York and Philadelphia looked warily at the New Deal, he recognized that a nationwide depression was not something that could be remedied by Catholic Charities. He applauded the National Recovery Act and Social Security. He and Roosevelt, both collectors, traded stamp books. Tommy "The Cork" Corcoran, FDR's jack-of-all-trades, became a political liaison between St. Mary's and Pennsylvania Avenue. It can be assumed that Mundelein's attacks on Father Coughlin were likely instigated by Roosevelt. In 1935, Roosevelt was asked to speak at the University of Notre Dame and likely asked Mundelein to introduce his speech for a nationally televised audience. Mundelein did in glowing praise, noting that since he was the only cardinal west of the Alleghenies, he was also the only cardinal between New York and China.

Yet, Mundelein was not a great liberal. His biographer, Edward R. Kantowicz, notes that while he was an unabashed supporter of Franklin Roosevelt, he deplored the birth control advocacy of Eleanor Roosevelt. He was the nation's leading opponent of indecent movies, and his efforts turned the Catholic Legion of Decency into a censorship body. An even more serious flaw in his liberal credentials, Kantowicz declared, was his insensitivity to Negroes. In one of his first acts as archbishop he designated St. Monica's parish on the South Side as the Negro church. He did this simultaneously with his efforts to dismantle all the Polish, Croatian, Slovenian, and German parishes.

Kantowicz concludes that above all Mundelein was pragmatic. His political gifts were not unlike his friend Roosevelt's. He understood what people cared about. He knew people did not want the government interfering in church business in the 1920s. He knew the average Catholic did not care much about the plight of Negroes in the 1920s. He knew labor unions were considered anarchist in the 1920s. And in the 1930s he recognized that the people's attitudes had changed, and he changed with them.

His legacy was the richest, most efficient diocese in America. He paved the way for Francis Cardinal Spellman of New York to succeed him as the White House's favorite churchman. And his glittering shows and splendid buildings boosted the pride of Catholics, who, after Mundelein, never considered themselves inferior to other Americans because of their religion.

5 ▨

WUNDERKIND:
ROBERT MAYNARD HUTCHINS

The great event of 1929 was the stock market crash. It was also the year that Ernest Hemingway wrote *A Farewell to Arms*, Heinrich Himmler became head of the Gestapo, and Samuel Insull opened his castlelike opera house. It was the year of the St. Valentine's Day Massacre and the year William Wrigley's Cubs went to a World Series and blew an 8–0 lead in the ninth inning en route to losing it.

The great crash of 1929 in American education was the landing of Robert Maynard Hutchins at the University of Chicago, where at the age of thirty the "boy wonder" was appointed president of a university that in forty years had already become one of the most prestigious academic institutions in America.

In the next two decades, Hutchins would become the most influential educator in America and one of its most outspoken and controversial characters. Hutchins would not be surprised that America continues to bemoan the state of its higher education five decades after he left Chicago. He envisioned an academic environment where the standards were so high that no one could ever achieve them, which he said was the whole point.

Hutchins was a breath of fresh air and a serpentine gale that swept through educational, social, and political worlds. He scorned the theories of John Dewey, who had scripted the format for twentieth-century American education at Chicago in 1899. He was publicly critical of Franklin Delano Roosevelt's policies and then tried to become FDR's running mate. He was an outspoken pacifist, which briefly endeared him to Colonel McCormick's *Tribune,* and then became the general contractor for atomic bomb research. He was fearless in his defense of the freedom to teach even when caught in the "red scare" of McCarthyism, and it was the faculty he defended who thwarted so many of his innovations and finally drove him to leave Chicago.

Hutchins had a tyrannical aversion to the concept of education as a vocational school, and he refused to consider establishing an engineering school at Chicago. He ridiculed the idea of allowing students to choose electives in any random fashion that suited them, and he thought grading and counting credits were worthless means to measure academic success. He introduced the Chicago Plan, which allowed students to be admitted without high school diplomas if they passed the admissions test. Students could take final examinations any time they felt prepared for them, and he introduced a short-lived program that allowed students to graduate after their sophomore year.

He infuriated the faculty, whose fame rested on the school's graduate and research programs, by demanding an emphasis on undergraduate education.

From the beginning he lashed out at what he called the trivialization of higher education with its emphasis on sports, fraternities, and sororities.

Hutchins was tall, handsome, witty, sophisticated, and usually broke, although he summered with the Rockefellers and traveled with the Vanderbilts.

Hutchins was born in 1899 in Brooklyn, New York, where his father, William James Hutchins, was pastor of the Bedford Presbyterian Church. Eight years after Robert was born, his father was appointed a professor of theology at Oberlin College in Ohio and the family moved there. Hutchins entered Oberlin when he was sixteen, and although he was a pacifist he volunteered in 1917 for service with the Army Ambulance Corps, the unit that also attracted Hemingway, Walt Disney, and Ray Kroc.

He graduated from Yale with high honors, working his way through school, and finished law school there in 1925 while he was working as secretary of the university. He was appointed dean of the law school two years later at age twenty-eight and began his revolution by joining the new reformers preaching legal realism. He introduced economics, social sciences, history, and philosophy to a curriculum that had been devoted exclusively to case studies. He hired future Supreme Court Justice William O. Douglas, one of the foremost radicals of legal realism, as a professor. Later, Hutchins advocated similar changes at the University of Chicago, and a latter-day successor, Edward Levi, would note, "The 1937 program made the philosophy of law an essential part of the law curriculum. It inaugurated a bold attempt to integrate economics with the law."

Hutchins's most controversial educational proposal was the Great Books course. Hutchins had met Mortimer Adler, a psychologist at Columbia University, who convinced him that a true liberal education involved prolonged exposure to the original works of the greatest minds from Socrates to Freud.

He was one of the earliest and most prescient opponents of intercollegiate sports, and he was covered more on Chicago's sports pages than on the front pages when he shocked the city by eliminating the University of Chicago's once-proud football program in 1939. "It is possible to earn twelve letters without ever knowing how to write one," Hutchins remarked, erroneously certain that schools like Harvard and Yale would first follow his example and that ultimately intercollegiate sports would return to pure amateurism.

The University of Chicago was filled in the 1930s with left-wing views, and Hutchins was forever defending his faculty's right to discuss Marxism, communism, socialism, and anything else they felt they should illuminate. At an Illinois legislative hearing looking into such nefarious doings, Hutchins was asked, "Are you really teaching communism in the political science department?" He replied, "We are indeed, and we are teaching cancer in the medical school."

His most famous remark concerning academic freedom was, "No faculty member can ever be fired except for rape or murder committed in broad daylight before three witnesses."

Hutchins was an early and frequent guest on the NBC radio show *Roundtable of the Air*, where throughout the Depression years he attacked Roosevelt's policies of foreign involvement, ultimately becoming one of the leading antiwar activists.

But when Harry Hopkins, FDR's right-hand man, approached Hutchins in 1940 about possibly joining Roosevelt on the ticket, he immediately began a campaign to land the job, which ultimately went to Henry Wallace.

In 1942, he was approached by Hopkins again to turn the University of Chicago into the research center for the development of the atomic bomb. Outside of the scientists involved and the highest government officials, Hutchins was the only civilian who knew that in December 1942 the first nuclear chain reaction was achieved under the stands of the football stadium that Hutchins had made obsolete.

Within weeks after the dropping of the atomic bomb on Hiroshima and Nagasaki, he called for a civilian agency to be placed in charge of nuclear development and foresaw what fifty years later would be labeled one-world diplomacy.

In 1944, he effectively ended whatever hopes he had of transforming Chicago into a great liberal arts, medieval institution that focused on learning for its own sake. He proposed that all outside earnings by faculty members be turned over to the institution, that all faculty rank be eliminated, and that faculty members be paid on the basis of need. These things, he said, would free the faculty to spend all their time concentrating on academic and teaching matters. The faculty revolted and Hutchins moved up to chancellor, where he remained until 1951, when he took the number-two spot at the Ford Foundation. From there he founded the Center for the Study of Democratic Institutions in Santa Barbara, California, where he remained until his death in 1977.

Whenever a computer science student balks at a course on Aristotle, whenever a law student becomes enthralled with the theories of John Stuart Mill, whenever a premed student discovers James Joyce, it is because of Robert Maynard Hutchins. He didn't change the world of higher education nearly as much as he would have liked, but he changed it more than anyone else in the last seventy years, and he changed it for the better.

His friend and biographer, Martin Mayer, said, "I know he has not succeeded in changing the world, but I know something much more marvelous than that: I know that the world has not succeeded in changing him."

6

IOLA:
IDA WELLS BARNETT

Jane Addams, Enrico Fermi, Charles Dawes, George Mundelein, and Robert Hutchins were all buried by the *New York Times* on page one. Ida Belle Wells wasn't buried by the *New York Times* at all. Nor was she buried by the *Chicago Tribune* in her hometown.

Of all the political warriors, mercantile buccaneers, soulful poets, and crusading writers mentioned on these pages, no one had more guts than Ida B. Wells.

About the only person in these lists that Ida B. Wells had anything in common with is Mother Cabrini. They both had Chicago public housing complexes named after them. That may not be the only similarity.

Ida B. Wells was talking Black Power before Stokely Carmichael's mother was born. Ida B. Wells was talking Black Pride before any American dreamed that such a phrase would make a legitimate presidential contender out of Jesse Jackson.

Sixty years before the historic and landmark *Brown v. Topeka Board of Education* decision there was *Ida B. Wells v. Chesapeake and Ohio*.

Five years before Booker T. Washington opened Tuskegee Institute in 1881, Ida B. Wells was teaching black children in schoolhouses that had no floors and no doors.

Ida Belle Wells was born forty miles south of Memphis near Holly Springs, Mississippi, in 1862 and was an orphan with five younger siblings to support by age fifteen. She refused to let relatives raise her brothers and sisters and moved them to Memphis, where she found a teaching job and took classes at Fisk University. In 1884, a year after

the U.S. Supreme Court had ruled the Civil Rights Act of 1875 uncon-
stitutional—opening the way for a return to total segregation in the
South—Ida Wells boarded a Chesapeake, Ohio, and Southwestern
Railway car and took a seat in the first-class coach. She was ordered to
leave the "whites only" car. She refused and was finally dragged off the
train at the next stop. There were not a lot of twenty-two-year-old
Negro women in the South who would think of suing a railroad. Ida
Wells did. She won and was awarded five hundred dollars in damages.

Then she began thinking about a career in journalism. She began
writing a column under the name Iola for black newspapers. In 1891 she
started a campaign documenting the awful conditions of black schools.
She was fired from her teaching job and became a full-time journalist,
taking over the *Memphis Free Speech* and continuing her column, which
appeared in most of the two hundred black newspapers in America.

In 1892, Thomas Moss, one of Wells's best friends, was lynched in
Memphis. Although it was common for black men to be lynched
throughout the South, usually on charges they had tried to rape a
white woman, Moss's crime was worse. He and two partners had
opened a small store and were quietly taking away business from a
white competitor.

Wells began the first antilynching crusade in America. She traveled throughout the South interviewing the families of victims, hiring
detectives, and compiling her own statistics, most of them proving
that the so-called "rape" charges were usually false and without any
basis. She listed the horrifying numbers of Negro men and women
lynched with no legal recriminations. She even raised the possibility
that some white women liked to consort with black men.

She was more than persona non grata in Memphis and most
southern cities. Newspapers unabashedly wrote that she was likely to
be lynched herself if she showed up in their neighborhood.

Wells was personally disappointed in 1896 when the Supreme
Court issued its "separate but equal" doctrine in the 1896 *Plessy v. Ferguson* decision, the case that eventually was overruled by *Brown v.
Topeka. Plessy v. Ferguson* also reversed her victory against the Chesapeake and Ohio a dozen years earlier.

By the early 1900s, Wells had become a major figure in many of
the black civil rights organizations that were sprouting. She was the

antilynching crusade chairman of the National Afro-American Council, and she founded the first black's women's club in Chicago.

She moved to Chicago in 1895 on her marriage to Ferdinand Lee Barnett, a prominent attorney who became the first black appointed assistant state's attorney in Cook County. Barnett also owned a newspaper, which his wife took over. She later organized the Negro Fellowship League and was one of the early founders of the NAACP, but she eventually withdrew from participating in its activities because she thought the leadership mirrored too closely the subservient policies of Booker T. Washington, who preached that blacks would achieve equality through education rather than militancy.

Ida Wells had seen too many charred bodies hanging from trees to be anything but militant.

She believed that equal rights were guaranteed Negroes by the Constitution that she taught her pupils, not something to be granted by the whim of whites or even obtained by trying to accommodate whites, although her campaign for women's suffrage led her often to Hull House, where she and Jane Addams had a mutual respect and friendship. She raised four children and was the first woman in Chicago to be appointed a probation officer. After World War I she was in the thick of investigations following the flurry of racial riots in Chicago, Tulsa, Houston, and other cities. She was often appointed to official investigating bodies and undertook her own investigations when she was not. She was instrumental in obtaining acquittals for blacks who had been charged as scapegoats in the aftermath of some riots.

In 1929 she decided to run for state senator. She lost to the black incumbent. She died in 1931 at the age of sixty-nine. She had raised four children and a nation's conscience.

7

CHICAGO'S SAINT: FRANCES CABRINI

More than fifty years after her death, Saint Frances Xavier Cabrini was a legend in Chicago newsrooms when Chicago newsrooms themselves were legendary. As the century wears down, there are fewer newsrooms and fewer legends and fewer newspaper people interested in them. But for years they used to tell the story of a young reporter named Harry Reutlinger, who in 1915 was given one of those Ben Hecht–type assignments to sneak into Columbus Hospital to get a wedding picture of a patient who had just killed his wife and then wounded himself. As Kenan Heise and Ed Baumann relate the story in *Chicago Originals*, Reutlinger was sneaking down a hallway when he came face to face with a tiny nun mopping the floor. "Mother Cabrini sent me," the reporter blurted. The nun whipped the mop across his face.

Mother Cabrini was not always a saint.

But the fact that she would become one led to the other newspaper legend. In 1938, Colonel Robert R. McCormick fired one of his star women reporters, Virginia Gardner, who was arrested while picketing in an effort to help the Newspaper Guild organize at two Chicago newspapers owned by William Randolph Hearst, never a McCormick ally but an obvious spiritual soul mate of antiunionism.

The Newspaper Guild appealed her firing to the National Labor Relations Board, which reinstated her with back pay. McCormick, vengeful and furious, relegated her to city news, forbidding the city desk to give her any bylines. But Cardinal George Mundelein, who

liked her spirit, deliberately gave Gardner a major scoop, that a former Chicago nun, Mother Cabrini, was going to be beatified. It was a
front-page story and called for a byline. McCormick relented and
allowed her to have one.

Gardner's fellow reporters were gleefully reading her story,
which noted that proof of two miracles were required for full sainthood. "She's halfway home," one observed. "She got Virginia's byline
back in the *Tribune*."

The church must have found at least one more miracle in the next
eight years, because on July 7, 1946, following the relatively brief
ecclesiastic period of twenty-nine years after her death, she was canonized by Pope Pius XII, the first American citizen to attain sainthood.

And the church never wanted her around.

Maria Francesca Cabrini was born in 1850 in Sant' Angelo Lodi-
giano near Milan, Italy. She was a tiny, sickly child whose continued
insistence that she would be a servant of God was dismissed because
of her fragility. She was rejected by several convents, and at age
twenty-four she founded the Institute of Missionary Sisters of the
Sacred Heart, determined she would minister to the heathens in far-
off China. But her work in Italy, opening orphanages and building hospitals, came to the attention of Pope Leo XIII, who urged her to continue her missionary work overseas. "China?" she hoped. "New York,"
he said.

In March 1889, Mother Cabrini and six assistant nuns arrived in
New York City, where she was greeted by the archbishop. "Go back to
Italy," he said. No one knows what Mother Cabrini said, and if they
did it was not a word that saints use. She found a filthy tenement
building near the Italian section of the lower East Side and scrubbed
it, begged, borrowed, and prayed until it was ready to be an orphanage
for Italian-American waifs. The archbishop said the dedication mass.

She gradually expanded the order's activities to include work
among the poor in every major industrial city in the country. Cabrini
possessed diplomatic skill and remarkable managerial abilities, to
which she added financial resourcefulness as she built schools, orphanages, and hospitals. In 1905, she moved to Chicago and built Columbus
Hospital, followed by Cabrini Hospital. She reportedly was infuriated
at the construction delays on the latter project, so she fired the general

contractor and took on the job herself. Old-time residents of the West Side talked of seeing her swinging a pick and shovel and hearing Italian phrases that sounded distinctly unsaintly. In 1909, Mother Cabrini became a naturalized American citizen. By the time she completed thirty-seven years as leader of the Sacred Heart Sisters, she had crossed the Atlantic thirty times, established strong bases in Chile and Argentina, and founded more than sixty convents with four thousand members.

She died December 22, 1917, in Columbus Hospital. The room where she died was preserved when the hospital was rebuilt and exists as a shrine, where some of the more than fifty thousand members of the Mother Cabrini League visit it each year. More than one hundred thousand people filled Soldier Field to celebrate her canonization, which was a momentous event in the American church at the time. The subsequent deemphasis in the Catholic Church on devotions to individual saints and the general secularity throughout organized religion in America has reduced the once-heroic nature of the tiny Italian nun whose name remains an everyday phrase in Chicago, where one of the nation's biggest public housing enclaves was named for her. Although her influence on America was probably restricted to a single religion and although even that influence has diminished, it is indisputably noteworthy that the city whose image is mayhem produced a woman who worked such miracles.

8

THE ORGANIZATION TOWN:
PHILIP KLUTZNICK

Levittown was a misnomer. William Levitt never built any towns. He did build the cluster of cookie-cutter houses that popped up all over America in the post–World War II years, and he created the model for affordable housing that moved returning GIs, and millions of young families out of the inner cities into homes that sold for $7,800 and led to America's suburban sprawl. But he built subdivisions, homes, and streets, and sewers.

Phil Klutznick built a town.

Park Forest was a swamp twenty-eight miles south of Chicago's downtown when Phil Klutznick first stepped into its mud in 1946. Eight years later it was awarded *Look* magazine's then-prestigious all-American city designation.

For a half century Philip M. Klutznick was so much a part of Chicago that most people never knew he was born in Kansas City, the son of Polish immigrants who began at age thirteen saving nickels for the establishment of Israel. He went to the University of Kansas and Creighton Law School in Omaha, where he began practice in 1929 and because of an article in the *New York Times* became one of the century's leading developers.

Developers are usually the forgotten men behind great projects that are either renowned for the architects who built them or the public officials who did the ribbon cutting. Developers usually get rich and get criticized. Phil Klutznick got rich, but he was more widely praised than criticized for a variety of projects that changed the way Americans lived and shopped.

In 1934, Klutznick was appointed an assistant city attorney in Omaha. The city was broke, but Klutznick read an article in the *New York Times* about a provision in the new National Industrial Recovery Act that provided $100 million—big federal money then—for slum clearance. Klutznick went to Washington, cut through the red tape, and obtained the money that rejuvenated Omaha. The government, however, would transfer it only to a public housing authority, which neither Omaha nor Nebraska had. Klutznick told the federal officials not to be concerned. He wrote the bill and in ten days the Nebraska Housing Authority Act sailed through the legislature.

Klutznick quickly became known as a public housing expert and served on various government boards during the 1930s and 1940s, ultimately being appointed commissioner of the Federal Public Housing Authority in 1944, where he supervised the massive construction of GI housing and national defense housing.

As World War II was winding down, two Chicagoans, Nathan Manilow and Carroll Sweet, visited Klutznick to ask his help in building a town.

Klutznick noted in his autobiography, *Angles of Vision*, that he did not want to participate in another mad scramble to construct houses that "were no better than pup tents."

He agreed to join the plan if his partners agreed that the project would be immediately incorporated as a town and the residents be self-governing. Klutznick and his fellow developers incorporated as American Community Builders and bought twenty-four hundred acres of cornfield, abandoned golf course, and swamp south of Chicago. Ground was broken on August 27, 1947, for the first clusters of rental apartments and ranch-style homes around a central shopping center. Klutznick's group made only modest profits from the housing, but profited more from water sales and its cut of shopping-center sales. American Community Builders also provided land and money for the first schools. Klutznick moved his own family to Park Forest, and his oldest son, Tom, was in the first graduating class of Rich High School.

Klutznick once recalled in a *Chicago Tribune* interview, "Living there was a big mistake for me. We had plenty of problems—mud streets, unfinished work, tenants renting before the plaster was on. It was day and night work, and then we got hit with something we hadn't experienced—inflation. It almost broke us."

By January 1950, 3,010 townhouses had been built and occupied at rentals between $75 and $117 a month. As the community grew and the young families were growing in income, houses were offered for sale beginning at $11,000. A few five-bedroom homes were sold for $19,000.

The fledgling community set the standard for many Chicago-area municipalities in the widespread suburbanization of the metropolitan area. The new town would have plenty of open space and parks, a shopping center, churches and public buildings, and schools within walking distance. "Homes, laid out in staggered clusters around a cul-de-sac, are being arranged so that every mother from her kitchen window can keep an eye on her youngster in centrally located and fenced-in tot yards," the *Tribune* reported in an article that year.

By 1950, Park Forest had become a haven for young families: Nine out of ten couples living there were parents, and nine out of ten children were under thirteen years of age. The plans called for a population of 25,000, living in 5,500 rental, cooperative, and single-family units. Four decades later, Park Forest was remarkably similar: The 1990 population was about 24,660, and only a few homes had not been in the original plans for the town.

In his midcentury social classic *The Organization Man*, William H. Whyte Jr. chronicled the lives of Park Forest's residents and singled out the community as the most successful attempt to restructure living patterns after World War II:

"People went to Park Forest because it was the best housing for the money," Whyte wrote. But it was different from all the other similarly priced housing developments in America, because it was conceived as a town that would be managed by the people who lived in it, "creating something above the original bargain . . . a social atmosphere of striking vigor."

Phil Klutznick would be the prime developer in many innovative and successful projects, such as the open-mall shopping centers at Old

Orchard on the North Shore and Oak Brook in DuPage County. He scribbled the $10 million land-acquisition deal for Water Tower Place on a single page and created the first modern vertical mall that anchored the Michigan Avenue renaissance. He combined with an old friend, Ferd Kramer, to create the Dearborn Park project. In between, he dedicated years and dollars to the nation of Israel. "He is considered by many to be the leading Jew in the U.S.," said Rabbi Seymour Siegel, director of the U.S. Holocaust Memorial Council. He was prophetic during the 1980s in insisting that the Palestine Liberation Organization be included in the Middle East peace process, an unpopular position among many Jews.

He was secretary of commerce under Jimmy Carter, Ambassador to the United Nations Economic and Social Council under President Kennedy, Federal Housing Commissioner under FDR, president-emeritus of the World Jewish Congress, and honorary president of B'nai B'rith International.

He will always be known as the man who built a town.

9 ▧

STUDS, TOO:
STUDS TERKEL

Louis "Studs" Terkel is Chicago's minstrel, author, interviewer, actor of the live theater, actor of stage and film, cabaret philosopher, radio personality, sports reporter, television pioneer, and historian. He might, some will observe, be listed as a literary figure or a media figure or a small business. He would fit perfectly in a category of inventors because he invented himself.

Along the way he became a Pulitzer Prize winner who didn't write a book until he was past fifty and a White House honoree who used to be shadowed by the FBI. A street was named after him in a town where the cops used to roust him. He was on blacklists and red lists and wound up on everyone's list of Chicago institutions.

For the five or six Chicagoans who have never seen him, M. W. Newman described him in a 1994 *Chicago Tribune* story:

> At 82 he's as ruddy-cheeked as ever: raspy-toned, ready-spouting, outracing his shadow on the calendar. Terkel is a free-floating civic landmark in a city where the official landmarks are nailed down. His crimson scarf tags behind him as he leans into the wind of North Michigan Avenue. His legs may be stubby, but he bucks the constraints of space/time, to say nothing of Establishment stuffed shirts and whatever else gets in his way.

Almost everything seems to have gotten in Studs's path since his birth in New York City in 1912, the year, he liked to point out, that the *Titanic* went down.

Terkel was raised in a rooming house his mother ran and that he has memorialized at Wells and Grand. It was there that he loved to listen to all the voices of the city that eventually he tried to recapture in oral histories that began with *Division Street, USA* in 1966 and continued with the publication in 1995 of his tenth book, *Coming of Age*. His oral history of the World War II years, *The Good War*, won him a Pulitzer Prize in 1985.

As a teenager, Terkel became fascinated and infatuated with James Farrell's "Studs Lonigan" to the point where people began calling him Studs. "It stuck like flypaper," he often remarked.

Terkel went to the University of Chicago and then law school before trying his hand at acting on the stage and then as a gangster in the soap-opera heyday of 1930s radio. He appeared on such daytime melodramas as *Ma Perkins* and *Helen Trent*, where he undoubtedly began aping Jimmy Cagney and other celluloid hoods, leaving him with that perpetual sneer in his voice.

He joined the WPA writer's group, where he worked with Richard Wright and met Saul Bellow. But his literary idol was Nelson Algren, who Terkel championed, befriended, and will eulogize without prompting or hesitation as Chicago's great poet.

Terkel became part of media history in 1950 hosting *Studs' Place*, an early network-television show that took place in a fictional cafe, was unrehearsed, and featured his folksinging, guitar-strumming cohort, Win Strake. It was pioneer television, and it might have lasted longer. "I couldn't keep my mouth shut, so we lost our network show," Terkel has recalled. "It was the McCarthy era and I had signed petitions for everything. They wanted me to say I was duped and the show would continue. I wasn't duped."

From television Terkel moved back to radio, landing at WFMT, Chicago's fine arts station, where he played folk music, discovered Mahalia Jackson (he denied it), and began interviewing anybody who would talk into his tape recorder, many of them the greatest artists of blues, jazz, theater, and politics of the time. It was in the radio interviews that Terkel developed his approach to interviewing that he used so successfully in his books.

By the end of the 1960s and its decade of civil rights, urban war, violent protest, and general societal transformation, Terkel was hardly a radical. His books had pushed him into the category of historian and elder raconteur. The tardy discovery by everyone else of such musical legends as Woody Guthrie and Bill Broonzy suddenly made Studs, who had praised them long before mainstream America heard of them, a new prophet. Of course, he was pushing seventy at the time.

His standard uniform, once a symbol of nonconformity, became charming. His casual dismissal of authoritarian figures, which the FBI once thought subversive, was refreshing. And his books were best-sellers all over America. If Ben Hecht had been the minstrel who turned Chicago into a fictional slapstick during the first half century, Terkel was the stenographer who gave America the real thing. And he never mellowed. Or never stopped playing soap operas.

When the producer of the movie *Eight Men Out*, the story of the Black Sox scandal, asked Studs to play a sportswriter, he at first declined, but on second thought accepted. "We got to get Comiskey," he rasped.

STREET SMART:
SAUL ALINSKY

No one else mentioned in this collection was called as many derogatory names as Saul Alinsky, who probably appreciated most of them.

Alinsky was not a likable fellow. He was not pleasant to look at or to be with. "Abrasive" was one of the nicer things people said about Alinsky. "Radical," "Commie," and "Nigger Lover," were the most common. His closest friends, and few remained that way forever, couldn't figure out whether Alinsky was premeditatedly antagonistic or just naturally mean.

He was the greatest community organizer of the last half century, and he sparked the civil rights movement in the northern cities, where both its violence and aftermath disgusted him but nevertheless made him a critical figure in the development of urban societies.

No one person who had so much impact on Chicago was more despised by its establishment. When Alinsky died in 1972, a liberal alderman introduced a resolution to name a city park after him. The council voted 35–8 to refer the motion to a committee, where Mayor Richard J. Daley conveniently and purposely forgot it.

Critics and students of Alinsky trace his social contrariness to an unsettled childhood on Chicago's West Side, where his father was an aloof figure who ultimately divorced his much younger second wife, leaving young Saul in the smothering embrace of an overbearing mother.

Sanford Horwitt, his biographer, believes all that Alinsky did and all that he was stemmed from a simple conviction that people should be allowed to determine their own fate, that poverty should not mean subservience, that race should not mean disenfranchisement.

The feeling was hardly universal in the 1930s when Alinsky graduated from the University of Chicago and began work as a sociologist in the Illinois prison system. But it was not unique. There were people in the 1930s who began to question the role that the establishment played in dividing the American wealth. Cardinal Mundelein once observed that while both political parties were interested in the same objectives, the Democrats thought the people were capable of governing themselves and the Republicans didn't. One of those who thought he could do a better job than either political party was John L. Lewis, who had organized the United Mine Workers to seize power from mine owners. Then he organized the American Federation of Labor (AFL) to seize power from all big business. Then he organized the Committee of Industrial Organizations (CIO) to seize power from the AFL. It's no wonder he became Alinsky's idol.

Alinsky's first job was with the Institute for Juvenile Research, where he became an expert on the youth gangs in Chicago's Little Italy and became friendly with enough thugs that he was able to regale friends in later years with stories of the Capone era. He spent three years working as a parole officer at the old Joliet prison before he decided that was not the kind of sociology he wanted to practice.

In 1939, he was back with the Institute and was assigned to organize a youth program in a tough South Side neighborhood known as the Back of the Yards, a neighborhood of ninety thousand people, many of them new immigrants, almost all of them employed in the Union Stockyards, which Upton Sinclair had labeled "the jungle" three decades earlier.

It was there that Alinsky invented the community-organizing method that flourishes in urban America at the close of the century.

Alinsky began by talking to everybody and compiling what amounted to a doctoral thesis on the neighborhood: who lived there, how it worked, who controlled what, and the dynamics of the opposing social forces. He noticed the street gangs and the taverns and the churches. He copied the methods of the CIO organizers who had moved to the community to organize the packing-plant workers against Swift, Armour, and Cudahy.

They taught Alinsky the skills of mass organizing: how to set up a large community meeting, to focus people's attention on troublesome issues, to agitate them to the point of action.

But he also learned about the power of the churches, since many of the Catholic pastors in Back of the Yards opposed the CIO on the popular notion that the labor group was a communist front and most of the priests abhorred godless communism far more than underfed parishioners. Alinsky formed an alliance with Auxiliary Bishop Bernard Sheil, who was Mundelein's spearhead in the support of the labor movement. Alinsky and Sheil began converting the neighborhood priests.

Alinsky organized a convention representing more than one hundred local organizations in July 1939, and the Back of the Yards Neighborhood Council was born. Its first act was to give unanimous support to the Packinghouse Workers Union. Two nights later the newly elected Back of the Yards leaders marched to the Chicago Coliseum for a CIO rally, where Bishop Sheil led the prayers and John L. Lewis roared. The meatpackers agreed to the union demands.

P. David Finks, the author of *The Radical Vision of Saul Alinsky*, wrote, "For the first time, Back of the Yards residents stood shoulder-to-shoulder in a common cause—Lithuanians, Poles, Slovaks, Czechs, Germans, Irish, Mexicans; Catholics, Protestants, Jews; the Chamber of Commerce and the CIO; housewives, school teachers, priests; whites and blacks—all stood up and with a single voice won a great community victory. Saul Alinsky was delighted. He had found his new career."

In 1940, with the support of Bishop Sheil and the money of Marshall Field III, Alinsky founded the Industrial Areas Foundation (IAF), which would support his work for the next thirty years as an itinerant community organizer.

During the next ten years, he organized neighborhood councils in Kansas City, Kansas, South St. Paul, Minnesota, and Omaha, Nebraska. In 1946, Alinsky wrote *Reveille for Radicals*, a statement of his radical American political faith.

On the West Coast, one of his thirty-five-dollar-a-week organizers was a young Mexican American, Cesar Chavez, who later founded the United Farm Workers of America.

During the next half-dozen years, Alinsky and his IAF organizers built three major community organizations in Chicago: the

Organization for the Southwest Community (OSC), The Woodlawn Organization (TWO) in that all-black South Side district, and the Northwest Community Organization (NCO) in West Town, an old, white ethnic neighborhood.

The Woodlawn Organization was the first black urban community organization in the nation. It brought forth a new generation of black leaders in Chicago and blocked the University of Chicago from dispossessing Woodlawn's residents to extend the campus. Charles Silberman, editor of *Fortune* magazine, called TWO "the most important and most impressive experiment affecting Negroes anywhere in the United States." It was at TWO that Alinsky drew the ire of Mayor Daley and the Chicago Democrats. He hauled hundreds of Negroes in buses to register at city hall, and he threatened to continually bring more busloads unless Daley acted as a mediator in the urban-renewal dispute between TWO and the University of Chicago, which wanted to "renew" the entire area.

In the mid-1960s, Alinsky sent his organizers to work in troubled racial communities in Kansas City, Buffalo, and Rochester, New York. When they returned to Chicago in 1968, it was to open the IAF Institute, a training facility for young organizers.

Oddly, but not surprisingly, Alinsky had little to do with the New Left of the 1960s. He thought their rejection of middle-class values was silly, since he had spent his life teaching people how to gain middle-class stature.

Alinsky was married three times and visiting his second wife, who suffered from multiple sclerosis, when he dropped dead on a street in Carmel, California, a most unlikely setting for a man who had spent most of his life on the streets of slums and ghettos.

Across the U.S., new Alinsky-style organizations were formed in the 1970s and 1980s among farmers, ranchers, big- and small-city dwellers, and minority groups. In Texas, a third generation of Alinsky organizers built Mexican-American citizens into critical voting blocs in San Antonio and Houston. California, with all its ballot propositions and activism, is a virtual statewide legacy to Alinsky.

Irv Kupcinet composed the most deft epitaph for Alinsky: "Here lies the man who antagonized more people than any contemporary American." He would consider it high praise.

■ ■ ■ BIBLIOGRAPHY

Abraham, Henry J. *Justices and Presidents*. Oxford and New York: Oxford University Press, 1992.

Addams, Jane. *Twenty Years at Hull House*. New York: New American Library, 1914.

Allen, George. *Pro Football's 100 Greatest Players*. Indianapolis: Bobbs-Merill Co., 1982.

Angle, Paul M. *Philip K. Wrigley*. New York: Rand McNally and Co., 1975.

Ashmore, Harry S. *Unseasonable Truths: The Life of Robert Maynard Hutchings*. Boston: Little, Brown and Co., 1989.

Baker, Carlos. *Ernest Hemingway*. New York: Charles Scribner's Sons, 1969.

Banks, Ernie, and Jim Enright. *"Mr. Cub."* Chicago: Follett Publishing Co., 1971.

Baum, Lawrence. *The Supreme Court*. Washington, D.C.: Congressional Quarterly, 1995.

Bauman, Ed, and John O'Brien. *Getting Away with Murder*. Chicago: Bonus Books, 1991.

Berger, Miles L. *They Built Chicago*. Chicago: Bonus Books, 1992.

Blasi, Vincent. *The Burger Court*. New Haven, Conn.: Yale University Press, 1983.

Branch, Edgar M. *James T. Farrell*. Minneapolis: University of Minnesota Press, 1963.

Berkow, Ira. *Maxwell Street*. Garden City, N.Y.: Doubleday and Co., 1977.

Bly, Nellie. *Oprah*. New York: Kensington Publishing Corp., 1993.

Brickhouse, Jack. *Thanks for Listening*. South Bend, Ind.: Diamond Communications Inc., 1986.

Ciccone, F. Richard. *Daley: Power and Presidential Politics*. Chicago: Contemporary Books, 1997.

Collier, James Lincoln. *Benny Goodman and the Swing Era*. New York: Oxford University Press, 1989.

————. *Louis Armstrong: An American Genius*. New York: Oxford University Press, 1983.

Condit, Carl W. *The Chicago School of Architecture*. Chicago and London: University of Chicago Press, 1964.

Cook, Bruce. *Listen to the Blues*. New York: Charles Scribner's Sons, 1973.

Cooper, Philip J. *Battles on the Bench*. Lawrence, Kans.: University Press of Kansas, 1995.

Cowley, Malcolm. *And I Worked at the Writer's Trade*. New York: The Viking Press, 1978.

Cutler, Irving. *The Jews of Chicago*. Urbana, Ill.: University of Illinois Press, 1996.

Davis, Francis. *The History of the Blue*. New York: Hyperion, 1995.

Dedmon, Emmett. *Fabulous Chicago*. New York: Atheneum, 1981.

Donohue, H. E. F. *Conversations with Nelson Algren*. New York: Hill and Wang, 1964.

Douglas, Paul H. *In the Fullness of Time*. New York: Harcourt Brace Jovanovich, 1971.

Drew, Bettina. *Nelson Algren, a Life on the Wild Side*. New York: G. P. Putnam's Sons, 1989.

Duster, Alfreda. *Crusade for Justice: The Autobiography of Ida B. Wells*. Chicago: University of Chicago Press, 1970.

Elliot, Emory. *Columbia Literary History of the United States*. New York: Columbia University Press, 1988.

Fermi, Laura. *Atoms in the Family*. Chicago: University of Chicago Press, 1953.

Freeman, Lucy. *Before I Kill More*. New York: Crown Publishers Inc., 1955.

Fucini, Joseph J., and Suzy Fucini. *Entrepreneurs.* Boston: G. K. Hall and Co., 1985.

Gallico, Paul. *The Golden People.* Garden City, N.Y.: Doubleday and Co., Inc., 1965.

Garr, Ian, Digby Fairweather, and Brian Priestly. *Jazz, the Rough Guide.* London: Rough Guides, Ltd., 1995.

Gelbert, Doug. *So Who the Heck Was Oscar Mayer?* New York: Barricade Books, Inc., 1996.

Gibson, Donald B. *Five Black Writers.* New York: New York University Press, 1970.

Gies, Joseph. *Colonel of Chicago.* New York: E. P. Dutton, 1979.

Girardin, G. Russell, with William J. Helmer. *Dillinger, the Untold Story.* Bloomington: Indiana University Press, 1994.

Golenbock, Peter. *Wrigleyville.* New York: St. Martin's Press, 1996.

Goreau, Laurraine R. *Just Mahalia, Baby.* Waco, Tex.: Word Books Publisher, 1975.

Graham, Bruce. *Bruce Graham of Som.* New York: Rizzoli International Publications, Inc., 1989.

Green, Paul M., and Melvin G. Holli. *The Mayors.* Carbondale, Ill.: Southern Illinois University Press, 1987.

Gropman, Donald. *"Say It Ain't So, Joe!"* Boston: Little, Brown and Co., 1979.

Gross, Daniel. *Forbes Greatest Business Stories.* New York: John Wiley and Sons, Inc., 1996.

Grossvogel, David I. *Dear Ann Landers.* Chicago: Contemporary Books, 1987.

Gunther, John. *Taken at the Flood, the Story of Albert D. Lasker.* New York: Harper and Brothers, 1960.

Halas, George, with Gwen Morgan and Arthur Veysey. *Halas by Halas.* New York: McGraw-Hill Book Co., 1979.

Halper, Albert. *The Chicago Crime Book.* Cleveland: World Publishing Co., 1967.

Hanson, Harry. *Midwest Portraits.* New York: Harcourt, Brace and Co., 1923.

Harris, Leon. *Upton Sinclair, American Rebel.* New York: Thomas Y. Crowell Co., 1975.

Hart, James D. *The Oxford Companion to American Literature*. New York: Oxford University Press, 1983.

Hart, Philip. *Fritz Reiner*. Evanston, Ill.: Northwestern University Press, 1994.

Heise, Kenan, and Ed Baumann. *Chicago Originals*. Chicago: Bonus Books, 1990.

Helyar, John. *Lords of the Realm*. New York: Villard Books, 1994.

Higdon, Hal. *Crime of the Century*. New York: G. P. Putnam and Sons, 1975.

Hillkirk, John, and Gary Jacobson. *Grits, Guts and Genius*. Boston: Houghton Mifflin Co., 1980.

Hogan, John. *A Spirit Capable, the Story of Commonwealth Edison*. Chicago: Mobium Press, 1986.

Hoge, Cecil C. *The First Hundred Years Are the Toughest*. Berkeley, Calif.: Ten Speed Press, 1988.

Horwitt, Sanford. *Let Them Call Me Rebel: Saul Alinsky—His Life and Legend*. New York: Alfred Knopf, 1989.

Hovde, Jane. *Jane Addams*. New York: Facts on File, 1989.

Howard, Robert P. *Illinois: A History of the Prairie State*. Grand Rapids, Mich.: William B. Eerdsman Publishing Co., 1972.

———. *Mostly Good and Competent Men*. Springfield, Ill.: Illinois State Historical Society, 1988.

Jackson, Mahalia, with Evan McLeod Wylie. *Movin' on Up*. New York: Hawthorn Books, Inc., 1966.

Johnson, Haynes, and David S. Broder. *The System*. Boston: Little, Brown and Co., 1996.

Judson, Clara Ingram. *City Neighbor*. New York: Charles Scribner's Sons, 1951.

Kantowicz, Edward R. *Corporation Sole*. South Bend, Ind.: University of Notre Dame Press, 1983.

Kazin, Alfred. *An American Procession*. New York: Alfred A. Knopf, 1984.

Katz, Donald R. *The Big Store*. New York: Viking Press, 1987.

Kenney, William Howard. *Chicago Jazz*. New York: Oxford University Press, 1993.

Klutznick, Philip M. *Angles of Vision*. Chicago: Ivan R. Dee, 1991.

Knappman, Edward W. *Great American Trials*. Boston: New England Publishing Associates, Inc., 1994.

Kobler, John. *Capone*. New York: G. P. Putnam and Sons, 1971.

Kogan, Herman. *Traditions and Challenges, History of Sidley Austin*. Chicago: R. R. Donnelly and Co., 1983.

Kramer, Dale. *Chicago Renaissance*. New York: Appleton-Century, 1966.

Landers, Ann. *Wake Up and Smell the Coffee*. New York: Villard Co., 1996.

Larson, George, and Jay Pridmore. *Chicago Architecture and Design*. New York: Harry N. Abrams Inc., 1993.

Lerner, Gerda, ed. *Black Women in White America*. New York: Pantheon Books, 1979.

Lindberg, Richard. *Who's on 3rd?* South Bend, Ind.: Icarus Press, 1993.

Linedecker, Clifford. *The Man Who Killed Boys*. New York: St. Martin's Press, 1989.

Lomax, Alan. *Mister Jelly Roll*. New York: Grove Press, 1950.

Love, John F. *McDonald's: Behind the Arches*. New York: Bantam Books, 1986.

Lyttleton, Humphrey. *The Best of Jazz: Basin Street to Harlem*. New York: Taplinger Publishing Co., 1968.

Marsh, Barbara. *A Corporate Tragedy*. Garden City, N.Y.: Doubleday and Co., 1985.

Martin, John. *Ruth Page: An Intimate Biography*. New York: Marcel Dekker, Inc., 1977.

Martin, John Bartlow. *Adlai Stevenson and the World*. Garden City, N.Y.: Doubleday and Co., 1977.

————. *Adlai Stevenson of Illinois*. Garden City, N.Y.: Doubleday and Co., 1976.

Mayer, Milton. *Robert Maynard Hutchins*. Berkeley, Calif.: University of California Press, 1993.

McDonald, Forrest. *Insull*. Chicago: University of Chicago Press, 1962.

McGrady, Patrick M. *The Love Doctors*. New York: Macmillan Co., 1972.

McPhaul, John J. *Deadlines and Monkeyshines: The Fabled World of Chicago Journalism*. Englewood Cliffs, N.J.: Prentice-Hall Inc., 1962.

Melamed, Leo. *Leo Melamed on the Markets*. New York: John Wiley and Sons, 1993.

Melamed, Leo, and Bob Tamarkin. *Escape to the Futures*. New York: John Wiley and Sons, 1996.

Miller, Ruth. *Saul Bellow*. New York: St. Martin's Press, 1991.

Morgan, Gwen, and Arthur Veysey. *Poor Little Rich Boy*. Carpentersville, Ill.: Crossroads Communication, 1985.

Muller, Herbert J. *Adlai Stevenson: A Study in Values*. New York: Harper and Row, 1967.

Murray, George. *Madhouse on Madison Street*. Chicago: Follett Publishing Co., 1966.

Newcombe, Jack. *The Fireside Book of Football*. New York: Simon & Shuster, 1964.

Petrakis, Harry Mark. *The Founder's Touch*. New York: McGraw-Hill Book Co., 1965.

Pleasants, Harry. *The Great American Popular Singers*. New York: Simon and Shuster, 1974.

Pottker, Jan, and Bob Speziale. *Dear Ann, Dear Abby*. New York: Dodd, Mead & Co., 1987.

Regnery, Henry. *Creative Chicago*. Evanston, Ill.: Chicago Historical Bookworks, 1992.

Roemer, William F. *Accardo, the Genuine Godfather*. New York: Donald I. Fine, 1995.

Rooney, James. *Bossmen: Bill Monroe & Muddy Waters*. New York: The Dial Press, 1971.

Rust, Art, Jr. *"Get That Nigger off the Field."* New York: Delacorte Press, 1976.

Schapp, Richard. *The Olympics*. New York: Alfred A. Knopf, 1963.

Schapsmeier, Edward L., and Frederick Schapsmeier. *Dirksen of Illinois*. Urbana and Chicago: University of Illinois Press, 1985.

Schulze, Franz. *Mies van der Rohe*. Chicago: University of Chicago Press, 1985.

Schwartz, Herman. *The Burger Years*. New York: Viking Books, 1987.

Secrest, Meryle. *Frank Lloyd Wright*. New York: Alfred A. Knopf, 1992.

Segre, Emilio. *Enrico Fermi Physicist*. Chicago and London: University of Chicago Press, 1970.

Slappey, Sterling G. *Pioneers of American Business*. New York: Grosset and Dunlap, 1973.

Smith, Carl S. *Chicago and the American Literary Imagination*. Chicago: University of Chicago Press, 1984.

Smith, Richard Norton. *The Colonel*. Boston, New York: Houghton Mifflin, 1997.

Smith, Sam. *The Jordan Rules*. New York: Simon & Schuster, 1992.

Sterling, Dorothy. *Black Foremothers, Three Lives*. Old Westbury, N.Y.: The Feminist Press, 1979.

Stevens, Mark. *The Big Six*. New York: Simon and Schuster, 1991.

Stone, Irving. *Clarence Darrow for the Defense*. Garden City, N.Y.: Doubleday and Co., 1941.

Swanberg, W. A. *Dreiser*. New York: Charles Scribner's Sons, 1965.

Tamarkin, Bob. *The Merc, Emergence of a Global Financial Powerhouse*. New York: Harper Business, 1993.

Terkel, Studs. *Talking to Myself*. New York: Pantheon Books, 1977.

Thomas, Henry and Dana Lee. *Famous Women*. Garden City, N.Y.: Blue Ribbon Books, 1946.

————. *50 Great Modern Lives*. Garden City, N.Y.: Hanover House, 1951.

Thorndike, Joseph J., Jr. *Three Centuries of Notable American Architects*. New York: American Heritage Publishing Co., 1981.

Tierney, Kevin. *Darrow, a Biography*. New York: Crowell Publications, 1979.

Timmons, Bascom N. *Portrait of an American: Charles G. Dawes*. New York: Henry Holt and Co., 1953.

Tingley, Donald F. *The Structuring of a State: The History of Illinois, 1899 to 1928*. Urbana: University of Illinois Press, 1980.

Twombly, Robert. *Frank Lloyd Wright: An Interpretive Biography*. New York: Harper and Row, 1973.

————. *Louis Sullivan*. New York: Viking Penguin, 1986.

Vass, George. *The Chicago Black Hawks Story*. Chicago: Follett Publishing Co., 1970.

Wald, Alan M. *James T. Farrell*. New York: New York University Press, 1978.

Waldrop, Frank C. *McCormick of Chicago*. Englewood Cliffs, N.J.: Prentice-Hall Inc., 1966.

Walker, Margaret. *Daemonic Genius*. New York: Amistad Press, Inc., 1988.

Werner, M. R. *Julius Rosenwald*. New York: Harper and Brothers Publishers, 1939.

Woodward, Bob. *The Brethren*. New York: Simon and Schuster, 1979.

Worthy, James C. *Shaping an American Institution*. Urbana: University of Illinois Press, 1984.

Zukowsky, John. *Chicago Architecture and Design 1923–1993*. Chicago: Art Institute of Chicago, 1993.

———. *Mies*. Chicago: Art Institute of Chicago, 1986.